POWER SHIFT? POLITICAL LEADERSHIP AND SOCIAL MEDIA

Power Shift? Political Leadership and Social Media examines how political leaders have adapted to the challenges of social media, including Facebook, Instagram, Twitter, and memes, among other means of persuasion. Established political leaders now use social media to grab headlines, respond to opponents, fundraise, contact voters directly, and organize their election campaigns. Leaders of protest movements have used social media to organize and galvanize grassroots support and to popularize new narratives: narratives that challenge and sometimes overturn conventional thinking. Yet each social media platform provides different affordances and different attributes, and each is used differently by political leaders.

In this book, leading international experts provide an unprecedented look at the role of social media in leadership today. Through a series of case studies dealing with topics ranging from Emmanuel Macron and Donald Trump's use of Twitter, to Justin Trudeau's use of selfies and Instagram, to how feminist leaders mobilize against stereotypes and injustices, the authors argue that many leaders have found additional avenues to communicate with the public and use power. This raises the question of whether this is causing a power shift in the relationship between leaders and followers. Together the chapters in this book suggest new rules of engagement that leaders ignore at their peril.

The lack of systematic theoretically informed and empirically supported analyses makes *Power Shift? Political Leadership and Social Media* an indispensable read for students and scholars wishing to gain new understanding on what social media means for leadership.

Richard Davis is Professor of Political Science and Director of the Office of Civic Engagement at Brigham Young University, USA. He is the author of several books on the Internet and American politics, including *Twitter and Elections Around the World: Campaigning in 140 Characters or Less* (2016), *Covering the Courts in the Digital Age* (2014), *The Symbiotic Relationship Between the U.S. Supreme Court and the Press* (2014), and many more.

David Taras is Professor of Communication Studies and holds the Ralph Klein Chair in Media Studies at Mount Royal University, Canada. Before coming to Mount Royal, David taught at the University of Toronto, the University of Amsterdam, and, most recently, the University of Calgary, where he served as the Ernest C. Manning Chair in Canadian Studies. While there, he received the Students' Union Award for Teaching Excellence five times and was inducted into the Teaching Excellence Awards Hall of Fame in 2011. He was President of the Canadian Communications Association and served two terms on the Board of Governors of the University of Calgary. He received the Alberta Centennial Medal in 2005. A leading expert in the area of Canadian media policy and its relationship to Canadian identity and democracy, he is the author of *The Newsmakers: The Media's Influence on Canadian Politics* (1990) and of *Power & Betrayal in the Canadian Media* (2001). He is co-author of *The Last Word: Media Coverage of the Supreme Court of Canada* (2006).

"Taras and Davis have put together a collection of scholars that represent a who's who of researchers focused on the now ubiquitous role of social media in modern politics. The result is, as expected, successful. The essays in this volume provide a unique look into social media and political leadership. Has there been a foundational shift in the underpinnings guiding leadership, or does the song remain the same? Addressing multiple related topics, this collection grapples with that fundamental question."

—**Jason Gainous**, *Professor, co-author of* Tweeting to Power

"More scholarship has been available about uses of social media by political publics than by political leaders. That makes this volume a welcome addition. It presents a range of useful analyses on national leadership in the US, Canada, Europe, and South Africa. It should be useful to scholars interested in a more complete picture of social media in politics as well as those interested in important comparative questions."

—**Bruce Bimber**, *Professor, Center for Information Technology &*
Society, and Department of Political Science,
University of California – Santa Barbara

"Taras and Davis have assembled some of the top scholars in the area of digital politics and leadership. This book provides an important foundation for anyone who wants to understand how modern leadership has changed in the Internet Age."

—**Kevin Wagner**, *Professor of Political Science,*
Florida Atlantic University

"This book offers a timely and refreshingly diverse array of perspectives on social media and political elites. It's a must-read for anyone interested in understanding leadership and strategic political communication and in today's media environment."

—**Johanna Dunaway**, *Associate Professor,*
Texas A&M University

POWER SHIFT?
POLITICAL LEADERSHIP
AND SOCIAL MEDIA

Edited by
Richard Davis & David Taras

NEW YORK AND LONDON

First published 2020
by Routledge
52 Vanderbilt Avenue, New York, NY 10017

and by Routledge
2 Park Square, Milton Park, Abingdon, Oxon, OX14 4RN

Routledge is an imprint of the Taylor & Francis Group, an informa business

© 2020 Taylor & Francis

The right of Richard Davis and David Taras to be identified as the authors of the editorial material, and of the authors for their individual chapters, has been asserted in accordance with sections 77 and 78 of the Copyright, Designs and Patents Act 1988.

All rights reserved. No part of this book may be reprinted or reproduced or utilised in any form or by any electronic, mechanical, or other means, now known or hereafter invented, including photocopying and recording, or in any information storage or retrieval system, without permission in writing from the publishers.

Trademark notice: Product or corporate names may be trademarks or registered trademarks, and are used only for identification and explanation without intent to infringe.

Library of Congress Cataloging-in-Publication Data
A catalog record for this book has been requested

ISBN: 978-1-138-60985-3 (hbk)
ISBN: 978-1-138-60988-4 (pbk)
ISBN: 978-0-429-46600-7 (ebk)

Typeset in Bembo
by Apex CoVantage, LLC

CONTENTS

List of Figures	*viii*
List of Tables	*ix*

1 Political Leaders and Social Media: An Introduction   1
   David Taras

PART 1
Leaders and the New Instruments of Media
Persuasion   **15**

2 The President Tweets the Press: President–Press Relations
   and the Politics of Media Degradation   17
   Joshua M. Scacco and Eric C. Wiemer

3 Vulgar Eloquence in the Digital Age: A Case Study of
   Candidate Donald Trump's Use of Twitter   33
   Jennifer Stromer-Galley

4 "Delete Your Account"? Hillary Rodham Clinton
   Across Social Media Platforms in the 2016 U.S. Presidential
   Election   49
   Shannon C. McGregor and Regina G. Lawrence

vi Contents

5 The Visually Viral Prime Minister: Justin Trudeau, Selfies,
   and Instagram   63
   Chaseten Remillard, Lindsey M. Bertrand, and Alina Fisher

6 Tweeting the Agenda: Policy Making and Agenda Setting
   by U.S. Congressional Leaders in the Age of Social Media   76
   Jacob R. Straus and Raymond T. Williams

PART 2
Twitter, Leaders, and Populism   95

7 Populism and Social Media Popularity: How Populist
   Communication Benefits Political Leaders on
   Facebook and Twitter   97
   Sina Blassnig, Nicole Ernst, Sven Engesser, and Frank Esser

8 A Marriage of Twitter and Populism in the French
   Presidential Campaign? The Twitter-Discourse of
   Challengers Macron and Le Pen   112
   Peter Maurer

9 Political Communication Patterns and Sentiments
   Across Time on Twitter in the 2017 Election in the
   Netherlands   126
   Maurice Vergeer

PART 3
Social Media and Grassroots Politics   151

10 'Twitter was Like Magic!': Strategic Use of Social Media
    in Contemporary Feminist Activism   153
    Kaitlynn Mendes

11 #Unsettling Canada 150, One Tweet at a Time:
    How Indigenous Leaders Use Twitter to Resist and
    Reframe Mainstream News in Canada   167
    Brad Clark

Contents **vii**

12 Fanning Flames of Discontent: A Case Study of Social
Media, Populism, and Campaigning 187
Patrick McCurdy

13 Not a Leader! Theresa May's Leadership Through the
Lens of Internet Memes 202
Mireille Lalancette and Tamara A. Small

14 Twitter and Student Leadership in South Africa: The Case
of #FeesMustFall 220
Tanja Bosch, Thierry M. Luescher, and Nkululeko Makhubu

Conclusion 235
Richard Davis

About the Contributors *243*
Index *250*

FIGURES

2.1	Network Visualization of "Fake News" Instances in Trump's Tweets Since Entering Office	24
2.2	Network Visualization of "Real News" Instances in Trump's Tweets Since Entering Office	25
4.1	Clinton Campaign Social Media Posts, January 1, 2016–November 8, 2016	52
4.2	Clinton Campaign Instagram Post, September 29, 2016	54
4.3	Clinton Campaign Facebook Post, November 7, 2016	55
4.4	Clinton Campaign's Policy Messaging on Instagram	57
4.5	Clinton Campaign Attacks on Donald Trump on Twitter and Instagram	58
9.1	Electoral Volatility in the Netherlands 19xx–2017	128
9.2	Candidates' Types of Tweets During the Election Campaign	135
9.3	Time Series of Expressed Sentiments During the Election Campaign by Party Leader and Regular Candidates	136
11.1	A Tweet from the @Resistance150 Twitter Account with the Hashtag #Canada150	172
11.2	A Tweet from @Apihtawikosisan with the Hashtag #Canada150	175
11.3	A Tweet from the @Resistance150 Account	176
11.4	A Screen Shot of the Unsettling Canada 150 Home Page	177
13.1	Generic Image Macro Meme	207
13.2	Examples of Theresa May Memes	211

TABLES

6.1	Topics Discussed Surrounding President Trump's 2017 Joint Address	81
6.2	Topics Discussed Surrounding President Trump's 2018 State of the Union Address	82
7.1	Factors Influencing the Number of Popularity Cues a Post Receives. (Predictions Based on Negative Binomial Regression [N = 566])	103
9.1	Growth Curve Analysis of Broadcasting, Directed, Replies and Retweets	137
9.2	Interaction Effects for Populism (Differences in Marginal Means)	139
9.3	Interaction Effects for Type of Political Party (Differences in Marginal Means)	139
9.4	Growth Curve Analysis of Sentiments in Tweets	141
9.5	Interaction Effects for Populism (Differences in Marginal Means)	143
9.6	Interaction Effects for Type of Political Party (Differences in Marginal Means)	144
9.7	Political Parties and Their Leaders in the 2017 Parliament Elections	146
11.1	Tweets using Hashtags Associated with Canada 150 between January 1 and July 2, 2017	174
13.1	Meme Focus Coding Definitions	208

1

POLITICAL LEADERS AND SOCIAL MEDIA

An Introduction

David Taras

Leadership, like beauty, is in the eye of the beholder. In her book on leadership, political scientist and former president of Duke University, Nannerl Keohane, remarks on the number of political leaders that she has met, who, as she puts it, "couldn't lead a gaggle of seven year olds to an ice cream counter," or who were so ill-suited to their positions that defeat or disaster was all but inevitable (Keohane, 2010, p. 2) To Keohane, political leadership is largely situational; some of the great leaders of the 19th century probably couldn't get zoning by-laws through city councils in Hamburg, Zurich or Los Angeles today, and business leaders thinking that the rules of the road are the same often fail miserably when they make a transition to politics. Different political systems require different sets of skills. Forging a coalition government made up of three or four political parties, as is the case in the Netherlands or Germany; being an effective parliamentary leader amidst the storm bursts of Question Period; and being a congressional leader in the divisive atmosphere that now pervades and has scarred American politics call for very different qualities. Keohane also cautions that, for leaders, success or failure is often the product of blind luck or bizarre circumstances. With just a few more votes in Broward county, Al Gore would have been elected president in 2000; the United States would almost certainly have not invaded Iraq and would have given far greater priority to environmental issues. A difference of just one half of 1 per cent of the vote in the 1995 referendum on Quebec sovereignty, and arguably Canada would be two countries today, and Prime Minister Jean Chretien's legacy and reputation, which are considerable today, would be all but destroyed. As Machiavelli reminds us, the whims of fortune, or "fortuna," are often the hinges on which fate rests.

Despite the limitations imposed by circumstances and systems, scholars such as Max Weber, Richard Neustadt, James David Barber, Fred Greenstein, James

2 David Taras

MacGregor Burns and Archie Brown, among a host of others, have been able to hypothesize about what leadership means. At the very least, leaders clarify goals. They also use symbols, stir passions and, at some level, command obedience from others. According to Burns, true leaders lift or inspire their followers and promote policies that are transformational; they reach for the skies in terms of advocating change, even if they sometimes crash down to earth. Leadership also involves a ceremonial element in which the leader presides over moments of celebration or injury. At such moments, they must embody and signify something larger than themselves, have a sense of grace and a gift for oratory. Interestingly, Samuel Popkin has observed that while business leaders are highly successful if they capture 5 or 10 per cent of a particular market, political leaders have to win close to or more than 50 per cent of the vote. Getting to 50 per cent requires making compromises and building coalitions of followers in a jigsaw puzzle that might not fit together for very long. Just getting elected often requires something close to a herculean effort.

Leaders also emerge because they are able to use the media effectively. The media is at once a means for achieving power, the stage on which they perform that power and a check on their power. The media sets the conditions in which leadership takes place. Economist Harold Innis was among the first scholars to argue that the means of communication have the capacity to distribute and redistribute power in fundamental ways. The printing press was the great democratizing medium. Through the publishing of books and eventually newspapers, control over knowledge and therefore power was transferred from a cloistered religious elite to what would become a burgeoning merchant class. The telegraph had just as important an effect in redistributing power. According to James Carey, the telegraph nationalized political life in the United States by breaking down the barriers of time and regional differences. Local dialects and colloquialisms fell into disuse as a common language and culture took hold. Radio had much the same effect, except that radio created a new kind of intimacy so that listeners could feel that political leaders were talking directly to them. Radio also allowed leaders to bypass the filter of press coverage and speak directly to their publics. Famously, Franklin Roosevelt's "fireside chats" played a decisive role in easing fears during the onslaught and misery of the Great Depression. Charles de Gaulle's broadcasts to the French people via the BBC played an important role in mobilizing resistance to German occupation during the Second World War and in establishing his position as head of the resistance and eventually leader of France. Mastering the subtleties of the airwaves became a key to political power.

Each means of communication shifts power in fundamental ways. Each technology has different affordances and different attributes and demands different skills from leaders. Fail to communicate in the way that the times and publics demand, and leaders are unlikely to survive for long.

A galaxy of scholars, including Kathleen Hall Jamieson, Peter Dahlgren, Des Friedman, Austin Ranney, Philip Schlesinger, Thomas Patterson, Robert Entman, Michael Grossman and Martha Kumar, Jay Rosen and Richard Davis, have studied leadership and media politics in the TV era – an era that, despite the emergence of digital media, has not yet passed. One has to be careful to distinguish between a number of different TV eras; there were only a handful of TV networks in the period from the 1960s to the 1980s, and together they could reach a mass audience. The culture of TV would change dramatically, however, with the explosion of cable and satellite specialty channels that began in the 1980s and 1990s.

The rules that governed the first TV era still survive today. Grossman and Kumar have argued that the relationship between the US president and the press, and arguably leaders and journalists in all political systems, is one of conflict and symbiosis. Journalists are at once deadly opponents who can filter and alter the messages that leaders want to send and the vital connecting link to the public. Using, cajoling, bypassing, negotiating with and out-manoeuvring journalists is part of the game that political leaders must play and must play well. When it comes to TV, political leaders attempt to set the media and hence the political agenda by using the elements that TV news most requires. They wrap their messages in pithy sound bites, attractive and flashy visuals and dramatic attacks. Political leaders try to control the narrative by producing what is in effect a daily TV show. They write the stories for the journalists that cover them in the hope that they will take the bait; and they often do. Stage management became and still is integral to the art of political persuasion.

Of course, the desire for ratings at all costs that pervades almost all of journalism is part of the calculation. Case in point. Michael X. Delli Carpini estimates that Donald Trump received roughly $5 billion in free air time during his run for the presidency based on his ability to give TV reporters and commentators what they craved: nightly performances based on sensationalism, the politics of outrage, vicious attacks and outlandish conspiracy theories. Those who ran against him for the Republican nomination almost never made the news unless they had been attacked by Trump.

Another development was the growth of an adversarial press. While shaming and attacking the powerful had been part of journalism since at least the penny press of the 1850s, in the aftermath of the Vietnam War and Watergate, taking out politicians, claiming their scalps and exposing their failings had become deeply embedded in the journalistic culture. The effects of this continuous hazing on political leaders were dramatic. Respect and deference were in short supply. Christopher Arterton has argued that reporting had become so corrosive that virtually every political campaign underwent what he described as a "press crisis": a time when reporters set the agenda and leaders were under scrutiny and persistent attack (Arterton, 1978, pp. 48–49).

Political leaders would find themselves in a kind of "dead zone" without the oxygen that they need to survive. As Popkin has observed about media politics: "If you don't enter the process humbly, you will leave it humbly (Popkin, 2012, p. 52)."

In parliamentary democracies, question periods became the main theatres of politics during the era of mass audience TV. A leader's standing often depended

4 David Taras

on how well she or he performed in Question Period. Be caught unprepared or be embarrassed too often and a leader's fortunes could quickly capsize. Not only was Question Period the stage on which much of politics took place but winning the battle of Question Period day after day also required a skill set, a talent for showmanship that not all leaders possessed.

Journalists and news organizations were part of the show. They famously conspired with favoured parliamentarians by feeding them questions based on the stories that they were working on and then happily covered the fireworks that in effect they themselves had set off.

A number of forces have combined to lessen the influence of these models of political NB Change reporting. Perhaps most importantly, with the growth of satellite and cable TV in the 1980s and 1990s, audiences became fragmented. In his book on "post-broadcast democracy," Markus Prior was able to demonstrate that with a smorgasbord of specialty channels their disposal, large numbers of viewers avoided watching news shows almost entirely and as a consequence became less well informed and were less likely to vote. Most critically, the advent of 24-hour all-news channels changed the nature of news and journalism and hence politics. Political leaders were now faced with an accelerated news cycle that demanded responses throughout the day. They soon found themselves in a "permanent campaign" in which the demand for news making as well as other political activities never stopped. Arguably, social media has sped up the news cycle even more dramatically. Political leaders and parties are always on, always in overdrive, always having to react and perform.

Cable news networks, in the United States at least, soon realized that they could be profitable by appealing to a small cadre of ideologically driven viewers rather than to a mass audience. News didn't have to be objective or even informative; it just had to appeal to viewers' preconceived beliefs and prejudices. Daniel Kreiss has gone as far as to contend that Fox News, for instance, is "much less about information than about family": more the political equivalent of appealing to sports fans who want to see the home team win than to the needs of citizens (Kreiss, 2018, p. 94). A number of scholars have found that news shows would reward political leaders who took extreme positions by giving them far more coverage that they did to leaders who took middle of the road positions or who wanted to compromise. In a sense, news and politics on American TV had become "Europeanized." In Europe, the press has long been parsed along party and ideological lines so that identity proceeded and pre-determined news choices.

Joshua Meyrowitz has argued that TV by its very nature has had a levelling effect on leaders. Where the leaders of the past were largely distant from public view and could project a sense of unreachable and even mythical authority, TV has erased the majesty that came with distance. As Meyrowitz observed,

> the camera unthinkingly records the flash of anger and the shiver in the cold; it determinedly shadows our leaders as they trip over words or down

stairs. And . . . words and actions recorded on electronic tape are impossible to deny (Meyrowitz, 1986, p. 272).

He argued that "the familiarity fostered by electronic media all too easily breeds contempt." TV's intimacy is a double-edged sword. It has the capacity to both project and solidify power and, if not used well, to erode and weaken it.

Shifting Ground: Political Leaders and Digital Media

One of the most important power shifts in political and economic life has come from the development of high-powered search engines. This is because "search" has distributed and re-oriented power in at least two fundamental ways. First, it has distributed power upwards by giving a handful of media behemoths such as Google, Facebook, Amazon and Twitter extraordinary power. They are now the hosts and gatekeepers through which other media must pass in order to reach their publics. Even the most prominent news organizations now find themselves in a deadly game; if they are not on Facebook, for instance, they literally cease to exist for much of the public. If, on the other hand, they have negotiated an agreement with Facebook, they face the threat of brand extinction because users tend to see their posts as being part of Facebook. These giant media platforms have also been able to accumulate extraordinary power because they have been able to collect, analyse and package massive amounts of data. Google, for instance, has thousands of data points on every one of its users, and its powerful algorithms are able to devise messages that target individual users right down to their favourite colours, the words and symbols and music that they like and the tone that should be used in ads or prompts. As former Google President Eric Schmidt once bragged, "We know where you are. We know where you've been. We can more or less know what you are thinking about."

Data analytics has allowed Google and Facebook in particular to dominate online and mobile advertising to such a degree that newspapers in particular have been either severely weakened or have already disappeared. In Canada, for instance, advertising losses have been so catastrophic that a number of reports have predicted that virtually all of the traditional media will disappear by the middle of the next decade. While the press in Europe and Asia is not yet at the edge of a cliff in the same way that it is in Canada, alarm bells have been rung almost everywhere. But it must also be noted that countries with sturdy public broadcasters such as Germany, Ireland, Japan, the UK and the Scandinavian countries are not exposed to the same level of emergency, although younger viewers and listeners are not nearly as loyal to these broadcasters as their parents were.

The point made above with respect to Meyrowitz's observation that TV never forgets applies even more to social media. Words posted in haste or in the white heat of emotion can never be erased. It does not take much for a political rival to

6 David Taras

track down zany comments or awkward photos posted years earlier. The political leaders of today can never outrun their pasts. Every photo, tweet, video, ad, sarcastic comment or misstep is now part of the public record. Their worst moments are sometimes the first things that people see.

Another fundamental shift in the geological plates brought by search engines is that we now see the world through "filter bubbles" based on our previous searches. Facebook will post stories and ads based on what its famous algorithms say about our likes and interests and those of our friends; it knows, apparently, which posts are likely to make us feel good and which posts we are likely to share. Twitter's "trending topics" are tweaked to reflect what it knows about the interests of each of its users, and answers and topics are listed on Google based on what its analytics have calculated from our previous searches. This means that liberals and conservatives, feminists and environmentalists, sports and music fans all have different googles. The problem, as Eli Pariser has expressed it, is that "you get stuck in a static, ever-narrowing version of yourself – an endless you-loop." In the end, "the user becomes the content" (Pariser, 2011, p. 47).

Just as "search" has pushed power upward to giant monopolies, it has also pushed power downward to individual users by giving them the capacity to create their own highly individualized media eco-systems. Where news used to move only from the top down, from producers to consumers, today we each have the capacity to be our own producers. We not only choose the TV programmes, news sites, playlists, podcasts and video networks that we prefer but also post, like, mash up, spread, comment on, tweet, create Instagram stories, make our own videos and receive steady streams of messages and content from friends. The key to this new media world, according to Henry Jenkins and his colleagues, is that culture is participatory and spreadable. It is not just that citizens receive news stories, videos or commentaries from others; it is what they do with them when they get them that's crucial. Some stories or messages go "viral"; they spread quickly, gain traction and for a moment at least penetrate the membranes of popular culture. In her chapter in this volume, Kaitlynn Mendes describes Carolyn Criado Perez's astonishment when her tweet evoked a mass response: "Twitter was like magic." Of course, most posts do not hit the raw nerve endings that produce a mass response and, like snowflakes, disappear almost as quickly as they land.

The new "attention economy" has produced yet another power shift. While political leaders are almost guaranteed exposure and headlines because of their positions as policy-makers and the ceremonial roles that they play, they cannot control the message to nearly the same extent as they did when there were fewer media outlets and a mass audience. Political leaders must compete for space in ways that were unimaginable just short time ago. The vast kaleidoscope of media alternatives that people now have at their disposal means that reaching their publics, cutting through the noise, is more difficult than ever. Moreover, as scholars such as Neil Postman, Markus Prior and Robert Putnam have pointed out, the explosion of entertainment choices in particular has meant that large numbers of people, perhaps even a majority of the population, avoid the news entirely, pay little attention to politics except when there are elections or sensational stories and have little knowledge about their own communities. There is evidence that media abundance has produced a less rather than more knowledgeable public.

At the same time, the demand side for leaders has increased exponentially. It is not enough to give speeches or win the daily battle to set the conventional news agenda; leaders must now tell Instagram stories, be ever-present on Twitter, post on regularly on Facebook and even, in the case of Barack Obama, place ads on billboards that appear in video games. In their chapter in this book, Shannon C. McGregor and Regina G. Lawrence describe how Hillary Clinton's campaign for president in 2016 used and adjusted to the "affordances" demanded by each platform. She had to mount multiple strategies and campaigns and needed a phalanx of workers and volunteers in order just to be in the game.

Even if their messages get through, political leaders have no control over the power that users have to spread, mash up, meme or culturally jam their messages. They also have no guarantee that their daily messages and packaging will get past Facebook's gatekeeping algorithms and make it onto Facebook's news feeds, let alone reach target audiences. They have little control over news prompts on mobile phones, perhaps the most influential connector to audiences that now exists.

To make matters worse, they have little time for contemplation or even decision making. The media churn is now so fast and all consuming that leaders have little time to think or consult before responses are expected. The art of delay that was intrinsic to Lincoln, Churchill or Roosevelt's leadership, and to Obama's, is arguably no longer possible. Leaders now find themselves playing in a high-speed game that never stops and in which the players never rest.

The great generals in history have been masters of logistics. Without effective transportation and ample supplies of weapons and ammunition, food, clothing and blankets, no army can prevail. Similarly, unless the "backend of politics" goes well in terms of fund-raising; organizing rallies, events and get-togethers; collecting and using voters' lists; creating databases; and getting supporters to the polls, campaigns will fall apart. Here again social media has become a key to success. Social media sites not only spread messages but also, if used wisely, help to build organization. Presumably, political leaders, like generals, know that logistics matter and that the old political style based on personal contacts, backroom deals and phone conversations, while still critical, may not be nearly enough.

One of the effects of social media has been to allow people who once felt disconnected from and alone in their communities to contact and sustain each other. Environmentalists, student activists, feminists, passionate conservatives, gay rights advocates and people from every imaginable background and cause could now create their own meeting places and online worlds. As a result, the fires of grassroots political action are everywhere and inescapable. Chapters in this book describe student activists in South Africa, the role that online feminist leaders

8 David Taras

played in organizing *SlutWalk*, the battle by online Indigenous leaders in Canada to reshape the narrative of Canadian political life and the energy industries' attempts to change the symbolic landscape in their battle against environmentalists. All were successful to some degree.

In terms of the larger tableau, Manuel Castells, Malcolm Gladwell, Paolo Gerbaudo and Zeynep Tufecki, among others, have described the successes and failures of social movements that have changed the dynamics of politics from Iceland to Egypt, Hong King to Spain. Castells argues that what we are seeing is a new style of politics and leadership. Even if they do not translate into immediate success in elections or on the streets, although they sometimes do, online campaigns created by activists can be transformative nonetheless because they have the capacity to change the political narrative. Once narratives change, everything else can change. Gladwell is much less sympathetic to grassroots movements that have formed online. He criticizes the instant coffee politics that these movements have spawned: a politics without leaders, clear policies or even the ability to negotiate coherently with governments. Once these movements hit the real world of the public square, they tend to shatter quickly. Real progress can only come through elections, in legislatures and with the development of policies that are often the result of long effort and compromises. All else is illusion, the short and frantic politics of make-believe.

Yasha Mouck is concerned that online movements have nurtured and fostered extremists and empowered outsiders with anti-democratic views. They have helped "de-consolidate" democracy by delegitimizing and bypassing established and venerable institutions.

Tufecki takes a middle position. She believes that social movements that largely form online, in what she terms "the networked public sphere," have the ability to challenge existing narratives and disrupt how institutions operate but often do so in the best interests of democracy. The strategy of "protest first, organize later," however, signals both strengths and weaknesses and can only be taken so far. As Tufekci observes, "capabilities are like muscles that need to be developed: digital technologies allow 'shortcuts' which can be useful for getting to a goal, but bypass the muscle development that might be crucial for the next step." (Tufekci, p. 269) She is also aware that online technology can cut both ways. Governments have become much more skilled at surveillance, disruption and intimidation than was the case even two or three years ago. This has made the networked public sphere a more dangerous place for protesters and dissidents.

Political Leaders, Social Media and Grassroots Politics

The question at the end of the rainbow is whether social media represents a shift in power, a re-calculation of the skills and governing styles needed by leaders to emerge and succeed. Or to put it differently, does social media both produce new types of leaders and signal the end of those who cannot navigate in its sometimes treacherous waters?

Donald Trump seemed like an unlikely candidate from virtually every point of view. He was opposed by party elites, spent less than the other candidates, had an only rudimentary organization and had seemingly little understanding of data analytics. His strengths were a flamboyant personality, bombastic language and a simple message that revolved around "making America great again," "draining the swamp" in Washington and building a wall along the border with Mexico, all of which brought torrents of coverage from the conventional media. There was also Twitter. While Trump's supporters were the least likely to use social media, what Jennifer Stromer-Galley has described as Trump's "vulgar eloquence" on Twitter allowed Trump to set the media agenda, demean his opponents and attract almost endless attention to himself.

Stromer-Galley argues in her chapter that Trump has an extraordinary and instinctive understanding of the rhythms and cadences demanded by Twitter and how tweets are received and interpreted by users. According to Stromer-Galley, his tweets have a unique poetic structure and "a signature style." His uses repetitive language, including applying adjectives to the names of his opponents; crooked Hillary, Rubio "a choker" etc., enthymemes that force users to fill in the gaps and thus better remember his tweets and tropes of outrage. He positions himself as a common man, one of the people, compliments his audience by telling them that they are smart and "in the know" and ends his tweets with blunt conclusions that are unique to his Twitter style, such as declaring something or someone "Sad," "a total joke" or "Bad."

In their analysis of Trump's tweets about the news media from his inauguration as president on January 20, 2017 until April 10, 2018, Joshua M. Scacco and Eric Wiemer conclude that Trump's use of Twitter was unique in yet another way. Trump set himself up as a kind of national editor-in-chief or, in their words, "a sort of pseudo-news network." He used Twitter to refute critical stories, harshly and viciously attack reporters and news sources that he didn't like and re-direct followers to alternative news sources and facts. In a sense, Trump had inverted the usual dynamics of presidential–press relations. While the press' job is to report on the president, now the president was reporting on the press. The irony was that his relentless and often stream-of-consciousness attacks on journalists and news organizations often made news.

Moving beyond the particular politics of Twitter and Donald Trump, in the chapter that follows Shannon McGregor and Regina Lawrence argue that each social media platform has different affordances and audiences and that social media cannot be lumped together into a single category. In their study of Hillary Clinton's online campaign during the 2016 US presidential election, they found that the Clinton campaign used Facebook, Twitter and Instagram in different ways and for different purposes. Facebook was seen as a vehicle for reaching a mass audience and was useful for testing different messages and approaches. It also allowed

10 David Taras

the campaign to target particular ethnic or civic groups. Twitter attracted a more elite audience and was a main instrument for reaching journalists. Hence, it was the preferred platform for releasing policy statements and daily talking points. Instagram was for telling the campaign's backstory and humanizing Hillary through photos and happy moments. McGregor and Lawrence's main point is that each of these new instruments of persuasion demands different skills and strategies, and the staffing and skills needed to run a multifaceted campaign. The social media game has to be played on a number of different chess boards at the same time.

In another chapter, Chaseten Remillard and his colleagues describe Justin Trudeau's use of selfies and Instagram during the 2015 Canadian federal election. They point out that Trudeau's selfie campaign and Instagram account were used very differently from his Twitter and Facebook accounts. Selfies were meant to convey accessibility, warmth, youthfulness and a "joyful public" and had an authentic feel because it was the very people who appeared with Trudeau in the photos, and not the campaign, who sent them viral. Instagram involved a different kind of photo bombing. The Instagram campaign was designed to display the Liberal party's values by showing Trudeau in different settings: ones involving cultural diversity, urban chic, caring for nature and the environment, humanism and policy activism. The party's message was "condensed in Trudeau."

A last chapter in the first section describes how Twitter was used by 17 US congressional leaders a month before and after President Trump's address to Congress in 2017 and State of the Union address in 2018. According to Jacob Straus and Raymond Williams, Twitter accomplished a number of key tasks for congressional leaders. It allowed them to connect with constituents, reach journalists with their messages and, most crucially, perhaps, gauge how the public was responding to issues and events. On this last point, Straus and Williams note that as few as 30 similar tweets from constituents was sometimes enough to move leaders to pay attention. Twitter was also used to enforce party discipline. Those members whose tweets did not reflect the same positions as the leaders could be quickly spotted and dealt with. The heightened power of congressional leaders to monitor their colleagues through Twitter undoubtedly discourages ordinary members from compromising, staking out middle-of-the-road positions or dealing with the other side. Twitter helps keep congressional politics both divisive and frozen in place.

Strauss and Williams found, not surprisingly, that congressional leaders shifted positions to support or oppose the policies of the president but "in a more limited way than we might have suspected."

The next section of the book describes how populist leaders in Europe have used Facebook and Twitter to reach disgruntled publics. Here politics is anything but frozen in place. The first chapter by Peter Maurer analyses the Twitter campaigns of Emmanuel Macron and Marine Le Pen in the year before and for a month after the French presidential election of 2017. Maurer argues that Twitter is by far the most popular social media platform in French political life. It has

Political Leaders and Social Media **11**

become the basic currency of political exchange. Maurer attempts to gauge the degree to which the two main candidates used populist appeals on Twitter during the election. He defines populism as an ideology that distinguishes the people who are fundamentally honest and pure from a corrupt elite that is corrupt, detached from the people and illegitimate. The people are the "collective we" that makes France sovereign and good, but there are other groups that do not belong. His conclusion is that while Le Pen's Twitter feed was replete with populist-like messages and Macron's more cautious in that his appeals were encased in a rejection of the party system and therefore the party elites, both candidates were careful not to use inflammatory language, insults or appeals to raw emotions. Their tweets were rational and conditioned by the need to reach the 50 per cent of the vote demanded by the presidential system.

Sina Blassnig and her colleagues surveyed the social media messages of 36 leaders in six countries: – France, Germany, Italy, Switzerland, the United Kingdom and the United States – during a three-month period in 2015 when there were no election campaigns. The sample consisted of the leaders of the four largest parties in the parliaments of each of the countries surveyed. The study matched the number of popularity cues – Facebook likes and shares and Twitter favourites and retweets – with populist messages in order to determine whether populist messages resonated more strongly with users. Their conclusion was that while Facebook was a better instrument for conveying populist messages than Twitter, all political leaders did better on both mediums when their posts and tweets contained populist appeals.

It's difficult to know whether these results echo the times and the vast discontent that seemed to pervade much of Europe during this period or whether there is an intrinsic connection between social media and populist rhetoric.

Maurice Vergeer does a similar examination of Twitter use in Dutch politics. His findings are very different, however. In a political system in which political parties have to share power in coalition governments, populist appeals and negative attacks on opponents are muted. The system as whole imposes a "normalization" that ensures that the political leaders play by rules long accepted in Dutch politics.

The last section of the book examines leadership, social media and grassroots politics. We begin with Kaitlynn Mendes' analysis of feminist activism online. According to Mendes, in the absence of money, organization, offices, support from established women's groups, attention from the conventional media and status, activists had little choice but to forge links online. In the case of SlutWalk, Mendes credits Facebook's algorithms with spreading the message to would-be activists quickly. Another of Facebook's affordances is that it not only spreads news about scheduled events cheaply and effectively but also allows users to see who else was "interested" or "attending." Seeing whether their friends were going was often decisive in getting others to come. Facebook thus helped to produce a cascading effect. The question is whether SlutWalk, for instance, would have been nearly as successful without Facebook.

12 David Taras

Those who led the charge online sometimes faced considerable danger. They were often trolled and harassed and felt exposed and vulnerable. They could do little to escape their enemies, who could follow them for days and even years from the protective cover of anonymity. Online leaders also succumbed to burn-out and fatigue and some withdrew from the cause.

It's important to note that more than a few journalists, who have to continually tweet, argue and defend themselves on Twitter, also report being exhausted by the process. The attacks never seem to come to an end and a kind of PTSD sets in. Some have had to take themselves off Twitter just to recover.

Mendes also argues that the real success of feminist activism online is that it has created a "discursive activism": a "political speech . . . that intervenes in hegemonic discourses, and that works at the level of language to change political cultures." Like Castells, Mendes believes that change comes by altering the narratives that guide society.

Brad Clark makes the same point in his examination of the activities of online Indigenous leaders in Canada during the country's 150th anniversary celebrations, which took place in 2017. Their online campaign attempted to counter the commanding narrative of government celebrations and indeed of national life in Canada by re-writing the script to reflect the injustices experienced by Indigenous peoples. According to Clark, they succeeded to a remarkable degree in part by influencing coverage in the mainstream media. Remarkably, online leaders all but bypassed the established native leadership. The lesson may be that governments can no longer be certain that their narratives will go uncontested even when it comes to expensive and highly choreographed national celebrations.

This is also the point made in Tamara Small and Mireille Lalancette's chapter on how former British Prime Minister Theresa May was depicted in Internet memes. Created by ordinary grassroots users, memes marry images and text and if they go viral can explode the images carefully crafted by leaders and campaigns with devastating force. Their power comes from the fact that they often use the ideas and trends in popular culture to ridicule those in power. Political leaders such as Theresa May have little defence against the politics of mockery because the very act of defending oneself will validate and call further attention to the memes. While Small and Lalancette remind us that little is known about who creates memes or the types of memes that go viral, if we are looking for a shift in power created by social media, then memes are certainly a poignant and powerful example.

Patrick McCurdy's chapter describes the battle that is being fought between the oil and gas industry and environmental groups in Canada and by inference across the globe. His particular focus is on an online campaign launched by the oil and gas industry to preserve the Centennial Flame that presides over Parliament Hill in Ottawa, a flame powered by natural gas. McCurdy describes the goal of #KeepCanadasFlame as attempting to transform the "Centennial flame from an

Political Leaders and Social Media **13**

empty signifier into a focal point, and a rallying point for the fossil fuel lobby and its supporters." The industry in effect was attempting to reverse the usual power dynamic by waging a grassroots campaign from the top down.

The key for McCurdy is Paolo Gerbaudo's argument that social media has created a new style and type of leader: "soft leaders" who "set the scene" and "construct an emotional space within which collective action can unfold." Those who devised the industry's online campaign did precisely that. While hardly the type of leadership that would impress admirers of Churchill or de Gaulle, one can argue that these campaigns cannot be easily dismissed. Others would argue that leaders who cannot be easily identified by the public, are not running for office and do not take strong positions themselves are not leaders at all.

In the last chapter, Tanja Bosch and her colleagues describe the #FeesMustFall campaign that mobilized students across South Africa to oppose a proposed rise in university tuitions in 2016. Here again social media helped ignite and galvanize mass protests that would force the government into headlong retreat. The authors compare Facebook with Twitter, crediting Facebook with being more of a connecting link, particularly for poorer African students. Twitter was used principally for public relations and for communicating with the media and the broader public.

While one can argue that social media have shifted the demands on and instruments available to leaders in important ways, one can also argue that in other ways much has stayed the same. Political leaders still rely to a large degree on the traditional media, have many levers of institutional power at their disposal and usually have the money, resources and standing needed to organize sophisticated online campaigns. Yet there can be little doubt that social media has empowered both citizens and social movements and created a new culture of activism and protest. They have also altered political campaigning in fundamental ways. A campaign based solely on old media would likely sink as quickly as dingy boats in a hurricane.

Patrick McCurdy ends his chapter by speculating about whether the "relentless stream of outrage politics and manufactured crises designed to illicit outrage" and "the practice of soft leadership" have damaged civic debate. While there is great concern that social media have enlivened and propelled extremists and placed traditional institutions that were designed for deliberation and consensus building under great strain, it is also the case that leaders are now forced to confront the critical issues and compelling narratives that social media campaigns sometimes represent. At the very least, they ignore them at their peril.

Reference

F. Christopher Arterton, "The Media Politics of Presidential Campaigns," in *Race for the Presidency*, James David Barber ed. (Englewood Cliffs, NJ: Prentice-Hall, 1978).

Keohane, Nannerl O. *Thinking about leadership*. Princeton University Press, 2012.
Kreiss Daniel, "The Media Are about Identity, Not Information" in *Trump and the Media* edited by Pablo Boczkowski and Zizi Papacharissi MIT Press, 2018.
Meyrowitz Joshua, *No Sense of Place*, Oxford University Press, 1986.
Pariser Eli, *The Filter Bubble*, Penguin, 2011.
Popkin Samuel, *The Candidate*, Oxford, 2012.

PART 1

Leaders and the New Instruments of Media Persuasion

2

THE PRESIDENT TWEETS THE PRESS

President–Press Relations and the Politics of Media Degradation

Joshua M. Scacco and Eric C. Wiemer

On Thursday, August 16, 2018, the editorial boards of more than 100 newspapers in the United States published editorials criticizing President Donald Trump's systematic attacks on the press. Coordinated by the *Boston Globe*, this effort was designed to highlight "the dangers of the administration's assault on the press" (Stelter, 2018). This effort by various media outlets occurred in the wake of a meeting between President Donald Trump and the publisher for the *New York Times*, A.G. Sulzberger, wherein Sulzberger urged Trump to stop referring to journalists and the news media as "the enemy of the people" (Lander, 2018). These pointed attacks on the press by a sitting president of the United States warrant careful contextualization within the present political moment, changes to institutional presidential communication, and political leadership in general.

A changing, high-choice media environment has had consequences and implications for the president's relationship with the press. The president, facing competitive pressures from other political elites, news outlets, and everyday citizens for the public's attention, has adopted a ubiquitous communication presence (Scacco & Coe, 2016). This presidential presence touches many areas of life in an attempt to stay relevant and harness the reigns of political leadership. Yet this ubiquitous posture evokes costs. The president's (and the public's) use of digital and social media technologies threatens the messaging monopoly over which presidents once presided. For instance, even in the midst of the Watergate scandal, President Richard Nixon could still carefully control the flow of political information to the press because the media system was less differentiated than at present (Lang & Lang, 1983). Amid a panoply of media options for producers and consumers of information to choose from, the modern presidency strains at times against the affordances of emergent media platforms.

18 Joshua M. Scacco and Eric C. Wiemer

Enter Donald Trump into the middle of this evolution of the presidency and media system. The case we document is one leadership response President Trump has had to these circumstances: the degradation of the news media and communicative positioning of himself and friendly information sources as the arbiters of "truth" amid a sea of "fake news." We categorize Trump's communicative approach to the news media as a form of rhetorical leadership because it is part of his process of presidential influence. The president has shown an incredible command of constituting and polarizing a loyal base of supporters already distrustful of mainstream news sources. Data from the Pew Research Center recorded a 35-point drop among Republicans between 2016 and 2017 on the belief that news media criticism prevents "political leaders from doing things that shouldn't be done" (Barthel & Mitchell, 2017). By stepping into a breach full of (mis)information from various sources, the president communicatively constructs unitary information management and control – particularly for his Republican base.

Even amid this influence on segments of the American electorate, we note that not all exercises in leadership are positive ones and more space in political communication research should be devoted to negative rhetorical leadership. President Trump is not the first president to engage in pointed attacks on the news media. As we document later in this chapter, Abraham Lincoln called for the imprisonment of newspaper publishers during the Civil War. Richard Nixon's attacks on "such outrageous, vicious, distorted reporting" had a chilling effect on initial coverage of the Watergate break-in during the 1972 presidential campaign (Lang & Lang, 1983, p. 106). Yet it is precisely for these reasons – historical and contemporary – that we seek to better understand *this moment* in negative presidential leadership.

In this chapter, we examine the Twitter activity of President Trump in the first year and a half of his presidency with regard to his relationship with the press. Through a network analysis of how Trump treats what he deems *fake news* compared to sources of information deemed trustworthy, or *real news*, we discover consistent patterns in how Trump protects his administration, delegitimizes mainstream news sources, and elevates himself as well as friendly information sources as unitary forces for truth. We first turn to briefly discussing digital information management by the president in a complicated media environment.

Digital Information Management and Executive Leadership

An important component of public rhetorical leadership is the ability to exercise influence (Stuckey, 2010; Zarefsky, 2004). At the root of these influence processes is message control. As Walter Lippmann (1922/1997) wrote regarding the need for an elite class to guide and manage public opinion, "without some form of censorship, propaganda in the strict sense of the word is impossible. Access to the real environment must be limited, before anyone can create a pseudo-environment that he thinks wise or desirable" (p. 28). Organizations then attempt to control their information environment by engaging in strategic public relations efforts (Bernays, 2015).

Yet mass censorship of information and centralization of information sources seems unlikely (or near impossible) in the contemporary American media environment. As communication researcher William Eveland (2003) observes, newer communication technologies hand over message control from producers to consumers. Individuals can choose the speed by which they encounter content or even alter said content altogether by reposting and sharing it via social media. Political elites from news organizations (Stroud, Scacco, Muddiman, & Curry, 2015) to interest groups (Bimber, Flanagin, & Stohl, 2012) to the president (Scacco & Coe, 2016) have all strained against the inversion of power relationships in traditional communication processes.

Our concern here is with the presidency, specifically Donald Trump's and how he navigates these challenges to information control. One trend facing his presidency, and the institution in general, is the inverse relationship between internal and external information control. Internally, the presidency post-Franklin Roosevelt became more bureaucratic: a larger, professionalized staff handling and centralizing policymaking power in the Executive Branch (Burke, 2010). White House communications post-Lyndon Johnson also grew to manage an increasing number of presidential public events (Kumar, 2007). Yet externally, the media environment (from the 1980s to the present) fragmented and created abundant choice options for consumers. This trend scattered presidential audiences and made it much more difficult for the president to have guaranteed network air time for official pronouncements (Baum & Kernell, 2009). The integration of digital communication platforms, including social media, further challenged presidential influence over messaging.

Recent research suggests that changes in the media environment and the American population pushed presidential communication toward a more ubiquitous footing (Scacco & Coe, 2016). In this model, the president finds publics as they are, wherever they are – segmented in political and non-political media silos. Information management, as a result, becomes more difficult and potentially more frenzied as the president seeks to reach disparate audiences. Amid these challenges, the modern presidency continues to struggle to shape the news in its favor (Farnsworth, 2018).

Emergent media that invert messaging control. A disinterested and scattered public. A seemingly disinterested yet competitive news media system. These elements confront all contemporary political officials. As we turn to next, elites in government, political campaigns, and journalism have turned to several possible responses to the information management challenges they face. We review these responses and how Donald Trump's press attacks illustrate his own approach to confronting the messaging challenges his administration faces.

Elite Responses to Information Management Challenges

In a seemingly uncontrollable information environment with digital communication technologies roiling more traditional modes of public outreach, political elites have confronted messaging challenges in various ways. These adaptations vary, including *embracing* new platforms and ways of communicating, *misusing* the available means of new media, creating *illusions* of adaptation to technological change, or completely *shutting down* emergent avenues of elite–public communication online. Each of these ways of confronting digital and social media attempts to gain some control over the messaging process, even if the final outcome leaves message control unlikely. Contemporary political elites, including President Trump, lean on each of these four approaches at different points. After reviewing these responses to information management challenges, we turn our attention to a fifth approach to confronting these challenges that we label *constitutive control*.

The first approach political elites have taken to information management is to fully embrace the affordances of emergent media, or the unique technological components of what a digital or social media platform can actually do (Kreiss, Lawrence, & McGregor, 2018). This tact is akin to "if you can't beat them, join them." With the public using many spaces to create a political, social, and cultural "wild west," the logic behind this approach is to bring *more* message control and elite influence to online spaces that embrace flatter, more interactive flows of communication. Research on comment sections suggests such elite modeling of good discursive behavior in these digital spaces can be beneficial to the quality of online discussions (Stroud et al., 2015). For many political elites, embracing technological affordances involves participating in the real time conversations the governors can have with the governed – what communication scholar Jennifer Stromer-Galley calls interactivity as process (2004). President Barack Obama participated in Reddit Ask Me Anythings to convey connectedness with the public and to showcase adaptability to the technologies rapidly challenging presidential communication (Katz, Barris, & Jain, 2013). Although rare, Donald Trump, as a presidential candidate, did engage more in transactional communication on social media than his Democratic opponent Hillary Clinton (Rossini & Stromer-Galley, 2016). Some politically-engaged audiences appreciate such accessibility, reporting that presidential connectedness is a necessary component of executive communication (Scacco & Coe, 2017).

Political officials also may choose to misuse newer means of communication technology. Strategic public communication efforts, whether related to war propaganda (Bernays, 2015) or the general management of public opinion (Lippmann, 1922/1997), emphasize the need to use all available means of communication technology to reach the public. Yet in the rush to accomplish this task, some political leaders may choose to leave the affordances of an emergent platform unused. This approach appears most prominently when political elites use an interactive platform only for the purposes of one-way communication (i.e., broadcasting). Members of Congress, for example, have a tendency to use Twitter as a bullhorn for their press releases – tweeting links in order to direct individuals back to a member's website (Hemphill, Otterbacher, & Shapiro, 2013). In President Trump's media-related tweets examined later in this chapter, he included hyperlinks in 10 percent of his tweets—a marker of this broadcast style.

Related to the misuse or even non-use of interactive media's affordances, political leaders also may choose to construct an illusion of interpersonal connectedness with the public and other political actors. Jennifer Stromer-Galley (2014) has observed this process take shape in the controlled interactivity of contemporary political campaigns. Controlled interactivity leans on the medium-specific affordances of a platform that do not involve person-to-person conversational elements (i.e., buttons, hyperlinks). By controlling interactions to those between an individual and a technological interface, political elites open up some channels of connectivity while leaving digital face-to-face interactivity at a premium. The Obama administration's much vaunted "We the People" petitions were a good example of this illusory interactivity. Individuals could e-petition the White House on any issue, but a formal response required 100,000 signatures and took between 34 and 271 days on average to receive a response once the signature threshold was achieved (Hitlin, 2016).

Should the embrace, misuse, or the illusion of interactivity not suit a political official, a final possibility is the complete shutdown of communications on a particular platform. This tact can be observed in how news outlets, failing to manage the toxicity of comment sections housed on their websites, completely remove commenting spaces altogether. Donald Trump has done similar, as well. The "We the People" petition platform was largely unattended at first in the Trump administration before being temporarily shut down (Rosenberg, 2017).

Although political leaders can avail themselves of these four approaches for information management – independently or in tandem depending on the communication strategy – we turn our attention to another approach that we observe in the Trump administration. President Trump assumed an institutional office buffeted by the tides of technological and societal change (Scacco & Coe, 2016; Stuckey, 2010). The presidency can no longer exercise command-and-control over external political messaging and still must manage a sprawling bureaucratic operation in the White House where internal information coordination is already quite difficult (Burke, 2010). From the demand perspective, intense competition among political actors and news media outlets places audience attention at a premium (Stroud, 2017). To gain some attention, the presidency increasingly adopts a ubiquitous persona to maintain relevancy and influence (Scacco, Coe, & Hearit, 2018). One outcome, we observe in this chapter, is how Donald Trump communicatively constitutes information control, particularly for his Twitter audience.

A constitutive approach calls for an understanding of how a communicator socially constructs reality. Communication theorist James Carey explained that "we first produce the world by symbolic work and then take up residence in the world we have produced. Alas, there is magic in our self deceptions" (1989,

p. 30). Examining the constitutive components of Donald Trump's tweets during the first year and half of his administration, we observe how the president uses social media to communicatively construct control over his environment by degrading press sources and positioning himself as a central arbiter of reliable information. The resulting picture is one where Donald Trump assumes the role of pseudo-news reporter: refuting what he deems misinformation, assessing the credibility of sources, and acting as informational gatekeeper for favorable information.

Method

Data Collection

In order to examine President Trump's messages regarding the press, his tweets from the inauguration (1/20/17) until April 10, 2018 were collected using a social media metrics and archival platform, Crimson Hexagon. This platform allows subscribers access to the universe of public tweets (except deletions) along with metrics regarding each tweet, such as retweets, replies, and potential impressions. We downloaded all of the tweets sent from Trump's personal Twitter account, @realDonaldTrump ($n = 1,776$).

Next, we narrowed down this data to include only tweets that referenced the news media in some way. Our criteria for relevant tweets included any mentions of the press, news media, news stories, or journalists in any context, as well as general mentions of fake news and the mainstream media (e.g., MSM). All of Trump's tweets were content analyzed for these criteria (Krippendorff's $\alpha = 0.97$). A total of 317 tweets were determined to be media-related.

Data Analysis

Once the corpus of media-relevant Trump tweets was coded, we employed text mining on all media-related Trump tweets. Text mining allowed us to efficiently clean and narrow the scope of the text (Lambert, 2017). AutoMap, a software developed for text mining, has the ability to take large sets of textual data and perform preprocessing techniques (Carley, 2001; Carley, Columbus, Bigrigg, Diesner, & Kunkel, 2010). Here, we used AutoMap to remove noise words (e.g., with, so, but), misspellings, and punctuation. Then, we constructed a custom delete list and thesaurus to fit this specific data. The custom delete list got rid of words and metadata that are common among text derived from tweets, such as hyperlinks and @ symbols in front of usernames. The custom thesaurus was created to combine various iterations of the same word into a single instance. For example, the *New York Times* and *NYTimes* can both be transformed into simply *NYT*. AutoMap then allowed us to export the preprocessed textual data into a co-occurrence semantic list. A semantic list enumerates every pair of words that occur in any given tweet either five words before or after one another and the frequency with which that particular pair occurs in the entire corpus of text.

Following the preprocessing of tweet data, semantic network analysis methods using NodeXL took the connections and instances of words in the co-occurrence semantic list and constructed networks and visualizations (Doerfel, 1998; Wasserman & Faust, 1994; Smith et al., 2010). Each word in the semantic list is represented by a node in the network, and a connection between two words in the semantic list is represented in a network by a line, or edge, connecting those two nodes together (Wasserman & Faust, 1994).

After reviewing this initial network visualization and the corresponding semantic list, we wanted to differentiate the network between tweets associated with fake news and tweets associated with real or honest news. This differentiation allowed us to later qualitatively examine for emergent themes. Semantic connections between words that included mentions of fake news, dishonest news, witch hunt, and other related constructions were classified as fake news tweets. Such connections were highlighted in the overall semantic network of media-related tweet data and exported to their own semantic network consisting only of mentions of fake news terms and the connections those terms have with other words. Real news word associations included mention of outlets or commentators that Trump has favored, including *Fox News*, *Fox & Friends*, and specific anchors, such as Sean Hannity and Tucker Carlson. Similarly, these connections were also highlighted in the overall semantic network and exported into a separate semantic network. Figures 2.1 and 2.2 show the network visualizations for each of the two new semantic networks representing *fake news* and *real news*, respectively. The size of each node in the network is determined by the degree centrality of that word in the network, or the number of connections that word has with other words in the network, such that a bigger-sized node denotes a higher degree centrality (i.e., more connections; Wasserman & Faust, 1994).

Cross-checking the semantic network visualizations, co-occurrence lists, and tweets, we arrived at themes using emergent category designation, a qualitative approach where latent theory is used to form categories (Erlandson, Harris, Skipper, & Allen, 1993). In this instance, we focused on how the president's tweets communicatively constituted efforts at information management and control.

Results

The president's tweets reveal a recurring effort to *protect* his administration against problematic information, *delegitimize* the sources of said problematic information, and *promote* an alternative set of venues for news information. By returning to these constructions in his tweets, the president attempts to communicatively

24 Joshua M. Scacco and Eric C. Wiemer

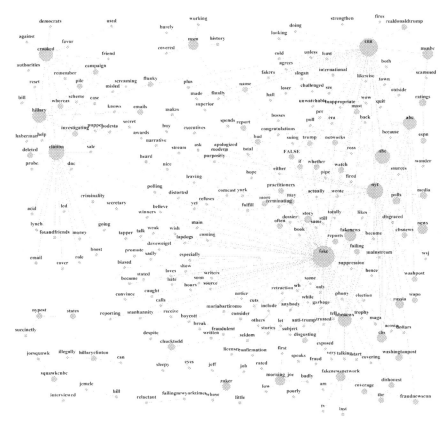

FIGURE 2.1 Network Visualization of "Fake News" Instances in Trump's Tweets Since Entering Office

Source: Figure created by Authors

constitute informational control for his audience in a maelstrom of socially-mediated information.

Protection Against Problematic Information

In a competitive political environment, an important portion of a presidency's messaging strategy involves protection against criticism. Indeed, the protective tone has been observed at various points across different presidencies, including in presidential press conferences (Hart & Scacco, 2014). Donald Trump's administration is no different in this regard.

A dual approach Trump uses to control unwelcomed news information and thus fortify his standing is inoculation followed by refutation and deflection. Rhetorical inoculation attempts to protect an audience from future persuasive

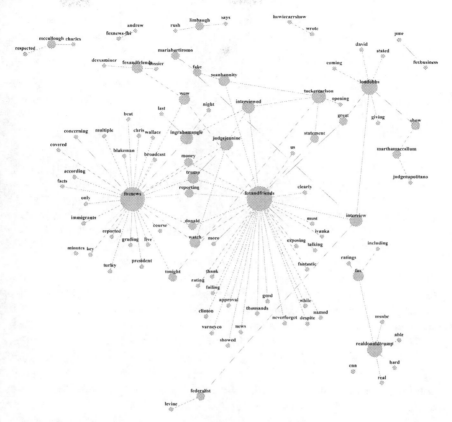

FIGURE 2.2 Network Visualization of "Real News" Instances in Trump's Tweets Since Entering Office

Source: Figure created by Authors

efforts, much like a communicative vaccine (Stiff & Mongeau, 2016). However, this approach carries risks. Political consultant Frank Luntz (2007) argues that when you evoke the opposition's message, you give that message greater visibility. Refutation and deflection are the immediate denial and reframing of a particular situation – a common strategy in political debates and press conferences (Hart & Scacco, 2014). We can see this approach made manifest in Donald Trump's tweets.

For a message to serve as a tool of inoculation, it must first frame (or even repeat in some instances) a form of the opposition's argument. Donald Trump, for example, tweeted in March 2018 an attack on the *New York Times* over its reporting of his legal woes.

> The Failing New York Times purposely wrote a false story stating that I am unhappy with my legal team on the Russia case and am going to add

26   Joshua M. Scacco and Eric C. Wiemer

> another lawyer to help out. Wrong. I am VERY happy with my lawyers, John Dowd, Ty Cobb and Jay Sekulow. They are doing a great job . . .
>
> *(3/11/18)*

The tweet repeats the *Times'* reporting and then advances a message favorable to the administration. We can see a similar tact at work when Donald Trump rewrites a *Washington Post* headline he disagrees with (4/5/18) or uses capitalization to draw attention to a story about "CHAOS" in the White House (3/6/18).

Following the delivery of an unfavorable message, the president then refutes it. One form of immediate refutation is the statement that news information is "wrong." Trump employs this approach 13 times in his media-related tweets (4%). The approach mirrors how media fact checkers assess the accuracy of statements. Another form of refutation is for the president to explicitly say "Don't believe" a particular story or news source as well as to pose a rhetorical question about belief in news information ("Do you believe that the Fake News Media is pushing hard on a story that I am going to replace A.G. Jeff Sessions with EPA Chief Scott Pruitt . . . ?"; 4/6/18). The rhetorical question serves to highlight the perceived extremity of individuals who would believe such information ("Do people really believe this stuff?" 4/6/18), an approach designed to marginalize oppositional arguments as unintelligible inaccuracies.

Once the oppositional message has been delivered and refuted, it is then deflected via correction. The push to "correct the record" is common in political arenas. For instance, political campaigns devote sections of websites or even whole political advertisements to correcting "claims" made by the opposition. The rise of a nascent form of fact checking in the 1988 presidential campaign that appeared on television news, called the Ad Watch, served as a means to take negative campaign advertisements and correct them for users (Gladstone, 2012). In the tweet regarding Trump's attorneys, the president ends with "They are doing a great job . . ." (3/11/18). When criticizing another *Times* story, the president fumed "Another false story, this time in the Failing @nytimes, that I watch 4–8 hours of television a day – Wrong! Also, I seldom, if ever, watch CNN or MSNBC, both of which I consider Fake News" (12/11/17). Much as news fact checkers correct the record once a claim has been labeled inaccurate, President Trump also engages in a parallel form of correcting the record. The extent to which these efforts lead to success for the president, as opposed to ensconcing messages he dislikes in the minds of the public, is an effect that scholars and practitioners should further examine.

Delegitimation of News

Distrust and dislike of the news media is certainly not a new phenomenon. In fact, political scientist Jonathan Ladd (2012) claims that politicians who desire support from the public are inherently threatened by an independent news media

The President Tweets the Press **27**

and therefore often do what they can to dismiss news claims. As a result, political elites, including the president, issue statements of dislike toward the media in hopes that the public will bypass unfavorable claims made by the media. Even President Abraham Lincoln, freer of slaves and preserver of the Union, issued an executive order calling for the arrest of the editors and publishers of the *New York World* and *New York Journal of Commerce* over content deemed "treasonable [in] nature, designed to give aid and comfort to the enemies of the United States and to the rebels now at war against the Government and their aiders and abettors . . ." (Lincoln, 1864). Although the Trump administration has not called for the imprisonment of press officials in his attacks on the press, his tweets reveal the ways in which he seeks to delegitimize it through name-calling, legal threats, and appeals to popularity.

One of the most recognizable ways in which President Trump attempts to delegitimize the press is through *ad hominem* attacks, or name-calling. The semantic connections of the "Fake News" network reveal negative labels for news outlets, coverage, and journalists, including "disgusting," "loser," "unwatchable," "lapdogs," and "fraudulent," among others. This approach to press degradation also is repeatedly employed in the labels of "fake" news (163 mentions), "fail(ing)" (31 mentions), "bias" (9 mentions), and "enemy" (2 mentions). By repeating these descriptors, as well as associating particular characteristics with each news outlet – failing *New York Times*, Amazon *Washington Post*, Fake News Network (CNN), the president attempts to make his press attacks memorable for the public while directing individuals away from these sources. These labels are not just ascribed to news organizations, but to journalists as well. The president has referred to NBC journalist Chuck Todd as "sleepy eyes" (4/1/17) and a CNN reporter as "Crazy Jim Acosta" (1/28/18) in attempts to stunt the credibility of news individuals.

The press attacks escalate from name-calling to *ad baculum*, or overt threats, in some instances. Presidential threats against news organizations are designed to bring press officials to heel. In the Trump case, such threats are towards the news media as an institution. "Network news has become so partisan, distorted and fake that licenses must be challenged and, if appropriate, revoked. Not fair to public!" (10/11/17). The president threatened the licenses of news organizations twice and called for changes to libel laws once in the time frame examined here. If the president were to follow through on these threats, the changes would make it much more difficult for news outlets to report information critical of the Trump administration.

A third delegitimation approach seen in Trump's tweets is *argumentum ad populum*, or appeal to popularity (or lack thereof). Focusing on television ratings, Trump signals to his Twitter followers that "good" news and popularity are linked while critical coverage of his administration makes an outlet unpopular. The president also fallaciously equates popularity with accuracy. "Bad ratings @CNN & @MSNBC got scammed when they covered the anti-Trump Russia rally wall-to-wall. They probably knew it was Fake News but, because it was a rally against

28 Joshua M. Scacco and Eric C. Wiemer

me, they pushed it hard anyway" (2/20/18). By engaging in delegitimation via popularity appeals, the president may hope to direct individuals away from more critical television news programming.

Promotion of a Real News Network

The Trump campaign and administration devote considerable time to promoting particular sources of information. For instance, the Trump–Pence 2020 campaign launched a webcast in July 2017 called "Real News Update" designed to broadcast favorable coverage of the administration on Twitter and Facebook (Vitali, 2017). In the first "news" update, President Trump's daughter-in-law Lara Trump announces the purpose of the webcasts as truth teller in an information environment full of lies. "I bet you haven't heard about all the accomplishments the president had this week because there's so much fake news out there." Such messaging carries over into the president's Twitter communications as well.

When turning to the president's tweets, we see that Donald Trump goes to great lengths to promote the credibility of particular news sources, stories, and journalists he deems helpful to the administration's efforts. The real news semantic network weaves a tight web around Fox News and its related programming, including *Fox & Friends* (mentioned 36 times), Tucker Carlson (5 times), Laura Ingraham (4 times), and Sean Hannity (3 times). Interestingly, Donald Trump also has a prominent node in the network (9 mentions) – indicating that his discourse positions himself as a source of real news, as well. In holding up these sources as exemplars, the president creates an alternative news ecosystem to compete with the one he has attacked.

The communicative construction of real news promotion takes several different forms: thanks, discovery, and juxtaposition. First, the president thanks outlets and programming he sees as favorable toward his agenda or critical of his opponents. "Thank you to @foxandfriends for the great timeline on all of the failures the Obama Administration had against Russia, including Crimea, Syria and so much more" (2/20/18). In the 317 media-related tweets examined, Trump uses the phrase "thank you" 21 times (6.6% of tweets) to laud particular coverage. These communications toward favorable news anchors and organizations are remarkably positive, featuring words such as "good," "fantastic," and "respected."

Second, President Trump's tweets frame the existence or discovery of "real news" that he sees as hidden from the public and necessary for him to publicize. "The Fake News Media works hard at disparaging & demeaning my use of social media because they don't want America to hear the real story!" (5/28/17). The phrases "real story" or "real news" appear only seven times, but his attacks on "fake news" serve to implicitly highlight the existence of some truth that the president has discovered. It is in these moments that the president positions himself as breaker of news. Seven of the eight mentions of "social media" in Trump's tweets construct a need for him to use Twitter to "fight" and "go around" mainstream

The President Tweets the Press **29**

news outlets. This approach echoes the frustrations previous presidents have felt with the national news media as well as the drive to "go public" directly to individuals with official appeals (see Kernell, 2007).

Third, the president's promotional tweets juxtapose what he considers to be real news against misleading news information. "Such amazing reporting on unmasking and the crooked scheme against us by @foxandfriends. 'Spied on before nomination.' The real story" (4/3/17). What counts as "real" news for President Trump? The scandalous behavior of the FBI ("the leaking of classified information" 3/20/17), Hillary Clinton and the Democratic Party's loss in 2016 ("They lost the election, and now they have lost their grip on reality . . ." 3/2/17), or the accomplishments of his administration. Trump attempts to act as an informational gatekeeper for his Twitter followers – highlighting (mis)information he deems to be important from trusted sources of information. In a cluttered information environment online, such gatekeeping efforts may indeed provide important consumption signals for some segments of his audience.

Conclusion

When the president tweets the press, his messages attempt to constitute information control for his audience. Donald Trump's tweets reveal a president attempting to protect his administration from critical news stories, delegitimize news outlets, and promote an alternate network of news truth tellers. In the process, the president also positions himself on Twitter as the hub for trusted and favorable news – a sort of pseudo-news network where he fact checks, vets credible sources, and promotes particular information. These efforts may have the effect of winnowing down an abundance of media options for segments of his audience to ones that favor his administration – a tactic that feeds the tendency to seek out likeminded political information (Stroud, 2011).

The presidential communicative behavior we document in this chapter, although reflecting a potentially effective use of public rhetorical leadership on the part of the president, nonetheless invites two sobering questions about the sustainability of an independent press against an almost daily executive onslaught. First, how might the president's critiques and outright attacks on the press influence the accountability relationship between the chief executive and news outlets? The news media hold the powerful accountable for their actions and are a vital component to what presidency scholar Bruce Buchanan (2012) calls the *presidential accountability system*. Not only is this press accountability function largely supported across segments of the American public (Barthel & Mitchell, 2017), but it also is a vital component to the steeling of executive leadership. Yet, Trump's approach to media degradation shows the means by which the president can re-orient the accountability function while disseminating particular messages. By using social media to reveal "the real story," the president attempts to avoid press scrutiny while challenging news accounts – an inversion of the accountability

30 Joshua M. Scacco and Eric C. Wiemer

function. The president holds the press accountable on behalf of the public (i.e., his supporters) by correcting the record and using the bully pulpit to compete as a pseudo-news outlet. The reaction from journalists, including meta-coverage of the president's treatment of the press, then serves as the grist by which the president can continue attacks and encourage the public to distrust the media. What these results may mean for public views of the press becomes an urgent endeavor to further understand.

Second, how might forms of hostile press-directed communication constitute a broader discursive environment unfavorable to the news media's central function in democratic life? Even prior to the rise of Donald Trump, the digital and social media environment placed substantial stress on newsrooms, particularly local ones (Stroud, 2017). News outlets continue to face these financial stresses, but also must operate at a time when basic public support for their functions falls along ideological boundaries (Barthel & Mitchell, 2017) and press criticism is unrelenting in socially mediated spaces. Extremists have targeted news outlets in the United States during the first two years of Trump's administration, including a domestic terrorist who – inspired by the president's attacks – mailed improvised explosive devices to CNN. The end of the Trump presidency will not signal an end to these underlying financial issues nor the echoes of Trumpian attacks on the press. Although the normative rules for press treatment may have shifted slightly, the financial rules for news have not. The long-term concern is whether the current confluence of financial and political difficulties test the future ability of the press to maintain its watchdog function in democratic life. Any faltering on the part of the press may have unintended consequences for how future presidents "perform" executive fitness from the steeling that comes from press critique.

References

Barthel, M., & Mitchell, A. (2017, May 10). Americans' attitudes about the news media deeply divided along partisan lines. *Pew Research Center*. Retrieved from www.journalism.org/2017/05/10/americans-attitudes-about-the-news-media-deeply-divided-along-partisan-lines/

Baum, M. A., & Kernell, S. (2009). How cable ended the golden age of presidential television: From 1969–2006. In S. Kernell & S. S. Smith (Eds.), *Principles and practice of American politics: Classic and contemporary readings* (4th ed., pp. 311–326). Washington, DC: CQ Press.

Bernays, E. L. (2015). *Crystallizing public opinion*. New York, NY: Open Road Media.

Bimber, B., Flanagin, A. J., & Stohl, C. (2012). *Collective action in organizations*. New York, NY: Cambridge.

Buchanan, B. (2012). *Presidential power and accountability: Toward a presidential accountability system*. New York City, NY: Routledge.

Burke, J. P. (2010). The institutional presidency. In M. Nelson (Ed.), *The presidency and the political system* (9th ed., pp. 341–366). Washington, DC: CQ Press.

Carey, J. (1989). *Communication as culture*. London, UK: Routledge.

Carley, K. (2001). AutoMap (version 3.0.10.41) [Computer software]. Pittsburg, PA: CASOS, Carnegie Mellon University. Retrieved from www.casos.cs.cmu.edu/projects/automap/index.php

Carley, K. M., Columbus, D., Bigrigg, M., Diesner, J., & Kunkel, F. (2010). AutoMap User's Guide 2010 (CMU-ISR-10). Carnegie Mellon University. Retrieved from www.casos.cs.cmu.edu/publications/papers/CMU-ISR-10-121.pdf

Doerfel, M. L. (1998). What constitutes semantic network analysis? A comparison of research and methodologies. *Connections, 21*, 16–26.

Erlandson, D. A., Harris, E. L., Skipper, B. L., & Allen, S. D. (1993). *Doing naturalistic inquiry: A guide to methods.* Thousand Oaks, CA: Sage.

Eveland, W. P. (2003). A "mix of attributes" approach to the study of media effects and new communication technologies. *Journal of Communication, 53*(3), 395–410.

Farnsworth, S. J. (2018). *Presidential communication and character: White House news management from Clinton and cable to Twitter and Trump.* New York, NY: Routledge.

Gladstone, B. (2012, October 19). Fact-checking done right. *WNYC Studios.* Retrieved from www.wnycstudios.org/story/244942-fact-checking-done-right/

Hart, R. P., & Scacco, J. M. (2014). Rhetorical negotiation and the presidential press conference. In R. P. Hart (Ed.), *Communication and language analysis in the public sphere* (pp. 59–80). Hershey, PA: IGI Global.

Hemphill, L., Otterbacher, J., & Shapiro, M. (2013, February). What's Congress doing on Twitter? In *Proceedings of the 2013 conference on Computer supported cooperative work* (pp. 877–886). ACM.

Hitlin, P. (2016, December 28). 'We the people': Five years of online petitions. *Pew Research Center.* Retrieved from http://assets.pewresearch.org/wp-content/uploads/sites/14/2016/12/27154442/PI_2016.12.28_We-the-People_FINAL.pdf

Katz, J. E., Barris, M., & Jain, A. (2013). *The social media president: Barack Obama and the politics of digital engagement.* New York, NY: Palgrave Macmillan.

Kernell, S. (2007). *Going public: New strategies of presidential leadership* (4th ed.). Washington, DC: CQ Press.

Kreiss, D., Lawrence, R. G., & McGregor, S. C. (2018). In their own words: Political practitioner accounts of candidates, audiences, affordances, genres, and timing in strategic social media use. *Political Communication, 35*(1), 8–31.

Kumar, M. J. (2007). *Managing the president's message: The White House communications operation.* Baltimore, MD: Johns Hopkins University Press.

Ladd, J. M. (2012). *Why Americans hate the news and how it matters.* Princeton, NJ: Princeton University Press.

Lambert, N. J. (2017). A text mining tutorial. In A. Pilny & M. S. Poole (Eds.), *Group processes: Computational and data driven approaches* (pp. 93–118). New York, NY: Springer Press.

Lander, M. (2018, July 29). New York Times publisher and Trump clash over president's threats against journalism. *The New York Times.* Retrieved from www.nytimes.com/2018/07/29/us/politics/trump-new-york-times-sulzberger.html

Lang, G. E., & Lang, K. (1983). *The battle for public opinion.* New York, NY: Columbia University Press.

Lincoln, A. (1864). Executive order – Arrest and imprisonment of irresponsible newspaper reporters and editors. American Presidency Project. Retrieved from www.presidency.ucsb.edu/ws/index.php?pid=70018&st=newspaper&st1

Lippmann, W. (1922/1997). *Public opinion.* New York, NY: Free Press.

32 Joshua M. Scacco and Eric C. Wiemer

Luntz, F. (2007). *Words that work: It's not what you say, it's what people hear*. New York, NY: Hachette.

Rosenberg, E. (2017, December 19). White House takes down 'We the People' petitions site before responding to a single one. *The Washington Post*: The Fix. Retrieved from www.washingtonpost.com/news/the-fix/wp/2017/12/19/ white-house-takes-down-we-the-people-petitions-site-without-responding-to-a-single-one/?utm_term=.daf994543979

Rossini, P., & Stromer-Galley, J. (2016, August 2). Online activation: The role of citizen engagement on social media in the 2016 presidential election. *Illuminating 2016*. Retrieved from http://illuminating.ischool.syr.edu/blog/view/Online-activation-The-role-of-citizen-engagement-on-social-media-in-the-2016-presidential-campaign

Scacco, J. M., & Coe, K. (2016). The ubiquitous presidency: Toward a new paradigm for studying presidential communication. *International Journal of Communication, 10*, 2014–2037. doi:1932–8036/20160005

Scacco, J. M., & Coe, K. (2017). Talk this way: The ubiquitous presidency and expectations of presidential communication. *American Behavioral Scientist, 61*(3), 298–314. doi:10.1177/0002764217704321

Scacco, J. M., Coe, K., & Hearit, L. B. (2018). Presidential communication in tumultuous times: Insights into key shifts, normative implications, and research opportunities. *Annals of the International Communication Association, 42*(1), 21–37. doi:10.1080/238089 85.2018.1433962

Smith, M., Ceni, A., Milic-Frayling, N., Shneiderman, B., Mendes Rodrigues, E., Leskovec, J., & Dunne, C. (2010). NodeXL: A free and open network overview, discovery and exploration add-in for Excel 2007/2010/2013/2016. Retrieved from http://nodexl.codeplex.com/

Stelter, B. (2018, August 11). More than 100 newspapers will publish editorials decrying Trump's anti-press rhetoric. *CNN*. Retrieved from https://money.cnn.com/2018/08/11/media/boston-globe-free-press-editorial/index.html

Stiff, J. B., & Mongeau, P. A. (2016). *Persuasive communication*. New York, NY: Guilford Publications.

Stromer-Galley, J. (2004). Interactivity-as-product and interactivity-as-process. *The Information Society, 20*(5), 391–394.

Stromer-Galley, J. (2014). *Presidential campaigning in the internet age*. New York, NY: Oxford University Press.

Stroud, N. J. (2011). *Niche news: The politics of news choice*. New York, NY: Oxford University Press.

Stroud, N. J. (2017). Attention as a valuable resource. *Political Communication, 34*(3), 479–489.

Stroud, N. J., Scacco, J. M., Muddiman, A., & Curry, A. (2015). Changing deliberative norms on news organizations' Facebook sites. *Journal of Computer-Mediated Communication, 20*(2), 188–203. doi:10.1111/jcc4.12104

Stuckey, M. E. (2010). Rethinking the rhetorical presidency and presidential rhetoric. *Review of Communication, 10*, 38–52. doi:10.1080/15358590903248744

Vitali, A. (2017, August 7). Fake news? Trump launches 'real news' series. *NBC News*. Retrieved from www.nbcnews.com/politics/white-house/fake-news-trump-launches-real-news-series-n790241

Wasserman, S., & Faust, K. (1994). *Social network analysis: Methods and applications*. Cambridge, UK: Cambridge University Press.

Zarefsky, D. (2004). Presidential rhetoric and the power of definition. *Presidential Studies Quarterly, 34*, 607–619. doi:10.1111/j.1741–5705.2004.00214.x

3

VULGAR ELOQUENCE IN THE DIGITAL AGE

A Case Study of Candidate Donald Trump's Use of Twitter[1]

Jennifer Stromer-Galley

Modern political campaigns enable candidates to demonstrate to the public the leadership qualities they will take with them into public office (Trent, Friedenberg, and Denton 2019). Public commentators, journalists, and scholars raised concerns about the leadership qualities of candidate Donald Trump. On the stump, Trump's campaign speeches were rife with non-sequiturs and parentheticals that made his points hard to follow (Wang and Liu 2017). An article on Vox,[2] for example, pulled a snippet from a Trump campaign rally on July 21, 2015 when he talked about an Iranian nuclear deal negotiated under then-President Barack Obama:

> Look, having nuclear – my uncle was a great professor and scientist and engineer, Dr. John Trump at MIT; good genes, okay, very smart, the Wharton School of Finance, very good, very smart – you know, if you're a conservative Republican, if you were a liberal, if like, okay, if I ran as a liberal Democrat, they would say I'm one of the smartest people anywhere in the world – it's true! – but when you're a conservative Republican they try – do, do they do a number – that's why I always start off: Went to Wharton, was a good student, went there, went there, did this, built a fortune – you know I have to give my like credentials all the time, because we're a little disadvantaged – but you look at the nuclear deal, the thing that really bothers me – it would have been so easy, and it's not as important as these lives are (nuclear is powerful; my uncle explained that to me many, many years ago, the power, and that was 35 years ago; he would explain the power of what's going to happen, and he was right – who would have thought?)

Trump's main thesis was meant to be an argument that the Obama-era Iran deal was bad for the United States (for some reason never specified), yet it

34 Jennifer Stromer-Galley

seemed so incoherent with tangents about his uncle and his credentials as to neglect the main idea.

In addition to seemingly incoherent expression, Trump's campaign discourse ran counter to the historical precedence of decorum and the burdens of argumentation expected of presidential candidates. Jamieson and Taussig (2017) argue that Trump's "rhetorical signature" is "spontaneity laced with Manichean, evidence-flouting, accountability-dodging, and institution-disdaining claims" (p. 620). During the campaign, prominent websites kept a count of all of the people Trump had verbally attacked during his run for president in the 2016 elections, and those counts continued when he assumed the presidency.[3] Trump's favorite communication medium for his attacks was the social media platform, Twitter, where in 140 and then 280 characters he could lambast his opponents, the news media, immigrants, and the political establishment to his millions of followers. For political observers, candidate Trump could not fit into a class of political speakers that we might judge as eloquent because of his roguish style.

Yet, Trump's Twitter oratory worked powerfully because it conveyed what I describe as a vulgar eloquence. Today, *vulgar* tends to mean crude, anti-normative, and talk about the body or sex. Its etymology, however, points to a slightly different meaning. In the 14th century, *vulgar* was used to describe the common person, the lower classes, a crowd or a throng of people. Trump's Tweets are *vulgar* in the sense that they appeal to ordinary people in the vernacular used in the communication technology that conveys his messages. His Tweets signify through their grammar and style that he is ordinary, that he is a common man – he is just like the rest of us. He speaks to us through our mobile devices the way our friends do. For example, on December 9, Trump sent this note: ".@Mayor_Nutter of Philadelphia, who is doing a terrible job, should be ashamed for using such a disgusting word in referring to me.Low life!" (12/09/2015). And the next day, he sent this message: "Why does @CNN bore their audience with people like @secupp, a totally biased loser who doesn't have a clue. I hear she will soon be gone!" (12/10/2015). His language in both of those Tweets is informal, in a cultural slang that fits the medium and the messenger.

In this chapter, I lay out the case that candidate Donald J. Trump demonstrated a kind of eloquence in his leadership style – what I characterize as *vulgar eloquence*. By this, I mean that Trump's rhetorical style as evidenced in his Twitter feed is a symptom of the digitally mediated attention economy that exists in our increasingly mediatized reality (Couldry and Hepp 2017). Twitter's short message architecture and follower network promote new forms of communication that extend even to political candidates. Trump's rhetorical style on Twitter is uniquely reflective of this new medium of communication. Through it, he conveys a crude, no-holds-barred emotional expressiveness meant to rile his base and enact his rhetorical argument that he is not a typical politician. He used several styles of speech that demarcate his unique rhetorical style. He had a propensity to rely on hyperbole (exaggerated claims), and for enthymematic arguments, where the audience fills in parts of the argument, as well as synecdochic speech, where single phrases stand in for entire arguments. He also had a penchant for memorable phrases, vivid, colorful language, and a poetic structure that is distinctly his own. Although I cannot speak to Trump's intentions to be eloquent, I argue that his unique turns of phrase convey a style of eloquence that is befitting the digital medium of his personal Twitter account.

In this chapter, I detail the concept of eloquence and explain how it is a socially constructed quality of expression that is mediated by the communication environment. Then, I analyze Trump's Tweets between December 2015 until the election in November 2016, looking at his persuasive Tweets for indications of eloquent expression, describing the ways that Trump's Tweets exhibit dimensions of eloquence befitting the medium, the messenger, and the rhetorical audience.

Eloquence

We have long expected political leaders to produce eloquent discourse, especially when the context gives rise to this need. Although not all leaders meet such ideals of discourse, there are hundreds of moments when leaders rose to the rhetorical challenge and then produced eloquent speech. Fields' (1996) analysis of presidential speech reminds us that the president both speaks *for* and *to* the people. For example, we attribute eloquence to the speeches of John F. Kennedy, such as in his inaugural address, where he declared: "Ask not what your country can do for you, but what you can do for your country." Or Abraham Lincoln's Gettysburg Address; its sheer simplicity, while simultaneously capturing the horrors of a country torn in two, made it eloquent. Candidate Barack Obama was also heralded on the 2008 campaign trail for his eloquent "A More Perfect Union" speech. In the speech, he addressed his controversial pastor's racialized speech, and the style is viewed as a contemporary example of eloquent speech (Terrill 2009). For example, in describing his own racial mixture, Obama explains that he is the "son of a black man from Kenya and a white woman from Kansas," and he notes that he "has seared into my genetic makeup the idea that this nation is more than the sum of its parts – that out of many, we are truly one." By contrast, Trump's chant "Build that wall," or his claims that the Iranian nuclear deal was "a really bad deal. The worst deal" seem crude by comparison.

Eloquence, however, is not well defined. Defining it is similar to how Scott (1973) defines rhetoric in his foundational article "On Not Defining 'Rhetoric.'" He explains that it is challenging to fully define rhetoric, but we have a sense of it that is rooted in our lived experiences. The same holds for eloquence; in the moment, we recognize when we are experiencing it, even if we cannot fully explain what it is that makes the message and its delivery eloquent. Nevertheless, it is helpful to at least draw some boundaries around what eloquence might be. Donoghue (2008) defines eloquence simply as that which "has no aim: it is a play of words or other expressive means. It is a gift to be enjoyed in appreciation and

36 Jennifer Stromer-Galley

practice" (p. 3). This definition, however, is problematic; eloquence often does have some aim to construct the speaker or the audience in specific ways, or to capture the moment in rhetorical expression to help construct a common understanding of an event. In other words, eloquence works in the service of persuasion. I find Bryant's (1973) definition more satisfying: it brings together "natural genius, greatness or importance of idea and circumstance, power of mind or intellectual quality of thought, and special activity of imagination and emotion incarnated in fine and appropriate language [for the audience]" (p. 122). This definition better captures the persuasive function and also the aesthetic qualities of eloquent speech.

Some might be hard pressed to consider "Tweets" – posts on the Twitter platform – as having the capacity to express greatness, importance, or demonstrate quality of thought through beautiful words. Twitter has specific affordances that seem designed to force public discourse to either be plain or to be provocative, but not eloquent. The 140 (and then 280) character limit forces a succinctness that does not lend itself to "fine and appropriate language."

Yet, eloquence is neither a given nor fixed in time. In *Eloquence in the Electronic Age*, Jamieson (1988) explains that what is considered eloquence is co-constructed by leaders, the public, the communication technologies that deliver elite discourse to the public, and the electoral system within which these actors operate, including the publicity engine that is the news media. Thus, eloquence is not a fixed ideal but a changing quality of leadership communication structured by the context within which leaders and the public find themselves.

Jamieson wrote *Eloquence* in the mid-1980s, at a time when the full impact of mass media was being felt, when the political party system, party platforms, and political issues were being supplanted by the figureheads of the parties, and when our nation's first movie star president, Ronald Reagan, was elected. Jamieson explains that the oratory in the mass media era was noteworthy for increased personal anecdote and storytelling in speeches: "television is a medium conducive to autobiographical, self-disclosive discourse" (p. 63), she explains. In the mass media era, the eloquent speaker is one who can distill an idea into a 30-second or less soundbite.

Communication Technology and Eloquence

Through her analysis of Reagan, Jamieson suggests that eloquence has changed over time – how speakers manifest it and also how receivers identify it. She provides analysis of speeches by politicians in the pre-mass media age, including references to oratory by ancient Greeks. Through her analysis, she argues that oratory in the pre-mass media era was often fiery, both in its words and in its delivery. Its power could bring people to war.

The communication technologies that channel messages from political leaders to the public have changed dramatically over the last two centuries. The age of

Vulgar Eloquence in the Digital Age **37**

print media — newspapers, billboards, fliers, and pamphlets — shaped thought in important ways (Ong 1982). Writing forces a more formal, explicit, and logical mode of expressing ideas. Part of the reason for this is the lack of cues that support oral expression: tone of voice, the location and nature of pauses, rapidity of speech, eye and facial expressions, gestures, and the like. When we are in conversation with others, our sentences are shorter and we interrupt our line of thinking with asides and embellishments. Indeed, the Trump stump speech excerpt at the start of this chapter highlights how oral discourse is more likely to be structured. In person, the audience follows the train of thought because of the supportive cues that go along with the speech to help the audience maintain understanding. Converted into print, such conversational expression seems almost incoherent.

Stump speeches, the political candidate's direct medium for communication in the era before mass media, invited a conversational and often fiery style of expression. Campaign stump speeches were meant to emotionally engage and energize the audience, with the goal of cementing support by those in attendance. Before mass media, candidates and political parties largely relied on social networks, who in face-to-face conversations would work to persuade voters (Ryfe 1999). Jamieson explains that the 19th-century understanding of political speech was that logic alone was not sufficient to persuade; the effective leader must also use eloquence to incite the passions. Even during the mass media and current digital ages, the campaign stump speech is still the setting where audiences can experience fiery rhetoric meant to excite and impassion through heated language and forceful verbal delivery.

Yet, radio and television, as they ushered in an age of mass media, shifted the experience of speech-making, leading to a style of delivery that Jamieson described as "cool." In the mass media age, viewers watching television in the intimacy and quiet of their living rooms were turned off by the boisterous, impassioned delivery of the stump speech. Instead, they favored candidates with a cooler, calmer, and more intimate delivery style.

This idea — of mass media inviting a cooler delivery and style — is perhaps best captured by President Franklin Roosevelt's fireside chats, in which he weekly talked to Americans who sat around their radios in their living rooms to hear his thoughts on the state of the economy or the war. Ryfe notes that the style of discourse of early radio was scripted yet conversational. The style that Roosevelt adopted was that of conversing with "the friend next door," according to Ryfe (p. 89). Jamieson argues that Roosevelt's "chats" ushered in a new mode of eloquent speech where "one person in a private space of his living room [is] chatting with millions of other individuals in theirs" (p. 55). Roosevelt's chats set the early archetype of presidential discourse in the mass media era.

If Roosevelt established the style of discourse for mass media, Ronald Reagan epitomized it with his masterful understanding of the medium of television. Reagan, who grew up in the age of radio and television, and played movie roles in Westerns, seemed especially able to understand the medium of television.

38 Jennifer Stromer-Galley

Jamieson notes that Ronald Reagan, at least when she wrote the book in the 1980s, was not considered an eloquent speaker. Yet, he had mastered the medium of television; so, while his words tended to be plain, he understood the power of visuals and of what she characterized as a style to convey his vision and policy positions to the public via stories and anecdotes rather than facts and logical–deductive argumentation. His folksy, plain-speaking narrative style fit the expectations audiences had of the medium.

So, if FDR was to radio and Reagan was to television, perhaps Trump is to digital media. Prior candidates in the digital era have been heralded for their digital communication skills. Howard Dean, who ran for the Democratic nomination for the 2004 presidential race, was the first candidate to fully embrace the interactive nature of digital media, enabling blogging on his campaign website, dedicating staff to cultivating a community online, and appealing to his online supporters as the driving force of his "people powered" campaign (Stromer-Galley 2019). Yet, he failed to understand other communication media, especially television. He fed into the popular narratives about his fiery-ness at his concession speech after placing third in the Iowa caucuses, with his full-throated declaration that his campaign would head on to the next states and then to victory, yeehah! Cable news pundits and television audiences were taken aback by the intensity and strangeness of the display. Barack Obama, in the next campaign cycle, followed the strategically useful practices of the Dean campaign (Kreiss 2012) and embraced the fledgling social media outlets of MySpace and Facebook. His campaign also created its own social media platform called MyBO to help his online supporters organize themselves and work in a coordinated way with the campaign. Although both Dean and Obama appealed to their online supporters through the common styles of campaigns, the candidate's *rhetorical styles* were not especially noteworthy online.

Trump's rhetorical style through digital media was noteworthy. If Reagan, in the words of Jamieson, "shows and tells in the visual bites that television cameras crave" (p. 119), what was candidate Trump doing to similarly capture the mediated reality we now live in so profoundly? To answer that question, I unpack Trump's discursive proclivity in the context of his preferred communication medium and the larger campaign.

Twitter is considered a "micro-blog" in the large body of scholarship on Twitter and on blogging, inviting the referent of a blog in condensed form. Blogs are chronologically inverted entries on a website, often informal musings or pontifications, diary-style observations, or sharing news and events. On Twitter, the expectation is similarly that the author is opining, documenting, sharing, but in once 140 and now a luxurious 280 characters (or fewer). While fiery and hateful rhetoric existed in the past, it did not have the reach of the contemporary digital communications landscape. Here I focus on Twitter, since that is Trump's preferred mode of communication.

Twitter holds several affordances that enable Trump's message to reach and reverberate in powerful ways. Twitter's social media platform, like Facebook's,

Vulgar Eloquence in the Digital Age **39**

capitalizes on network relationships. Unlike Facebook, which tends to privilege friends and acquaintance networks, Twitter's network profile is more public. People "follow" others and try to gain followers in the architecture of the platform. Those followers are as likely as not to be strangers. When a person "Tweets" – writes a post to Twitter – it appears on the person's account and followers will see the post on their Twitter news feed. Users can "Retweet" something they have seen from a follower to share it with their own network. They can also reference another person within or outside of their network using their unique Twitter handle.

Academics mused when Twitter came on the scene back in 2006 that its restricted character limit might have significant negative implications on the public sphere. Indeed, I wondered back then what it would mean for argumentation and persuasion when one's message was so constrained. The form necessarily restricts logical argumentation in a single Tweet, leading to discourse that is more emotive and expressive than rational–critical in a Habermasian deliberative sense, in which people hold their personal needs aside in order to engage in rational debate with others for the common good. Twitter, however, was not designed to be a communication platform for persuasion. Its original design was based on short-message service (SMS) texts for friends to stay connected and keep tabs on each other.[4] The first prompt on Twitter was "what's happening?" Early commentators wondered what the point of such a social networking service might be and derided the banality of the likely messages that would circulate there (Stromer-Galley 2019. As the service grew, the platform became the place to watch celebrities, with Ashton Kutcher and Justin Bieber growing massive followings on the platform. It also became a useful venue for bloggers and political commentators to share their opinions and observations about the world. Using their blogs and websites as home base, they could Tweet to their followers on Twitter what their latest article or opinion was and link back to the website to drive traffic. Twitter became a useful push medium to pull followers to websites.

Trump's Eloquence

To examine Trump's discourse on Twitter, and to explain how I arrived at the description of Trump's Tweets as conveying vulgar eloquence, I used the Illuminating 2016 project website[5] (Stromer-Galley, Hemsley, Tanupabrungsun et al. 2016) to analyze all messages by Trump on Twitter that were categorized as attack or as advocacy between December 1, 2015 and Election Day, November 8, 2016.[6] I read closely the messages by Trump, ignoring Retweeted messages, such as this one from December 20, 2015: ".@blueeyd2020: @JebBush reminds me now of @BobbyKindal but no one cares Jeb! You lost your chance. #Trump2016 @ realDonaldTrump." In total, I analyzed 2,672 Tweets. Trump's Tweets used several styles of speech that demarcated his unique rhetorical style, which I argue should be considered eloquence in our current culture. Trump relies on a unique poetic

40 Jennifer Stromer-Galley

structure, memorable phrases and repetition, hyperbole (exaggerated claims), enthymeme (arguments where the audience supplies premises), and synecdochic speech (where a phrase or element of an argument stands in for the whole argument). I provide example Tweets to support my argument, and I have preserved typographical and punctuation errors that were in the original.

A Unique Poetic Structure

Trump developed a signature poetic style to his campaign Tweets. They were typically three sentences. The first two were negative, emotion-laden opinion statements, and the third was a short, punctuated emotive expression. Some examples:

> February 8: "Now that Bush has wasted $120 million of special interest money on his failed campaign, he says he would end super PACs. Sad!"
> April 25: "Lyin' Ted and Kasich are mathematically dead and totally desperate. Their donors & special interest groups are not happy with them. Sad!"

Although "sad" (with exclamation point) is the most common ending, Trump found other emotive expressions to fit the context. For example:

> February 14: "Even though every poll, Time, Drudge, etc., has me winning the debate by a lot, @FoxNews only puts negative people on. Biased – a total joke!"
> February 23: "Ted Cruz does not have the right "temperament" to be President. Look at the way he totally panicked in firing his director of comm. BAD!"
> March 22: "Obama, and all others, have been so weak, and so politically correct, that terror groups are forming and getting stronger! Shame."

A Tweet on April 11, which expresses frustration at the way delegates to the Republican Party convention were chosen in Colorado, was couched to convey the anger of his followers, not him: "How is it possible that the people of the great state of Colorado never got to vote in the Republican Primary? Great anger – totally unfair!"

This style of Tweet was unique to Trump, making it a signature style. Comedians and commentators recognized the lyrical and wholly negative expression in this structure and commented upon it.[7] His "sad" rejoinder even has an entry on the website "Know Your Meme."[8]

Memorable Phrases, Vivid Language

Commentators and pundits noted early in Trump's candidacy that his usage of Twitter was remarkable, in part because of the strong, repetitive language he used to describe his opponents and his policy positions. Prior analyses suggest that

Vulgar Eloquence in the Digital Age **41**

Trump's discourse used more negative emotional expressions as compared with his general election opponent Hillary Clinton (Savoy 2018), even though Clinton produced a greater volume of attack messages as compared with Trump (Stromer-Galley, Robinson, and Rossini 2016). Over the course of the campaign, for example, he repeatedly attacked Democratic primary candidate, and eventual nominee for the Democratic Party, former Secretary of State Hillary Clinton, on her qualities to lead. On December 16, 2015, for example, he Tweeted: "Hillary Clinton is weak and ineffective – no strength, no stamina." He repeated the "no strength, no stamina" message in several Tweets:

> December 20, 2015: "We need a #POTUS with great strength & stamina. Hillary does not have that. #Trump2016"
> January 2, 2016: "Hillary Clinton doesn't have the strength or stamina to be president. Jeb Bush is a low energy individual, but Hillary is not much better!"

This line of attack disappeared from his rhetoric during the primary and caucus voting stage, but as his campaign pivoted to a general election stance, he again took up concerns that she was weak. On July 6, for example, he Tweeted: "Crooked Hillary Clinton is unfit to serve as President of the U.S. Her temperament is weak and her opponents are strong. BAD JUDGEMENT!" In the general election campaign, he returned to questioning her stamina. On September 1, he Tweeted: "Hillary Clinton didn't go to Louisiana, and now she didn't go to Mexico. She doesn't have the drive or stamina to MAKE AMERICA GREAT AGAIN!" This gendered attack constructed Clinton as frail and questioned her physical ability to handle the office, using repetition to underscore his argument.

Another noteworthy dimension to Trump's Tweets was the labels he used for all his opponents. He did not just refer to his opponents by their first names, but also applied adjectives to characterize what he saw as essential, negative attributes. For example, in January as the Iowa caucuses and New Hampshire primary were around the corner, Trump aggressively attacked Texas Republican Senator Ted Cruz, who also was vying to be the Republican nominee for president and who was ahead in public opinion polling. On January 16, 2016, Trump sent a series of Tweets attacking Cruz for being a Canadian citizen and for failing to disclose bank loans, such as this: "Ted is the ultimate hypocrite. Says one thing for money, does another for votes." Out of this set of attacks, he branded Cruz as "lyin' Ted" and used that label nearly every time he Tweeted about Cruz. He applied adjectives to his other key Republican rivals, although without the same consistency as Cruz. For example, he described Representative Marco Rubio as "a choker" for being nervous during a February debate and not forcefully attacking Trump. On February 26, Trump Tweeted: "Lightweight choker Marco Rubio looks like a little boy on stage. Not presidential material!" followed by: "Lightweight Marco Rubio was working hard last night. The problem is, he is a choker, and once a

42 Jennifer Stromer-Galley

choker, always a choker! Mr. Meltdown." The labels "lightweight," "choker," and "little" all were used repeatedly to describe Rubio during the primaries.

Hyperbole

Hyperbole and exaggeration can serve as eloquent speech because of the often extremeness of the language used to over-state the situation. By way of illustration, I highlight Trump Tweets attacking two large American cities:

> December 7: "N.Y.C. has the worst Mayor in the United States. I hate watching what is happening with the dirty streets, the homeless and crime! Disgrace."
> July 12: "Crime is out of control, and rapidly getting worse. Look what is going on in Chicago and our inner cities. Not good!"

These two Tweets, both about cities with Democrats as mayors, articulated Trump's stark vision of life there. Of New York, he described "dirty streets, homeless, and crime" created by "the worst Mayor," not a bad or an incompetent mayor, but the mayor who Trump characterized as being the most inferior mayor of any city in the country. Of Chicago, he described crime as "out of control" and also at the same time "getting worse," which served to intensify the extent of crime in the city. These hyperbolic statements painted a picture of grim urban centers worthy of our disdain and even fear. Yet, Trump provided no evidence for the degradation of these cities, and indeed, New York's murder rate was at noteworthy low levels at the time,[9] and neither made the list of the 100 most dangerous cities in the U.S. in 2015 or 2016.[10]

In December 2015, Trump received negative news coverage from the *Washington Post*, and he generated a set of hyperbolic attacks on the owner as a result. Jeff Bezos, Amazon.com founder and CEO, purchased the newspaper in 2013, and his motives for doing so were unclear. Candidate Trump offered his own theory. On December 7, he Tweeted: "The @washingtonpost, which loses a fortune, is owned by @JeffBezos for purposes of keeping taxes down at his no profit company, @amazon." He continued: "The @washingtonpost loses money (a deduction) and gives owner @JeffBezos power to screw public on low taxation of @Amazon! Big tax shelter." And then: "If @amazon ever had to pay fair taxes, its stock would crash and it would crumple like a paper bag. The @washingtonpost scam is saving it!" Trump's argument was that Bezos was using declared losses from the *Washington Post* to offset the income gains of his primary company Amazon. Although the allegations were unsubstantiated, of note is the hyperbolic way he made the argument. He characterized Bezos' efforts as attempts to evade paying taxes, which would "screw the public," a strong and sexually crude statement of the effects of Amazon not paying its fair share in taxes. He then followed this claim by suggesting that if Amazon actually paid its fair share, the "stock would crash" and Amazon would "crumple like a paper bag." Both of these striking and

Vulgar Eloquence in the Digital Age   **43**

dramatic descriptions greatly overstated the effects of more taxation on the online retail behemoth.

Enthymeme

Trump's Tweets routinely argued through enthymeme. These are arguments where the receiver must complete elements of the argument, supplying claims (premises) that complete the argument in support of the conclusion. Jackson and Jacobs (1980) remind us that enthymemes are "social productions" (p. 262); the parties to the discussion co-constructing the argument via assumed knowledge and dispositions. Furthermore, communication via Twitter is forced to rely on enthymematic argument because Tweets are so short. Policy stances by candidates and attacks on opponents' character or policy positions depend upon on the recipient filling in major and minor premises to complete the argument. In some cases, the audience must even fill in the conclusions, which are left unstated while the premises are articulated.

Trump made enthymematic arguments on policy, especially his arguments about illegal immigration and its ties to terrorism and crime. His announcement speech explicitly argued that illegal immigrants were criminals, "rapists and murderers," which set the argumentation context for his later Tweets. In December 2015, he laid the groundwork that further connected immigration and terrorism. On December 9, he Tweeted: "Our country is facing a major threat from radical Islamic terrorism. We better get very smart, and very tough, FAST, before it is too late!" Later that day he continued: "Wow, what a day. So many foolish people that refuse to acknowledge the tremendous danger and uncertainty of certain people coming into the U.S." The phrase "certain people" in this sentence requires the audience to understand that Trump is arguing that there are terrorists entering the United States, likely through illegal channels. It also highlights the "foolish people" who do not share Trump's prescience. Trump's audience is neither of these groups, situating them as a special group that, like him, knows the truth.

After one of the largest mass shootings in U.S. history occurred at a gay nightclub in Orlando, Trump Tweeted on June 12: "Horrific incident in FL. Praying for all the victims & their families. When will this stop? When will we get tough, smart & vigilant?" The unstated argument in this Tweet is that the shooting was an act of terrorism, and based on his prior arguments, that also implied that the terrorist was an illegal alien. In fact, however, this mass shooting incident was an act of domestic terrorism. The shooter was born in the U.S., and although ISIS claimed that an ISIS fighter was the shooter, the evidence to connect him to the group was weak, with the probability much higher that he was simply mentally ill. Nevertheless, Trump repeatedly made the argument on Twitter that he would use the words Radical Islamic Terrorism when his opponents would not, further amplifying an implied link between the nightclub shooting and an act of terrorism by Islamic fighters.

44 Jennifer Stromer-Galley

Synecdoche

One of Trump's rhetorical proclivities on the campaign trail was for synecdoche, which is a style of speech where a statement or discursively constructed image stands for or characterizes a larger argument or idea. Jamieson (1988) explains that synecdoche is the hallmark of an eloquent speaker. They are "those epitomizing phrases and sentences" that are "most generative of collective assent" (p. 91). They also challenge opponents and critics because they forestall debate (p. 91) by building on an often complex history of events and sentiments that are then encapsulated in a memorable phrase. Counter-argument of such eloquent memes requires a complex unpacking of all the premises and assumptions that underlie the phrase, many of them generated by assent from a constructed history shared by the community.

One of the synecdochic arguments that Trump relied on in his stump speeches, and referenced in some of his Tweets, was his catch-phrase "build that wall!" It became a stand-in for a complex policy stance that implicates immigration along the U.S. southern border, national security and sovereignty, and priorities for federal spending. For example, on April 1 he wrote: "We must build a great wall between Mexico and the United States!" Here he amplifies his wall into an actual entity that can have ascribed to it a description of its grandeur: a great wall. On September 1 he further explained who would pay for this great wall: "Mexico will pay for the wall!" Someone completely inattentive to the political landscape who read that Tweet would wonder what wall Trump was talking about and why Mexico would pay for such a thing. Trump's audience, however, knew this and filled in the missing context to understand that in Trump's policy on immigration, the cost of border enforcement would be limited for the United States taxpayer because Mexico is paying.

Trump's characterization in simplistic yet negatively dramatic ways of people and policies he disliked (e.g. lyin' Ted, little Rubio) also served as synecdochic arguments that succinctly captured purported weaknesses of his opponents. He labeled Hillary Clinton "crooked Hillary" early in the primaries, attacking her for a range of what he considered bad deeds, including an email scandal that would plague her campaign and raise questions about her judgment. He continued with that label throughout the campaign, sometimes referring to her simply as "Crooked": "So terrible that Crooked didn't report she got the debate questions from Donna Brazile, if that were me it would have been front page news!" His pejoratives effectively and singularly characterized his opponents' characters, defining them for the news media and the electorate while simultaneously restricting the range of responses his opponents could muster to counter the characterization.

Trump's Vulgar Eloquence

Trump's rhetorical style, especially the style via enthymeme and synecdoche, cultivated community, as the community completes the argument by virtue of

Vulgar Eloquence in the Digital Age **45**

sharing the understanding of the larger knowledge and attitude base. They are "in the know," as it were. Enthymeme thus can be powerfully effective at cultivating community when the speaker understands the arguments that can be made implicitly because the community shares the premises. Enthymeme also gives the audience license to fill in their own premises or conclusions, enabling a widening of the rhetorical community for the speaker. Furthermore, synecdoche specifies the "grounds to which the community assents and by stipulating patterns of language whose use speaks the communal bond" (Jamieson 1988, 92). In other words, synecdoche especially creates a *rhetorical community*: it brings together a set of people who share a common language and understanding, values and norms, and history. Although academics and political watchers might like to say that Trump's discourse violates rhetorical norms, there are aspects of his discourse that rely on long-honed traditions of oratory. "Build that wall" is not "Ask not what your country can do," but both work synecdochally and powerfully at creating a community via the practices of demonizing an outgroup: immigrants.

Trump's vulgar eloquence also worked because he speaks in the key of outrage. Twitter, it has been said, is a progenitor of "outrage culture," the means for amplifying consternation, anger, and vitriol at a target, which is vulgar in the sense that it activates crowds or throngs to embrace and further amplify their anger, indignation, and fear. Outrage discourse, according to Sobieraj and Berry (2011), is used to bypass "the messy nuances of complex political issues in favor of melodrama, misrepresentative exaggeration, mockery, and improbable forecasts of impending doom" (p. 20). The more provocative the better to feed the throng of followers.

Trump relied heavily on tropes of outrage culture to attack his opponents. Attacking media outlets was especially one of Trump's common outrage targets during the presidential campaign. He targeted individual writers, anchors, and journalists, especially *Morning Joe* on MSNBC, and he repeatedly attacked the *Washington Post*, CNN, the *New York Times*, and even conservative news outlets, such as the *National Review* and Fox News. He often characterized these news outlets as "dishonest" and as "failing." I pull out two Tweets attacking a particular female journalist to illustrate. In a Tweet on December 1, 2015, he declared: "Highly untalented Wash Post blogger, Jennifer Rubin, a real dummy, never writes fairly about me. Why does Wash Post have low IQ people?" Three days later, he continued, ".@jRubinBlogger one of the dumber bloggers @washingtonpost only writes purposely inaccurate pieces on me. She is in love with Marco Rubio." Both of these Tweets denigrated an opinion writer of a prominent national newspaper, and he posed a rhetorical question inviting his audience to further question the quality and utility of a news outlet that would have such an incompetent employee. He more famously attacked Fox News anchor, Megyn Kelly, after a televised debate in August 2015, in which she said, "You've called women you don't like fat pigs, dogs, slobs and disgusting animals" and then asked him about his treatment of women. He disliked the question, and after the debate he obsessively

46 Jennifer Stromer-Galley

attacked her on Twitter, using unsubstantiated critiques that her show was "failing" and that she "bombed" as an anchor. Kelly, in an interview a year after the incident, said that Trump even threatened to unleash his "beautiful Twitter following" on her,[11] suggesting Trump's awareness of the power of carrying a tune of outrage that he groomed among his followers in the key of vulgar eloquence through his favorite communication.

On policy matters, he cultivated outrage around illegal immigration. He tied it to terrorism and crime, both of which threaten our fundamental need for safety. Moreover, his arguments on terrorism were routinely structured with an interrogative: "when will we get smart?" "When will we defend our borders?" For example:

> June 28: "Yet another terrorist attack. This time in Turkey. Will the world ever realize what is going on? So sad."
> July 14: "Another horrific attack, this time in Nice, France. Many dead and injured. When will we learn? It is only getting worse."

The implication of his rhetorical question was that we are not getting smart, defending our borders, realizing what is going on, and learning from our mistakes. He also positioned himself as having had prescience; he understood what the rest of the world did not. Rhetorically, he constructed himself as an insightful leader who had the solutions. He also situated those who did not understand and who would not defend us as idiots who deserve our frustration, our disdain; in short, they deserved our outrage.

Leaders cannot be leaders without their followers (Fairhurst and Connaughton 2014). Candidate Trump constructed a reality where he was in the right and his supporters were with him. On December 25, he Tweeted: "Does everyone see that the Democrats and President Obama are now, because of me, starting to deport people who are here illegally. Politics!" His entreaty, "does everyone see," invited his audience to share with him what he so obviously sees. Then on May 2, he Tweeted: "Everybody is talking about the protesters burning the American flags and proudly waving Mexican flags. I want America First – so do voters!" He constructed a reality in which "everybody" is discussing the protests in California against Trump, and he constructed the protestors as outsiders because they are flying Mexican flags. True Americans would never fly another country's flag. He also spoke on behalf of "The American people," as in this Tweet from May 22: "The American people are sick and tired of not being able to lead normal lives and to constantly be on the lookout for terror and terrorists!" In these Tweets, he expressed his outrage, while simultaneously inviting that outrage to be shared among his followers. His anger and frustration in what from his mind was so clearly wrong constructs his rhetorical audience as sharing in his prescience and his righteous indignation.

Concluding Thoughts

Although the public does not necessarily require leaders to be eloquent, often leadership is associated with the ability to produce the memorable phrase that captures the moment in meaningful ways. Trump's campaign Tweets produced a vulgar eloquence through a unique rhythm that became a trademark of a Trump campaign Tweet and used nasty but colorful language and memorable phrasing, as well as enthymeme and synecdoche, to activate a narrative in the minds of his audience, constructing a rhetorical community and enabling and empowering them to share his outrage. Vulgar eloquence works in the context of Twitter, where the platform invites short, emotive messages that followers can easily transmit to their networks in a demonstration of their anger and their rightness. As our expectations of what constitutes an ideal leader is co-constructed and situated in time, so too is our sense of what is eloquent. Trump's Tweets embody a new kind of eloquence – a vulgar eloquence.

Notes

1 Acknowledgments: I would like to thank Angela Ray, Roc Myers, and Brian McKernan for helpful feedback on earlier versions of this manuscript. Special thanks to the Illuminating project team, including Jeff Hemsley, Feifei Zhang, and Patricia Rossini.
2 www.vox.com/2016/8/18/12423688/donald-trump-speech-style-explained-by-linguists
3 www.nytimes.com/interactive/2016/01/28/upshot/donald-trump-Twitter-insults.html
4 www.lifewire.com/history-of-Twitter-3288854
5 The Illuminating 2016 project collected and classified via supervised machine learning all of the presidential candidates' social media messages from their announcement until they dropped out or won the election. Visit http://illuminating.ischool.syr.edu.
6 For a description of the categorizations, see Zhang et al. (2017).
7 https://people.com/politics/donald-trump-things-called-sad-Twitter/; www.theverge.com/2017/6/26/15872904/trump-Tweet-psychology-sad-moral-emotional-words
8 https://knowyourmeme.com/photos/1161118-donald-trump-s-sad-Tweets
9 www.nytimes.com/interactive/2016/05/18/us/chicago-murder-problem.html
10 www.insurancejournal.com/news/national/2016/01/28/396750.htm
11 www.usatoday.com/story/news/politics/elections/2016/11/15/megyn-kelly-memoir-donald-trump-roger-ailes-president-fox-news/93813154/

References

Bryant, Donald C. 1973. *Rhetorical Dimensions in Criticism*. Baton Rouge, LA: Louisiana State University Press.

Couldry, Nick, and Andreas Hepp. 2017. *The Mediated Construction of Reality*. New York: Polity.

Donoghue, Denis. 2008. *On Eloquence*. New Haven, CT: Yale University Press.

Fairhurst, Gail, and Stacey Connaughton. 2014. "Leadership: A Communicative Perspective." *Leadership* 10, no. 3: 7–35.

Fields, Wayne. 1996. *Union of Words: A History of Presidential Eloquence*. New York: Free Press.

Jackson, Sally, and Scott Jacobs. 1980. "Structure of Conversational Argument: Pragmatic Bases for the Enthymeme." *The Quarterly Journal of Speech* 66, no. 3: 251–265.

Jamieson, Kathleen Hall. 1988. *Eloquence in the Electronic Age: The Transformation of Political Speechmaking.* New York: Oxford University Press.

Jamieson, Kathleen Hall, and Doron Taussig. 2017. "Disruption, Demonization, Deliverance and Norm Destruction: The Rhetorical Signature of Donald J. Trump." *Political Science Quarterly* 132, no. 4: 619–650. Doi: 10.1002/polq.12699

Kreiss, Daniel. 2012. *Taking Our Country Back: The Crafting of Networked Politics from Howard Dean to Barack Obama.* New York: Oxford University Press.

Ong, Walter. 1982. *Orality and Literacy: The Technologizing of the Word.* New York: Routledge.

Ryfe, David Michael. 1999. "Franklin Roosevelt and the Fireside Chats." *Journal of Communication* 49, no. 4: 80–103.

Savoy, Jacques. 2018. "Trump's and Clinton's Style and Rhetoric During the 2016 Presidential Election." *Journal of Quantitative Linguistics* 25, no. 2: 168–189.

Scott, Robert L. 1973. "On Not Defining 'Rhetoric.'" *Philosophy & Rhetoric* 6, no. 2: 81–96.

Sobieraj, Sarah, and Jeffrey M. Berry. 2011. "From Incivility to Outrage: Political Discourse in Blogs, Talk Radio, and Cable News." *Political Communication* 28, no. 1: 19–41.

Stromer-Galley, Jennifer. 2019. *Presidential Campaigning in the Internet Age.* 2nd Ed. New York: Oxford University Press.

Stromer-Galley, Jennifer, Jeff Hemsley, Sikana Tanupabrungsun, Feifei Zhang, Patricia Rossini, Lauren Bryant, Nancy McCracken, Yatish Hegde, Bryan Semaan, Sam Jackson, Olga Boichak, Yingya Li, Mahboobeh Harandi, and Jerry Robinson. 2016. *Illuminating 2016 Project.* Available http://illuminating.ischool.syr.edu.

Stromer-Galley, Jennifer, Jerry Robinson, and Patricia Rossini. July 27, 2016. "Candidates Control Their Own Social Media. What Message Are They Sending?" *The Conversation* Available https://theconversation.com/candidates-control-their-own-social-media-what-message-are-they-sending-62949

Terrill, Robert E. 2009. "Unity and Duality in Barack Obama's 'A More Perfect Union.'" *The Quarterly Journal of Speech* 95, no. 4: 363–386. Doi: 10.1080/00335630903296192.

Trent, Judith, Robert, Friedenberg and Robert Denton, Jr. 2019. *Political Campaign Communication: Principles and Practices.* 8th Ed., New York: Rowman & Littlefield Publishers.

Wang, Yaqin, and Haitao Liu. 2017. "Is Trump Always Rambling Like a Fourth-Grade Student? An Analysis of Stylistic Features of Donald Trump's Political Discourse During the 2016 Election." *Discourse & Society* 29, no. 3: 299–323. Doi: 10.1177/0957926517734659

Zhang, Feifei, Jennifer Stromer-Galley, Sikana Tanupabrungsun, Yatish Hegde, Nancy McCracken, and Jeff Hemsley. 2017. "Understanding Discourse Acts: Political Campaign Messages Classification on Facebook and Twitter." *Proceedings of the 2017 International Conference on Social Computing, Behavioral-Cultural Modeling & Prediction and Behavior Representation in Modeling and Simulation* (SBP'17). Washington, DC: George Washington University.

4

"DELETE YOUR ACCOUNT"? HILLARY RODHAM CLINTON ACROSS SOCIAL MEDIA PLATFORMS IN THE 2016 U.S. PRESIDENTIAL ELECTION[1]

Shannon C. McGregor and Regina G. Lawrence

On April 12, 2015, Hillary Clinton released a two-minute video announcing her bid (once again) for the U.S. presidency. She had also announced her candidacy via video in 2008, when she previously had thrown her hat in the presidential ring. But by 2015, a variety of social media platforms had become an important source of information and conversation among many Americans.

Clinton's announcement on Twitter, with its (at that time) strict 140-character-per-post limit, concisely echoed the main theme of her video: "I'm running for president. Everyday Americans need a champion, and I want to be that champion." Signed simply "H," the tweet included a link to Clinton's campaign website along with a flattering black-and-white profile photograph showing Clinton looking upward with a wide smile. The tweet was viewed 3 million times within its first hour online. Her announcement via the campaign's new Facebook account, featuring the video, generated over 10 million likes, comments, shares, and other interactions within its first 24 hours (Velencia, 2015). In contrast, the campaign's announcement via Instagram did not come until June, when its account opened with a photo of a clothes rack hung with red, white, and blue pantsuits, with a caption (echoing the title of her 2014 memoir) saying simply "Hard choices."

Candidates' Social Media Strategies Across Platforms

As evidenced by Clinton's multi-platform announcement, which took different forms across various platforms, campaigns must now implement multiple concurrent strategies across social media sites. Politicians' use of social media has become a prominent focus of political communication research, as the rise of social media has forced campaigns to rethink and revamp their communication strategies while providing them new opportunities for reaching, mobilizing, and persuading potential voters. Some studies of contemporary campaigns generalize from research based on a single social media platform, such as Facebook (Larsson, 2016; Williams & Gulati, 2013) or Twitter (e.g. Conway, Kenski, & Wang, 2015; Gervais & Morris, 2018; Golbeck, Grimes, & Rogers, 2010). Far fewer studies have looked at how campaigns might use different social media platforms differently. That kind of research requires taking into account the differences across platforms.

As we argue in a recently published study with Daniel Kreiss (Kreiss, Lawrence, & McGregor, 2018), campaigns' use of social media may vary by platforms based on the *audiences* best reached through each; the platforms' *affordances* (that is, the platform's particular functionalities and the types of activities it readily enables); the *genres* of communication perceived to be appropriate to each; and the *timing* of social media use within the electoral cycle – as well as each candidate's particular persona and comfort with social media engagement. Candidates' social media strategies must therefore take into account who can best be reached with what kinds of messages and imagery, depending on what platform is being utilized, and also must strategize within the tools available on each platform. For example, Facebook has evolved as a video-heavy platform that allows easy sharing across users' own social networks, and its back-end analytics make it useful for A/B testing how different messages resonate with audiences; Instagram, in contrast, has primarily been a platform featuring rich visual imagery, and in the 2016 campaign, at least, did not allow for linking outside that platform. As campaigns' social media use becomes more prolific and sophisticated, it is worth examining how they may communicate differently, with different kinds of messages, images, and strategic goals across social media platforms.

Our previous research, involving in-depth interviews with staff from most of the major 2016 presidential campaigns (Kreiss, Lawrence, & McGregor, 2018), suggests campaigns tend to see Twitter primarily as a vehicle to influence the news agendas and story frames of journalists, rather than as a way to reach the general public. Campaigns reported that they used Twitter to introduce the policy stances of their candidate and highlight key talking points for the media. In contrast, campaigns that used Instagram in 2016 (not all did, given the smaller, more skewed audiences prevalent on that platform at the time) tended to see it as a particularly promising way to humanize their candidates by offering behind the scenes glimpses of candidates' personal lives and experiences on the campaign trail. Facebook was seen by campaigns as a vehicle to reach mass audiences as well as to run targeted advertising to appeal to specific demographic groups (using Facebook's unique targeting capabilities). Our research found that campaigns also think about the expectations of each platform's audience and the norms of use on each platform. For example, our interviews revealed that campaign staff thought of both Facebook and Instagram as platforms for humanizing their candidates, and at the same time thought of Instagram as a platform whose users expected photos and storytelling, not official campaign statements.

"Delete Your Account"? Hillary Rodham Clinton   **51**

Campaigns' presentations of candidates on social media are therefore interesting in several ways. In this chapter, we examine how the 2016 Hillary Clinton campaign strategically communicated across three social media platforms: Twitter, Facebook, and Instagram. We ask:

What communication strategies were distinct to particular social media platforms and which were carried across social media platforms? In other words, what was the candidate using each platform to do?

We offer here an initial set of findings, based on a qualitative analysis of the Clinton campaign's Twitter, Facebook, and Instagram feeds. We compiled all of the Twitter, Facebook, and Instagram posts from the Hillary Clinton campaign's official accounts from January 1, 2016 to the day of the general election, November 8, 2016. The resulting database included over 10,000 social media posts (Twitter $n = 6645$; Facebook $n = 2979$; Instagram $n = 556$). We collected Instagram data independently; Jenny Stromer-Galley and her "Illuminating 2016" project[2] team kindly shared with us the Clinton campaign's Facebook and Twitter data. From that rich store of data, we sampled across time, selecting one post per platform every other day throughout the campaign. On days when the campaign posted more than one post on any platform, we selected one random post from that day to be included in the sample. The final sample analyzed here includes 2,525 posts from Twitter, 783 posts from Facebook, and 281 from Instagram, for a total sample of 3,589 (see Figure 4.1).

While our future research will examine these data quantitatively, for the current study we utilized a qualitative examination that was to some degree inductive but also informed by basic categories of content analysis that appear frequently in studies of campaign communication. Previous studies of campaign websites, for example, have identified several key strategies in candidates' online communication (Bystrom et al., 2005), including *mobilization* (messaging designed to drive voters to the polls, to donate, or to support the candidate in other tangible ways); *policy statements* (messages that convey the candidate's issue stances); *attacks* on the candidate's opponent or the opposing political party; and *character* claims (messages about the candidate's professional experience and personal characteristics). This last category includes content that has been described in other studies as "humanizing," "personalizing," or "intimizing" (McGregor, Lawrence, & Cardona, 2017; Stanyer, 2013) – that is, content that showcases the candidate's backstage and personal life.

After an initial reading of the sample, tracking the themes that emerged, we examined the data again, looking for these four types of strategies. We then compared our notes across the three platforms, looking for visual and textual strategies that were unique to a particular platform and those that were carried across more than one.

What follows is descriptive data that sketch some of the main social media strategies we observed, organized in terms of the basic categories of analysis

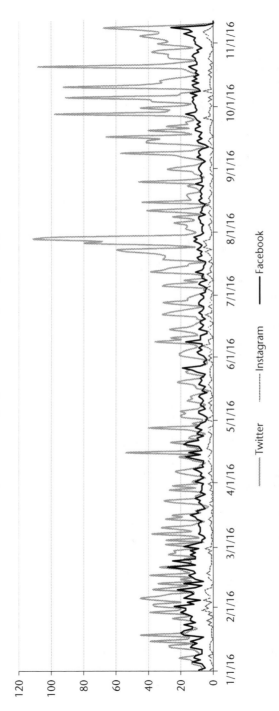

FIGURE 4.1 Clinton Campaign Social Media Posts, January 1, 2016–November 8, 2016

Source: Figure created by Author

"Delete Your Account"? Hillary Rodham Clinton **53**

described above, and how they were pursued and modified across Twitter, Facebook, and Instagram. Together, these initial findings suggest that the Clinton campaign used all three platforms for mobilizing voters, staking out policy stances, attacking opponents, and showcasing the candidate's personal qualities, but the particular ways the campaign did these things varied to some degree across the three platforms.

Findings

Mobilizing

The Clinton campaign social media feeds exhibit several varieties of posts designed to mobilize voters. One frequently-appearing type of post was the *stump speech*, conveying imagery and messaging from Clinton's public appearances. These posts were common across platforms and almost formulaic, generally featuring an image of the candidate in front of a large crowd (in a style that Grabe and Bucy [2009] have labeled "populist campaigner" imagery). On Twitter as well as on Facebook, these posts often included a pull quote from the candidate's stump speech along with embedded video of the speech itself (or, at times, a more highly produced campaign video that was not limited to that day's appearance). On Instagram, the classic campaigner imagery was often accompanied by lengthier passages from a Clinton campaign speech.

Another standard variety of social media mobilizing strategy was the post designed to convey *enthusiasm* for the candidate. On every platform, we found posts that announced the campaign's fundraising totals or high-profile political endorsements, for example, though these traditional markers of political support were more prevalent on Twitter and Facebook than on Instagram. The campaign's Facebook posts in this category often featured text captions urging people to text or to take some other online action; placards urging people to caucus or vote, often including the dates and times of caucusing or deadlines for registering to vote, or urging people to "commit" to voting; or infographics showing voting rules and procedures in a particular state (recall that Facebook allows that kind of geographic targeting). On all three platforms but especially on Facebook and Instagram, photographs were used to symbolically signal *who* was supporting Hillary Clinton, including frequent images of young people, people of color, and women, along with photographs of her celebrity endorsers, such as athlete LeBron James, Latina actress Eva Longoria, and celebrity power couples Beyoncé and Jay-Z, and Kim Kardashian and Kanye West.

Another standard social media post designed to both mobilize and convey enthusiasm were those featuring candidate *surrogates* – high profile political figures who speak "for" the candidate. Hillary Clinton's most frequently featured surrogates were Barack and Michelle Obama along with Bill Clinton. On Twitter, surrogate posts often appeared in the form of surrogates' tweets that were retweeted by the

Clinton campaign – an affordance heavily used on Twitter (during the 2016 campaign, Instagram did not have a similar functionality). On Facebook, where video was prevalent, surrogate posts often featured professionally edited videos produced by the campaign that included clips of surrogates' speeches supporting the candidate. On Instagram, photographs of surrogates often featured a text overlay, such as a snippet from a campaign speech or campaign tag lines like "I'm With Her" or "Stand With Her"; Instagram posts also featured much longer passages of surrogates' speeches than typically included on either Twitter (with its strict word limits) or Facebook. Along with frequent imagery of the candidate interacting with huge crowds, these surrogate images performed the work of communicating *who* would be "With Her," as the campaign's tag line went, and associated enthusiasm for Clinton's endorsers and surrogates with enthusiasm for Clinton herself (see Figure 4.2).

Although there were differences in how each platform was leveraged for voter mobilization, it is also important to note that the campaign sometimes used virtually identical imagery and messaging across platforms on a particular day. For example, on November 7, 2016, the day before Election Day, all three of the Clinton social media feeds featured posts with a black-and-white photo of Hillary Clinton on stage, a large audience in the background, with her hand crossed over her heart, with bold white text reading "I'm with her because it's time to make history" – an unveiled appeal to gender equality values. On the Facebook version (see Figure 4.3), the caption carried the message the "Share this if you're voting," with a link to a page on the campaign website designed to help voters "make a plan" for voting on Election Day; on Twitter, the caption urged followers to "RT [retweet] this if you're voting," with a link to the page on the site that assisted voters with finding polling places. The Instagram caption contained that same link, but with the message, "Tomorrow, we have the chance to stand up for the America we believe in."

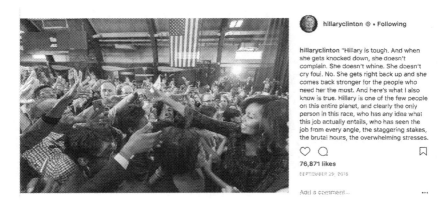

FIGURE 4.2   Clinton Campaign Instagram Post, September 29, 2016

Source: Hillary Clinton Instagram https://www.instagram.com/p/BK9ml8uApeE/

"Delete Your Account"? Hillary Rodham Clinton 55

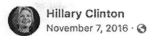

Tomorrow, we have the chance to stand up for the America we believe in. Share this if you're voting. hillaryclinton.com/makeaplan

FIGURE 4.3 Clinton Campaign Facebook Post, November 7, 2016

Source: Hillary Clinton Facebook www.facebook.com/hillaryclinton/photos/a.889773484412515/1320311824692010/?type=3&theater

Policy Messaging

As predicted by the literature on campaign communication, one strand of social media messaging by the Clinton campaign (though not necessarily the predominant one) focused on conveying the candidate's *policy stances*. The form this policy messaging took was notably distinct across the three platforms. On Twitter, these posts tended to include a short policy statement with a link out to the candidate's website, sometimes with a photo but often with no visual imagery. On Facebook, policy stances were usually communicated not just through text but through campaign-produced videos featuring Clinton's stance on a related set of issues, such as health care or gun control, or equal rights.

For example, Clinton campaign posts from the Democratic candidate debate on February 12, 2016 took noticeably different forms. On Twitter, a photo of Clinton at the debate was paired with one sentence from her remarks there: "I am not a single issue candidate, and I do not believe we live in a single issue country," along with the hashtag "#DemDebate." On Facebook, a text caption carried a fuller version of her remarks:

> We don't live in a single-issue country. If we solved our problems with Wall Street and campaign finance reform tomorrow, we'd still have discrimination and barriers holding too many Americans back. We need to tackle all of those problems, too.

The visual component was a campaign-produced video complete with musical soundtrack that paired Clinton's full closing remarks with imagery of people representing each group Clinton mentioned, including Black Americans, gays and lesbians, and working women. None of this material was featured on Instagram; in fact, the campaign did not post to Instagram on February 12.

That doesn't mean that the Clinton campaign never used Instagram for policy messaging. They did, but in a distinctive visual style that was pegged less to day-to-day campaign trail events and more to the presumably shared policy values of Clinton's Instagram followers. Whereas Twitter was the campaign's preferred platform for one-sentence policy statements, and Facebook was their platform for policy-oriented (and other) videos, the Clinton Instagram feed not infrequently featured policy messages characterized by bold text overlaying background imagery or infographics. One way to understand the differences in how these messages were differentially crafted is through the distinct audiences that campaigns aim to appeal to on individual platforms (Kreiss, Lawrence, & McGregor, 2018). One-sentence appeals on Twitter fit well with the targeted audience of journalists on the site, whereas vivid images with punchy text overlay on Instagram appear designed for that site's primarily younger audience. In another pattern, the campaign's Instagram posts occasionally featured essentially the same textual messaging as the campaign's Twitter and Facebook posts, but featured "backstage" images of supporters meeting with or waiting in anticipation of the candidate. The images, in other words, performed the humanizing work (see below) while the text performed the policy work (see Figure 4.4).

Attacks

As Stromer-Galley's research has indicated,[3] the Clinton campaign engaged in frequent attacks on Republican candidates, and on Donald Trump in particular as he surged in the Republican primaries and emerged as her main opponent.

"Delete Your Account"? Hillary Rodham Clinton   57

FIGURE 4.4   Clinton Campaign's Policy Messaging on Instagram

Source: Hillary Clinton Instagram www.instagram.com/p/BDwkMY4EPi9/?utm_source=ig_web_copy_link

Clinton frequently used Twitter to stage these attacks and to respond in real time to Trump's attacks upon her – most memorably in her famous "delete your account" tweet. Using Twitter for attacks on an opponent is predictable, given what we know about how campaigns use Twitter to target journalists in order to influence news coverage, but the Clinton campaign used Facebook and Instagram to attack her opponents as well. The campaign's Facebook attacks often featured imagery and videos that denigrated Trump's policy stances, experience, and temperament. On Instagram in particular, attacks were often drawn along gendered lines and focused on his treatment of women and seeming disregard for children and families, aligning well with audience demographics on the platform that skew female and younger (see Figure 4.5).

Character, Qualifications, and Intimizing Imagery

It is this last area of standard campaign communication strategies where differences across social media platforms become most clear. As much previous research indicates (e.g. Fenno, 1978), campaigning is as much about telling voters about the candidate's personal qualities as it is about conveying their policy stances. Candidates often seek to portray themselves as empathetic and compassionate; contemporary campaigning often features "intimizing" portrayals that seemingly lift the curtain on candidates' backstage lives in order to make them seem more approachable and relatable (McGregor, Lawrence, & Cardona, 2016; Stanyer, 2013). While a main theme of the Clinton campaign messaging overall was that she was tough, highly qualified, and ready to assume the responsibilities of the presidency, the

58 Shannon C. McGregor and Regina G. Lawrence

FIGURE 4.5 Clinton Campaign Attacks on Donald Trump on Twitter and Instagram

Source: Hillary Clinton Twitter and Instagram: https://twitter.com/hillaryclinton/status/740973710593654784?lang=en www.instagram.com/p/BMX0FLyg7Ok/?utm_source=ig_web_copy_link

campaign used social media – especially Facebook and Instagram – to also convey a strong sense of empathy and compassion.

The campaign also used social media to remind voters of Clinton's history of working for women's rights; and on Instagram in particular, to send messages of women's empowerment. Our initial analysis suggests (though more thorough quantitative analysis is required) that the Clinton campaign conveyed these types of gendered messages most noticeably on Instagram, to a lesser extent on Facebook, and more infrequently on Twitter. With its rich visual affordances and the premium its users place on a sense of spontaneous intimacy (Kreiss, Lawrence, & McGregor, 2018), Instagram seems to have invited a particularly gendered style of messaging. Using the throwback genre on Instagram to feature photos throughout one's life, the Clinton campaign repeatedly reminded voters – in a highly personal way – that she has long been working to support women and families. It was in these intimizing posts on Instagram that it was most clear that Clinton ran explicitly as a woman, in stark contrast to her 2008 bid for the Democratic nomination. On Clinton's Instagram feed we see perhaps most clearly how campaigns perceive they can best communicate with their audiences. As our previous research shows (Kreiss, Lawrence, & McGregor 2018), campaigns see social media in general and Instagram in particular as valuable vehicles for "humanizing" candidates, especially for young people who are less likely to engage with campaigns via traditional media.

Discussion

In this chapter, we have begun to explore apparent differences in the ways the Hillary Clinton campaign used different social media platforms in the 2016 presidential election. Our analysis, though preliminary, suggests that the rise of social media has not re-invented campaign strategy, but that well-worn campaign strategies do look somewhat different across the platforms now available to campaigns.

"Delete Your Account"? Hillary Rodham Clinton   **59**

As the traditional campaign literature would predict, the Clinton campaign used Twitter, Facebook, and Instagram to mobilize voters, publicize policy stances, and convey a sense of the candidate's personal qualities. But these classic campaign strategies looked a bit different depending on the affordances, genres, and audiences of each platform.

If we were to generalize from these preliminary findings, we would conjecture that from the campaigns' perspective, Facebook is for everything and everybody. As interviews with 2016 campaign staffers suggest (Kreiss, Lawrence, & McGregor, 2018), campaigns see Facebook as a general platform for reaching wide audiences and a main avenue for communicating with likely supporters. Moreover, in 2016, that platform was evolving to feature a wealth of video content – and that video-forward strategy was being pushed by Facebook staffers working with campaigns (McGregor, 2018). The Clinton Facebook feed therefore featured many videos and a wide variety of content. Indeed, on November 7, 2016, the day before Election Day, the Clinton campaign shared dozens of posts to its Facebook account, running the gamut from brief policy statements and get-out-the-vote messages from the candidate to lengthy, highly produced videos featuring everything from white union workers to Latino-Americans to a glossy video featuring concert footage and pro-Hillary campaign messaging from Beyoncé and Jay-Z.

Our work here also further cements the idea that campaigns use Twitter to speak mostly to the press (Kreiss, 2016; Kreiss, Lawrence, & McGregor, 2018). The Clinton Twitter feed featured standard fare like brief policy statements. The campaign also took advantage of journalists' proclivity to draw meaning of key media events from the platform (McGregor, 2019) to insert Clinton into broader conversations – for example, tweeting reactions to GOP debates with the debate hashtag. These attempts to drive the news cycle also took the form of tweets reacting to current events. Both of these strategies gave journalists rather easy access to a quote from Clinton about political events and/or breaking news events. On the other hand, many of the Clinton campaign's prolific tweets were geared towards mobilizing, though it's unclear *why* as a small minority of the public is on Twitter. We have two working theories as to why this may be, both of which should be examined further in future work. A press theory posits that these mobilizing posts are intended to communicate enthusiasm to the press and/or designed to be repeated by the press, thus reaching a broader and larger audience. A supporter theory suggests that the campaign understood relatively strong supporters to be on Twitter, a platform whose audience skews toward the politically interested public, and that these people in particular needed to be mobilized to donate or volunteer.

As our previous work has suggested, campaigns are not quite sure what exactly to *do* with Instagram (Kreiss, Lawrence, & McGregor, 2018), although they recognize it as a platform especially useful in "humanizing" candidates; other research has shown that, with its lush visual affordances and intimate feel, Instagram is an ideal platform for "intimizing" politics (McGregor, Lawrence, & Cardona, 2017.

60 Shannon C. McGregor and Regina G. Lawrence

While the Clinton campaign did not post as frequently on Instagram as compared to Facebook or Twitter, the campaign cultivated a particularly warm and personal space there. The intimizing dynamics of Clinton's campaign strategy were most apparent on Instagram, where the campaign leveraged the platform's visual affordances to effectively humanize a candidate who has often struggled with "likeability." In fact, the implied audience for Clinton's Instagram account was one to be reassured of their choice in a candidate. The Clinton campaign also leveraged the platform's expectations for "authenticity" to quite explicitly run as a woman.

Given the traditional advice to women to avoid "running as a woman" and given that the 2008 Hillary Clinton presidential campaign exhibited a somewhat confused strategy with respect to gender (Lawrence & Rose, 2010), the depth of gendered messaging on Clinton's social media feeds in 2016 is noteworthy. Many of the examples we have provided thus far also show the 2016 Clinton campaign's gender strategy (Lawrence & Rose, 2010) at work: exhortations to voters to "make history" by voting for her (Figure 4.3); policy messages focusing on equal pay and sex discrimination (Figure 4.4); and messaging and imagery conveying Clinton's history of advocating for women and children (Figure 4.5). Looking across platforms, we do see some differences. The campaign used Twitter for generalized and less gendered mobilization messaging, while on Instagram, the campaign crafted a deliberately gendered space. A regular Twitter follower would certainly know Clinton's position on women's issues from her messaging on that platform, but would not have nearly the same sense of the campaign as a regular Instagram follower. A Clinton Instagram follower who had exclusively encountered the candidate via that platform and then entered the campaign's Twitter feed would emerge a bit bewildered from the warm, enveloping circle of girl power to the campaign's cool, mechanical, institutionalized messaging on Twitter.

One explanation for these very different uses of social media by the same campaign is offered by "strategic stereotype theory," which argues that female candidates, who in the past were often encouraged to downplay their gender and gendered messaging, will seek to capitalize on positive gender stereotypes about warmth, caring, and trustworthiness when they sense a political context favorable to that messaging (Fridkin & Kenney, 2014). In 2016, we suspect, the Clinton campaign sized up a contest against a frankly misogynist opponent as an environment favorable for running as a woman. But this argument needs greater nuance, precisely because we see such different social media messaging across different platforms. The gendered space created on the Clinton Instagram feed was not replicated on Twitter, we theorize, for two reasons.

First, the different affordances and genres of the platforms allowed and encouraged rather different messaging. The Clinton campaign leveraged Instagram's rich visual affordances to the hilt, investing in higher-than-average production values to create a visually stunning stream of imagery. Second, the various social streams seem to have been produced for different audiences. For example, on Instagram, the campaign "risked" a higher degree of gendered messaging and imagery – precisely because, we suspect, the campaign calculated that the audiences were so different across platforms. Instagram in general skews younger and more female (Pew Research Center, 2018), whereas, previous research suggests, "Twitter is for journalists" and politicos. The Clinton campaign used Twitter to communicate more masculine ideals of leadership (decisive, experienced) along with its gender equity messaging.

As we have previously theorized, campaigns use social media platforms differently, depending on their understanding of each platforms' audiences, affordances, and genres of communication (Kreiss, Lawrence, & McGregor, 2018). As we show here, this does not mean that today's campaigns employ radically different communication strategies compared to well-documented, long-utilized strategies such as mobilizing messages and communicating policy stances, although social media do invite increased attention to intimizing communication (McGregor, Lawrence, & Cardona, 2017). But in looking deeply at one campaign, we see how classic campaigning tropes necessarily adapt to the particular audiences, affordances, and genres on any given social media platform. At the same time, unique campaign strategies (even styles) on individual platforms are shaped by what audiences can be reached, the platforms' actual and perceived affordances, and the genres of communication perceived to be appropriate to each.

Notes

1 The authors would like to acknowledge Michelle Alexander for her assistance in gathering and analyzing the data presented here.
2 http://illuminating.ischool.syr.edu/#/platforms/1,2/dates/2016-11-01,2016-11-08/candidates/10,5/types/8&9,5&6
3 http://illuminating.ischool.syr.edu/#/platforms/1,2/dates/2016-11-01,2016-11-08/candidates/10,5/types/8&9,5&6

References

Bystrom, D. G., Robertson, T., Banwart, M. C., & Kaid, L. L. (2005). *Gender and candidate communication: Videostyle, webstyle, newstyle.* Abingdon: Routledge.
Conway, B. A., Kenski, K., & Wang, D. (2015). The rise of Twitter in the political campaign: Searching for intermedia agenda-setting effects in the presidential primary. *Journal of Computer-Mediated Communication, 20*(4), 363–380.
Fenno, R. F. (1978). *Home style: House members in their districts.* HarperCollins.
Fridkin, K., & Kenney, P. (2014). *The changing face of representation: The gender of US senators and constituent communications.* Ann Arbor: University of Michigan Press.
Gervais, B. T., & Morris, I. L. (2018). *Reactionary Republicanism: How the Tea Party in the House Paved the Way for Trump's Victory.* Oxford: Oxford University Press.
Golbeck, J., Grimes, J. M., & Rogers, A. (2010). Twitter use by the U.S. Congress. *Journal of the American Society for Information Science and Technology, 61*(8), 1612–1621.
Grabe, M. E., & Bucy, E. P. (2009). *Image bite politics: News and the visual framing of elections.* Oxford: Oxford University Press.

Kreiss, D., Lawrence, R. G., & McGregor, S. C. (2018). In their own words: Political practitioner accounts of candidates, audiences, affordances, genres, and timing in strategic social media use. *Political Communication, 35*(1), 8–31.

Kreiss, D. (2016). Seizing the moment: The presidential campaigns' use of Twitter during the 2012 electoral cycle. *New Media & Society, 18*(8), 1473–1490.

Larsson, A. O. (2016). Online, all the time? A quantitative assessment of the permanent campaign on Facebook. *New Media & Society, 18*(2), 274–292.

Lawrence, R. G., & Rose, M. (2010). *Hillary Clinton's race for the White House: Gender politics and the media on the campaign trail*. Boulder, CO: Lynne Rienner Publishers.

McGregor, S. C. (2018). *Social (media) construction of public opinion by Elites* (Doctoral dissertation).

McGregor, S. C. (2019). Social media as public opinion: How journalists use social media to represent public opinion. *Journalism*.

McGregor, S. C., Lawrence, R. G., & Cardona, A. (2017). Personalization, gender, and social media: gubernatorial candidates' social media strategies. *Information, Communication & Society, 20*(2), 264–283.

Pew Research Center. (2018). *Social Media Use in 2018: A majority of Americans use Facebook and YouTube, but young adults are especially heavy users of Snapchat and Instagram*. https://www.pewinternet.org/2018/03/01/social-media-use-in-2018/

Stanyer, J. (2013). *Intimate politics: Publicity, privacy and the personal lives of politicians in media saturated democracies*. Hoboken, NJ: John Wiley & Sons.

Velencia, J. (2015). Hillary Clinton's 2016 announcement caused Twitter to freak out. *HuffPost*, April 13. www.huffingtonpost.com/2015/04/13/hillary-clinton-announcement-on-social-media_n_7057020.html

Williams, C. B., & Gulati, J. (2013). Social networks in political campaigns: Facebook and the congressional elections of 2006 and 2008. *New Media & Society, 15*(1), 52.

5

THE VISUALLY VIRAL PRIME MINISTER

Justin Trudeau, Selfies, and Instagram

Chaseten Remillard, Lindsey M. Bertrand, and Alina Fisher

A Prime Ministerial Photobomb and a Selfie

On May 19, 2017, Prime Minister Justin Trudeau took to the Vancouver seawall for a run. The seawall is an idyllic setting, backdropped by both the city and the ocean; the wall circumscribes Stanley Park and is a popular location for tourists and locals alike. Trudeau was in Vancouver to participate in a "roundtable with technology leaders" to promote his government's Canada Child Benefit, and meet with ethnic communities in nearby Surrey and Abbotsford (Justin Trudeau, Prime Minister of Canada 2017a, 2017b). Known for his athleticism, Trudeau's decision to jog along the seawall was not, in itself, noteworthy. However, as he passed a group of students gathered for their graduation celebration, something unique took place. Adam Scotti, official Photographer for Prime Minister's Office (PMO), who would sometimes join the PM for his runs, captured a photo of Trudeau running past the prom-goers.

The image is subtle. Foregrounded is a group of nearly 20 young people. Dressed to celebrate their graduation, the young women are in gowns and dresses, the young men in suits. In the middle of the image, seemingly spontaneously emerging from behind the group is a man in a black T-shirt, black running shorts; he's in mid-stride, his focus on the road ahead of him. The man, of course, is the Prime Minister. Without proper introduction, or without the recognition of Justin Trudeau in the frame, the image would be a throwaway, a test shot of a soon-to-be orchestrated group picture. Part of what makes the image remarkable, then, is the unremarkable nature of its composition. Of course, once we recognize the true subject of the image, this appearance dissolves quickly.

We can imagine that someone in the group of graduates recognized the jogger as Justin Trudeau. The recognition led to another photograph. This second

64 Chaseten Remillard et al.

image clearly has the Prime Minister as the focus. His arms around the group, he is embraced by the students. The focus distance is short. The image filled with smiling faces, thumbs-up, and phones out – a hallmark selfie.

Both images were originally broadcast on social media. Adam Scotti's image was posted to his Twitter and Instagram accounts. The Twitter post caption read, "Prom season in #Vancouver" (Scotti 2017a). The selfie was posted by prom photographer Cam Corrado on his personal Instagram (Corrado 2017). Scotti's image was "liked" by over 7,000 people and shared by nearly 2,000 on Twitter, and was "liked" by over 1,600 on Instagram. Corrado's post garnered nearly 1,500 "likes" and over 60 comments. Beyond social media impressions, the images were featured or mentioned in over 384 news stories around the world, and coverage included the agencies such as the British Broadcast Corporation (BBC), *Harper's Bazaar*, Canadian Broadcast Corporation (CBC), *Vancouver Sun*, and *Montreal Gazette*.

The seawall photograph and its selfie companion speak to a new form of political communication. The expansion of social media as a primary source of information for the public and the retrenchment of traditional or legacy media have allowed politicians the ability to engage with voters more easily and more directly. For some politicians, such engagement is in the form of text-based tweets; for others, such as Prime Minister Trudeau, social media offers an expanded ability to visually communicate his political brand and influence the agenda in traditional media.

The Campaign Selfie and Beyond

Justin Trudeau's confirmation as leader in 2013 began the Liberal Party of Canada's ascent back to power from an all-time low. Trudeau came from a notable political pedigree. As the son of one of Canada's most famous prime ministers, Pierre Elliott Trudeau, his name captured the national imagination in Canada in a manner comparable to the Kennedy name in the United States (Marland 2013; Leung 2016). However, in 2013, Justin Trudeau was untested as a leader and his success was far from certain.

With the 2015 election looming, the Conservative Party responded to the nomination of Trudeau with a great deal of personal criticism and attack ads, which characterized Trudeau as "just not ready" (Conservative – Conservateur 2015). He was too young, too inexperienced, too good looking to assume the role of Prime Minister (Messamore 2016; Proudfoot 2016). Trudeau's campaign responded by doubling down on Trudeau's personality. The campaign resisted the temptation "to stuff [Trudeau] into charcoal suits and park him behind campaign lecterns to emphasize his seriousness" and instead emphasized his strengths, putting out unrelentingly positive images of that emphasized their candidate's easy and outgoing nature (Proudfoot 2016). Trudeau was often pictured outdoors, with sleeves rolled up, performing physical feats, and/or engaging with everyday Canadians (see Hopper 2015; Markovinovic 2016; Lalancette and Raynauld 2018).

The Visually Viral Prime Minister **65**

Justin Trudeau's use of social media was also remarkably different than what had occurred before in Canadian politics (Marland, Lewis, and Flanagan 2017; Small 2016). In the "selfie election" of 2015, Trudeau was unrivalled (McDiarmid 2015). The selfie became nearly synonymous with Trudeau during the campaign, so much so that his party released a Liberal-branded selfie-stick, which retailed for $15.99 CDN (Hopper 2015). For Trudeau, the use of selfies as a political communication tactic leveraged the power of social media in a unique way. People post selfies as an expression of "self-definition" to those who are members of their online networks (Murray 2015, 490). The proximal nature of the subject from the camera and the visible extension of the arms tells the viewer "see this, here, now, . . . see me showing you me" (Frosh 2015, 1610). A selfie with Trudeau was less about Trudeau, and more about the person who posed with Trudeau. In so doing, a selfie blurs the lines between personal and professional and invites a sense of intimacy and seemingly shared values (Karadimitriou and Veneti 2016).

Selfies are also understood and received as unscripted, and so express a fundamental "truth" about the photographic subject (Coladonato 2014). The selfie is posed, to be sure, but importantly, a selfie is initiated by the person who takes it and posts it. The decision to make the image public is out of the hands of the politician and their communication team. As such, the selfie is seems more authentic and has an "unpretentious nature especially in comparison with traditional political photos" (Karadimitriou and Veneti 2016, 330).

The selfie is a great equalizer, in this sense. Unscripted, composed, and controlled by the citizen, user-generated and distributed, the selfie forces the politician to engage with the public on their terms, and in an "ordinary" way. This capacity is only accelerated by the ease of sharing selfies on social media. Social media unifies its users through a shared sense of identity and purpose and allows users to actively co-create culture rather than act as passive consumers (Adria 2007; Cross 2011). Social media enables people to create meaning collectively through a shared communicative act, one that may take place instantaneously, and that relies on one's own social network and capital. A selfie with a politician becomes an articulation of personal, not political, culture.

By taking seemingly spontaneous selfies with everyday people, Trudeau both positioned himself as one of the people and projected an image of "democratic accessibility" (Marland 2018). The use of social media platforms, where it is difficult to determine who authored any given post on the PMO account or whether it was vetted, edited, or posted immediately, also contributed to making the images appear to be free from the influence of political marketers, giving a feeling of more direct connection between Trudeau and those who follow or interact with his social media (Lalancette and Cormack 2018).

The opportunities associated with political selfies do not come without risks. During the 2015 election, Trudeau was labelled as narcissistic and image-obsessed for his supposed encouragement of campaign selfies (Pedwell 2015). After the election, criticism of that kind continued, and expanded to claim his government was more image than substance. On National Selfie Day, June 21, 2016, then interim Conservative Party leader Rona Ambrose took the opportunity to crystalize such sentiments in her pointed comment:

> While on the international stage we saw leaders of the Western world come together, coalescing around the fight against ISIS, the impression that was left with Canadians and the international community was that our prime minister was consumed with taking selfies.
>
> *(Canada 2015)*

Perhaps most infamously, Trudeau suffered a minor public relations crisis when he stopped to pose for a selfie on his way to former finance minister Jim Flaherty's funeral in April 2017. The so-called funeral-selfie incident raised a familiar discourse from opponents of Trudeau and his use of the photographic tactic and, for a number of members of the public, it also called into question the quality of his character (see The Huffington Post Canada 2014; QMI Agency 2014).

A different form of controversy took place when, in January 2017, Trudeau was invited to take a selfie with two Dalhousie University students in Halifax. Once he entered the frame of their camera for the photo, one of the students asked "whether he plans on implementing the United Nations Declaration on the Rights of Indigenous Peoples," a Liberal campaign promise. Caught off guard, and on video, Trudeau stepped out of frame, answered affirmatively that the government will, and immediately received a follow-up question by the second student, "Does that mean requiring consent for natural resource projects?" (Dunham 2017). Composed, Trudeau turned to the camera and responded that a broad range of communities need to be consulted. The video later appeared online.

The selfie functions as an expression of personal identity, is controlled in both composition and distribution by the citizen (and not the politician), and is shared across personal networks of users who share values and experiences; the selfie seems to escape the spin of more official political portraits and communications. As a tactic of political communication, therefore, the selfie is capable of leveraging social media to create an intimate image of a politician as approachable, authentic, and down-to-earth. At the same time, the selfie suffers from an association with narcissism and superficiality. Politicians engaged in selfie culture run the risk of opening themselves up to these criticisms and characterizations. Moreover, the ease of image capture and the foregone control of composition and distribution that make a selfie such a powerful force are also precisely the elements that create risk for a politician. As Trudeau experienced at the Flaherty funeral and in Halifax, unscripted and impromptu interactions with the public can compromise a politician's public image.

The Visually Viral Justin Trudeau

Trudeau is personally well suited for visual communication. He has a flair for the dramatic and an ability to appear authentic on camera. For example, Trudeau is

The Visually Viral Prime Minister **67**

known for a particularly endearing "baby trick," in which he balances a standing toddler on one hand. Trudeau has boxed a political opponent for charity (Raj 2013; Mandel 2015) and demonstrated how to fall down a flight of stairs as a "party trick" (Jvalicen 2015). On Halloween 2017, he went to Parliament dressed as Clark Kent. Dressed in a blue suit, white shirt, and red tie, hair combed down and parted to the side, and black-rimmed glasses, before answering any questions from reporters, he unbuttoned his shirt to reveal a Superman logo and commented, "It had to be done" (The Canadian Press Staff 2017).

Trudeau's dramatic acts provide excellent visual content for social media. Raised in the public eye, Trudeau is acclimatized to media attention, crowds, and engaging with high-profile officials and celebrities, all the while having his picture taken. In an interview with the *Globe and Mail*, the Prime Minister's official photographer, Adam Scotti, praised Trudeau's understanding of the importance and purposes of visual communication: "He is attuned to what I need to do my job.... It's not his first rodeo" (Andrew-Gee 2016). Whether Trudeau is pictured laughing with the Irish Taoiseach about the colour of socks (Dangerfield 2017), posing with his shirt off for a boxing match weigh-in, kayaking, canoeing, surfing, hiking, or balancing a baby, Trudeau manages to project a positive image of leadership defined by athleticism, friendly jokes or pranks, engagement with public, and overall joyful public persona (Raj 2013; Lalancette and Raynauld 2017).

These types of images are ripe for virality on social media. The phenomenon of virality, where something is shared and spread rapidly from one person to another, much like a contagion (Berger 2013), can be difficult to predict. Engagement with online content can be influenced by message framing, aspects of communicator credibility, and communication persuasion. Message uptake can be affected by social media channel-specific behaviours (Suh et al. 2010), communicator social capital (Recuero, Araujo, and Zago 2011), popularity and homophily (Macskassy and Michelson 2011), resonance with popular culture (Nisbet and Scheufele 2009), and concision (Cook, Cook, and Landrum 2013). However, viral content typically displays one or more traits that trigger a sense of value to the person sharing and receiving the content. The value may be an increased social currency and visibility because of the qualities of content, particularly in cases where content elicits a positive emotional response (Botha and Reyneke 2013; DelVicario et al. 2016), is humorous, and/or tells a compelling story that is more likely to have a greater reach on social networks (McDonald 2009; Berger 2013).

The so-called swooning Ivanka photos by Saul Loeb are a prime example of this type of viral capacity (Cresci 2017). In February 2015, both Prime Minister Justin Trudeau and American First Daughter Ivanka Trump attended a White House roundtable on female business leaders. In one of the images from the event, Ivanka Trump is pictured looking at Justin Trudeau out of the corner of her eyes. Justin Trudeau is blurred in the image, as the focus is on Ms. Trump's gaze. The original tweet by Philip Lewis was captioned "Get you someone that looks at you the way Ivanka Trump looks at Justin Trudeau" (Lewis 2017). The combination of the words and image combine to imply that Ivanka Trump's look was more

68 Chaseten Remillard et al.

admiring than professional. Originally posted on February 13, 2017, the tweet has been liked over 44,000 times and shared nearly 23,000 times. Moreover, the image has given rise to flood of traditional media coverage in the *Guardian*, *Vanity Fair*, *Huffington Post*, TMZ, the *Mirror UK*, and more.

Trudeau is undeniably photogenic and good looking. Shortly after winning the 2015 election, Trudeau was featured in *Vogue* magazine as one of the "10 Unconventional Alternatives to the Sexiest Man Alive." Trudeau is featured in the magazine with the caption, "Sexy, feminist, and capable of balancing a baby on one hand: Prime Minister Trudeau gets our vote" (Garcia 2015). In another representative article about Trudeau's handsomeness, an image of him taking the stage at an event is captioned "the internet collectively swooned over pictures of the Canadian PM's impressive bubble-butt" (Le Messurier 2017). Trudeau's good looks have made the pages of many other publications; *CBS News* featured Trudeau on a list of "Sexiest world leaders" (CBS News 2018), the *Mirror* asked if he is the "sexiest politician in the world" (Smith 2015), the *Guardian* argued that he "looks like a fairytale prince," at least for a politician (Freeman 2017), *InStyle* magazine referred to him as "very attractive" and a "political thirst trap" (Jones 2017), and even *Time Magazine* called Trudeau a "confirmed heartthrob" (Lang 2016), to name only a few.

As the popularity and accessibility of social media sites increases annually (Miller 2017; Smith and Anderson 2018), the potential to extend message reach, engage audiences, and achieve virality also increases. Observability of social media content creates a form of behavioural residue (a permanent record of behaviour) that in turn can act as social credential. The availability heuristic leads audiences to believe that a popular topic is something valuable to know about (Zuckerman 2013): the more we see it, the more credibility it seems to have, irrespective of the validity of the content (McDonald 2009; Thaler and Shiffman 2015; Del Vicario et al. 2016). So, the importance of content that is initially widely shared is further reinforced through repeated exposure (Berger 2013). In other words, in a way, the more the internet tells us Justin Trudeau is good looking, the more we want to share content that reinforces that collective opinion.

Thus, the initial image of Justin Trudeau and Ivanka Trump not only invigorates an already existing discourse about the leader's youthful good looks but also leads to further images that reinforce that knowledge. On February 14, 2017, a day after Philip Lewis' original tweet, another user, @DannyDutch, posted a tweet that featured four pictures of other world leaders and celebrities looking at Justin Trudeau with similarly suggestive facial expressions, including Ivanka Trump (again), Kate Middleton, Emma Watson, and Donald Trump (Dutch 2017). The caption of his tweet reads: "No one is safe from PM Steal Yo Girl!" This tweet received nearly 160,000 retweets and over 300,000 likes.

The redoubling effect of the internet validates collective conclusions through repetition, amplifies and reinforces a positive image of Trudeau as the leader of Canada, and builds social capital for retweeters (as they demonstrate cultural knowledge related to political knowledge). Beyond his policies, Trudeau's physical appearance becomes a point of national pride, a testimony to the power of youth to make an impact, and a counterpoint to traditional politics. As some have commented, "coupled with Canada's reputation for being polite and progressive (if a little bland), Trudeau's handsomeness has become a virtue in and of itself, a sign of general Canadian goodness" (Giese 2017). To others, Trudeau's physical qualities are a more aggressive form of Canadian power; as Samantha Bee, Canadian-born comedian and host of *Full Frontal*, posted, "Sending Trudeau to stand attractively next to Trump while speaking French is actually the closest thing Canada has to saying 'fuck you'" (Bee 2017). In either case, images of Trudeau on social media perform powerful political and cultural functions.

The First Prime Minister of the Instagram Age

With more to do and less time to do it, and with increased pressure to produce stories that can be used in media across jurisdictions and platforms, reporters have become more likely to accept "information subsidies" – stories carefully prepared for the press by public relations workers in the Prime Minister's Office, among others – focused on nationally recognizable leaders such as Trudeau. With increased competition from online sources and social platforms, and a 24-hour news cycle that demands frequent updates to stories, reporters are also under more pressure to focus their attention on leaders' performances in order to make their stories more spectacular, relatable, and/or easily digestible (Street 2004).

Beyond his status as an internet phenomenon, therefore, the Prime Minister has a strategic impetus to leverage social media to shape traditional media coverage of his politics and political brand and to communicate directly to his base supporters. The @justinpjtrudeau Instagram account has over 2.3 million followers and is used for significantly different content than that found on his official Twitter and Facebook accounts. Content on Instagram does not promote events or broadcasts but rather focuses on documenting events or meetings that have already happened. For the Prime Minister, Instagram is more about personal connection, featuring photos of him holding his daughter, hugging his wife, and various family photos, for example. Trudeau's Instagram feed also promotes cultural diversity and shares photos of meetings with global dignitaries, visible minorities, and cultural events.

The platform thereby communicates the values of the Liberal Party of Canada (LPC) and what the LPC believes to the predominant values of the nation itself (Lalancette, Drouin, and Lemarier-Saulnier 2014). Image management on Instagram has been shown to promote the perception of wanted qualities in politicians, "including honesty, intelligence, friendliness, sincerity, and trustworthiness" (Lalancette and Raynauld 2017, 1). Images of Trudeau are used to attempt to represent his party and nation's political values in a deeper way than policy-making or other governing activities could – by indicating that whatever his governing

70 Chaseten Remillard et al.

actions may be, they are informed by a moral, grounded, and authentic character (Street 2004; Lalancette, Drouin, and Lemarier-Saulnier 2014). In other words, the Liberal Party's values are "condensed" in Trudeau and extended "beyond the limits of their sphere of practice" (Corner 2000, 398).

While images of Trudeau's personal and family life are often what go viral or are highlighted in the media, images of official duties are more often posted than those of his family, and the majority of Instagram posts relate to government activity connected to the categories of "employment and social development" or "the economy" (Lalancette and Raynauld 2017). While these images are seen less often, the frequency at which they are posted suggests that the PMO attempts to use Instagram to position Trudeau as being as serious about economic matters (such as the ones highlighted in the Liberal platform) as he is friendly and approachable. Per Instagram, Trudeau is a loving husband and father (Lalancette and Cormack 2018), connected and comfortable with a wide variety of communities (Lalancette and Raynauld 2017), who both works hard and plays hard, and who speaks with a personal, authentic, and consistently Canadian voice.

Indeed, the Trudeau brand's appeal has held relatively strong through its first years (Mckenna 2018). This is perhaps unsurprising, given the powerful and well-resourced communications team in the PMO, and the weakness of opposition parties following the 2015 election (both the NDP and Conservative Party have since replaced their leaders) (Marland 2017). However, that is not to say that the honeymoon did not cool: eventually gaffes and controversial decisions would be made. Key controversial decisions included breaking the Liberals' promise of electoral reform (in February 2017), advancing an unpopular small business tax at a time when the finance minister was under investigation for impropriety relating to his personal wealth (in December 2017), and spending billions to pursue a controversial pipeline expansion project, despite opposition from environmentalists, Indigenous peoples, and the government of British Columbia (in May 2018).

While these controversies were significant, however, they did not go so far as to eliminate Trudeau's celebrity status: positive images of Trudeau have continued to be widely seen and shared on social and mainstream media, particularly as Trudeau has faced off against US President Trump over trade disputes (Slaughter 2018), and polling suggests the Liberal Party would win another majority if an election were held as of this writing (Grenier 2018).

However, one particular controversy was pronounced more vividly and visually on social media. In February 2018, Trudeau, his family, and key members of his leadership team travelled to India. In alignment with both Trudeau's flare for the dramatic and his brand of content on Instagram, images of the Trudeaus were posted on the Prime Minister's account as they participated in cultural events and wore traditional clothing. Press coverage of the images and antics was not positive; one commentator claimed that "he paraded around his costumed family and danced the bhangra like a bad impression of Phil Dunphy after his first yoga lesson" (Urback 2018), making a comparison to the slightly dim-witted and over eager father figure of popular sitcom *Modern Family*. Other articles claimed Trudeau wore the attire of a bridegroom, that Canadians were outraged at the cost of the clothes to taxpayers, or questioned whether the Prime Minister's costumes reflected cultural appreciation or appropriation (The Canadian Press 2018). The trip was problematic beyond the ridicule for wearing over-the-top traditional garb, as Trudeau was rumoured to have been snubbed by the Indian prime minister and had accidentally invited a convicted attempted murderer to an event hosted by the Canadian High Commissioner in Mumbai.

Nevertheless, for precisely the same reasons as his previous successes on social media occurred, Trudeau now suffered because of the visually viral elements of his political brand. Suddenly the playful "dressing up" of the Prime Minister as Clark Kent, his dramatic flare, and his youthful enthusiasm seemed like gaudy self-promotion. More damaging, his choice for a visually dramatic event even rekindled questions of his readiness and seriousness as a leader. As columnist Paul Wells expressed,

> perhaps the next time the PM goes over fun wardrobe ideas for a foreign trip, somebody on his staff could ask whether he also plans to bring any project serious enough to counterbalance the elevated likelihood of coming off like a giggling schoolboy.
>
> *(Wells 2018)*

Perhaps this is the fate of the new age of political communication: viral content and compelling Instagram stories enable politicians to control and shape their image, the public engages in amplifying that content, and the traditional media (understaffed and overworked) is left to comment and criticize. In this new age, when "media cycles end, but the Internet never forgets" (Yiannopoulos 2016), a politician such as Trudeau, whose brand is so pervasively linked to visual social media, both enjoys the benefits of such exposure and can never fully distance himself from his social-mediated past. The echo of Trudeau's posted past continuously shapes and colours interpretations of his present political brand.

References

Adria, Marco. 2007. "The ontology of Facebook: Popular culture and Canadian identity." *Canadian Issues* (Winter): 36–40.

Andrew-Gee, Eric. 2016. "The unmediated photo is the message." *The Globe and Mail*, August 12. www.theglobeandmail.com/news/national/the-unmediated-photo-is-themessage/article31389091/.

Bee, Samantha (@FullFrontalSamB). 2017. "Sending Trudeau to stand attractively next to Trump while speaking French is actually the closest thing Canada has to saying "fuck you."" Twitter, February 13. https://twitter.com/fullfrontalsamb/status/831229156411187200.

Berger, Jonah. 2013. *Contagious: Why things catch on*. New York: Simon & Schuster.

Botha, Elsamari, and Mignon Reyneke. 2013. "To share or not to share: The role of content and emotion in viral marketing." *Journal of Public Affairs* 13, no. 2: 160–171.

Canada. 2015. *House of Commons Debates*. December 7 (Hon. Rona Ambrose, Leader of the Opposition, CPC). www.ourcommons.ca/DocumentViewer/en/42-1/house/sitting-3/hansard#t1110.

The Canadian Press. 2017. "Justin Trudeau dresses as Clark Kent for Question Period, reveals Superman costume after." *Global News*, October 31. https://globalnews.ca/news/3835267/justin-trudeau-superman-halloween-2017/.

The Canadian Press. 2018. "Taxpayers not on hook for Trudeau family wardrobe: Documents." *Global News*, April 17, 2018. https://globalnews.ca/news/4150482/justin-trudeau-india-trip-wardrobe-documents/.

CBS News. 2018. "Sexiest world leaders and royals." *CBS News*, June 1. www.cbsnews.com/pictures/sexiest-world-leaders/.

Coladonato, Valerio. 2014. "Power, gender, and the selfie: The cases of Hillary Clinton, Barack Obama, Pope Francis." *Comunicazioni sociali* 3, no. 3: 394–405.

Conservative – Conservateur. 2015. "The Interview." YouTube Video, 1:03, May 25. www.youtube.com/watch?v=c86-9HitWg0.

Cook, Bryan G., Lysandra Cook, and Timothy J. Landrum. 2013. "Moving research into practice: Can we make dissemination stick?" *Exceptional Children* 79, no. 2: 163–180.

Corner, John. 2000. "Mediated persona and political culture: Dimensions of structure and process." *European Journal of Cultural Studies* 3, no. 3: 386–402.

Corrado, Cam (@crrdo). 2017. Selfie of prom-goers with Trudeau on Seawall. Instagram photo, May 20. www.instagram.com/p/BUU3bInAqp4/.

Cresci, Elena. 2017. "Pictures of 'swooning' Ivanka Trump and Justin Trudeau go viral." *The Guardian*, February 15. www.theguardian.com/media/shortcuts/2017/feb/15/pictures-of-swooning-ivanka-trump-and-justin-trudeau-go-viral.

Cross, Mary. 2011. *Bloggerati, Twitterati: How blogs and Twitter are transforming popular culture.* Santa Barbara, CA: ABC-CLIO.

Dangerfield, Katie. 2017. "Irish leader shows off socks with maple leaves, Mounties to Justin Trudeau." *Global News*. July 4. https://globalnews.ca/news/3573396/justin-trudeau-socks-irish-leo-varadkar/.

Del Vicario, Michela, Alessandro Bessi, Fabiana Zollo, Fabio Petroni, Antonio Scala, Guido Caldarelli, H. Eugene Stanley, and Walter Quattrociocchi. 2016. "The spreading of misinformation online." *Proceedings of the National Academy of Sciences* 113, no. 3: 554–559.

Dunham, Jackie. 2017. "PM Trudeau lured with selfie, caught on question of indigenous rights." *CTVNews.ca*, January 18. www.ctvnews.ca/politics/pm-trudeau-lured-with-selfie-caught-on-question-of-indigenous-rights-1.3245966.

Dutch, Danny (@DannyDutch). 2017. "No one is safe from PM Steal Yo Girl!" *Twitter*, February 14. https://twitter.com/DannyDutch/status/831575882972196864.

Freeman, Hadley. 2017. "Justin Trudeau: How did a Canadian PM become a style superhero?" *The Guardian*, February 27. www.theguardian.com/fashion/2017/feb/27/justin-trudeau-how-did-a-canadian-pm-become-a-style-superhero.

Frosh, Paul. 2015. "The gestural image: The selfie, photography theory, and kinesthetic sociability." *International Journal of Communication* 9: 1607–1628.

Garcia, Patricia. 2015. "Canada's feminist Prime Minister appoints gender-equal cabinet." *Vogue*, November 4. www.vogue.com/13368129/canada-feminist-prime-minister-justin-trudeau-cabinet.

Giese, Rachel. 2017. "Justin Trudeau's butt won't quit – Just like double standards in politics." *Chatelaine*, March 3. www.chatelaine.com/opinion/justin-trudeaus-butt-double-standards/.

Grenier, Éric. 2018. "Poll Tracker: Federal poll averages and seat projections." *CBC News*. Last modified August 7. www.cbc.ca/news/politics/poll-tracker-federal-poll-averages-and-seat-projections-1.4171977.

Hopper, Tristin. 2015. "The Trudeau manipulation: Behind the most image-conscious campaign in Canadian history." *National Post*, October 12. https://nationalpost.com/news/politics/the-trudeau-manipulation-behind-the-most-image-conscious-campaign-in-canadian-history.

The Huffington Post Canada. 2014. "Justin Trudeau criticized for posing for photo before Flaherty funeral." *The Huffington Post Canada*, April 17. www.huffingtonpost.ca/2014/04/17/justin-trudeau-jim-flaherty-funeral-selfie-photo_n_5167866.html.

Jones, Isabel. 2017. "Justin Trudeau reached peak Justin Trudeau at Toronto pride parade." *InStyle*, June 26. www.instyle.com/news/justin-trudeau-prime-minister-canada-pride-parade-socks.

Justin Trudeau, Prime Minister of Canada. 2017a. "Itinerary for the Prime Minister, Justin Trudeau, for Thursday, May 18, 2017." Last modified May 17. https://pm.gc.ca/eng/news/2017/05/17/itinerary-thursday-may-18-2017.

Justin Trudeau, Prime Minister of Canada. 2017b. "Itinerary for the Prime Minister, Justin Trudeau, for Friday, May 19, 2017." Last modified May 18. https://pm.gc.ca/eng/news/2017/05/18/itinerary-friday-may-19-2017.

Jvalicen. 2015. "Canadian Prime Minister Justin Trudeau falling down stairs." YouTube Video, 0:43, October 20. www.youtube.com/watch?v=tRHNqRyaLcs.

Karadimitriou, Achilleas, and Anastasia Veneti. 2016. "Political selfies: Image events in the new media field." In *The Digital Transformation of the Public Sphere*, edited by Athina Karatzogianni, Dennis Nguyen, and Elisa Serafinelli, 321–340. London: Palgrave Macmillan.

Lalancette, Mireille, Alex Drouin, and Catherine Lemarier-Saulnier. 2014. "Playing along new rules: Personalized politics in a 24/7 mediated world." In *Political communication in Canada: Meet the press and tweet the rest*, edited by Alex Marland, T. Giasson, and Tamara Small, 144–159. Vancouver: University of British Columbia Press.

Lalancette, Mireille, and Patricia Cormack. 2018. "Justin Trudeau and the play of celebrity in the 2015 Canadian federal election campaign." *Celebrity Studies*: 1–14.

Lalancette, Mireille, and Vincent Raynauld. 2017. "The power of political image: Justin Trudeau, Instagram, and celebrity politics." *American Behavioral Scientist*: 0002764217744838.

Lalancette, Mireille, and Vincent Raynauld. 2018. "Instagram, Justin Trudeau, and political image-making." *Policy Options*, April 9. http://policyoptions.irpp.org/magazines/april-2018/instagram-justin-trudeau-and-political-image-making/.

Lang, Cady. 2016. "Prince Harry and Justin Trudeau's meeting is the political summit of our dreams." *TIME*, May 2. http://time.com/4314849/prince-harry-justin-trudeau-met/.

Le Messurier, Danielle. 2017. "From Emmanuel Macron to Justin Trudeau, these are the sexiest young world leaders." *The Daily Telegraph*, May 7. www.dailytelegraph.com.au/business/work/from-emmanuel-macron-to-justin-trudeau-these-are-the-sexiest-young-world-leaders/news-story/9df1affb77472017507d00fabc29d215.

Leung, Marlene. 2016. "'Anti-Trump' and 'Canada's JFK': American media's fascination with Trudeau." *CTVNews.ca*, March 9. www.ctvnews.ca/world/anti-trump-and-canada-s-jfk-american-media-s-fascination-with-trudeau-1.2810108.

Lewis, Philip. 2017. "Get you someone that looks at you the way Ivanka Trump looks at Justin Trudeau." *Twitter*, February 13. https://twitter.com/Phil_Lewis_/status/831280292379910144.

Macskassy, Sofus A., and Matthew Michelson. 2011. "Why do people retweet? anti-homophily wins the day!" In *Proceedings of the Fifth International AAAI Conference on Weblogs and Social Media*, 209–216. San Francisco, CA: Association for the Advancement of Artificial Intelligence. www.aaai.org/ocs/index.php/ICWSM/ICWSM11/paper/viewFile/2790/3291.

Mandel, Charles. 2015. "Justin Trudeau's fight for the top." *National Observer*, August 25. www.nationalobserver.com/2015/08/25/news/justin-trudeaus-fight-top.

Markovinovic, Monika. 2016. "Justin Trudeau Debuts Shirt with Pre-Rolled Sleeves from New 'JT By Justin Trudeau' Collection." *The Huffington Post Canada*, April 1, 2016. https://huffingtonpost.ca/2016/04/01/justin-trudeau-pre-rolled-shirt_n_9586660. html.

Marland, Alex. 2013. "What is a political brand?: Justin Trudeau and the theory of political branding." Paper presented at *The 2013 annual meetings of the Canadian Communication Association and the Canadian Political Science Association*, Victoria. June 6. www.cpsa-acsp. ca/papers-2013/Marland.pdf.

Marland, Alex. 2017. "Government communications under Trudeau." *Policy Options*, April 18. http://policyoptions.irpp.org/magazines/april-2017/government-communications-under-trudeau/.

Marland, Alex. 2018. "The brand image of Canadian Prime Minister Justin Trudeau in international context." *Canadian Foreign Policy Journal*: 1–6.

Marland, Alex, J. P. Lewis, and Tom Flanagan. 2017. "Governance in the age of digital media and branding." *Governance* 30, no. 1: 132–133.

McDiarmid, Margo. 2015. "It's the selfie election and party leaders have to grin and bear it." *CBC News*, September 27. www.cbc.ca/news/politics/canada-election-2015-selfie-election-1.3244475.

McDonald, Susan. 2009. "Changing climate, changing minds: Applying the literature on media effects, public opinion, and the issue-attention cycle to increase public understanding of climate change." *International Journal of Sustainability Communication* 4: 45–63.

Mckenna, Barrie. 2018. "New poll shows deterioration in approval ratings for Trudeau Liberals." *The Globe and Mail*, January 14. www.theglobeandmail.com/news/politics/new-poll-shows-deterioration-in-approval-ratings-for-trudeau-liberals/article37601246/.

Messamore, Barbara J. 2016. "Justin Trudeau and Canada's 2015 election." *The Round Table* 105, no. 1: 81–84.

Miller, Vincent. 2017. "Phatic culture and the status quo: Reconsidering the purpose of social media activism." *Convergence* 23, no. 3: 251–269.

Murray, Derek Conrad. 2015. "Notes to self: The visual culture of selfies in the age of social media." *Consumption Markets & Culture* 18, no. 6: 490.

Nisbet, Matthew C., and Dietram A. Scheufele. 2009. "What's next for science communication? Promising directions and lingering distractions." *American Journal of Botany* 96, no. 10: 1767–1778.

Pedwell, Terry. 2015. "Baby kissing, selfie taking: Photo phenomenon new campaign mainstay." *The Globe and Mail*, September 28. www.theglobeandmail.com/news/politics/baby-kissing-selfie-taking-photo-phenomenon-moves-into-political-campaign-mainstream/article26558223/.

Proudfoot, Shannon. 2016. "Selling a PM: The marketing of Justin Trudeau." *Maclean's*, August 11. www.macleans.ca/politics/ottawa/marketing-justin-trudeau/.

QMI Agency. 2014. "Justin Trudeau, Rob Ford stop for selfies at Jim Flaherty's funeral." *Toronto Sun*, April 17. https://torontosun.com/2014/04/17/justin-trudeau-criticized-for-selfie-at-jim-flahertys-funeral/wcm/bbf74cf9-1732-4d78-b446–172bd236d0a9.

Raj, Althia. 2013. *Contender: The Justin Trudeau Story.* The Huffington Post Canada. http://big.assets.huffingtonpost.com/ContenderV2.pdf.

Recuero, Raquel, Ricardo Araujo, and Gabriela Zago. 2011. "How does social capital affect Retweets?" In *Proceedings of the Fifth International AAAI Conference on Weblogs and Social Media*, 305–312. San Francisco, CA: Association for the Advancement of Artificial Intelligence.

Scotti, Adam (@AdamScotti). 2017a. "Prom season in #Vancouver." *Twitter*, May 19. https://twitter.com/AdamScotti/status/865734843870568448.

Slaughter, Graham. 2018. "Majority of Canadians support Trudeau's trade tactics with Trump: Nanos survey." *CTVNews.ca*, July 8, 2018. www.ctvnews.ca/politics/majority-of-canadians-support-trudeau-s-trade-tactics-with-trump-nanos-survey-1.4005105.

Small, Tamara A. 2016. "Parties, leaders, and online personalization." In *Twitter and elections around the world: Campaigning in 140 characters or less*, edited by Richard Davis, Christina Holtz Bacha, Marion R. Just. New York: Routledge.

Smith, Aaron, and Monica Anderson. 2018. "Social media use in 2018." *Pew Research Center*, March 1. www.pewinternet.org/2018/03/01/social-media-use-in-2018/.

Smith, Mikey. 2015. "Is Justin Trudeau the sexiest politician in the world?" *Mirror Online*, October 20. www.mirror.co.uk/news/uk-news/justin-trudeau-sexiest-politician-world-6666495.

Street, John. 2004. "Celebrity politicians: Popular culture and political representation." *The British Journal of Politics & International Relations* 6, no. 4: 435–452.

Suh, Bongwon, Lichan Hong, Peter Pirolli, and Ed H. Chi. 2010. "Want to be retweeted? Large scale analytics on factors impacting retweet in twitter network." In *IEEE International Conference on Privacy, Security, Risk and Trust*, 177–184. Minneapolis, MN: Institute of Electrical and Electronics Engineers.

Thaler, Andrew David, and David Shiffman. 2015. "Fish tales: Combating fake science in popular media." *Ocean & Coastal Management* 115: 88–91.

Urback, Robyn. 2018. "Trudeau went all the way to India and all he got was this lousy diplomatic incident." *CBC News*, March 1. www.cbc.ca/news/opinion/trudeau-india-trip-1.4556209.

Wells, Paul. 2018. "Justin Trudeau in the real world." *Maclean's*, February 22. www.macleans.ca/politics/ottawa/justin-trudeau-in-the-real-world/.

Yiannopoulos, Milo. 2016. "Full Text: Milo at West Virginia University on what Trump means." *Breitbart*, December 21. www.breitbart.com/milo/2016/12/01/full-text-milo-west-virginia-university-trump-means/.

Zuckerman, Ethan. 2013. *Rewire: Digital cosmopolitans in the age of connection.* New York: WW Norton & Company.

6

TWEETING THE AGENDA

Policy Making and Agenda Setting by U.S. Congressional Leaders in the Age of Social Media

Jacob R. Straus and Raymond T. Williams

In recent years, leaders of the House and the Senate have augmented already significant power to set Congress' public agenda, including what legislative measures are considered. In fact, some have argued that the agenda control exercised by current congressional leaders might equal Speaker Joe Cannon's (R-IL) power prior to the 1910 "revolt" against his autocratic rule (Everett 2018). Today's centralized leadership agenda power comes after decades of committee government. Many factors precipitated the shift back to powerful leaders, including the landmark 1994 mid-term election that gave Republicans majority control of the House for the first time in 40 years. In 1995, the new Speaker, Newt Gingrich (R-GA), consolidated and centralized House leadership. Gingrich's successor, Dennis Hastert (R-IL), further emphasized that the job of the Speaker (and by extension the congressional leadership) "is to rule fairly, but ultimately to carry out the will of the majority" (Green 2010).

Politicians, including congressional leaders, have always engaged in political messaging. Even before the Constitution was ratified, the Founding Fathers wrote the *Federalist Papers* to convince New York to join the Union (Hamilton, Madison, and Jay 1787). While the *Federalist Papers* are frequently consulted to provide insight into the meaning of Constitutional provisions, there was also a concerted effort by James Madison, Alexander Hamilton, and John Jay to have "an effect . . . on attitudes toward the use of power" (Schudson 1997, 311), including why the Constitution was at the core of America's democratic experiment. Today, Members of Congress, especially congressional leaders, have a variety of tools available to help enunciate a political message and to steer the political agenda toward their goals.

Political messaging does not only occur in Congress. In fact, congressional leaders must set the House and Senate agenda in light of the president's ability

Tweeting the Agenda **77**

to command media and constituent attention (Dickinson 2014) and "go public" (Kernell 1993). This power is often described as the president's power of persuasion (Neustadt 1990). To account for the president's "bully pulpit," this chapter provides two case studies of congressional leaders' use of Twitter to augment what has been identified as a shift toward the president's agenda after his annual address to Congress (Rutledge and Larsen Price 2014, 443). Using a unique dataset of tweets sent by congressional leaders (for one month before and after both President Trump's 2017 joint address to Congress and his 2018 State of the Union address),[1] this chapter evaluates how congressional leadership messaging – a proxy for agenda setting – changes in response to the president's message. While a month can be a long time in politics, our analysis also considers that other factors could produce policy windows or focusing events (Kingdon 1995; Birkland 1997, 1998), which can shape the topics congressional leaders choose to push both before and after the president's speech.

Congress and Social Media

Social media, particularly Twitter, has become central to political messaging. Members of Congress tweet, the president tweets, and reporters actively follow government officials to generate news stories (Vis 2013; Vande Panne 2017). Within this context, past examinations of congressional social media have focused on political campaigns (Hong and Nadler 2012; Vargo et al. 2014; Williams and Gulati 2017), the adoption of social media (Straus et al. 2013), the content of tweets (Glassman, Straus, and Shogan 2009; Golbeck, Grimes, and Rogers 2010; Greenberg 2013), and why some political elites use social media more than others (Straus et al. 2016). These works, however, do not place social media usage in the larger context of political messaging and agenda setting by congressional leaders.

The analysis of social media as part of overall political messaging is challenging, partly because it requires gathering empirical data on various messaging methods that are not in the public realm. For example, no public database of internal party meetings in the House and Senate exist, so it is virtually impossible to understand how congressional leaders might use those settings to gauge interest from co-partisans and decide what policy issues and legislation to advance. Social media provides an opportunity to evaluate public political messaging by congressional leaders.

Generally, Members of Congress use social media to connect with constituents (Gulati and Williams 2010, Lassen and Brown 2011, Shapiro and Hemphill 2017) and to gather information on constituent preferences. In the context of this chapter, congressional social media usage focuses on official, non-campaign accounts. This is an important distinction for two reasons. First, House and Senate rules prohibit the use of official congressional resources to support campaign activities.[2] Violation of these provisions can result in disciplinary action both within Congress and by the Department of Justice (Schmidt 2013; Tully-McManus 2018).

Second, Members use official accounts as a way to gather information from geographic constituents, individuals who belong to surrogate groups (e.g., an African-American congressman representing African-American interests more broadly), and from other interested parties (Mansbridge 2003). Social media has been shown to move congressional opinions. At least one study found that no more than 30 similar comments is enough for some offices to pay attention and potentially influence the Member's position (Congressional Management Foundation 2015). If congressional offices can be moved by as few as 30 similar posts, then the potential for constituents and non-constituents alike to influence Congress is potentially greater today than in previous eras when fewer communications tools were available.

Unlike the president, who speaks with a single voice, Congress speaks with many voices. To reign in potentially competing ideas, Members of Congress empower the majority and minority party leaders to make agenda setting decisions. This is especially important as politicians increasingly take their message public through social media (Sunstein 2017; Wigglesworth 2017). These leaders' posts create the foundation of our analysis and allow us to see how political messaging and congressional agenda setting occur given the president's power to focus congressional parties on his priorities.

Congressional Leadership and Agenda Setting

Political parties play an essential role in defining the structures and procedures of the House and Senate. They provide a built-in set of cues for Members as they navigate myriad policy positions (Brady and Buckley 1994; Beck 1997, 306–310; Evans 2012; Green and Bee 2016), they influence Members' reelection chances, and they are pathways to gain power within the House or Senate (Mayhew 1974; Arnold 2017). The ultimate expression of power is being elected by their peers to the party's leadership (Schickler 2001; Green 2010).

Leadership is both a thankless and desirable job (Dodd 2012). Congressional leaders must "devote much effort and time to assembling and reassembling coalitions of members that enable legislation to be brought to the floor and acted upon" (Dove 1992, 19). Leaders must use both positive and negative incentives to motivate party colleagues (Peabody 1981; Smith and Gamm 2009). Through that lens, majority party leaders generally will only schedule legislation that they know their co-partisans will support. Minority party leaders strive to promote their priorities and mobilize their members in opposition to the majority's proposals (Poole and Rosenthal 1997).

Time is perhaps the most important commodity in Congress. Time management is embedded in the process, thus causing party leaders to work to control the legislative agenda. The Senate majority leader and the Speaker of the House are empowered by their party to set the agenda and allocate time to issues that they believe may have a chance to pass the House or Senate. Traditionally, House and Senate schedules have been publicly available by visiting leadership webpages or access to official House or Senate documents. Social media, like Twitter, allows individuals to observe congressional leadership announcements via social media, in real time. This capability, however, potentially suffers from selective exposure and requires citizens to actively seek out information (Feezell 2016).

Theoretical Framework

Political scientist David Mayhew identified reelection as Members' main goal. To achieve reelection, Members utilize three supporting activities: advertising, credit claiming, and position taking (1974). How Members behave within the confines of the House or Senate to support potential reelection is, in many ways, the foundation of Gary Cox and Mathew McCubbin's *Cartel Theory* (1993), which posits that the majority party wants to maintain its majority and the minority party wants to become the majority. Cox and McCubbin wrote their theory specifically for the House, where a majority of representatives can control both the operation of the chamber and the agenda. Their principles may also apply to the Senate because certain advantages (e.g., scheduling) exist for the majority party despite the significant power the minority party and each individual Senator can wield (Lee and Oppenheimer 1999; Sinclair 2001).

Party performance within Congress is essential for a Member's chance at reelection, prompting them to promote the party brand through public policy position taking and executive branch oversight. Party leaders, empowered by their co-partisans, use their messaging and agenda setting power to ensure that bills not meeting party goals do not reach the floor even if a majority of the whole chamber would vote to pass it. This practice, often called the *Hastert Rule* after former Speaker Hastert (R-IL), generally constrains Republican leaders from scheduling legislation that a majority of the party does not support (Richman 2015). Some majority party Members have come to rely on this informal practice to prohibit bipartisan cooperation on major policy legislation (McCabe 2017; Leubsdorf 2018).

Party cohesion within Congress may also influence the strength of messaging and agenda setting by political leaders. The more cohesive the party, the more likely its leadership can control the legislative agenda and push for the party's ideal policy position (Rohde 1991; Krehbiel 1998, 167; Aldrich and Rohde 2001; Dodd 2012). "Party leaders, especially on the majority side, have been granted powers greater than those granted at any time since early in the twentieth century" (Aldrich and Rohde 2001, 269). Subsequently, party leaders will often pivot toward the median (political center) member of their party, even if that moves potential policy opportunities away from the chamber median and possible bipartisan compromise. In fact, the shift toward the party median rather than the chamber median reflects the strength of leadership control over the agenda. The party leadership is empowered to make decisions that benefit the party and help ensure

Data and Methodology

Modern politics rewards cohesive party messaging. Given that individual Members seek reelection, party leaders want to maintain power, the majority party wants to preserve majority status, and the minority party wants to become the majority, we expect that the president's congressional co-partisans shift their messages and the congressional agenda to promote the president's policy preferences *after* his address to Congress. The opposition party leaders do the opposite. During 2017 and 2018, therefore, we expect Republican leaders to reorient their messaging and the congressional agenda to align with the president's stated goals after his joint address/State of the Union. Democratic leaders will unify their message in direct opposition.

Using President Trump's 2017 joint address to Congress (February 28, 2017) and his 2018 State of the Union address (January 30, 2018) as diverging events,[3] congressional leadership tweets were collected for one month before and one month after each speech. This time period allows for an evaluation of congressional leadership messaging leading up to the president's speech and also how that message might change after the president uses his bully pulpit to potentially direct the policy agenda. The length of this time period, however, does allow other events to shape the topics congressional leaders choose to promote. These are discussed below as warranted.

Congressional leaders were identified by using House of Representative and Senate leadership webpages. A total of 17 leaders were identified (U.S. Congress, House 2018; U.S. Congress Senate 2018).[4] Tweets for their official, non-reelection campaign accounts were downloaded from Twitonomy.com.[5] A total of 9,869 tweets were collected: 5,158 for 2017 and 4,711 for 2018.[6]

A hashtag analysis was then conducted. Evaluating hashtags allowed us to observe how congressional leaders used Twitter to drive their party's message and agenda. A total of 6,777 hashtags were initially identified. Any hashtag used only once was removed from the dataset, as unique hashtags do not provide insight into the potential for coordinated messaging (Shapiro and Hemphill 2017). After identifying duplicates, we found that congressional leaders used 1,260 unique hashtags.

The list of hashtags was then coded for content using 29 issue areas.[7] At this stage, hashtags that did not contain any policy content were also removed, leaving a total of 4,948 hashtags (73% of the total). The hashtags were then arranged in chronological order and analyzed in relation to the 2017 joint address and the 2018 State of the Union speech.

The texts of President Trump's 2017 address before a joint session of Congress and his 2018 State of the Union speech were obtained from the Government

Tweeting the Agenda **81**

TABLE 6.1 Topics Discussed Surrounding President Trump's 2017 Joint Address

Before joint address to Congress (February 1 to February 28, 2017)	
Republicans	Democrats
Healthcare 34% *obamacare, repealandreplace*	Healthcare 29% *aca, protectourcare*
Gorsuch 27% *scotus, neilgorsuch*	Administration 27% *sessions, devos*
Joint session 12% *jointsession, jointaddress*	Immigration 11% *muslimban, dreamer*
Administration 9% *confirmdevos, cra*	Marginalized groups 7% *blm, protecttranskids*
Environment/Energy 7% *wotus, epa*	Russia 7% *followthefacts, russia*

President Trump's joint address to Congress (February 28, 2017)
Healthcare 16%
Foreign affairs/National security 15%
Administration 10%
Economy 10%
Military 7%
Immigration 7%

After joint address to Congress (March 1 to March 31, 2017)	
Republicans	Democrats
Healthcare 67% *obamacare, repealandreplace*	Healthcare 56% *trumpcare, paymoreforless*
Gorsuch 11% *scotus, confirmgorsuch*	Joint session 8% *jointsession, jointaddress*
Joint session 6% *jointsession, jointaddress*	Administration 6% *sessions, zinke*
Events 3% *aipac2017, nrisummit17*	Immigration 6% *nobannowallnoraids, muslimban*
Environment/Energy 3% *wotus, keystonexl*	Russia 5% *followthefacts, russia*

Source: Table created by Authors

Publishing Office's (GPO) *Daily Compilation of Presidential Documents* (U.S. President [Trump] 2017, 2018). While the text can be found from multiple sources, the *Daily Compilation of Presidential Documents* provides both the official text and includes a subject index of topics. The subject index was coded using the same 29 issue areas employed to code hashtags. Results of the hashtag and speech analysis can be found in Table 6.1 (2017) and Table 6.2 (2018).

Tweeting the Agenda

The president might have a unique ability to frame the policy agenda, but he cannot introduce legislation or force the House or Senate to address policy in a proscribed manner. Instead, only Members of Congress can introduce legislation and, through the majority leadership, schedule debate on a proposed policy. As a coequal actor, however, Congress tends to listen when the president speaks. The president can potentially alter what Congress is discussing and how the narrative

82 Jacob R. Straus and Raymond T. Williams

TABLE 6.2 Topics Discussed Surrounding President Trump's 2018 State of the Union Address

Before the State of the Union address (January 1 to January 30, 2018)	
Republicans	Democrats
Taxes 44% *taxcutsandjobsact, taxreform*	Immigration 38% *dreamers, protectdreamers*
Budget 19% *schumershutdown, shutdown*	Budget 19% *trumpshutdown, doyourjob*
Healthcare 8% *chip, medicareforall*	Taxes 10% *goptaxscam, goptaxplan*
Abortion 8% *marchforlife, prolife*	SOTU 9% *sotu*
SOTU 6% *sotu*	Healthcare 8% *chip, getcoverednyc*

President Trump's State of the Union address (January 30, 2018)
Foreign affairs/National security 27%
Military 10%
Healthcare 9%
Immigration 9%
Economy 9%

After State of the Union address (February 1 to February 28, 2018)	
Republicans	Democrats
Taxes 54% *taxcutsandjobsact, taxreform*	Guns 17% *neveragain, endgunviolence*
SOTU 13% *sotu*	Immigration 14% *protectdreamers, dreamers*
Events 10% *teamusa, pyeongchang2018*	Net Neutrality 12% *netneutrality,*
Immigration 7% *daca, immigration*	*savetheinternet*
Military 2% *veterans, fundourtroops*	Marginalized Groups 10% *blackhistorymonth,*
	stophr620
	Taxes 10% *goptaxscam, withabuckfiftyaweek*

Source: Table created by Authors

is framed. Analysis of the tweets sent surrounding the president's address to Congress provides an opportunity to evaluate congressional messaging.

Joint Address to Congress 2017

On February 28, 2017, President Trump made his first address to a joint session of Congress (Krieg 2017). Watched by approximately 48 million people (Nielsen 2017), President Trump used the speech to "challenge the orthodoxy of both political parties" and to ask for an increase in military spending, recommend paid family leave, and increase infrastructure spending (Pindell 2017).

Congressional Messaging on Twitter Before the Joint Address to Congress

The 115th Congress (2017–2018) began with a focus on healthcare (repeal of the Affordable Care Act or "Obamacare") and the confirmation of presidential appointments and a Supreme Court justice (Neil Gorsuch). In the month before President Trump's joint address, the most widely used hashtags (30%) addressed healthcare. Overall, 34% of Republican hashtags and 29% of Democratic hashtags focused on healthcare. While healthcare was the most prominent hashtag for both parties, Democrats and Republicans framed the issue differently. For example, Republicans generally expressed their desire to repeal the Affordable Care Act (i.e., Obamacare), using tags such as #Obamacare or #RepealandReplace. Democrats defended the law using tags such as #ACA or #ProtectOurCare.

Beyond healthcare, the only other topics discussed by both parties were administrative-related issues, specifically the confirmation of presidential nominees. Predictably, Republicans tweeted in favor of the president's nominees (#ConfirmDevos), while Democrats were opposed (#Sessions; #Devos). These hashtags generally reflected the Senate's division over nominations and the administration's direction (McGill 2017). Furthermore, Republicans focused their tweets on support for Supreme Court nominee Neil Gorsuch (27% of tweets), talking about President Trump's speech (12%), and environmental and energy related issues (7%). Democrats tweeted about immigration (11%), marginalized groups (7%), and the investigation into Russian interference in the 2016 election (7%). A list of the most frequent hashtags in each category can be found in Table 6.1.

President Trump's Joint Address

President Trump's speech referenced many public policy areas, including healthcare (16%), foreign affairs and national security (15%), administration (10%), the economy (10%), military (7%), and immigration (7%). The president's comments on healthcare focused on repealing the Affordable Care Act, the opioid epidemic, and drug costs, issues he campaigned on in the 2016 presidential election (Woodward and Colvin 2018). His remarks about foreign affairs and national security focused on terrorism and international relations, specifically Israel and NATO.

Congressional Messaging on Twitter After the Joint Address to Congress

After President Trump's address, party leaders increased their focus on healthcare. As part of their effort to repeal and replace Obamacare, Republican leaders used 67% of their post-speech hashtags to focus on healthcare, with #Obamacare and #RepealandReplace the most popular. Similarly, Democrats focused their tweets on trying to block efforts to repeal or amend Obamacare by devoting 56% of their hashtags to healthcare, with #Trumpcare and #PayMoreForLess the most popular.

The popularity of healthcare hashtags following President Trump's speech represents a 33% increase for Republicans and a 27% increase for Democrats over the pre-speech period. This increase occurred simultaneously with the House's consideration of H.R.1628, the American Health Care Act of 2017, which ultimately did not pass (Pear, Kaplan, and Haberman 2017). The Republican hashtags on the confirmation of Neil Gorsuch to the Supreme Court declined from 27% to 11%, even though the Senate Judiciary Committee began confirmation hearings in late March. Other Republican tweets focused on the joint session (6%), the environment and energy (3%), and specific events like the American Israel Public Affairs Committee (AIPAC) annual meeting (3%). For Democrats, their tweets focused on responses to the joint session (8%), administrative issues (6%), immigration (6%), and the Russian investigation (5%).

State of the Union Address 2018

On January 30, 2018, President Trump gave his first State of the Union address to Congress. It focused on the economy, the stock market, immigration, national security, and national anthem protests by football players (Stewart 2018). Table 6.2 lists the most popular hashtags for congressional tweets and subjects for the president's speech.

Congressional Messaging on Twitter Before the State of the Union Address

By January 2018, our analysis shows that congressional leaders had shifted message and policy focuses away from healthcare and administrative issues. Instead, Republicans tweeted most about taxes (44%) and the budget (19%). This aligns with the congressional agenda. In December 2017, the Tax Cuts and Jobs Act of 2017 (PL 115–97) was enacted. In early 2018, Republican leaders used Twitter to tout the law, often using examples of already-realized benefits, such as a reduction in federal taxes and bonuses paid by private companies to workers. Republican leaders also challenged Democratic criticism of the law.

Democratic hashtags focused on immigration-related issues (38%) and the budget (19%). Immigration was the Democrats' most prominent issue, as leaders pushed for legislation to protect DACA (Deferred Action for Childhood Arrivals) – an Obama-era policy that shielded undocumented immigrants who were brought to America as children from deportation (U.S. Citizenship and Immigration Services 2015). In September 2017, the Trump administration announced that the DACA policy would end in six months (Kopan 2017). By January, Democratic leaders were focused on a legislative solution for DACA recipients (i.e., "Dreamers"), using Twitter as one way to frame the issue. The Democratic leadership linked the DACA policy to the budget, threatening a government shutdown for leverage with President Trump.[8]

President Trump's State of the Union Address

In his 2018 State of the Union address, President Trump focused his speech on foreign affairs and national security (27%), pivoting from his 2017 address, which had focused primarily on healthcare. This change is emblematic of the "Two Presidencies" thesis, which states that there is a domestic and a foreign policy president. Presidents are more comfortable in the foreign policy role because they have more formal authority in that arena (Wildavsky 1966). The emphasis on foreign affairs and national security at this time primarily focused on relations with North Korea, Iran, and Russia. Although Republican leaders were focused on taxes in their pre-speech tweets, President Trump only used 6% of his speech to discuss taxes. Conversely, immigration, which was the number one issue for Democrats before the State of the Union, was tied for third most referenced issue in his address (9%).

Congressional Messaging on Twitter After the State of the Union Address

In the month following Trump's State of the Union address, Republican leaders continued to focus on taxes (54%), while Democrats focused on guns (17%), immigration (14%), net neutrality (12%), and marginalized groups (10%). For Republicans, the focus on taxes represented an increase of 10% in the use of tax related hashtags from the pre-State of the Union time period. The tax-related tweets continued to extol the benefits of the new tax law (Wells, Zhao, and Imbert 2018).

Unlike the Republicans, Democrats did not have a single dominant issue. Instead, the plurality of their hashtags dealt with guns, in response to the school shooting at Marjory Stoneman Douglas High School in Parkland, Florida (Laughland, Luscombe, and Yuhas 2018). This outcome serves as an example of how an intervening event can cause a shift in policy focus. In their tweets, Democrats primarily promoted background checks and other gun control measures to prevent future school shootings. Table 6.2 lists the most prominent topics and examples of hashtags before and after the 2018 State of the Union address.

Observations

While the Republican and Democratic leaders both used Twitter to address some topics like healthcare, they frequently took opposite positions. Unsurprisingly, Republicans tweeted in favor of Obamacare repeal and replacement and touted the benefits of the December 2017 tax cuts. Democrats focused on maintaining a healthcare status quo and highlighting the negative aspects of tax cuts. Since Twitter is a public platform, and Members, particularly leaders, use it to promote party positions, our analysis is a window into congressional messaging. From the hashtag analysis, several observations about Congress, messaging, social media, and agenda setting can be drawn. These include the nature of public messaging through Twitter and partisanship's role on agenda setting.

Public Messaging Through Twitter

Twitter is a public forum; what Members of Congress post is public record. Public policy action often occurs because an event creates opportunity for action (Kingdon 1995; Birkland 1997, 1998; Simmons et al. 1974; Hacker 2010). Lawmakers post on Twitter because of its public nature. Subsequently, the choice to focus on a particular policy issue is for both opportunity and interest. On the one hand, Members post because they see opportunity to score political points, stake out a particular position, or appeal to a group of supporters. Choosing to post on Twitter, however, is also about policy. Lawmakers are unlikely to make a public policy statement that they do not believe in. The public nature of Twitter ensures that any statement will exist as a lasting public record.

In 2017, following the president's joint address, Republican leaders refocused their Twitter attention on issues covered by the president and Democratic leaders generally refocused in opposition. In 2018, intervening factors, including special events (e.g., the Olympics) and other focusing events (e.g., the Parkland, FL, school shooting), played a more prominent role. Regardless of whether congressional leaders respond to the president or to other events, Twitter provides the ability to spotlight issues for both an internal audience (other Members of Congress) and an external audience (the general public).

Further, Twitter has become a way for congressional leaders to use social media to get traditional media coverage (Lapinski and Neddenriep 2004). Instead of being a replacement for traditional media, social media has resulted in journalists following congressional social media accounts to generate news stories. For example, the *Washington Post* routinely uses President Trump's tweets as sources for stories, and other publications have written stories about how Members are using social media (Kaczynski 2014). Consequently, social media has become a way for Members to push a message to constituents as well as a way to drive traditional media coverage of Member activity.

Partisanship

A popular narrative suggests that Congress has become more partisan (Mann and Ornstein 2006; Bump 2016). Our hashtag analysis provides data points that support that narrative. In general, Republican and Democratic leaders, even when they are talking about the same policy, do so in markedly different ways. For example, on healthcare Republicans primarily used the hashtags #Obamacare and #RepealandReplace, while Democrats used #ACA and #Trumpcare. These hashtags illustrate, without any nuance, the different positions that the parties have taken.

Overall, party positions did appear to shift from before to after the president's addresses. As expected, Republicans generally sent tweets in favor of the president's agenda and Democrats coalesced around opposition to the president's plans. The president's ability to influence congressional leadership tweets, however, appears to be more limited than we might have suspected. This was especially true in 2018, when 10% of Republican tweets focused on events (e.g., the Olympics) and not on substantive policy issues, especially after the president's speech. A focus on messages not included in the president's speech could be a coincidence of the time period in which tweets were collected, or it could suggest that some leaders wanted to shift away from some of the president's issues onto other noncontroversial topics, or focus on issues, like taxes, in preparation for reelection campaigns.

Republican and Democratic use of partisan hashtags also illustrates the divisive potential of social media. Past studies have found politically active Twitter users have "highly segregated, well-clustered, partisan community structures" (Conover et al. 2012). The closed nature of social media networks means that messages are not ideologically distributed; rather, they are designed for a narrow audience that does not want consensus (French 2017). A closed system has the potential to create an echo-chamber that reinforces partisan arguments and discourages the potential for compromise policy. Overcoming the potential for online groupthink might require users to follow and listen to each other, potentially even sharing hashtags that promote policy over position. Little evidence of that behavior appears in our dataset, and especially in 2018, Republican and Democratic leaders choose to tweet about different topics, with little overlap.

Conclusion

Congressional leaders control the legislative agenda, but they can be influenced by the president. In this chapter, we examined how congressional leaders use Twitter for political messaging and to set the congressional agenda. By evaluating how congressional leaders use Twitter hashtags, a picture of congressional messaging and agenda setting emerges. Overall, analysis of Twitter hashtags suggests that Republicans tended to promote the president's agenda, while Democrats tended to oppose it. This generally fits with the broader narrative that Republicans and Democrats view public policy from different political spaces (Miller and Schofield 2008; Brownstein 2016).

More specifically, the hashtag analysis shows that both Republican and Democratic leaders refocused their agendas after President Trump's 2017 speech. Additionally, we found evidence in 2018 that congressional leaders do not always follow the president's agenda and that intervening factors can drive messaging, especially when national attention is drawn to an event (e.g., the Parkland, FL, school shooting). The importance of intervening events should not be underestimated. Historically, many circumstances have fundamentally changed the focus on governmental action. Events can bring the president and both congressional parties together (e.g., September 11, 2001), serve as wedge issues that drive the branches and parties apart (e.g., the impeachment of President Clinton), or unite Congress against the president (e.g., Watergate). How Congress and the president react to these events can shape their future relationship and the balance of power.

We currently live in a hyper-connected society where citizens can be in constant contact with and receive constant feedback from others. Social media not only allows interaction between average citizens but also promotes contact between citizens and their nation's political leadership. Citizens can follow their leaders, respond to their postings, and observe policy debates. As we have shown in this chapter, congressional leaders tweet about their party's policy agenda. Social media provides an outlet that mirrors and amplifies real world politics without discrimination. As we have shown, leaders maintain party discipline on Twitter by posting partisan tweets. This has the potential to exacerbate the polarization that already exists in the real world and result in further gridlock.

It does not have to be this way. Elites can influence mass opinion (Zaller 1992). If congressional leaders wanted to push a more bipartisan agenda, they could start by using social media to promote cooperation, civility, and comity with other Members of Congress, constituents, and other followers. Not every news article, Facebook post, or Twitter threat needs to invoke Godwin's law (Godwin 2018); instead, they can promote participation and the sharing of policy options that could allow for bipartisan policy solutions. If that were to happen, Congress could become more productive and responsive.

The authors would like to thank Jose Godoy and Stephen Lippincott, undergraduate research assistants at the University of Maryland Baltimore County, for research and coding assistance, Bill Egar for his data assistance, and Walter Oleszek, Colleen Shogan, Darryl Getter, Shawn Reese, and James Saturno for their comments on earlier drafts. The authors received a 2018 University of Maryland Baltimore County Adjunct Faculty Advisory Committee award, which paid for this project's data and travel to Banff, Alberta, for the book's conference.

Notes

1 Article II, section 3 of the U.S. Constitution requires that the president "from time to time give to the Congress Information of the State of the Union, and recommend to their Consideration such Measures as he shall judge necessary and expedient" (U.S. National Archives and Records Administration 2018).

2 The House of Representatives has established rules for the use of official funds for many purposes, including communication via social media. For more information, see U.S. Congress, Committee on House Administration, *Member's Congressional Handbook*, at https://cha.house.gov/handbooks/members-congressional-handbook. The Senate has established a general internet policy, which in combination with ethics prohibitions against supplementing official accounts prohibits the mixing of campaign and official functions. U.S. Congress, Senate, *Internet Services and Technology Resources Usage Rules*, November 9, 2015, at www.senate.gov/usage/internetpolicy.htm.

3 In function, an address before a joint session of Congress and a State of the Union address are the same. The name difference is derived from recent presidents who preferred not to give a formal State of the Union address so close to their inauguration on January 20 and the inaugural address given at that time. For more information, see Kreiser, Maria, and Michael Greene. 2018. *History, Evolution, and Practices of the President's State of the Union Address: Frequently Asked Questions*, Congressional Research Service

report R44770 (Washington, DC: Library of Congress), at https://fas.org/sgp/crs/misc/R44770.pdf; and Diaz, Daniella. 2017. "Why Trump's Tuesday Speech Isn't a State of the Union Address," *CNN*, February 28, at www.cnn.com/2017/02/27/politics/donald-trump-address-not-state-of-the-union/index.html.

4   The congressional leaders include Rep. Paul Ryan (R-WI; Speaker of the House), Rep. Kevin McCarthy (R-CA; House majority leader), Rep. Steve Scalise (R-LA; House majority whip), Rep. Cathy McMorris Rogers (R-MI; House Republican Conference chair), Rep. Luke Messer (R-IN; House Republican Policy Committee chair), Rep. Nancy Pelosi (D-CA; House minority leader), Rep. Steny Hoyer (D-MD; House minority whip), Rep. Jim Clyburn (D-SC; House Assistant Democratic leader), Rep. Joe Crowley (D-NY; House Democratic Caucus chair), Rep. Jim Larson (D-CT; House Democratic Caucus chair), Sen. Mitch McConnell (R-KY; Senate majority leader), Sen. John Cornyn (R-TX; Senate minority whip), Rep. John Thune (R-SD; Senate Republican Conference chair); Sen. John Barrasso (R-WY; Senate Republican Policy Committee chair); Sen. Chuck Schumer (D-NY; Senate minority leader), Sen. Dick Durbin (D-IL; Senate minority whip); and Sen. Debbie Stabenow (D-MI, Senate Democratic Policy Committee chair).

5   Twitonomy is an independent website – unaffiliated with Twitter – that allows users to search for the Twitter history of accounts by entering a Twitter handle into a search box. Information on total number of tweets, followers, following, and other analytic statistics are then provided. Data are available for download with the payment of a monthly or yearly fee. For more information, see www.twitonomy.com.

6   For 2017, a total of 5,158 tweets were analyzed. This included 1,940 tweets sent in February 2017 before President Trump's joint address to Congress (1,291 by Democratic leaders and 649 by Republican leaders) and 3,218 tweets (1,715 by Democratic leaders and 1,503 by Republican leaders) sent after the president's February 28 address. For 2018, a total of 4,711 tweets were analyzed. This included 2,492 tweets sent in January 2017 before President Trump's 2018 State of the Union address (1,038 by Democratic leaders and 1,454 by Republican leaders) and 2,219 tweets (1,217 by Democratic leaders and 1,002 by Republican leaders) sent after President Trump's January 30 speech.

7   The 29 issues areas were: abortion, administration, agriculture, budget, crime, disaster, economy, education, environment/energy, events, foreign affairs/national security, free press, guns, healthcare, immigration, infrastructure, joint session, labor, marginalized groups, military, net neutrality, Russia, Gorsuch, service, social security, SOTU [State of the Union Address], taxes, technology, and trade.

8   The Democratic attempt to link DACA and the budget was ultimately not successful, as a partial government shutdown occurred after talks between President Trump and congressional leaders broke down (Stolberg and Kaplan 2018).

References

Aldrich, John H., and David W. Rohde. 2001. "The Logic of Conditional Party Government: Revisiting the Electoral Connection," in *Congress Reconsidered, 7th edition*, edited by Lawrence C. Dodd and Bruce I. Oppenheimer, 269–292. Washington, DC: CQ Press.

Arnold, R. Douglas. 2017. "The Electoral Connection, Age 40," in *Governing in a Polarized Age: Elections, Parities, and Political Representation in America*, edited by Alan S. Gerber and Erick Schickler, 15–34. New York: Cambridge University Press.

Beck, Paul Allen. 1997. *Party Politics in America, 8th edition*. New York: Longman.

Birkland, Thomas A. 1997. *After Disaster: Agenda Setting, Public Policy, and Focusing Events*. Washington, DC: Georgetown University Press.

Birkland, Thomas A. 1998. "Focusing Events, Mobilization, and Agenda Setting," *Journal of Public Policy* 18(1): 53–74.

Brady, David W., and Kara M. Buckley, "Coalitions and Policy in the U.S. Congress," in *The Parties Respond: Changes in America Parties and Campaigns*, edited by L. Sandy Maisel, 319–340. Boulder, CO: Westview Press.

Brownstein, Ronald. 2016. "America's Divides Aren't Just Partisan," *The Atlantic*, January 21, at www.theatlantic.com/politics/archive/2016/01/two-americas/425046/.

Bump, Phillip. 2016. "The Unprecedented Partisanship of Congress, Explained," *Washingtonpost.com*, January 13, at www.washingtonpost.com/news/the-fix/wp/2016/01/13/heres-why-president-obama-failed-to-bridge-the-partisan-divide-graphed.

Congressional Management Foundation. 2015. *#SocialCongress*, October 24, at www.congressfoundation.org/projects/communicating-with-congress/social-congress-2015.

Conover, Michael D., Bruno Goncalves, Alessandro Flammini, and Filippo Menczer. 2012. "Partisan Asymmetries in Online Political Activity," *EPJ Data Science* 1: Article 6, https://doi.org/10.1140/epjds6.

Cox, Gary W., and Mathew D. McCubbins. 1993. *Legislative Leviathan: Party Government in the House*. Berkeley: University of California Press.

Dickinson, Matthew J. 2014. "The President and Congress," in *The Presidency and the Political System, 10th edition*, edited by Michel Nelson, 406–447. Washington, DC: CQ Press.

Dodd, Lawrence C. 2012. *Thinking about Congress: Essays on Congressional Change*. New York: Routledge.

Dove, Robert. 1992. "Leaders and Policymaking," *The Public Manager* 21(Summer): 19–23.

Evans, C. Lawrence. 2012. "Parties and Leaders: Polarization and Power in the U.S. House and Senate," in *New Directions in Congressional Politics*, edited by Jamie L. Carson, 65–84. New York: Routledge.

Everett, Burgess. 2018. "Mitch McConnell's Record-Breaking Reign," *Politico*, May 31, at www.politico.com/story/2018/05/31/mitch-mconnell-senate-republicans-dole-611587.

Feezell, Jessica T. 2016. "Predicting Online Political Participation: The Importance of Selection Bias and Selective Exposure in Online Settings," *Political Research Quarterly* 69(3): 495–509.

French, David. 2017. "Increasingly Partisan Americans Don't Want 'Unity'," *National Review*, October 24, at www.nationalreview.com/2017/10/polarization-america-unity-both-sides/.

Glassman, Matthew Eric, Jacob R. Straus, and Colleen J. Shogan. 2009. "Social Networking and Constituent Communication: Member Use of Twitter During a Two-Week Period in the 111th Congress," September 21, R40823, *Congressional Research Service Report* (Washington, DC: Library of Congress).

Godwin, Mike. 2018. "Do We Need to Update Godwin's Law about the Probability of Comparison to Nazis?" *Los Angeles Times*, June 24, at www.latimes.com/opinion/op-ed/la-oe-godwin-godwins-law-20180624-story.html.

Golbeck, Jennifer, Justin M. Grimes, and Anthony Rogers. 2010. "Twitter Use by the U.S. Congress," *Journal of the American Society for Information Science and Technology* 61(8): 1612–1621.

Green, Matthew. 2010. *The Speaker of the House: A Study of Leadership*. New Haven, CT: Yale University Press.

Green, Matthew, and Briana Bee. 2016. "Keeping the Team Together: Explaining Party Discipline and Dissent in the U.S. Congress," in *Party and Procedure in the United States*

Congress, 2nd edition, edited by Jacob R. Straus and Matthew E. Glassman, 41–62. Lanham, MD: Rowman & Littlefield.

Greenberg, Sherri. 2013. *Congress + Social Media.* Austin, TX: LBJ School of Public Affairs.

Gulati, Girish J., and Christine B. Williams. 2010. "Congressional Candidates' Use of YouTube in 2008: Its Frequency and Rationale," *Journal of Information Technology & Politics* 7(2/3): 93–109.

Hacker, Jacob S. 2010. "The Road to Somewhere: Why Health Reform Happened: Or Why Political Scientists Who Write About Public Policy Shouldn't Assume They Know How to Shape It," *Perspectives on Politics* 8(3): 861–876.

Hamilton, Alexander, James Madison, and John Jay. 1787. *The Federalist Papers,* at www.congress.gov/resources/display/content/The+Federalist+Papers.

Hong, Souman, and Daniel Nadler. 2012. "Which Candidates Do the Public Discuss Online in a Presidential Campaign?: The Use of Social Media by 2012 Presidential Candidates and Its Impact on Candidate Salience," *Government Information Quarterly* 29(4): 455–461.

Kaczynski, Andrew. 2014. "88-Year-Old Member of Congress Probably the Best Person on Twitter," *Buzzfeed,* July 22, at www.buzzfeednews.com/article/andrewkaczynski/congressman-who-can-tweet.

Kernell, Samuel. 1993. *Going Public: New Strategies of Presidential Leadership, 2nd edition.* Washington, DC: CQ Press.

Kingdon, John. 1995. *Agendas, Alternatives, and Public Policies, 2nd edition.* New York: Harper Collins.

Kopan, Tal. 2017. "Trump Ends DACA But Gives Congress Window to Save It," *CNN.com,* September 5, at www.cnn.com/2017/09/05/politics/daca-trump-congress/index.html.

Krehbiel, Keith. 1998. *Pivotal Politics: A Theory of U.S. Lawmaking.* Chicago, IL: University of Chicago Press.

Krieg, Gregory. 2017. "A Tale of Two Speeches: Comparing Trump's Inaugural to His Address to Congress," *CNN.com,* February 28, at www.cnn.com/2017/02/28/politics/trump-joint-congress-inauguration-speech/index.html.

Lapinski, Daniel, and Gregory Neddenriep. 2004. "Using 'New' Media to Get 'Old' Media Coverage," *Press/Politics* 9(1): 7–21.

Laughland, Oliver, Richard Luscombe, and Alan Yuhas. 2018. "Florida School Shooting: At Least 17 People Dead on "Horrific, Horrific Day,'" *The Guardian,* February 15, at www.theguardian.com/us-news/2018/feb/14/florida-shooting-school-latest-news-stoneman-douglas.

Lassen, David S., and Adam R. Brown. 2011. "Twitter: The Electoral Connection?" *Social Science Computer Review* 29(4): 419–436.

Lee, Frances E., and Bruce I. Oppenheimer. 1999. *Sizing Up the Senate: The Unequal Consequences of Equal Representation.* Chicago, IL: University of Chicago Press.

Leubsdorf, Carl P. 2018. "Hastert Rule Stymies Congress," *Nueces County Record Star,* January 19, at www.recordstar.com/opinion/20180119/hastert-rule-stymies-congress.

Mann, Thomas E., and Norman Ornstein. 2006. *The Broken Branch: How Congress Is Failing America.* New York: Oxford University Press.

Mansbridge, Jane. 2003. "Rethinking Representation," *American Political Science Review* 97(4): 515–528.

Mayhew, David. 1974. *Congress: The Electoral Connection.* New Haven, CT: Yale University Press.

McCabe, Neil. 2017. "Rep. Gohmert: Speaker Ryan Promised Hastert Rule, No Amnesty, No Trade Deals," *Brietbart News*, January 3, at https://gohmert.house.gov/news/documentsingle.aspx?DocumentID=398403.

McGill, Andrew. 2017. "Who's Voting for Donald Trump's Cabinet Nominees?" *The Atlantic*, March 3, at www.theatlantic.com/politics/archive/2017/03/whos-voting-for-donald-trumps-nominees/515943.

Miller, Gary, and Norman Schofield. 2008. "The Transformation of the Republican and Democratic Party Coalitions in the U.S.," *Perspectives on Politics* 6(3): 433–450

Neustadt, Richard E. 1990. *Presidential Power and the Modern Presidents: The Politics of Leadership from Roosevelt to Reagan*. New York: The Free Press.

Nielsen. 2017. "Nearly 48 Million Americans Watch Pres. Donald Trump's First Address to Congress," March 1, at www.nielsen.com/us/en/insights/news/2017/nearly-48-million-americans-watch-president-donald-trumps-first-address-to-congress.html.

Peabody, Robert L. 1981. "Senate Party Leadership: From the 1950s to the 1980s," in *Understanding Congressional Leadership*, edited by Frank H. Mackaman, 51–116. Washington, DC: CQ Press.

Pear, Robert, Thomas Kaplan, and Maggie Haberman. 2017. "In Major Defeat for Trump, Push to Repeal Health Law Fails," *New York Times*, March 24, at www.nytimes.com/2017/03/24/us/politics/health-care-affordable-care-act.html.

Pindell, James. 2017. "Everything that Happened in Donald Trump's Address to Congress," *Boston Globe*, March 1, at www.bostonglobe.com/news/politics/2017/02/28/everything-that-happened-donald-trump-address-congress/HDTR1V1aSBsRfKQiBx-Q9wL/story.html.

Poole, Keith T., and Howard Rosenthal. 1997. *Congress: A Political-Economic History of Roll Call Voting*. New York: Oxford University Press.

Richman, Jesse. 2015. "The Electoral Costs of Party Agenda Setting: Why the Hastert Rule Leads to Defeat," *Journal of Politics* 77(4): 1129–1141.

Rohde, David W. 1991. *Parties and Leaders in the Postreform House*. Chicago, IL: University of Chicago Press.

Rutledge, Paul E., and Heather A. Larsen Price. 2014. "The President as Agenda Setter-in-Chief: The Dynamics of Congressional and Presidential Agenda Setting," *Policy Studies Journal* 42(3): 443–464.

Schickler, Eric. 2001. *Disjointed Pluralism: Institutional Innovation and the Development of the U.S. Congress*. Princeton, NJ: Princeton University Press.

Schmidt, Michael A. 2013. "Lavish Lifestyle of a Lawmaker Yields Federal Charges," *New York Times*, February 15, at www.nytimes.com/2013/02/16/us/politics/jesse-jackson-jr-charged-in-misuse-of-campaign-money.html.

Schudson, Michael. 1997. "Sending a Political Message: Lessons from the American 1790s," *Media, Culture, & Society* 19: 311–330.

Shapiro, Matthew A., and Libby Hemphill. 2017. "Politicians and the Policy Agenda: Does Use of Twitter by the U.S. Congress Direct *New York Times* Content?" *Policy & Internet* 9(1): 109–132.

Simmons, Robert H., Bruce W. Davis, Ralph J.K. Chapman, and Daniel D. Sager. 1974. "Policy Flow Analysis: A Conceptual Model for Comparative Public Policy," *Political Research Quarterly* 27(3): 457–468.

Sinclair, Barbara. 2001. "The New World of U.S. Senators," in *Congress Reconsidered, 7th edition*, edited by Lawrence C. Dodd and Bruce I. Oppenheimer, 1–20. Washington, DC: CQ Press.

Smith, Steven S., and Gerald Gamm. 2009. "The Dynamics of Party Government in Congress," *Congress Reconsidered*, edited by Lawrence C. Dodd and Bruce I. Oppenheimer, 141–164. Washington, DC: CQ Press.

Stewart, Emily. 2018. "5 Big Moments from Trump's State of the Union Address," *Vox.com*, January 31, at www.vox.com/policy-and-politics/2018/1/31/16954826/state-of-the-union-2018-big-moments-trump.

Stolberg, Sheryl Gay, and Thomas Kaplan. 2018. "Government Shutdown Ends after 3 Days of Recriminations," *New York Times*, January 22, at www.nytimes.com/2018/01/22/us/politics/congress-votes-to-end-government-shutdown.html.

Straus, Jacob R., Matthew Eric Glassman, Colleen J. Shogan, and Susan Navarro Smelcer. 2013. "Communicating in 140 Characters or Less: Congressional Adoption of Twitter in the 111th Congress," *PS: Political Science & Politics* 46(1): 60–66.

Straus, Jacob R., Raymond T. Williams, Colleen J. Shogan, and Matthew E. Glassman. 2016. "Congressional Social Media Communications: Evaluating Senate Twitter Usage," *Online Information Review* 40(5): 643–659.

Sunstein, Cass R. 2017. *#Republic: Divided Democracy in the Age of Social Media*. Princeton, NJ: Princeton University Press.

Tully-McManus, Katherine. 2018. "Duncan Hunter Indicted for Misuse of Campaign Funds," *Roll Call*, August 21, at www.rollcall.com/news/politics/rep-duncan-hunter-indicted-for-misuse-of-campaign-funds.

U.S. Citizenship and Immigration Services. 2015. "2014 Executive Action on Immigration," April 15, at www.uscis.gov/archive/2014-executive-actions-immigration.

U.S. Congress, House. 2018. "Leadership," at www.house.gov/leadership.

U.S. Congress, Senate. 2018, "Leadership & Officers," at www.senate.gov/senators/leadership.htm.

U.S. National Archives and Records Administration. 2018. "The Constitution of the United States: A Transcription," *America's Founding Documents*, at www.archives.gov/founding-docs/constitution-transcript.

U.S. President (Trump). 2017. "Address Before a Joint Session of Congress," *Daily Compilation of Presidential Documents*, February 28, at www.gpo.gov/fdsys/pkg/DCPD-201700150/pdf/DCPD-201700150.pdf.

U.S. President (Trump). 2018. "Address Before a Joint Session of Congress on the State of the Union," *Daily Compilation of Presidential Documents*, January 30, at www.gpo.gov/fdsys/pkg/DCPD-201800064/pdf/DCPD-201800064.pdf.

Vande Panne, Valerie. 2017. "Study Asks Whether Reporters are Influence by Who They Follow on Twitter," *Columbia Journalism Review*, August 16, at www.cjr.org/analysis/journalist-twitter-study.php.

Vargo, Chris J., Lei Guo, Maxwell McCombs, and Donald L. Shaw. 2014. "Network Issue Agendas on Twitter During the 2012 U.S. Presidential Election," *Journal of Communication* 64(2): 296–316.

Vis, Farida. 2013. "Twitter as a Reporting Tool for Breaking News," *Digital Journalism* 1(1): 27–47.

Wells, Nick, Helen Zhao, and Fred Imbert. 2018. "These Companies are Paying Bonuses with Their Tax Savings," *CNBC.com*, January 26, at www.cnbc.com/2018/01/26/us-companies-that-have-announced-bonuses-investments-after-tax-cut.html.

Wigglesworth, Alex. 2017. "Trump Defends Social Media Use in Tweet," *LA Times*, December 30, at www.latimes.com/politics/la-pol-updates-everything-president-1514673945-htmlstory.html.

Wildavsky, Aaron. 1966. "The Two Presidencies," *Trans-Action*, IV.

Williams, Christine B., and Girish J. "Jeff" Gulati. 2017. "Digital Advertising Expenditures in the 2016 Presidential Election," *Social Science Computer Review* Online First, September 8, at https://doi.org/10.1177/0894439317726751.

Woodward, Calvin, and Jill Colvin. 2018. "The Promises Trump Had Kept During His First Year in Office," *Chicago Tribune*, January 15, at www.chicagotribune.com/news/nationworld/politics/ct-trump-campaign-promises-20180115-story.html.

Zaller, John. 1992. *The Nature and Origins of Mass Opinion*. New York: Cambridge University Press.

PART 2
Twitter, Leaders, and Populism

7

POPULISM AND SOCIAL MEDIA POPULARITY

How Populist Communication Benefits Political Leaders on Facebook and Twitter

Sina Blassnig, Nicole Ernst, Sven Engesser, and Frank Esser

"Without the tweets, I wouldn't be here," Donald Trump told *Financial Times* journalists in the Oval Office on April 2, 2017. Claiming over 100 million Facebook, Twitter, and Instagram followers, he added, "I don't have to go to the fake media."

President Trump's open disdain for the established, traditional news media has been a recurring theme in his prolific social media output. Commentators readily label him a populist. But what exactly defines political leaders and parties as populist? And how is it that social media seem to have dealt them such a good hand?

Research has shown that social media is a particularly well-suited channel for distributing populist messages (Ernst et al. 2017; Groshek and Engelbert 2012; Stier et al. 2017). But do populist actors also garner more support on the internet than politicians who do not represent populist views or communicate in a populist way? If so, what will the political landscape look like if typically non-populist politicians compete by sending populist messages on social media?

In this chapter we address these questions. We set out a definition of populism that now has wide currency in the academic world. We describe a framework that allows populism to be measured in social media messages, and we review recent research. We describe what we learned when we analyzed the tweets and Facebook posts of 36 diverse political leaders in six countries over a three-month period. Finally, we consider the potential impact of populism on liberal democracies in the new-media world.

What is Populism?

For decades, populism was viewed as a "notoriously vague term" (Canovan 1999). It has been variously defined as an ideology, a political strategy, a style, or

98 Sina Blassnig et al.

a discourse (Hawkins 2010; Jagers and Walgrave 2007; Laclau 2005; Mudde 2004; Weyland 2017).

However, in the last few years scholars have increasingly come to a consensus in regarding populism as a "thin ideology" (Abts and Rummens 2007; Mudde 2004; Stanley 2008; Taggart 2000), as politicians can combine it with different ideological positions from the left to the right.

This thin populist ideology assumes a simplistic dichotomy between the pure, good people and a corrupt, aloof elite; and it demands that politics should be an expression of the unrestrained popular will. Populists present themselves as the only true representatives of the supposedly unheard public interests. Their ideology has three core dimensions: people-centrism, anti-elitism, and restoring sovereignty (e.g., Mény and Surel 2002).

What is Populist Communication?

How do we tell how populist someone is? Here we follow a "communication-centered approach" (Stanyer, Salgado, and Strömbäck 2017). This means that we study political leaders across the political spectrum and infer how populist each of them is, based on how often he or she uses a set of populist key messages. Building on the existing literature (Bos, van der Brug, and Vreese 2011; Cranmer 2011; Jagers and Walgrave 2007), nine populist key messages have been defined that can be assigned to the three core dimensions of populism (Wirth et al. 2016). Listed below, these key messages in political leaders' statements are seen as expressions of populist ideology (Ernst et al. 2017).

People-centrism, the first dimension, contains four key messages that advocate for the people. A politician can demonstrate that he or she is close to the people, stress their virtues, praise their achievements, or describe them as a homogenous group.

Anti-elitism, the second dimension, combines three hostile key messages towards the elite: discrediting them, blaming them, or emphasizing their detachment from the people.

Restoring sovereignty, the third dimension, is characterized by two key messages: advocating for the people's sovereignty, or denying that of the elite.

Populist Political Leaders on Social Media

Social media play a major role in the way all political leaders come across in a hybrid media system (Chadwick 2017). But, according to recent research, social media can particularly assist populist leaders or communication (Engesser, Fawzi, and Larsson 2017; Ernst et al. 2017).

Why is this? Firstly, politicians can communicate directly with the people, bypassing traditional gatekeepers such as journalists. Secondly, social media allow them to engage more closely with their followers and to come over as highly approachable. Thirdly, they can adopt a more personalized and emotionalized approach: they can share photos of their personal life and offer a look behind the scenes (see also Remillard in this volume on Trudeau's personalized use of Instagram). Finally, social media make it easier for political leaders to connect with specific target groups, like-minded people, or "kindred souls" (Jacobs and Spierings 2016) who share their political ideology. This, for example, lets populists use harsh words to attack a common enemy without being subjected to criticism from political opponents or critical observers (Engesser et al. 2017).

Despite these close theoretical connections, researchers have only recently started to examine populism with regard to social media. Most studies up to now focus on politicians who are already identified as populists. This is what Stanyer, Salgado, and Strömbäck (2017) call an "actor-centered approach." An early study by Groshek and Engelbert (2012) showed that leaders of the Dutch Party for Freedom and the US Tea Party Patriots (TPP) used social media for the typical populist strategy of "double differentiation" (Kriesi 2014). This means that they simultaneously distanced themselves from the political establishment as well as from extremist groups.

In a similar vein, Van Kessel and Castelein (2016) concluded that Dutch populist leaders used Twitter as an adversarial tool of opposition. Focusing on populist leaders in Latin America, Waisbord and Amado (2017) found that Twitter had not led to more dialogue between presidents and the public. Instead, they used the platform strategically to influence the news and public agenda. Like Dutch and American populist leaders, Latin American presidents also used Twitter to attack elites, and specifically journalists and the traditional news media. Other actor-centered studies have investigated who follows or supports populists on social media. Bartlett, Birdwell, and Littler (2011) and Heiss and Matthes (2017) came to similar conclusions that the average online supporter of populist politicians or parties was male and less educated. He displayed low levels of political trust but was highly motivated to participate in political discussions or activities.

Communication-centered studies that examine how a broad range of politicians use specific populist communication elements on social media are less common so far. Two earlier studies by ourselves (Engesser et al. 2017; Ernst et al. 2017) reinforce the assumption that social media are particularly well suited to spread populist ideology. They also show that the different elements of populist communication are communicated in a rather fragmented way on Facebook and Twitter. Politicians from extreme parties (both right-wing and left-wing) and opposition parties use more populist key messages. Furthermore, populist communication is more common on Facebook than on Twitter.

While we focused on the content of populist key messages, Bracciale and Martella (2017) analyzed the populist communication style of Italian political leaders. They showed that a specific style was linked to populist content. This mostly reflected the leader's political communication style and was less influenced by the political divide between left and right. This led to different combinations or nuances of populist styles.

100   Sina Blassnig et al.

Finally, there are studies that have investigated how populist communication on social media affects the populist attitudes of citizens (Hameleers and Schmuck 2017); or how citizens perceive populists' profiles and messages on social media (Enli and Rosenberg 2018). Interestingly, populist politicians come across as more authentic on social media than traditional politicians do, according to the study by Enli and Rosenberg (2018). Overall, the summarized studies support the theoretical assumptions that populists, as well as populist communication, have an affinity with social media.

Populism and Social Media Popularity Cues

While populism seems very compatible with social media, it is less well understood how populist communication affects the popularity or reach of social media messages.

Social media work to a distinctly different logic from that of traditional mass media (Klinger and Svensson 2015; Mills 2012). When users like or share politicians' tweets or Facebook posts, they help them to reach a wider audience beyond their direct followers and friends. This can be related to Vaccari and Valeriani's (2015) distinction between a *primary* and a *secondary audience* as well as to the model of a two-step flow of communication (Katz and Lazarsfeld 1955). Additionally, popularity on social media may win politicians more attention in traditional news media (Fürst and Oehmer 2018; Chadwick 2017). Consequently, political leaders have an incentive to post or tweet messages that they expect to elicit a lot of likes and shares.

In this chapter, following Porten-Cheé et al. (2018), we refer to user reactions such as likes, shares, favorites, and retweets as popularity cues, and interpret them as indicators of attention, relevance, or endorsement of social media messages. As such, we expect that specific characteristics of a message such as, for example, the occurrence of populist key messages, may have a positive influence on the number of likes and shares a Facebook post or tweet gets.

In general, there is not much research yet on which aspects of politicians' communication lead to higher numbers of popularity cues. However, amid a growing body of research on populism and social media, Bobba (2018) has conducted one of the few such studies. Examining the Facebook activity of Italy's populist Lega Nord and its leader, Matteo Salvini, Bobba's findings suggest that populist Facebook posts receive more likes than non-populist posts. Focusing on Switzerland, Keller and Kleinen-von Königslöw (2018) concluded that how successful politicians were on social media depended on their personal background, political activity, and media coverage, as well as their followership and the platform. Focusing on characteristics of individual messages, two studies by Bene (2017a, 2017b), based on Hungarian election campaigns, found that emotionally negative Facebook posts received more likes. A study by Heiss, Schmuck, and Matthes (2018) in Austria also found that negative content and emotional language increased

Populism and Social Media Popularity **101**

user reactions, but positive emotional expressions had a stronger impact on user engagement than negative ones.

Testing the Theory: Our Own Study

From here on in this chapter, we build on these initial studies and try to expand their findings by investigating the relationship between populist communication and popularity cues across different social media platforms (Twitter and Facebook), a wide spectrum of politicians, and several countries.

There are various reasons to expect that populist key messages could engender more popularity cues. Firstly, populism can motivate marginalized social groups to participate in political action (Jansen 2011). This could especially apply to social media popularity cues: liking or sharing a political message requires little resource or effort. Secondly, populism is often attributed a high news value or a high compatibility with the logic of news media (Mazzoleni 2008). As Trilling, Tolochko, and Burscher (2016) show, what renders a message *newsworthy* may also contribute to its social media *shareworthiness*. Thirdly, the studies described above empirically support the theory that populist content, or communication styles often associated with populism (emotionalization, negativity, and personalization), make Facebook posts more likely to be shared, liked, or commented on. Hence, we expect political leaders to receive higher numbers of popularity cues when they communicate populist key messages.

While we expect to find similar effects across the countries we study, we anticipate differences between social media platforms and different types of politicians. Firstly, we expect that populist communication would have a stronger positive effect on popularity cues on Facebook than on Twitter. The two platforms have different user demographics and serve different purposes for political leaders' communication. Furthermore, results of our earlier study (Ernst et al. 2017) indicated that politicians' Facebook content is more populist than that of their tweets. Secondly, we expect that leaders of political parties that are typically labeled as "populist" in the scientific literature would be more successful on social media and that they could also profit more from communicating populist key messages. We expect that politicians typically known as "populist" – for example, Nigel Farage or Marine Le Pen – also communicate in a more populist way on social media. Likewise, we assume that their followers or supporters on Facebook and Twitter also have more populist attitudes and therefore may be more inclined to like or share populist posts or tweets (Müller et al. 2017).

How We Did It: Method and Data

To investigate the research questions and formulated expectations, we analyzed the content of Facebook posts and tweets by 36 political leaders from six countries – Switzerland (CH), Germany (DE), the United States (USA), the United Kingdom

102 Sina Blassnig et al.

(UK), Italy (IT), and France (FR) – during three politically routine months from September to November 2015 without any election campaigns.[1]

For each country, we selected the leaders of the four largest parties in parliament across the left–right spectrum that could be assigned to the following categories: social democratic, economic liberal, conservative/Christian democratic, and green, as well as those of the most influential party commonly classified as populist in the scientific literature.[2] We defined political leaders as the politicians who held the highest position in the party hierarchy and/or country (party leader and/or head of government) in 2015. Based on these criteria, we investigated the verified Facebook and Twitter profiles of 36 political leaders. Our sample included political leaders of six parties that we identified as typically populist beforehand: Toni Brunner, Swiss People's Party (SVP/CH); Frauke Petry, Alternative for Germany (AfD/ DE); Marine Le Pen, Front National (FN/FR); Beppe Grillo, Five Star Movement (5S/IT); Nigel Farage, UK Independence Party (UKIP/UK); and Sarah Palin, Tea Party Patriots (TPP/USA).

We used Facepager (Jünger and Keyling 2013) to download all Facebook posts and tweets, including the number of popularity cues. We coded only tweets and Facebook posts in which a politician made an explicit statement on an issue or a target actor. The final sample included 345 Facebook posts and 221 tweets (N = 566).

Our dependent variable – social media popularity cues – was measured as the sum of likes and shares on Facebook, and the sum of favorites and retweets on Twitter. Additionally, we coded whether a social media message contained populist communication based on the nine key messages described above. For each populist key message, we coded whether it was present in a social media statement or not. The nine populist key messages were operationalized using a broad range of categories that are rooted in theory and build on existing empirical studies. (For more details, see Ernst et al. 2017 and Wirth et al. 2016.)

The material was coded by a team of intensively trained student coders, which reached acceptable levels of reliability. The average Brennan and Prediger's kappa across all populist key messages is .83. For a more detailed description of the methodological approach, see our previous study: Ernst et al. (2017).

Table 7.1 shows how the data were calculated, alongside a detailed account of the method and statistical analysis.

In brief, for each tweet and Facebook post, we counted popularity cues: Facebook likes and shares, and Twitter favorites and retweets. We also calculated whether at least one of the nine populist key messages was present in any post/tweet, and what proportion of tweets/posts per politician contained at least one populist message. We differentiated male from female politicians. We also took account of whether each subject's party was in government or opposition; and whether the party was typically classified as populist. We additionally took into account the general profile reach, counting how many Facebook page likes or Twitter followers a politician had.

TABLE 7.1 Factors Influencing the Number of Popularity Cues a Post Receives. (Predictions Based on Negative Binomial Regression [N = 566])

		Popularity cues			
		Model 1		Model 2	
		Incidence rate ratios (IRRs)	Confidence interval	Incidence rate ratios (IRRs)	Confidence interval
	(Intercept)	1.19	[0.69, 2.06]	1.21	[0.71, 2.09]
	Controls				
	Gender (male)	1.37	[0.93, 2.01]	1.32	[0.91, 1.93]
	Party incumbency	2.90***	[2.01, 4.19]	3.12***	[2.17, 4.49]
	Profile reach	1.00***	[1.00, 1.00]	1.00***	[1.00, 1.00]
	Country (Switzerland was set as baseline category)				
	Germany	25.08***	[13.19, 47.69]	25.93***	[13.55, 49.61]
	United Kingdom	26.78***	[15.56, 46.10]	24.84***	[14.57, 42.33]
	United States	25.30***	[13.85, 46.22]	23.10***	[13.00, 41.03]
	Italy	45.96***	[27.12, 77.90]	46.03***	[27.25, 77.76]
	France	14.28***	[7.84, 26.04]	13.20***	[7.30, 23.85]
	Independent variables				
A	Populism index	1.27	[0.80, 2.00]	0.31**	[0.151, 0.650]
B	Populism index (aggregated)	580.07***	[34.83, 9662.09]	1111.03***	[65.01, 18989.31]
C	Facebook	14.74***	[10.97, 19.81]	13.00***	[9.59, 17.61]
D	Populist leader	5.36***	[3.54, 8.12]	5.57***	[3.64, 8.53]
E	Facebook*populism index			5.52***	[2.43, 12.52]
F	Populist leader* populism index			1.28	[0.50, 3.25]
	Akaike information criterion (AIC)	8399.255		8391.380	
	Log likelihood	−44185.63		−4179.194	
	Omnibus-test	504.385*** (df = 12)		517.252*** (df = 14)	

Source: Table created by Author

Note: IRRs with confidence intervals in brackets. Values < 1 indicate a negative effect; values > 1 indicate a positive effect. ** $p < .01$, *** $p < .001$.

Table 7.1 displays the regression models. For the calculations, we used a populism index as independent variable, which was present if a Facebook post or tweet contained at least one of the nine populist key messages. The populism index was aggregated at the politician level, indicating the share of tweets or posts per politician that contained a populist key message. Furthermore, we coded whether a party was typically classified as populist in the literature (e.g., Aalberg et al. 2017; Van Kessel 2015) as dummy variable (1 for populist party, 0 for non-populist party). The models also contain dummy variables for Facebook (1 for Facebook, 0 for Twitter), gender (1 for male, 0 for female), and party in power (1 for government, 0 for opposition party), as well as a variable controlling for the general profile reach, which refers respectively

(Continued)

104 Sina Blassnig et al.

TABLE 7.1 (Continued)

to the number of Facebook page likes and the number of Twitter followers per politician. While the first model only looks at the main effects of the independent variables, the second model additionally incorporates interaction terms between the populism index and Facebook and populist leader respectively.

For the interpretation of the independent variables, we focus on the incidence rate ratios, which correspond to exponential B-coefficients. Values higher than 1 indicate a positive influence; values below 1 indicate a negative influence on popularity indicators. Values with a p-value below .05 (confidence interval does not include 1) are statistically significant.

What We Found

Political leaders in our sample received on average 2,649 popularity cues in response to each social media post. However, the numbers varied considerably. Most posts got few user reactions, while a small number got an exceptionally large response. Twenty-two posts were not liked, shared, favorited, or retweeted at all, whereas the most successful Facebook post in our sample was liked or shared 99,688 times in total.

There were also notable differences between the two platforms and the different types of popularity cues. Facebook posts prompted many more popularity cues (4,108 on average) than tweets (373 on average). On both platforms, users more often endorsed a message by liking or favoriting it than recirculated it by sharing or retweeting it (Facebook posts received on average 3,550 likes and 557 shares; tweets received on average 223 favorites and 150 retweets).

To test our expectations regarding the use of populist key messages and its combination with the platform and populist leaders, we calculated negative binomial regression models.[3] These models particularly fit the distribution of the dependent variable and allow the investigation of different effects and interactions while controlling for additional influences such as country differences, gender, party incumbency, and profile reach.

Firstly, we looked at the effect that populist communication has on popularity cues, regardless of the platform and the nature of the politician. Contrary to our expectations, an individual social media post with a populist key message did not receive significantly more popularity cues than a non-populist message (see Table 7.1, Model 1, line *A*).

However, we did find a significant influence from populist communication on the aggregated politician level (see Table 7.1, Model 1, line *B*). This means that the more often political leaders posted populist key messages, the more popularity cues their tweets or Facebook posts received. Thus, for followers it may matter more how populist a political leader's communication is overall than whether an individual message is populist. If a political leader regularly posts or tweets populist key messages, this may have a spillover effect on his or her non-populist posts.

Secondly, we examined the role of the social media platform. The regression models confirm that Facebook posts got significantly more popularity cues than tweets (see Table 7.1, Model 1 & 2, line *C*). And populist key messages were more successful on Facebook than on Twitter. According to the model, populist Facebook posts received 5.5 times more popularity cues than non-populist Facebook posts (see Table 7.1, Model 2, line *E*).

On Twitter, on the other hand, communicating populist key messages seemed to have the opposite effect. Political leaders actually got fewer popularity cues in response to populist tweets. Using populist key messages in a tweet led to only 30% of the popularity cues that a non-populist tweet would expect (see Table 7.1, Model 2, line *A*). This is rather surprising but may be explained by the characteristics of these two different platforms, and we discuss this more below.

Finally, we compared typically populist leaders with typically non-populist leaders. Overall, regardless of whether an individual post contained populist key messages, leaders of typically populist parties seemed to be more successful on both Facebook and Twitter than leaders of other parties. This means that social media posts by populist leaders were significantly more liked, shared, favorited, or retweeted than posts by non-populist leaders (see Table 7.1, Model 1 & 2, line *D*). This is in line with our expectations that being a populist may have a positive influence on political leaders' popularity and reach on social media.

However, contrary to our expectations, populist leaders did not profit more from posting populist key messages than non-populist leaders (see Table 7.1, Model 2, line *F*). Social media posts by political leaders of populist parties were overall more popular, regardless of whether the individual message was considered populist or not.

Looking back to our theoretical considerations (above), we expected that populist key messages would lead to more popularity cues and that this effect would be more pronounced on Facebook and for populist leaders. These expectations can only partly be supported by our analysis.

To summarize our findings: while populist posts received more popularity cues on Facebook, this was not the case for Twitter. However, messages by political leaders whose average communication was more populist did get higher popularity or reach on both platforms. The same was true for leaders of typically populist parties. Moreover, typically "populist" and "non-populist" political leaders alike received more popularity cues on Facebook when their posts included populist key messages.

As an aside, it is interesting to note how news media journalists may lend politicians enormous extra reach by republishing their social media posts. Two cases from our study illustrate this phenomenon.

Firstly, Nigel Farage, while leader of UKIP, posted the following message both on Facebook and on Twitter on October 12, 2015:

> It is not patriotic to give away control of our country to overseas bureaucrats, it is a surrender.

106 Sina Blassnig et al.

This statement carries an anti-elitist message against supranational institutions as well as a demand for the country's (and implicitly the people's) sovereignty. The post received relatively high popularity cues on Facebook, being liked by 3,397 followers and shared 654 times. On Twitter, the same message got only 398 favorites and 491 retweets. This is despite the fact that Mr. Farage then had more than twice as many followers on Twitter as on Facebook. Even more interestingly, the British tabloid newspaper *Daily Mail* cited this message on the same day that Mr. Farage had posted it on social media.

We found a similar example with Marine Le Pen, leader of Front National.[4] On September 30, 2015, she sent out the following statement, again both on Facebook and Twitter:

> Reduction of APL [housing assistance] to fund the reception of migrants: the foreign preference of the government in action! [Réduction des APL pour financer l'accueil des migrants: la préférence étrangère du gouvernement en action!]

Her anti-elitist populist message, this time against the national government, received even higher numbers of popularity cues on Facebook with 16,442 likes and 10,881 shares (but only 156 favorites and 366 retweets on Twitter). Again, it was picked up by the news media on the same day when the French edition of the *Huffington Post* published her tweet.

Thus, although earlier research suggests that, overall, only a small share of social media posts actually contain populist key messages (Ernst et al. 2017), they may garner disproportionate attention and reach, both directly on social media and indirectly through traditional news media.

Recap and Outlook

Social media give politicians an unfiltered communication channel to their followers. This fits populism's ideal of a direct connection to the people as well as populist leaders' self-perception as the voice of the people. With Facebook and Twitter, political leaders can circumvent the traditional news media, which populists often view as biased, hostile, or even, in Donald Trump's words, "the enemy of the people."

Thus, social media offer populists an ideal platform to appeal to the people, demand the people's sovereignty, and criticize the elite.

Social media also give an indirect advantage to populists in providing the means for disaffected citizens to express themselves and form online communities, which, in turn, lets politicians – particularly populist ones – tap into the potential of such partisan online crowds. It is another example, as Gerbaudo (2018) points out, of how well matched populism is with social media. This network effect is also a reason to continue exploring the relationship between populism and popularity cues.

Our empirical findings support earlier evidence that populism may help politicians of any stripe increase their social media popularity and reach. While leaders of typically populist parties were more successful overall with their Facebook posts and tweets, populist key messages from anyone had a positive influence on popularity cues.

However, this may depend on the platform. While Facebook posts with populist key messages received more likes and shares, populist tweets were actually less favorited or retweeted than non-populist tweets. This may be explained by the specific characteristics of these two platforms and their user demographics. Twitter is a more elite medium, which political leaders mostly use to interact with fellow politicians, journalists, or other elite actors. Facebook, in comparison, has a broader user base across different social groups and allows for closer and more personal interactions. (This observation is, of course, contradicted by Donald Trump's[5] often-populist Twitter use, which Stromer-Galley describes as *vulgar eloquence* in this volume).

However, our findings also show that political leaders who sent populist key messages more often overall also got more popularity cues on both platforms. Thus, while on Facebook the effect of populist communication could also be found for individual populist posts, on Twitter, the politician's image, or how populist he or she was overall, seemed to matter more to followers than what he or she actually said in an individual tweet.

Furthermore, we found that both typically "populist" and typically "non-populist" leaders could use populist key messages to gain popularity on social media, at least on Facebook. This could encourage politicians to use populist communication not only to gain reach on social media but also to gain visibility in mainstream media (see Chadwick 2017). The effect of populist communication on popularity cues in connection with the "network effect" of social media, which further pushes popular content, may also explain why the most outrageous tweets (e.g., by Donald Trump) or specifically populist Facebook posts attract enormous attention from the traditional news media and the public (see Gerbaudo 2018).

If social media actually give an advantage to populist leaders or encourage normally non-populist political leaders to use populist communication, this may be seen as problematic from the perspective of liberal democracy. Although populism may legitimately express criticism of a growing gap between governments and citizens, scholars have argued it threatens to undermine central pillars of a liberal democracy (Kriesi 2014; Abts and Rummens, 2007). This is because treating the people as a homogenous group denies the idea of a pluralist society in which minorities should receive special protection. The demand for unrestricted popular sovereignty challenges the division of powers. Also, the hostile juxtaposition between the people and the elite may hamper considered, fact-based deliberation and compromise. Thus, if social media give an advantage to populist leaders, they may have negative consequences for political communication in liberal democracies (see Waisbord 2018).

108 Sina Blassnig et al.

However, this of course also depends on how important social media will be for political communication in the future and whether or how much political leaders are willing to adapt their communication to gain higher popularity or reach on these platforms. Thus, besides extending the scope of our findings with regard to politicians, countries, and other contextual factors, there is a case for future research to explore whether non-populist political leaders adapt their communication to fit the network logic of social media. And to investigate what the actual impact is of online popularity cues on citizens' perceptions, attitudes, and political actions.

Notes

1 An exception is Switzerland, where national parliamentary elections were held on October 18, 2015. However, due to the Swiss direct democratic system, elections are seen as less important than the regular public votes on referenda on initiatives, of which none took place within the sampling period.
2 For the US, due to its party system, only four parties were chosen: the Democratic Party, the Republican Party, the Green Party, and the Tea Party Patriots.
3 We chose negative binomial regression due to the distribution of the dependent variable, which is, typically for count distributions, right-skewed and has a standard deviation larger than the mean. This choice is in line with other recent studies using popularity cues as dependent variable (Bene 2017a; Keller and Kleinen-von Königslöw 2018; Saxton and Waters 2014; Trilling, Tolochko, and Burscher 2016).
4 In June 2018, *Front National* changed its name to *Rassemblement National*.
5 As Mr. Trump did not hold any leader position in the party or country in 2015, he is not in our sample.

References

Aalberg, Toril, Esser, Frank, Reinemann, Carsten, Strömbäck, Jesper, and Claes de Vreese (Ed.). 2017. *Populist Political Communication in Europe*. New York: Routledge.
Abts, Koen, and Stefan Rummens. 2007. "Populism versus democracy." *Political Studies* 55 (2): 405–24.
Bartlett, Jamie, Jonathan Birdwell, and Mark Littler. 2011. *The new face of digital populism*. London: Demos.
Bene, Marton. 2017a. "Go viral on the Facebook! Interactions between candidates and followers on Facebook during the Hungarian general election campaign of 2014." *Information, Communication & Society* 20 (4): 513–29.
Bene, Marton. 2017b. "Sharing is caring! Investigating viral posts on politicians' Facebook pages during the 2014 General Election Campaign in Hungary." *Journal of Information Technology & Politics* 14 (4): 387–402.
Bobba, Giuliano. 2018. "Social media populism: Features and 'likeability' of Lega Nord communication on Facebook." *European Political Science*, 1–13.
Bos, Linda, Wouter van der Brug, and Claes de Vreese. 2011. "How the media shape perceptions of right-wing populist leaders." *Political Communication* 28 (2): 182–206.
Bracciale, Roberta, and Antonio Martella. 2017. "Define the populist political communication style: The case of Italian political leaders on Twitter." *Information, Communication & Society* 20 (9): 1310–29.

Canovan, Margaret. 1999. "Trust the people! Populism and the two faces of democracy." *Political Studies* 47 (1): 2–16.

Chadwick, Andrew. 2017. *The hybrid media system: Politics and power.* Second edition. New York: Oxford University Press.

Cranmer, Mirjam. 2011. "Populist communication and publicity: An empirical study of contextual differences in Switzerland." *Swiss Political Science Review* 17 (3): 286–307.

Engesser, Sven, Nicole Ernst, Frank Esser, and Florin Büchel. 2017. "Populism and social media: How politicians spread a fragmented ideology." *Information, Communication & Society* 20 (8): 1109–26.

Engesser, Sven, Nayla Fawzi, and Anders O. Larsson. 2017. "Populist online communication: Introduction to the special issue." *Information, Communication & Society* 20 (9): 1279–92.

Enli, Gunn, and Linda T. Rosenberg. 2018. "Trust in the age of social media: Populist politicians seem more authentic." *Social Media + Society* 4 (1): 1–11.

Ernst, Nicole, Sven Engesser, Florin Büchel, Sina Blassnig, and Frank Esser. 2017. "Extreme parties and populism: An analysis of Facebook and Twitter across six countries." *Information, Communication & Society* 20 (9): 1347–64.

Fürst, Silke, and Franziska Oehmer. 2018. "Twitter-Armies, Earned Media und Big Crowds im US-Wahlkampf 2016: Zur wachsenden Bedeutung des Nachrichtenfaktors Öffentlichkeitsresonanz." In *Strategische Politische Kommunikation im digitalen Wandel: Interdisziplinäre Perspektiven auf ein dynamisches Forschungsfeld*, edited by Michael Oswald and Michael Johann, 35–61. Wiesbaden: Springer Fachmedien Wiesbaden.

Gerbaudo, Paolo. 2018. "Social media and populism: An elective affinity?" *Media, Culture & Society* 40 (5): 745–53.

Groshek, Jacob, and Jiska Engelbert. 2012. "Double differentiation in a cross-national comparison of populist political movements and online media uses in the United States and the Netherlands." *New Media & Society* 15 (2): 183–202.

Hameleers, Michael, and Desirée Schmuck. 2017. "It's us against them: A comparative experiment on the effects of populist messages communicated via social media." *Information, Communication & Society*, 1–20.

Hawkins, Kirk A. 2010. *Venezuela's Chavismo and populism in comparative perspective.* Cambridge, NY: Cambridge University Press.

Heiss, Raffael, and Jörg Matthes. 2017. "Who 'likes' populists? Characteristics of adolescents following right-wing populist actors on Facebook." *Information, Communication & Society* 20 (9): 1408–24.

Heiss, Raffael, Desiree Schmuck, and Jörg Matthes. 2018. "What drives interaction in political actors' Facebook posts? Profile and content predictors of user engagement and political actors' reactions." *Information, Communication & Society*, 1–17.

Jacobs, Kristof, and Niels Spierings. 2016. *Social media, parties, and political inequalities.* New York: Palgrave Macmillan US.

Jagers, Jan, and Stefaan Walgrave. 2007. "Populism as political communication style: An empirical study of political parties' discourse in Belgium." *European Journal of Political Research* 46 (3): 319–45.

Jansen, Robert S. 2011. "Populist mobilization: A new theoretical approach to populism." *Sociological Theory* 29 (2): 75–96.

Jünger, Jakob, and Till Keyling. 2013. *Facepager: An application for generic data retrieval through APIs.* https://github.com/strohne/Facepager.

Katz, Elihu, and Paul F. Lazarsfeld. 1955. *Personal influence: The part played by people in the flow of mass communications.* New Brunswick, NJ: Transaction Publishers.

110 Sina Blassnig et al.

Keller, Tobias R., and Katharina Kleinen-von Königslöw. 2018. "Followers, spread the message! Predicting the success of Swiss politicians on Facebook and Twitter." *Social Media + Society* 4 (1): 1–11.

Klinger, U., and J. Svensson. 2015. "The emergence of network media logic in political communication: A theoretical approach." *New Media & Society* 17 (8): 1241–57.

Kriesi, Hanspeter. 2014. "The populist challenge." *West European Politics* 37 (2): 361–78.

Laclau, Ernesto. 2005. *On populist reason*. London: Verso.

Mazzoleni, Gianpietro. 2008. "Populism and the media." In *Twenty-first century populism: The spectre of Western European democracy*, edited by Daniele Albertazzi and Duncan McDonnell, 49–64. Basingstoke: Palgrave Macmillan.

Mény, Yves, and Yves Surel. 2002. "The Constitutive Ambiguity of Populism." In *Democracies and the populist challenge*, edited by Yves Mény and Yves Surel, 1–21. Basingstoke: Palgrave.

Mills, Adam J. 2012. "Virality in social media: The SPIN Framework." *Journal of Public Affairs* 12 (2): 162–69.

Mudde, Cas. 2004. "The populist Zeitgeist." *Government and Opposition* 39 (4): 542–63.

Müller, Philipp, Christian Schemer, Martin Wettstein, Anne Schulz, Dominique S. Wirz, Sven Engesser, and Werner Wirth. 2017. "The polarizing impact of news coverage on populist attitudes in the public: Evidence from a panel study in four European democracies." *Journal of Communication* 67 (6): 968–92.

Porten-Cheé, Pablo, Jörg Haßler, Pablo Jost, Christiane Eilders, and Marcus Maurer. 2018. "Popularity cues in online media: Theoretical and methodological perspectives." *SCM Studies in Communication and Media* 7 (2): 80–102.

Saxton, Gregory D., and Richard D. Waters. 2014. "What do stakeholders like on Facebook? Examining public reactions to nonprofit organizations' informational, promotional, and community-building messages." *Journal of Public Relations Research* 26 (3): 280–99.

Stanley, Ben. 2008. "The thin ideology of populism." *Journal of Political Ideologies* 13 (1): 95–110.

Stanyer, James, Susana Salgado, and Jesper Strömbäck. 2017. "Populist actors as communicators or political actors as populist communicators: Cross-national findings and perspectives." In *Populist political communication in Europe*, edited by Toril Aalberg, Frank Esser, Carsten Reinemann, Jesper Strömbäck, and Claes de Vreese, 353–64. New York: Routledge.

Stier, Sebastian, Lisa Posch, Arnim Bleier, and Markus Strohmaier. 2017. "When populists become popular: Comparing Facebook use by the right-wing movement Pegida and German political parties." *Information, Communication & Society* 20 (9): 1365–88.

Taggart, Paul. 2000. *Populism*. Concepts in the social sciences. Buckingham: Open University Press.

Trilling, Damian, Petro Tolochko, and Björn Burscher. 2016. "From newsworthiness to shareworthiness: How to predict news sharing based on article characteristics." *Journalism & Mass Communication Quarterly* 94 (1): 38–60.

Vaccari, Cristian, and Augusto Valeriani. 2015. "Follow the leader! Direct and indirect flows of political communication during the 2013 Italian general election campaign." *New Media & Society* 17 (7): 1025–42.

Van Kessel, Stijn. 2015. *Populist Parties in Europe. Agents of Discontent?* Basingstoke: Palgrave Macmillan.

Van Kessel, Stijn, and Remco Castelein. 2016. "Shifting the blame. Populist politicians' use of Twitter as a tool of opposition." *Journal of Contemporary European Research* 12 (2): 594–614.

Waisbord, Silvio. 2018. "Why populism is troubling for democratic communication." *Communication, Culture and Critique* 11 (1): 21–34.

Waisbord, Silvio, and Adriana Amado. 2017. "Populist communication by digital means: Presidential Twitter in Latin America." *Information, Communication & Society* 20 (9): 1330–46.

Weyland, Kurt. 2017. "Populism: A political-strategic approach." In *The Oxford handbook of populism*, edited by Cristóbal Rovira Kaltwasser, Paul A. Taggart, Paulina Ochoa Espejo, and Pierre Ostiguy, 48–72. Oxford: Oxford University Press.

Wirth, Werner, Frank Esser, Sven Engesser, Dominique Wirz, Anne Schulz, Nicole Ernst, Florin Büchel et al. 2016. *The appeal of populist ideas, strategies and styles: A theoretical model and research design for analyzing populist political communication*. Zürich: NCCR Democracy, Working Paper No. 88. Accessed July 27, 2018. www.nccr-democracy.uzh.ch/publications/workingpaper/wp88: 1–60.

8

A MARRIAGE OF TWITTER AND POPULISM IN THE FRENCH PRESIDENTIAL CAMPAIGN? THE TWITTER-DISCOURSE OF CHALLENGERS MACRON AND LE PEN

Peter Maurer

The French presidential election of 2017 shook up the political landscape and led to a re-alignment of parties and voters which was unprecedented throughout the 5th French Republic, in place since 1958. As a challenger of the political establishment without an affiliation to one of the major parties, relative political newcomer Emmanuel Macron was elected president on 7 May. He disputed the second ballot of the election against Marine Le Pen, an outsider of the political establishment from the far-right, who registered the highest share of votes for a presidential candidate of her party ever. While political scientists point to political reasons for these results (Escalona, 2017), this chapter argues that the reconfiguration of French politics that took place in this election also has a communicative side which is related to the efficient use of social media.

Online platforms and social media have played an increasing role in French elections from 2007 onward as tools for mobilization, building party platforms and influencing public opinion (Lilleker, 2016; Wells et al., 2016; Mercier, 2015; 2017a, 2017b). In this election, social media reached a new high in terms of impact as it allowed Macron and Le Pen to create powerful political movements outside traditional party organizations and to spread a coherent discourse independent of the political agenda and commentary of the traditional news media.

In this chapter, we shall analyse how the specific communication format of Twitter was used by Macron and Le Pen to set the tone of their respective campaign in order to drain the support bases of the traditional centre-left and centre-right parties that had dominated the political landscape up to that point. The focus is on Twitter, as it is arguably the most important social media platform for political campaigning in France (Mercier, 2015; Frame & Brachotte, 2015). Although the share of Twitter users in the French population is steadily growing

A Marriage of Twitter and Populism **113**

(between 10 and 15%), direct communication between sender and followers is only a small part of its real impact. For example, more than 4 million individuals visited Twitter every day in June 2017, which is more visits than any other online news platform (Frame & Brachotte, 2015; Médiametrie, 2017). Moreover, a significant percentage (53%) of French internet users declare to view political tweets, regardless whether they are themselves Twitter users or not, which indicates that the actual Twitter audience is much larger than the number of registered users (Frame et al., 2016). Publics might have also encountered political tweets on public affairs TV and radio programmes, where they are often discussed and put on display. Twitter stands out especially among social media because it is an open message board for the candidates where their messages reach followers, a wider public and journalists in very short time. In this respect, Tweets reach a larger, more elitist, less confirmed, and more metropolitan audience than Facebook postings. Facebook is a place where the dyed-in-the-wool supporters gather and more provincial.

Twitter's high adoption rate among the political elite is also telling with regard to the political influence of the platform. Virtually all significant French politicians, journalists and pundits use Twitter. About 60% of French members of parliament were active on Twitter in 2014 and the number is significantly higher in 2017. No prominent national political actor forgoes Twitter. The great appeal of Twitter for politicians consists in the possibility of communicating with a wide audience of followers without having to deal with journalistic gatekeepers, thereby keeping full control of the message. According to studies, French politicians use Twitter primarily to spread information and views, and to gauge public opinion almost in real time (Frame & Brachotte, 2015). The possibility to quickly publicize rebuttals, set the tone in a debate, and counter arguments made by others might be added to the list. Twitter was also heavily used in the 2017 campaign to promote candidates' media appearances and spread the statements they made in interviews with broadcast or print media or at public speeches more widely. A potential disadvantage of Twitter is the risk of attracting memes and satiric tweets for campaign gaffes that go viral. However, Macron and Le Pen were very professional and wary in their Twitter behaviour, such that no significant gaffes happened to them throughout the campaign. Apart from the general strategy, the content of the candidates' rhetoric is in the centre of this chapter: We will examine to what extent the Twitter campaigns of Macron and Le Pen bear a resemblance to *populism*, a political discourse that appeals to disgruntled and hitherto apathetic voters. This discourse is typically used by challenger candidates to attack the establishment (Bonikowski & Gidron, 2016; Taggart, 2002). Populist discourse unfolds especially on social media, as these media facilitate free, unfiltered expression of political views and thus give the speaker more leeway how to frame attacks on established parties than the mainstream news media would allow. Accordingly, scholars have detected strong populist elements in the social media campaigns of major challenger candidates in recent Italian (Movimento 5S, Salvini), Spanish

114 Peter Maurer

(Podemos), Dutch (Wilders), Indian (Modi) or US (Trump, Sanders) presidential or legislative campaigns (Bracciale & Martella, 2017; Gonawela et al., 2018; Mazzoleni & Bracciale, 2018). Hence, the Twitter communication of Macron and Le Pen in the French election campaign will be screened for elements of populism, especially people-centrism and anti-elitism. What do their tweets tell us about their conception of the people–elite relationship, the urgency for political change and national identity, another cherished theme by populists?

The Role of Twitter for Political Communication

Social media have become a new power resource for professional politicians and other political actors (e.g. Chadwick, Dennis & Smith, 2016; Karlsen & Enjolras, 2016; Mercier, 2017a; Frame & Brachotte, 2015; Frame et al., 2016). In the French political process, and particularly during election campaigns, Twitter has emerged as the most influential social media tool to set the tone in a campaign. Several of Twitter's affordances are important in this respect. First, using Twitter (and other social media platforms) for political communication means a disintermediation of the political communication process between politicians and the public (e.g. Frame, 2017; Chadwick, Dennis & Smith, 2016). While the messages can appear crude and less credible outside the journalistic context, they are also liberated from contexts that distract from the core information the sender wants to convey. In other words, Twitter provides politicians with a greater freedom of expression due to the absence of contradicting arguments that may be provided by gatekeepers.

Such a disintermediation is by no means trivial. The legacy or mainstream media, it must be remembered, are part of the entrenched power structure of a society and therefore tend to be protective of the established or mainstream political elite. That is why Donohue, Tichenor and Olien ([1995] 2018), in a groundbreaking article, called the mainstream media "guard dogs" rather than watchdogs of the political elite. Media acting as guard dogs means that the traditional mass media organizations filter and contextualize the communication of political speakers who seek access to the public. In so doing they can deemphasize statements that challenge an established order and confront them with divergent information and counterarguments. Media organizations were the gatekeepers of the largest part of the public sphere before social media had their breakthrough. Yet, the affordances of Twitter and other social media platforms have reduced this role, to the potential benefit of outsiders and challengers of established, 'mainstream' parties.

Twitter enables those outsiders and challengers to reach large and diverse audiences without passing through the mass media gates. Moreover, the platform gives them possibilities to engage with the audience in ways that can facilitate the build-up of political movements outside the member-based canvassing of mainstream parties. Features that enable community building are, for example, common hashtags (often suggested by the campaign) among supporters when specific issues are discussed. These become shared code words for people holding similar views, and tweeting around these hashtags strengthens their views and their feelings of internal efficacy. In other words, Twitter has features that can turn supporters of a candidate quickly into a political 'tribe' with a minimal need of resources. It must not be overlooked either that Twitter gives prominent politicians a reach beyond just active Twitter users. As Frame and colleagues (2016) argue, the role of passive participants on Twitter, who may not actively tweet or retweet but who nevertheless gather information for their own deliberation process from the tweets they encounter or actively seek, is important.

Another obvious advantage of Twitter over legacy media is that the senders select the topics and the tone, not an interviewer, talk show host or expert. Another advantage is that politicians can be more authentic in their communication, for example by using a personal linguistic style or by including photos or other links in the tweets that personalize the message (see also Enli & Skogerbø, 2013). This allows for what can be called a better self-promotion or "self-mediatisation" (Frame, 2017) strategy of political actors and, by the same token, strengthens their individual position vis-à-vis their parties (Karlsen & Enjolras, 2016) in the process of public communication, as Twitter handles are personal. The impact of these messages then depends on the number of followers a politicians' Twitter account has rather than on support by a party and its machine. Twitter thereby levels the playing field for political candidates who do not have the support of a mainstream party. The use of Twitter also enables direct rebuttals to attacks launched by others through the traditional media or other channels.

Twitter is, moreover, a means to building a following of people who are not used to engaging politically, as it also reaches passive "readers" or "lurkers" of political debates (Frame et al., 2016). In a way, Twitter democratized the public discussion, as it has been shown that non-party members use it to discuss politics informally to the same extent as party members (Vaccari & Valeriani, 2016). Hence, as a low-threshold participation channel, Twitter can serve to slowly introduce potential supporters and sympathizers to the discourse of new movements. Twitter offers the additional advantage of multiplier or snowball effects if followers share the messages with their own followers. As Vaccari and Valeriani put it, social media can "to some extent flatten rather than reinforce existing political hierarchies" (2016, p. 294).

So, taken together, Twitter is suitable for sending messages beyond the group of convinced followers and sympathizers and for familiarizing formerly apathetic publics with political views, including through accidental encounters with political messages.

Populism and Twitter

The full potential of Twitter as a medium for political mobilization and persuasion unfolds for challengers because it works as a political counter-public sphere in which polemical critique of institutions and elites often set the tone of the debate (Mercier, 2016, 2017a). As a communicative milieu, Twitter thus matches the style of populism, and more generally the needs of political challengers and outsiders.

Ott (2017) has argued that Twitter is so powerful in shaping messages that it has even begun to transform the character of public discourse. According to him, communication on Twitter is characterized by simplicity, impulsivity and incivility. Since harsh critique of the performance of elites and the functioning of institutions are main themes of populism, there could be a reinforcing spiral between Twitter and a populist tone in tweeted messages. Some observers point to such an elective affinity between the medium, Twitter, and the style of the political message (Gerbaudo 2018).

In essence, populism is a political logic utilizable in campaigns that claims to defend the "the people" against an "elite", a group of power holders which is said to disrespect popular sovereignty, to make deals with narrow interests and betray the people. So, in a nutshell, populist rhetoric denigrates the elite and praises the people (Stanley, 2008; Mudde, 2004). Populism is compatible with different ideological beliefs though. Laclau (1979) characterized populist rhetoric as popular democratic interpellations of the dominant ideology. However, what ideology or group is presented as 'dominant' and thus challenged in the name of the people depends on the political communicator. Since Macron and Le Pen both ran as challengers of the ruling parties and given that they both claimed to stand for renewal of political culture and dogmas, their respective bids for power bear a natural resemblance to populism.

However, as will be demonstrated in the analysis, the brand of populism that Macron and Le Pen employed in their Twitter discourse differed. As Mény and Surel (2002) have pointed out, "populism is, by itself, an empty shell which can be filled and made meaningful with whatever is poured into it" (p. 6). Indeed, in Le Pen's discourse, populist claims become coloured with elements from other ideologies. For instance, when talking about the antagonistic people–elite relationship, she incorporates socialist and "Rousseauian" radical democratic ideas in her arguments. Such conceptions of a general will of the people stand behind her repeated praise of referendums and her reject of the free mandate for the directly elected president.

On the other side, Twitter can be used for a communication strategy that seeks to create a broad coalition by repeatedly referring to qualities and potentials of "the people". This selective use of populism transforms it to a mere communicative strategy. Macron picked only the people-centric side of populism while omitting the anti-elitist aspects. The people-centric discourse was connected with the foregrounding of specific values that were central in his campaign. People-centrism fit with the strategy of Macron, which could be termed mildly populist.

We will examine the expressions of people-centrism and national identity on the one hand and anti-elitism on the other in the Twitter feeds of the candidates Macron and Le Pen. As others have convincingly argued (Bonikowski & Gidron,

2016), challengers like Macron and Le Pen find common ground with populism since it promotes overcoming a deprecated system of parties, elites and political institutions, as well as an old guard of incumbents. In addition, populist appeals to "the people" and national identity might have assisted the candidates to assemble a group of followers around common values.

Yet, people-centrism can be a slippery slope since it invites the question how "the people" are delineated from other groups. In that respect, the ideological positions of Macron and Le Pen differed since Macron is a confirmed cultural liberalist whereas Le Pen is close to a nativist creed. Did that difference play out in both candidates' people-centric rhetoric and their references to national identity?

Populist discourse has always been characterized by the *topos* of national identity. In this regard, we agree with the assumption that the production of national identity takes place primarily through discourse (Gerteis & Goolsby, 2005) and this naturally includes discourse on social media platforms. National identity has a lot to do with the construction of social boundaries, as, for example, Gerteis and Goolsby (2005) argue. The boundary between the people of the nation and those who do not belong to this group can be drawn on different bases, for example ethnic or civic. So-called ethnic national identity is based on ethnic bonds or sharing the same ethnic history, whereas "civic" refers to an identity based on "shared substantive vision of citizenship" (Gerteis & Goolsby 2005, p. 202).

Methodology

Tweets from Emmanuel Macron (now French president) and his opponent in the second round of the election, Marine Le Pen, collected during a 13-month period from 7 May 2016 to 7 June 2017, form the corpus for the analysis. Despite a quantitative overview of how often the outsiders tweeted about key concepts such as "elite" and "people", the main part of the analysis is qualitative and examines the tweets in-depth. Thus, the investigation will show to what extent the two outsiders' Twitter discourse was populist in comparison to their much more streamlined discourse in the mainstream news media.

The corpus consists of over 6,800 tweets in total. Macron issued more than 3,100 tweets and Le Pen more than 3,700. However, only part of these tweets contained elements of populist speech, as an automated search with a dictionary of populist expressions in the tweets revealed. The dictionary was compiled based on existing shorter wordlists used in previous populism studies and a careful qualitative pre-analysis of a subset of the tweets that led to adding terms. The search process was automated, meaning that a statistics program, R, was used to match the dictionary to the tweets. It turned out that Le Pen referred to the "elite" in an impressive 21% of her tweets, while Macron did so only in 9.7%. Le Pen also referred more often to the "people" (12.1%) followed by Macron (4.4%). In the remainder, the contents of the Twitter messages of both candidates will be further clarified in a qualitative analysis.

Results of the Qualitative Analysis

"The Elite" in the Tweets

Macron does not make many references to "the elite" in his Twitter discourse, perhaps because he wants to delineate himself from his populist competitor Le Pen. At the same time, this shows that Twitter does not automatically drag populist rhetoric with it. When Macron does mention elites, he subsumes the established political parties of the left and right with his label. He thereby tries to capitalize on the widespread mistrust towards political parties in the French population. Macron uses terms such as "system of old parties" or "the political landscape as we knew it" to designate the political elite and suggest its outdatedness. His tweets offer him the possibility to make clear that he delineates himself from these actors, but without attacking them too harshly.

Macron makes the same criticism of all the established parties, i.e. having allowed the FN to rise to a major political force. Unlike Le Pen, Macron does not single out specific politicians but rather addresses his critique to the established parties as an ensemble:

> C'est le système de vieux partis politiques qui a nourri le Front national tant et tant d'années. #JT20H". [It is the system of the old parties that has nourished the Front National for so many years.[1]]
>
> *(@EmmanuelMacron, tweet from 25 April 2017)*

Repeating that all established parties are equal in their incapability to act decisively against the decline in political trust was one aim of Macron's communication. For this, Twitter was the perfect medium because he could repeat this simple message in minor variations as often as he wanted and be sure that it reached the right audience. In the mainstream media, this would have been less convincing because those voters who distrust the political establishment also mistrust the legacy media and tend to not watch them. Macron shows his Twitter followers his disdain for the old political party elite by using the impersonal pronouns "eux" (they) and "les" (them), which have a pejorative connotation in this context:

> Ce qu'on est en train de faire les gêne tous. #Quotidien. [What we are doing disturbs *them* all.]
>
> *(@EmmanuelMacron, tweet from 13 March 2017)*

This language is a gentle way of othering and denigrating politicians from the existing and thus most dominant parties. The "we" in this opposition is of course those who decide to join Macron's movement.

In general, Macron's word choice in the tweets underlines his preference for reform rather than a radical shift. He thus uses words such as "retrouver" (recover), "refonder" (re-establish) and "renouvellement" (renewal) when talking about the French political system rather than using a more disruptive vocabulary, which some have said to be the norm on Twitter (Ott, 2017). Hence, in summary, while Macron is not very populist when discussing the political system on Twitter, he clearly is in one respect, namely in putting the existing parties in one basket and delineating his own candidacy from them. In that respect, he surely does use the medium to convey a very simple message about a complex relationship.

Compared to Macron, Le Pen adopts a more clearly populist style in her tweets, as she talks much more often about political elites and uses a more contemptuous vocabulary. Remember that 21% of Le Pen's tweets included terms that belong to the semantic field of "elite" versus barely 9% of Macron's. But her tweets are also much more in line with populism's claims about the nature of the elite and their relationship with the people than Macron's discourse.

Le Pen's Twitter discourse often pits "elite" and "people" against each other. In many tweets she sets herself on the side of the people in this conflict. The *topos* of treason by the elite to the detriment of the people's interest is very common, as in this example:

> Nos dirigeants ont cessé de croire en la France et professent des discours (. . .) de trahison. [Our leaders have stopped to believe in France and are holding (. . .) treacherous discourses.] #LilleMLP
>
> *(@MLP_officiel, tweet from 26 March 2017)*

The behaviour of the elite is described as illegitimate because they would be responsive to the interests of specific groups and actors rather than the people's interest. In many of Le Pen's tweets, elites are accused of having betrayed the people of their sovereignty and running on the orders of specific interests, for example of the European Union.

However, exactly who is the elite remains vague in Le Pen's tweets. In her characteristic style, she uses a vocabulary that attacks and delegitimizes political elites as a group – and which is thus very prone to being filtered by legacy media – such as the terms "oligarchy" and "system" (which reminds us of the "rigged system" phrase of Donald Trump's Twitter rhetoric). With the use of terms like "oligarchy", she suggests that political decision makers lack democratic legitimacy. According to Le Pen, "the system" of government in place particularly violates the democratic principle of popular sovereignty and shows a condescending attitude toward its constituency:

> Le système est une forme d'oligarchie qui méprise le peuple, et même gouverne contre lui et contre son avis. [The system is a sort of oligarchy, which dislikes the people, and which even governs against their opinions.] #BourdinDirect
>
> *(@MLP_officiel, tweet from 3 January 2017)*

120 Peter Maurer

Le Pen equates the elite with agents of the political, economic and media sectors who, however, remain hidden behind the scenes and send their candidates into the race as puppets. So, Le Pen attacks Macron for being the candidate of these obscure forces when she calls him "a candidate of the system that has already been established" (@MLP_officiel, tweet from 11 April 2017) or claims that Macron was "in the hands of financial powers (. . .)" (@MLP_officiel, tweet from 1 February 2017). She thereby also tries to discredit Macron's claim to stand for political renewal.

Le Pen also attacks specific politicians more often than Macron does. This is another strategy she can do best on social media. She especially targets Macron and the candidate of the centre-right party who followed her closely in the polls during the campaign. Her line of attack remains consistently on the theme of their alleged neglect of popular demands because they were captured by private interests. The tweets are emotionally charged but not uncivil. Here is a typical example of Le Pen's attack tweets:

> MM. #Macron et #Fillon sont sous influence. Ils ne sont pas libres. Ce sont des pantins dans les mains d'intérêts privés. [Mr. Macron and Mr. Fillon are influenced. They are not free. They are puppets in the hands of private interests.] #ChateaurouxMLP
>
> *(@MLP_officiel, tweet from 11 March 2017)*

"The People" and National Identity in the Tweets

In France, the national narrative has become a central part of political culture and discourse (e.g. Koukoutsaki-Monnier, 2010), and the term "people" has a positive connotation due to the myth of French Revolution. So, associating themselves with "the people" in their tweets seems a reasonable strategy of self-promotion and image projection by the candidates, as this should appeal widely. Macron refers to the people less often than Le Pen does, but still, a significant proportion (4.4%) of his tweets do contain words referring to this concept. Macron's style is in this regard mildly populist, but without the stronger elements. In Macron's political narrative, "the people" have a unifying character. For example, he expresses in a statement tweeted from a public rally that the French have always come together to be "frères" (brothers), "amis" (friends) and "citoyens" (citizens) (@EmmanuelMacron, tweet from 12 April 2017). This is underlined by using hashtags such as #LaFrancequiunit [#Francewhichunites] or simply #ensemble [#together].

According to his notion of the people as a group of individual citizens, Macron sees the tension between the people and institutional politics as grounded in citizens' lack of trust in political institutions, which can be overcome by allowing citizens more active participation in them. Unlike populism and simplified Twitter discourse, though, Macron does not suggest that there exists a fundamental contradiction between the policy of these institutions and the demands of the people. This reform-oriented approach is expressed in quite considerate content, as in tweets like this:

> Je veux un Parlement qui retrouve votre confiance, la confiance des citoyens, la confiance de la Nation. #MacronPrésident [I want a parliament that regains your trust, the trust of the citizens, the trust of the nation. #MacronPrésident]
>
> *(@EmmanuelMacron, tweet from 17 April 2017)*

Macron's tweets related to the people also reveal his conception of national identity, in particular how he draws boundaries between the French people and other groups. First, in correspondence to his unifying, understanding of the term "people", Macron's conception of national identity is relatively open and accessible to many, as he reiterates in the tweets. He clearly draws a boundary between the collective "we" and those who are not French citizens in a shared vision of citizenship. According to Gerteis and Goolsby (2005), Macron thus follows the civic concept of national identity. For Macron, being French is connected to attitudes or values, the most important of which are expressed in tweeted messages. As he explained in a big public rally and tweeted thereafter, being French for Macron means being faithful to the "promise of emancipation and empowerment" (@EmmanuelMacron, tweet from 26 October 2016). Those messages are also likely to being picked up by journalists since they allude to societal objectives, which the more liberal media also pursue.

It is worth noting that Macron adds another, namely cultural, aspect to the civic conception that also allows for diverse cultural communities within France to be included in "the people". He explicitly ties the notion of people to the existence of a cultural production that emanates from this community. In this regard, language is a crucial aspect: according to Macron, a people only exist because of their cultural output in terms of language and literature. This is remarkable as, by sending those types of messages, he uses the Twitter platform in the opposite way as Twitter critical scholars such as Ott (2017) predict.

Le Pen again adopts a more clearly populist discourse when it comes to references to the people. She consistently alludes to this central concept of populism, and the meaning conveyed is closer to classic ideas of populism about the people as victims of malicious elites. In the phraseology of her tweets, Le Pen suggests in a series of similar of tweets that "the people" suffer a severe crisis that can be summarized in three claims: (1) they have been dispossessed of their sovereignty; (2) they are unprotected against globalization and immigration, which threaten their national identity; (3) they are ripped off by national and international elites such as EU bureaucracy.

122 Peter Maurer

Unlike Macron, who tries to link the "people" to certain qualities, Le Pen emphasizes the common *possessions* of the people:

> Les Français ont une nation, une patrie, dont ils sont propriétaires. (. . .) [The French have a nation, a home country of which they are the *owners*.]
>
> *(@MLP_officiel, tweet from 4 April 2017)*

In line with many accounts of populism (Mény & Surel, 2002), Le Pen's tweets define the people by stating who is opposed to them or with which groups the people's interest stands in potential or actual conflict. She identifies four antagonist groups: the political elite, financial institutions, illegal immigrants and the EU. Thereby, it is characteristic of her Twitter style to mention the people and one of their antagonists in the same tweet, something which Macron seldom does. Here is an example:

> Je ne confondrai jamais un *peuple* avec ses *dirigeants*. (. . .) [I will never confound the *people* with their *leaders*.]
>
> *(@MLP_officiel, tweet from 17 January 2017)*

Finally, what can Le Pen's tweets tell us about her conception of national identity? This has been a main theme for the French (extreme) right since the 1980s at least (Noiriel, 2007; Charaudeau, 2011). How can she pick up this longstanding theme and actualize it in tweets so that it contributes to a 'softened' nationalist discourse that is capable of appealing to a wider coalition? Le Pen has a clear point of reference when she speaks about national identity in her tweets, namely French culture. It is French culture and mores rather than civic values or ethnic origin that she emphasizes as the most important criterion for delineating French citizens from others. So, in spite of her nationalist party background, Le Pen's discursive boundary-making on Twitter in terms of national identity is not fundamentally different from Macron's. While she certainly stresses the civic concept less, she does not speak about an ethnic or biological concept, either. In Le Pen's rhetoric, love of France is paramount for being French, insofar as French national identity is open to all who "love" France Of course, "aimer la France" can mean very different things, but by alluding to an attitude that is in principle accessible for everyone rather than to French descendance, Le Pen's discourse is clearly demarcated from nationalist right discourses of the past.

Conclusion

While Twitter already played a significant role in the 2012 elections, for example as a second screen to frame the online discussions around the big TV debate (Wells et al., 2016), in the 2017 election it represented a perfect opportunity for challenger candidates by providing them with a lot of latitude to cultivate their discourse of rupture and renewal. The Twitter activity of both Macron and Le Pen was equally strong, with almost ten tweets per day on average. However, many of the tweets making political claims are repetitions, in real time, of statements the candidates made on the radio, on television or at rallies. That means, for one thing, that their social media aides are behind a good deal of their tweeting activity, and that the Twitter discourse is not an entirely different animal than their political discourse on other platforms.

A comparison of Macron and Le Pen's tendencies to use elements of populist discourse in their tweets has clearly shown that Le Pen relied more on it than Macron. Twitter structurally encourages populism because it triggers impulsive messages of low complexity, often making strong claims or attacking groups or individuals. This was borne out in Le Pen's tweets.

However, according to our analysis, Le Pen has softened her discourse in another respect, i.e. her tweeted conception of national identity. She conveys in her tweets a preference for a cultural understanding of national identity, not a purely ethnic one, which would be less open and accessible to non-natives. It seems reasonable that Le Pen changes her nationalist discourse on Twitter some-what to appear more acceptable to moderates or hitherto apathetic voters who might encounter her tweets accidentally, for example when searching on the web, and must not be intimidated by an overly nationalist tone.

By contrast, we found very few instances of populism in Macron's discourse. We thus may assume that his liberal ideology trumps any populist ideas he may have and almost precludes the use of this style in public communication. He turned the impossibility of explaining his visions on Twitter into an advantage when he rephrased those visions in forceful but vague tweets around assembling concepts, often emphasized with hashtags. Ideologically, Macron might be best classified as a liberal – in his words a "progressist" – and he took great care to create this image with Twitter. That said, one might argue that he draws on a populist narrative when he delineates himself from the rest of the French party system. Yet, Macron never abandons the inclusive, reform-oriented tone in his communication overall (see also Escalona, 2017). The aim of this rhetoric is to present himself to his followers and swing voters as an optimistic leader and a unifier while remaining vague on policy. Twitter was a very useful channel for this type of discourse after all.

Finally, neither Le Pen nor Macron used insults, uncivil language, innuendo, word play, satire or the like, which are the stylistic elements other scholars have found are often used by populist politicians (Ott, 2017; Gonawela et al., 2018). Contrary to this assumption, we find that Macron and Le Pen's styles were rational, even though Twitter structurally does not allow complex arguments. We can conclude that the appeal to French voters of an intransigent populist discourse on Twitter remained limited, given that Macron won the second ballot by a relatively large margin. This might indicate the still greater power of legacy media when it comes to swaying election outcomes, as Macron's agenda was much more

124 Peter Maurer

supported there (Mercier, 2017b). His discourse and persona also were eventually much more appealing and acceptable to moderate voters. Hence, the result of the election should guard against exaggerated fears of the persuasive or manipulative power of social media platforms as such; they show that Twitter can be used in political discourse in a rather civil way.

Our last observation is that both candidates avoided gaffes in their tweeted discourse. The way to do that was, first, to use Tweets planned and, second, to employ Twitter as a one-way megaphone, not as a tool for any kind of 'dialogue'. Neither Macron's nor Le Pen's messaging was triggered by impulsive reactions but followed a thought-out strategy. Twitter as a tool was used to give coherence to the candidates respective campaign messages, not for engaging in in-fights with political opponents. It is also obvious that both candidates worked with a professional social media team in the background that helped them with the tweeting.

Note

1 All translations of tweets are done by the author.

References

Bonikowski, B., & Gidron, N. (2016). The populist style in American politics: Presidential Campaign discourse, 1952–1996. *Social Forces, 94*(4), 1593–1621. doi:10.1093/sf/sov120

Bracciale, R., & Martella, A. (2017). Define the populist political communication style: The case of Italian political leaders on Twitter. *Information, Communication & Society, 20*(9), 1310–1329. doi:10.1080/1369118X.2017.1328522

Chadwick, A., Dennis, J., & Smith, A. P. (2016). Politics in the age of hybrid media. In Bruns, A., Enli, G., Skogerbo, E., Larsson, A. O., & Christensen, C. (Eds.). *The Routledge companion to social media and politics*. London: Routledge. 7–22.

Charaudeau, P. (2011). Réflexions pour l'analyse du discours populiste. Mots. *Les langages du politique, 97,* 101–116.

Donohue, G. A., Tichenor, P. J., & Olien, C. N. (1995). A guard dog perspective on the role of media. *Journal of Communication, 45*(2), 115–132.

Enli, G. S., & Skogerbø, E. (2013). Personalized campaigns in party-centred politics: Twitter and Facebook as arenas for political communication. *Information, Communication & Society, 16*(5), 757–774.

Escalona, F. (2017). Le "moment Macron". *Cités* (4), 175–185.

Frame, A. (2017). Personnel politique et médias socionumériques: nouveaux usages et mythes 2.0. In Mercier A. (Ed.) *La communication politique* (pp.175–202). Paris: CNRS Editions.

Frame, A., & Brachotte, G. (2015). Le tweet stratégique: Use of Twitter as a PR tool by French politicians. *Public Relations Review, 41*(2), 278–287.

Frame, A., Mercier, A., Brachotte, G., & Thimm, C. (2016). General introduction. In Frame, A., Mercier, A., Brachotte, G., & Thimm, C. (Eds.), *Tweets from the campaign trail: Researching candidates' use of Twitter during the European Parliamentary Elections*. New York: Peter Lang.

Gerbaudo, P. (2018). Social media and populism: an elective affinity?. *Media, Culture & Society, 40*(5), 745–753.

Gerteis, J., & Goolsby, A. (2005). Nationalism in America: The case of the Populist movement. *Theory and Society*, *34*(2), 197–225.

Gonawela, A. N., Pal, J., Thawani, U., van der Vlugt, E., Out, W., & Chandra, P. (2018). Speaking their mind: Populist style and antagonistic messaging in the tweets of Donald Trump, Narendra Modi, Nigel Farage, and Gert Wilders. *Computer Supported Cooperative Work (CSCW)*. doi:10.1007/s10606-018-9316-2

Hawkins, K. A. (2009). Is Chávez populist?: Measuring populist discourse in comparative perspective. *Comparative Political Studies*, *42*(8), 1040–1067. doi:10.1177/0010414009331721

Koukoutsaki-Monnier, A. (2010). La construction symbolique de l'identité nationale française dans les discours de la campagne présidentielle de Nicolas Sarkozy. *Communication*, *28*(1), 11–39.

Karlsen, R., & Enjolras, B. (2016). Styles of social media campaigning and influence in a hybrid political communication system: Linking candidate survey data with Twitter data. *The International Journal of Press Politics*, *21*(3), 338–357.

Laclau, E. (1979). Politics and Ideology in Marxist Theory: Capitalism, Fascism, Populism. London: Verso.

Lilleker, D. G. (2016). Comparing online campaigning: The evolution of interactive campaigning from Royal to Obama to Hollande. *French Politics*, *14*(2), 234–253. doi:10.1057/fp.2016.5

Mazzoleni, G., & Bracciale, R. (2018). Socially mediated populism: the communicative strategies of political leaders on Facebook. *Palgrave Communications*, *4*(1), 50.

Médiametrie (2017). http://www.mediametrie.fr./ [May 2019].

Mény, Y., & Surel, Y. (2002). The constitutive ambiguity of populism. In Mény, Y., & Surel, Y. (Eds.), *Democracies and the populist challenge* (Vol. 1–21). Basingstoke: Palgrave.

Mercier, A. (2015). Twitter as a counter public sphere. Polemics in the Twittersphere during French electoral campaigns. In Frame, A., & Brachotte, G. (Eds.), *Citizen participation and political participation in a digital world* (pp. 139–152). London: Routledge.

Mercier, A. (2017a). Contestation et manipulations électorales en 140 signes. In Perrineau, P. (Ed.), *Le vote disruptif* (pp. 115–128). Paris: Presses de Sciences Po.

Mercier, A. (2017b). L'agenda médiatique de la présidentielle dominé par les médias traditionnels. *The Conversation France*. https://theconversation.com/lagenda-mediatique-de-la-presidentielle-domine-par-les-medias-traditionnels-79727.

Mudde, C. (2004). The populist Zeitgeist. *Government and Opposition*, *39*(4), 541–563. doi:10.1111/j.1477–7053.2004.00135.x

Noiriel, G. (2007). *À quoi sert « l'identité nationale »* ? Marseille: Agone.

Ott, B. L. (2017). The age of Twitter: Donald J. Trump and the politics of debasement. *Critical Studies in Media Communication*, *31*(1), 59–68.

Stanley, B. (2008). The thin ideology of populism. *Journal of political ideologies*, *13*(1), 95–110.

Taggart, P. (2002). Populism and the pathology of representative politics. In Mény, Y., & Surel, Y. (Eds.), *Democracies and the populist challenge* (pp. 62–80). London: Palgrave Macmillan UK.

Vaccari, C., & Valeriani, A. (2016). Party campaigners or citizen campaigners? How social media deepen and broaden party-related engagement. *International Journal of Press/Politics*, *21*(3), pp. 294–312, DOI: 10.1177/1940161216642152

Wells, C., Van Thomme, J., Maurer, P., Hanna, A., Pevehouse, J., Shah, D. V., & Bucy, E. (2016). Coproduction or cooptation? Real-time spin and social media response during the 2012 French and US presidential debates. *French Politics*, *14*(2), 206–233. doi:10.1057/fp.2016.4

9

POLITICAL COMMUNICATION PATTERNS AND SENTIMENTS ACROSS TIME ON TWITTER IN THE 2017 ELECTION IN THE NETHERLANDS

Maurice Vergeer

Introduction

Personal and direct communication has become more important in (post-)modern-day political campaigning. It is in sharp contrast to the strongly mediated way of communication in the pre-Internet era (Vergeer, Hermans, & Sams, 2013). To understand how candidates use social media during an election campaign, this chapter focuses on longitudinal communication activities by political candidates and leaders in the 2017 campaign for election of the Dutch parliament. Even though Twitter's user base has seemed to stabilize globally, with notable exceptions like Japan (Hale, 2017), Twitter is still very dominant as an online platform for political campaigning by candidates in the Netherlands. It is not only candidates that use Twitter extensively; people from the Netherlands are also very active, second after Sweden, according to the Pew Research Center (Poushter, 2017).

Candidates on social media can be understood from multiple perspectives: for instance, personalization, political performance, communication and media visibility. Because election campaigns are not static events, but events that evolve over time, some even talk about the permanent campaign (Blumenthal, 1980; Vergeer, Hermans, & Sams, 2013). During these campaigns, candidate and party visibility and popularity can shift dramatically over time. Whereas most studies use a static approach to understanding candidates' performance online, the present study will track candidates' social media activities and expressions over time. By comparing candidates, we can trace their online communication patterns and expressed sentiments.

The Dutch Political Landscape

The Netherlands' political system is a multiparty system. Since 2002, between 9 and 13 political parties populated the Dutch parliament. This characterizes the Dutch

Political Communication Patterns **127**

political system as a multiparty system with large diversity. Governments are always coalitions of multiple parties (sometimes up to four), because none of the political parties is able to secure a majority in the popular vote. As a result, parties will need to collaborate, in either the government or the opposition. This seems a plausible explanation for the lack of negative campaigning in the Netherlands (Walter, 2014).

The election system is proportional representative. Even though there are 20 election districts, the party ballots hardly differ across these districts. Some parties have so-called list pushers ("lijstduwers") at the last position of the ballot, such as celebrities (e.g. sportsmen, artists, known locals) that support the party by being candidates but do not expect to be elected. Their celebrity status aims to convince voters to vote for their party. In elections, many countries have two to four political parties in the elections (e.g. US, UK), but in the Netherlands (counting from the elections of 2002 onward), between 16 and 28 political parties have participated in the elections. As a result, people find it easy to switch between parties, because there is always a party ideologically close by.

Although voters who switch parties do not necessarily cause changes in the seat distribution in parliament, it can lead to significant changes. During the pillarized eras of the Netherlands (Lijphart, 1989), parliament's seat distribution was quite stable. After the influence of pillarization in Dutch society diminished and society modernized and individualized (1970s onward), switching parties became much easier, leading to increased changes in the power balance. This was particularly true for the early 2000s, which showed a rise of new (local) parties (LPF, Leefbaar Nederland and special interest parties for the elderly and for animal rights). Figure 9.1 shows the electoral volatility as a result of changes in the seat distribution in parliament. Up to the 1990s, the seat distribution did not change drastically. While the electoral volatility for entire political system remains high, electoral volatility for parties already in parliament only showed increased volatility during the LPF and Leefbaar Nederland period between 2002 and 2006. The sharp increase of electoral volatility roughly coincides with the rise of social media use in the Netherlands. Whether there is a causal relation is not clear.

As for political leaders in the Netherlands, most have long track records, e.g. Mark Rutte (PM and leader of VVD), Alexander Pechtold (D66), Sybrand Buma (CDA) and Emile Roemer (SP). There are, however, some notable newcomers. Jesse Klaver (born 1986; Groen Links) made quite an impression with a new campaign style. Not only was there a strong focus on social media, but his appearances in theaters were also very popular. He was compared to Canadian PM Justin Trudeau in style and appearance (Lang, 2017). Another notable new party leader is Thierry Baudet (FvD, flamboyant and controversial), as well as Sylvana Simons (Art1) a presenter turned politician fighting racism in the Netherlands.

Setting the Media Stage

Television is often named as one of the main causes of the decline of pillarization in the Netherlands. Although Dutch broadcasting had dedicated organizations for

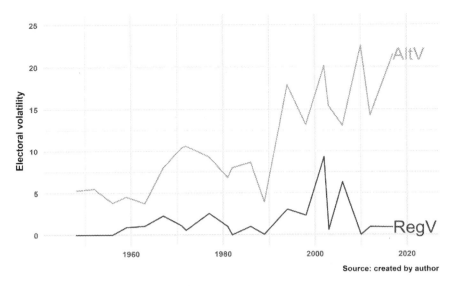

FIGURE 9.1 Electoral Volatility in the Netherlands 19xx–2017

Source: Figure created by Author

Note: RegV refers to electoral volatility, calculated as vote switching between existing parties, receiving at least 1% of the vote share in consecutive elections, including parties entering and exiting the party system from one election to the next one. AltV is similar to RegV but excludes entering and exiting parties. *Source:* Emanuele (2015)

each of the pillars in society, people could watch all programs and take note of different thoughts in society. Jumping to the 1990s and early 2000, the Internet became a new means for information sharing and news consumption and entertainment. This allowed politicians to circumvent journalists to reach a wider audience and for direct communication between politicians and citizens. In the Web 1.0 era, where websites and blogs were the dominant platforms, this was in effect still a one-sided broadcasting process (Bordewijk & Van Kaam, 1986; Van Dijk, 2012). The increased mediatization, reinforced by Web 2.0's social media, changed the political communication process even further. Political communication and campaigning became much more individualized and personalized, diminishing the role of the party apparatus: people and politicians are much more directly connected, although social relations on social media are often unreciprocated. As a result, social media are often still used as a means to broadcast and not so much to engage in discussions with all people online (Vergeer & Hermans, 2013). Mediatization of politics also entails increased personalization in political communication (Hermans & Vergeer, 2013; Kriesi, 2012). While in other countries there is strong evidence of "advanced personalizations" (cf. Berlusconi, Sarkozy and Blair; Helms, 2012), there is little evidence of advanced personalization in politics in the Netherlands. The only candidate that fits this label is Pim Fortuyn (killed in 2002), the flamboyant party leader of Lijst Fortuyn. Even though personalization may not be particularly present in the online realm of candidate campaigning in the Netherlands, personalization of politics seems to be a nonnegligible factor regarding party preference and vote choice (Gattermann & De Vreese, 2017). In the present study, we focus on candidates' behavior on Twitter. We raise the following research questions:

(1) How do candidates and party leaders in the Dutch elections of 2017 use Twitter?

    a   Types of communication patterns
    b   Types of sentiments

(2) How do communication patterns and sentiments change over time, in general and for specific conditions?

Understanding Candidates' and Leaders' Communication behavior in Social Media Campaigns

Political leaders are considered a special breed of people. They are deemed to share distinctive psychological traits, either because of their upbringing, their sex or even their gender. For instance, Andeweg and Berg (2003) show that first-borns and singletons are overrepresented among political leaders. This effect of being a first-born seems stronger among women as compared to men. O'Brien's (2015) comprehensive study on gender and political leadership shows that women rise to political leadership in minor opposition parties and parties that lost seats in the elections. They retain their position as long as the party is successful but leave when their party loses seats.

Defining leadership from a communication perspective takes a different turn. Ever since the arrival of social media, the increase of personalization of politicians in the media has taken hold and fallen under control of the individual politician. This is different for party leaders, who – at least for the larger parties – have assembled campaign teams to coordinate campaign efforts.

Communication Patterns

Dissecting communication behavior on social media entails distinguishing several communication dimensions. One dimension of tweets refers to different communications patterns. We distinguish four different types of mutually exclusive statuses. Broadcasting tweets are messages sent to no one in particular. These are often used to disseminate information or a candidate's viewpoint on a specific issue. Directed (@) tweets are specifically addressed to someone on Twitter. These types of tweets are a form of instigating a discussion or dialogue on

130 Maurice Vergeer

Twitter, or at least of informing someone on Twitter about an issue. It signifies a candidate is more extravert and more sociable. A third type of tweets are replies to someone's previously sent tweet, sometimes directly to a candidate, signifying a candidate's level of responsiveness and a willingness to engage with others on Twitter. A fourth type of tweet is a retweet: a candidate forwards a tweet sent by some else. It indicates the promotion, endorsement and support of a message sent by someone else. Previous research has shown that broadcasting tweets and replies are most common, while retweeting is less common (Graham, Jackson, & Broersma, 2016).

Sentiments in Tweets

Sentiment analysis is a relatively new method for analyzing content (Cambria, 2017). Candidates can be typified by not only the type of tweet but also the actual sentiment, irrespective of the topic being discussed. Candidates using specific sentiments in communication may lead people to create favorable attitudes towards them. In general, there are two overarching dimensions of sentiments: positive and negative. Research (Aaldering, van der Meer, & Van der Brug, 2018) shows that positive media portrayals of party leaders has a positive effect on people's intention to vote for the party. This effect is stronger in the campaign period. The reverse effect – negative portrayals of party leaders leading to lower voter intention – is present in off-campaign periods, but absent in campaign periods.

Explanations of Communication Patterns and Expressed Sentiments

To understand the differences in and causes of communication patterns and expressed sentiments, we will look at a party characteristics, candidate characteristics and how behavior and expressions change over time.

Populism

One particular aspect of political communication is populism. Mudde defines populism as "ideology that considers society to be ultimately separated into two homogeneous and antagonistic groups, 'the pure people' versus 'the corrupt elite', and which argues that politics should be an expression of the volonté générale (general will) of the people" (Mudde, 2004, p.543). Some additional characteristics that are tied to populism are thin-centered ideology, a charismatic leader, anti-establishment, direct communication to the people and personalization. Although populism doesn't seem to be increasing in Europe (Rooduijn, Lange, & Brug, 2014), it at least seems to have found a strong foothold. We expect that populism as a party and characteristic of leaders will be related how they use social media to communicate during the campaign.

Two parties in the Netherlands are considered to be populist: Party for Freedom, led by Geert Wilders; and the Socialist Party, led by Emile Roemer. Among the new political parties, three are considered ambiguous in terms of populism: Forum voor Democratie, GeenPeil and Voor Nederland. Experts disagree whether these parties are really populist (cf. Rooduijn, 2016), or, as Mudde (2018) argues, nativist (i.e. putting the native people first). Whether this has consequences for the way candidates from these parties use social media to communicate during the election campaign is unclear. Therefore, we will retain the following distinction: regular parties (non-populist), populist parties (PVV, SP) and the parties that are either populist or nativist. Because populist parties are anti-establishment, we expect that populist parties to be more negative in their online communication as compared to government parties. If nativist/populist parties are similar to populist parties (cf. Rooduijn, 2016), we expect them to be as negative towards government parties as populist parties.

Male and Female Communication

In the Netherlands the distribution of sex in party leadership is quite uneven. In the 2017 elections, of all 28 parties only four had female leaders. In parliament before the election of 2017, there were 57 women to 93 men. Female candidates are expected to communicate differently from male candidates. Women in general are expected to communicate more sociably and in more positive tone (Thelwall, Wilkinson, & Uppal, 2010). A reason why female candidates would want to use social media in electoral campaigning is to keep control over what others (e.g. newspapers) write about them (Bystrom et al., 2004).

Research on sex differences and social media use have produced inconsistent findings. Vergeer and Hermans (2013) show that female candidates were less likely to reciprocate in online social networking than male candidates. Otherwise, women are quite similar to men in their other types of online behavior (level of tweeting, connection to others and being followed by others). Web campaigning in general shows no difference between men and women either (Vergeer, Hermans, & Cunha, 2013). Carlson, Djupsund and Strandberg (2013) find female candidates to adopt blogging more often, as well as using it more extensively.

Experience in Parliament and on Twitter

One of the established perspectives on social media in political communication is the debate about normalization versus equalization: are social media able to change the power balance in the political playing field? So far, research seems to support the normalization thesis (Strandberg, 2013). The debate centers on who uses social media best and whether this is related to political power in terms of experience and incumbency.

132 Maurice Vergeer

Most candidates are no blank sheet when they enter the election campaign. Some have gained a lot of experience over the years in parliament, while others are political novices. Being an incumbent candidate and having gained experience in how to communicate in public may affect how social media are used. In terms of the amount of social media communication, incumbents might use social media to a lesser extent because their position in parliament is relatively safe. Their knowledge and experience in parliament and notoriety may give them an upper hand compared to challengers on the list. As a result, they might perceive it less urgent to actively campaign on social media. Moreover, social media use by an incumbent could, when misused, backfire and endanger their re-election for parliament. In a worst-case scenario, such a "social media fail" can turn into a social media meme, possibly damaging a politician's public image (cf. Haynes, 2014). Barisione (2009) argues that new and relatively unknown candidates (challengers) need to establish their public image to become salient for the constituency. Because they lack the easy access to traditional media channels incumbent parties have, new parties and candidates needs to resort to alternative and free options, such as social media and blogs, and present themselves as best as they can. This may be visible in the way candidates use sentiments in their tweets. Previous research on social media use by candidates shows mixed findings as to the role of incumbency and social media use. In Finland, incumbents use social media more extensively (Strandberg, 2013). In Germany, incumbent candidates are more likely to use Twitter; the use of Facebook is unrelated to incumbency (Metag & Marcinkowski, 2012).

Apart from experience in the political realm, candidates differ in the extent of experience on social media they have: what to tweet and what not, and how to tweet, as well as deciding when not to tweet. The length of time candidates have been active on Twitter might explain how candidates use Twitter. Previous research has shown that the time subscribed to Twitter increases the frequency of tweeting (Vergeer & Hermans, 2013). Whether this holds for different types of communication patterns and for sentiments as well is as yet unclear.

A different distinction is whether candidates are member of parties that are part of the government, or member of parties of the incumbent opposition, or are member of new parties. Some research has suggested that members of government parties in particular will not be active campaigners on social media, because – similarly to incumbent candidates – they have more to lose than to gain by social media campaigning. Members of opposition parties are similar to challengers in general and are therefore expected to be more active than candidates of government parties. Lastly, candidates of new parties are expected to campaign more extensively than members of government parties because these candidates are challengers and are not represented in parliament at all. We expect opposition parties not only to communicate more actively, but also to be positive in their communication in order to present themselves more favorably to voters. At the same time, they may also use negative communication when challenging other political parties or even criticize the establishment.

Twitter as a social medium also entails setting up online social networks. Although the number of followers is an important proxy for online popularity, candidates seeking out others on social media and connecting with potential voters reflects their willingness to engage with others or their inquisitiveness about what concerns people. We expect that seeking out more friends on Twitter will be positively related to engaging in types of communication patterns as well as positive expressions on Twitter.

We distinguish a number of statistical controls. First, ballot position: political parties rank their candidates' position on the ballot from high (party leader) to low (low-priority candidate), indicating the likelihood of being (re-)elected for parliament. Second, the number of followers candidates have on Twitter and, third, the number of times their Twitter account is listed — as proxies for their popularity on Twitter — are included as statistical controls.

Data, Measurements and Analysis

Sampling

The sample comprises all tweets (N = 254,369) by all candidates on Twitter (N = 902) in the period of January 1, 2017 to March 15, 2017 (Election Day). Candidates' tweets were collected using the R package rtweet (Kearney, 2016). Data on political parties and their candidates were obtained from the Election Committee (Kiesraad, 2017)

Measurements

We distinguish different *types of communication patterns* on Twitter: (1) tweets directed to no one specifically (19.1%), (2) tweets directed (@-tweets) to specific Twitter users (9.0%), (3) tweets as replies (24.3%) and (4) retweets (47.8%). Twitter's REST API indicates whether tweets are replies or retweets. Whether tweets were directed (@) or broadcasting tweets was based whether or not tweets contained an @-sign (but that were not replies). Subsequently, the binary measurements were aggregated at the candidate and day level. *Measurements of sentiment* were obtained by using a precompiled dictionary of words (NRC lexicon) reflecting degrees of sentiments (Jockers, 2017). These indicators point to eight sentiment dimensions. The *political leader* is defined as the candidate having the top position (i.e., number 1) on the ballot (i.e. the party leader). The classification of *populism* for parties was as follows: (1) populist parties, (2) nativist/populist parties and (3) regular parties (see Table 9.7 for classified parties). *Party type* was classified as follows: (1) government parties, (2) incumbent opposition parties and (3) new parties (see Table 9.7 for party classification). *Ballot position* of the candidates was obtained from the Election Committee as provided by the political parties. Position 1 on the ballot is reserved for party leaders, while higher ballot numbers refer

134 Maurice Vergeer

to less important candidates. *Candidate incumbency* was determined by comparing the candidate lists against the list of members of parliament. To measure *election events*, we distinguished seven election debates on radio and television and Election Day itself as specific days where candidates' activity on Twitter increases. The *number of followers* of candidates as well as the *number of times candidates' accounts were listed* on Twitter were obtained by use of Twitter's REST API.

Analysis

To test the expectations, we use growth curve analysis (Mirman, 2014). Because the dependent variables are count-measurements, we use negative binomial regression from the R package lme4 (Bates, 2010).

Findings

Descriptive Analyses

Figure 9.2 shows the average number of tweet for each communication pattern for regular candidates and party leaders over time. Overall, party leaders are more active than regular candidates across the campaign period. Over the course of the 2.5 months we see an increase of broadcasting tweets, directed tweets and retweets. Replies on Twitter seem to become less prevalent when Election Day comes closer. Interestingly, this finding is similar to online political discussions: the closer Election Day is, the fewer discussions take place in favor of broadcasting (Vergeer & Hermans, 2008).

Figure 9.3 shows the number of sentiments expressed in tweets by regular candidates and party leaders over the course of 2.5 months. All sentiments gradually increase, except for "disgust" and "fear", which level off close to Election Day. On Election Day, we see a sharp increase of all sentiments. Systematically, we see party leaders express sentiments more often than regular candidates do. Whether these differences persist when we take into account other explanations is determined in the following analyses.

Understanding Activities and Sentiments

Types of Tweets

Table 9.1 shows the findings regarding types of tweets. For all types of tweets, the closer Election Day comes, the more tweets are sent. This indicates that all types of activities increase across time. There are, however, no differences between party leaders and regular candidates regarding the use of these types of tweets.

Being a candidate from a populist party would suggest communicating more extensively, to vent discontent with the established political parties. The findings

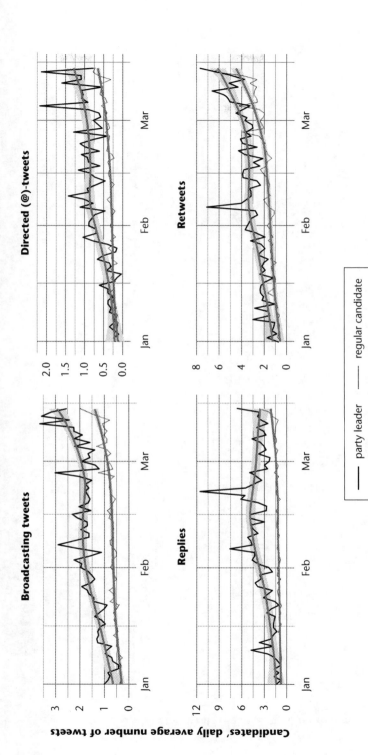

FIGURE 9.2 Candidates' Types of Tweets During the Election Campaign

Source: Figure created by Author

Note: Raw trends and smoothed trends (Loess) for party leaders and regular candidates.

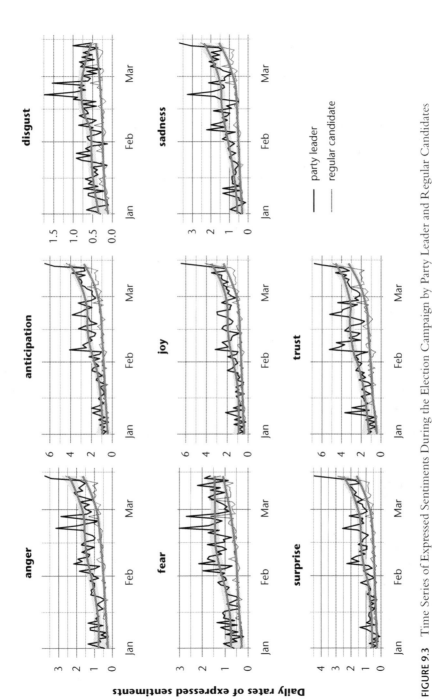

FIGURE 9.3 Time Series of Expressed Sentiments During the Election Campaign by Party Leader and Regular Candidates

Source: Figure created by Author

Note: Raw trends and smoothed trends (Loess) for party leaders and regular candidates.

TABLE 9.1 Growth Curve Analysis of Broadcasting, Directed, Replies and Retweets

	Broadcasting	Directed (@)	Replies	Retweets
Intercept	−1.823***	−3.288***	−3.119***	−0.921***
Date	58.838***	69.509***	74.973***	81.152***
Political leader (0=no, 1=yes)	−0.422	−1.204	−3.929	−1.075
Sex (0=male, 1=female)	−0.014	0.037	0.069	0.011
Populism				
populist		reference category		
non-populist	0.037	0.712***	0.636**	−0.251
nativist/populist	0.681**	1.600***	1.335***	0.846***
Party type				
government party		reference category		
opposition party	0.638***	0.807***	0.922***	0.956***
new party	0.517	0.527	0.915	0.997**
Incumbency	0.374*	0.094	0.184	0.31
Number of days on Twitter	0.219***	0.217***	0.272***	0.092
Ballot position	0.06	0.256	0.149	0.536***
Events	0.469***	0.345***	0.499***	0.532***
Number of friends[a]	0.401***	0.396***	0.515***	0.363***
Political leader*date	−21.868	12.58	−15.784	−19.3
Leader*sex	−0.282	−0.224	−0.865	0.803
Weekday				
Monday	−0.079***	−0.075***	−0.075***	−0.075***
Tuesday	0.069***	0.041**	0.079***	0.083***
Wednesday	0.127***	0.121***	0.204***	0.062***
Thursday	0.102***	0.127***	0.066***	0.080***
Friday	−0.006	0.014	−0.114***	−0.026*
Saturday	−0.013	0.113***	−0.002	0.062***
Sunday	−0.192***	−0.318***	−0.164***	−0.177***
Number of followers[a]	−0.078	−0.066	−0.277	−0.013
Number of times listed[a]	0.268*	0.238	0.535***	0.139
Log Likelihood	−52,707.40	−35,706.03	−46,102.89	−83,472.92
Akaike Inf. Crit.	105,476.80	71,474.05	92,267.77	167,007.80
Bayesian Inf. Crit.	105,753.90	71,751.19	92,544.91	167,285.00

Source: Table created by Author

Note: N candidates = 902, N days = 74; * $p < 0.1$; ** $p < 0.05$; *** $p < 0.01$; [a] original variables were divided by 10,000. Independent interval variables were mean centered.

show that populist candidates – as compared to non-populist and nativist/populist parties – distinguish themselves by sending fewer directed tweets and being less responsive (replies) than other candidates. This is contrary to expectation. Because populism serves the people, a question begs a reply, especially if the question originates from the people. Nativist/populist candidates, on the other hand, send significantly more original tweets, directed tweets, replies and retweets. As such, nativist/populist candidates seem to act more populist than established populists themselves. These findings suggest that the distinction between the established populist parties (PVV, SP) and the nativist/populist parties (VNL, GP, FVD) seems justified.

Candidates from opposition parties use different types of tweets more extensively than candidates from government parties. New parties do not utilize Twitter more than government parties, except for the easiest types of tweets to produce, namely retweets. This corroborates previously voiced interpretations that new parties lack the time and the skills to deploy social media as an election campaign tool, making it hard to make a change in the power distribution in parliament.

Candidate incumbency (political experience) shows only a positive effect for broadcasting tweets as compared to new candidates. However, they do not send directed tweets, replies or retweets more often than other candidates. As for Twitter experience, the longer a candidate is subscribed, the more original tweets, directed tweets and replies he or she will send. The number of retweets is unrelated to Twitter experience. These findings suggest that experienced Twitter users use more engaging and originally produced communication on Twitter, whereas newbies resort to "quick and dirty" retweets.

A candidate's position on the ballot shows a positive relation to retweets: the higher the ballot number (i.e., the less important the candidate is), the more retweets the candidate will send. A candidate's position on the ballot is unrelated to broadcasting tweets, directed tweets and replies.

Looking at specific events during the campaign, we see that on days with election debates and on Election Day itself, candidates are much more active on all types of tweets. Apparently, all candidates try to get the upper hand in terms of visibility and engagement in social media on these specific days.

Candidates that made a lot of friends on Twitter (i.e. following others) are also more active for all types of tweets, showing that creating online networks also entails more active communication with others. It signifies that being sociable is reflected in creating networks as well as more extensive communication.

Comparing weekdays to the weighted weekly average, we see that Mondays and Sundays are slow days: less than average activities for all types of tweets. Tuesdays, Wednesdays and Thursdays are most active for all tweet types. On Fridays, the engaging types of tweets (replies and retweets) are below the weekly average, while the original and directed tweets are equal to the weekly average. Saturdays only show above average activities for directed tweets and retweets.

As for the controls of online popularity, we see that attracting many followers on Twitter is unrelated to types of tweet activities. The more often candidates' accounts are listed, the more often candidates send tweet replies. Being listed is unrelated to candidates' activities of sending directed tweets and retweets.

Reviewing the interactions with party leadership, we see that the main effect of sex (which does not deviate from zero) is also absent for party leaders and regular candidates. Leadership does not interact with date either. For the interactions of leadership with populism and party type, we refer to Table 9.2 and Table 9.3. In the case of populism, the differences exist between types of parties and not

TABLE 9.2 Interaction Effects for Populism (Differences in Marginal Means)

	candidate			party leader		
	populist	populist	nativist/ populist	populist	populist	nativist/ populist
	nativist/ populist	non- populist	non- populist	nativist/ populist	non- populist	non- populist
broadcasting	−0.681	−0.037	0.643*	−2.118	0.016	2.134
directed	−1.600*	−0.713*	0.888	−2.883	−0.688	2.195
replies	−1.335*	−0.636*	0.699	−5.480*	−2.730	2.750
retweets	−0.846*	0.251	1.097*	−1.817	0.501	2.318

Source: Table created by Author

Note: * $p < 0.05$, two-tailed

TABLE 9.3 Interaction Effects for Type of Political Party (Differences in Marginal Means)

	candidate			party leader		
	government party	government party	incumbent party	government party	government party	incumbent party
	opposition party	new party	new party	opposition party	new party	new party
broadcasting	−0.638*	−0.518	0.121	−0.468	−1.141	−0.673
directed	−0.807*	−0.527	0.280	−1.424	−2.271	−0.847
replies	−0.922*	−0.915	0.007	−1.307	−3.017	−1.709
retweets	−0.956*	−0.997	−0.041	−1.714	−2.497	−0.783

Source: Table created by Author

Note: * $p < 0.05$, two-tailed

140 Maurice Vergeer

between candidates and party leaders. Interestingly, populist candidates are relatively silent as compared to those of nativist/populist parties (cf. directed, replies, retweets) and non-populist parties (cf. directed, replies). Nativist/populist party leaders are more responsive to reply than populist leaders. PVV's Geert Wilders particularly is known to rarely reply on Twitter. As for party type (Table 9.3), candidates of government parties are more silent than opposition parties in terms of broadcasting, directed tweets, replies and retweets.

Sentiments

Table 9.4 shows the models of expressed sentiments in tweets. All sentiments increase over time up to Election Day. The top four strongest increases over time are the negative sentiment of anger and the positive sentiments anticipation, joy and surprise. Party leaders do not differ from other candidates regarding their use of sentiments. Male and female candidates do not differ either regarding their expressed sentiments. Candidates from non-populist parties express fewer negative sentiments (disgust, fear, sadness) than populist parties, but they express positive sentiments at an equal rate. Candidates of nativist/populist express more sadness in their tweets as compared to populist parties but also express more positive sentiments overall (anticipation, joy, surprise and trust).

Distinguishing government, opposition and new parties, we see that candidates of opposition parties express more negative and more positive sentiments as compared to government party candidates. Candidates of new parties express themselves more positively and more negatively than candidates of government parties (except for disgust).

Incumbent candidates express more fear, while other sentiments are expressed equally as compared to new candidates. Experience on Twitter shows mixed results. More negative sentiments are expressed only for disgust and fear, while positive sentiments are expressed for anticipation, joy and trust.

The ballot position of candidates shows that the higher the position (the lower the number on the ballot), the less negative sentiments candidates express (except for disgust and sadness), and less positive sentiments across the board. Positive communication seems to be prevalent among these candidates.

On days of debates among party leaders and on Election Day, candidates express more positive and more negative tweets, as compared to other days. These events seem to engage candidates significantly.

Seeking out more friends on Twitter is related to the way candidates express themselves: more friends means expressing more positive and more negative sentiments. This suggests sociable candidates are also expressing more emotions.

To assess whether the day of the week affects the use of communication patterns, we compared these Twitter activities per day against the weighted mean. Sundays and Mondays are slow days for communicating specific sentiments. Positive sentiments are mostly prevalent on Tuesdays, Wednesdays and Thursdays.

TABLE 9.4 Growth Curve Analysis of Sentiments in Tweets

	anger	disgust	fear	sadness	anticipation	joy	surprise	trust
Intercept	−1.816***	−2.067***	−1.626***	−1.814***	−1.723***	−2.008***	−2.283***	−1.453***
Date	90.965***	32.865***	64.504***	75.753***	75.125***	79.977***	75.132***	67.204***
Political leader (0 = y, 1 = n)	−0.617	−0.619	−0.692	−0.726	−1.191	−1.676	−1.216	−1.451
Sex (0 = male, 1 = female)	−0.05	−0.001	0.003	−0.009	0.0002	0.023	−0.003	−0.003
Populism								
populist				reference category				
non-populist	−0.272	−0.667***	−0.513***	−0.363**	0.068	0.231	0.111	0.098
nativist/populist	0.709**	0.402	0.431	0.621**	0.901***	1.019***	1.057***	0.879***
Party type								
government party				reference category				
opposition party	0.821***	0.627***	0.781***	0.783***	1.002***	1.000***	0.910***	0.995***
new party	1.087***	0.55	0.913**	0.844**	1.354***	1.274***	1.053***	1.318***
Incumbency	0.317	0.137	0.370*	0.229	0.299	0.226	0.227	0.264
Number of days on Twitter	0.056	0.102*	0.103*	0.069	0.122**	0.111**	0.08	0.121**
Ballot position	0.359**	0.139	0.318**	0.219	0.548***	0.564***	0.424***	0.556***
Events	0.553***	0.471***	0.540***	0.704***	0.590***	0.585***	0.683***	0.580***
Number of friends	0.391***	0.367***	0.385***	0.399***	0.377***	0.384***	0.376***	0.383***
Leader*date	−31.059	−13.142	−22.02	−16.39	−4.927	−12.397	−16.234	−7.96
Leader*sex	−0.046	−0.407	−0.076	0.003	0.078	−0.03	−0.086	−0.067
Weekday								
Monday	−0.098***	−0.007	−0.097***	−0.064***	−0.088***	−0.116***	−0.078***	−0.081***
Tuesday	0.096***	0.028	0.059***	0.129***	0.114***	0.094***	0.114***	0.097***
Wednesday	0.157***	0.034	0.040*	0.121***	0.130***	0.137***	0.176***	0.118***
Thursday	0.059***	0.039	0.035	0.082***	0.094***	0.071***	0.063***	0.125***
Friday	−0.112***	−0.052*	−0.046**	−0.095***	−0.045**	−0.057***	−0.080***	−0.050***
Saturday	0.059***	0.01	0.074***	−0.027	0.025	0.066***	−0.021	0.055***
Sunday	−0.161***	−0.052*	−0.059***	−0.149***	−0.224***	−0.188***	−0.178***	−0.252***

(Continued)

TABLE 9.4 (Continued)

	anger	disgust	fear	sadness	anticipation	joy	surprise	trust
Number of followers	−0.105	−0.138	−0.125	−0.096	−0.051	−0.029	−0.07	−0.07
Number of times listed	0.246*	0.308**	0.268*	0.259*	0.191	0.176	0.226	0.225
Log Likelihood	−51,433.78	−31,999.50	−49,517.14	−48,095.85	−66,911.99	−61,717.04	−48,351.05	−76,220.55
Akaike Inf. Crit.	102,929.60	64,061.00	99,096.29	96,253.70	133,886.00	123,496.10	96,764.10	152,503.10
Bayesian Inf. Crit.	103,206.70	64,338.14	99,373.43	96,530.84	134,163.10	123,773.20	97,041.24	152,780.20

Source: Table created by Author

Note: N candidates = 902, N days = 74; * $p < 0.1$; ** $p < 0.05$; *** $p < 0.01$; [a] original variables were divided by 10,000. Independent interval variables were mean centered.

Expressing negative sentiments on the midweek days seems more random in the sense that there seems no consistency across different dimensions of sentiments: anger and sadness are expressed above average on midweek days, but disgust and fear are on par with the weekly average.

Reviewing the interaction effects between communication patterns on Twitter, we see that as Election Day comes closer, the expressed sentiments for leaders as compared to regular candidates does not increase or decrease. The combination of sex and leadership does not affect the expression of any sentiments. The interaction effects of populism and party type are reported in Table 9.5 and Table 9.6. Table 9.5 indicates that nativist/populist candidates are more expressive in terms of anticipation joy, surprise and trust, as compared to populist candidates. Populist candidates, however, are more expressive in terms of disgust and fear as compared to non-populist candidates. Nativist/populist candidates are more expressive as compared to non-populist candidates, except for fear. As for party leaders, nativist/ populist leaders are more expressive in terms of disgust, fear, sadness, and surprise.

Table 9.6 shows that government party candidates express fewer sentiments as compared to opposition parties. Compared to candidates of new parties, this applies to five of eight sentiments. This indicates that government party candidates are less expressive than candidates. Party leaders are mostly quite similar in how they express themselves. A few exceptions to the rule are new party leaders, who are more expressive in terms of anticipation, joy and trust, as compared to government party leaders.

TABLE 9.5 Interaction Effects for Populism (Differences in Marginal Means)

	candidate			party leader		
	populist	populist	nativist/ populist	populist	populist	nativist/ populist
	nativist/ populist	non-populist	non-populist	nativist/ populist	non-populist	non-populist
anger	−0.709*	0.272	0.981*	−1.594	0.645	2.239
anticipation	−0.901*	−0.068	0.832*	−2.040	−0.049	1.991
disgust	−0.402	0.667*	1.069*	−1.645	0.738	2.383*
fear	−0.431	0.513*	0.944	−1.541	0.679	2.220*
joy	−1.019*	−0.231	0.789*	−2.318	−0.380	1.938
sadness	−0.621	0.363	0.983*	−1.789	0.537	2.326*
surprise	−1.057*	−0.111	0.946*	−2.169	−0.032	2.137*
trust	−0.879*	−0.098	0.781*	−2.085	−0.197	1.888

Source: Table created by Author

Note: * $p < 0.05$, two-tailed

144 Maurice Vergeer

TABLE 9.6 Interaction Effects for Type of Political Party (Differences in Marginal Means)

	candidate			party leader		
	government party	government party	opposition party	government party	government party	opposition party
	-	-	-	-	-	-
	opposition party	new party	new party	Opposition Party	new party	new party
anger	-0.821*	-1.087*	-0.267	-1.184	-2.356	-1.172
disgust	-0.627*	-0.550	0.077	-0.835	-1.562	-0.727
fear	-0.781*	-0.913	-0.132	-1.082	-2.007	-0.925
sadness	-0.783*	-0.844	-0.061	-0.927	-1.965	-1.038
anticipation	-1.002*	-1.354*	-0.352	-1.523	-2.930*	-1.407
joy	-1.000*	-1.274*	-0.275	-1.958	-3.227*	-1.268
surprise	-0.910*	-1.053*	-0.143	-1.619	-2.697	-1.079
trust	-0.995*	-1.318*	-0.323	-1.705	-3.112*	-1.407

Note: * $p < 0.05$, two-tailed

Conclusion

This chapter set out to understand candidates' communication patterns and their use of sentiments during the 2017 election campaign in the Netherlands. We focused specifically on party leaders to determine whether they differed from regular candidates. The findings show that party leaders hardly distinguish themselves from regular candidates. Main effects as well as almost all interaction effects did not show any differences. There are a number of possible reasons. The first reason is that candidates and party leaders simply may not be that different from each other. The difference might not so much be the leader versus the candidate, but the politician versus regular citizen. Another – statistical – reason is that the sample of party leaders is quite small, namely 28 leaders. They need to be very different to stand out from all other candidates. Our study took a rigorous approach: besides including leadership as a distinguishing factor, we also included candidates' ballot positions. As a measurement of importance to the party, ballot position is a metric scale of importance in which candidate has a score, instead of two groups which lump non-leader party candidates in a single group. Even though leadership didn't surface as a distinguishing factor, ballot position shows that more important candidates for the party retweet more often, while also expressing more anger and fear as negative sentiments and anticipation, joy, surprise and trust as positive sentiments. These findings suggest that being higher up the ladder in the party distinguishes the candidate in aforementioned communication behavior, but the mere fact of being the party leader doesn't indicate exceptional communication behavior.

Besides the distinction in type of candidate, we also tested for sex differences. The Netherlands has an uneven representation of sex in parliament and among party leaders. But we see no sex differences in patterns of communication and expressed sentiments. This is in contrast to previous findings by Vergeer and Hermans (2013), who found women to be less responsive on Twitter, as well as other descriptive studies on gender roles in politics (Meeks, 2016). As for the longitudinal dimension of this study, we showed that Twitter activity steadily increased over time. We also identified regular weekly patterns in Twitter communication. Apart from these regular patterns, we also identified significant increases in Twitter activities on days when political debates were scheduled.

Besides the aforementioned conclusions about sex differences and leadership, probably the most striking differences are found regarding populism. Distinguishing three types of parties (non-populist, populist and nativist/populist), our study revealed that the nativist/populist parties in particular, and not the populist candidates as we expected, stand out as being particularly active as well as expressive in terms of sentiment use on Twitter. Populist candidates were less direct and less responsive in communication as compared to native/populist candidates. Populist candidates were also less expressive in using sentiments than nativist/populist candidates. But overall, nativist/populist parties have a distinct way of communicating on Twitter. Whether this means nativist/populist parties are more populist than the populist parties, or whether they are a different type of party (cf. nativist), additional content analysis of the tweets is necessary.

APPENDIX

TABLE 9.7 Political Parties and Their Leaders in the 2017 Parliament Elections

Abbreviation	Party leader	Party name in Dutch	Party name in English	Party type	Populism
50PLUS	Henk Krol	50Plus	50Plus	opposition	regular
Art1	Sylvana Simons	Artikel 1	Article 1	new	regular
CDA	Sybrand Buma	Christen Democratisch Appel	Christian Democratic Appeal	opposition	regular
CU	Gert-Jan Segers	ChristenUnie	Christian Union	opposition	regular
DBB	Ad Vlems	De Burger Beweging	The Civil Movement	new	regular
D66	Alexander Pechtold	Democraten 66	Democrats 66	opposition	regular
DENK	Tunahan Kuzu	DENK	DENK	opposition	regular
FvD	Thierry Baudet	Forum voor Democratie	Forum for Democracy	new	nativist/ populist
GP	Jan Dijkgraaf	GeenPeil	No Poll	new	nativist/ populist
GL	Jesse Klaver	Groen Links	Green Left	opposition	regular
JL	Florens van der Spek	Jezus Leeft	Jezus lives	new	regular
LP	Robert Valentine	Libertarische Partij	Libertarian Party	new	regular
LidK	Jan Heijman	Lokaal in de Kamer	Local in parliament	new	regular

Political Communication Patterns **147**

Abbreviation	Party leader	Party name in Dutch	Party name in English	Party type	Populism
MenS	Tara-Joelle Fonkl	MenS en Spirit/ Basisinkomen Partij/V-R	Man and Spirit/Basic Income Party/V-R	new	regular
NS	Peter Plasman	Niet Stemmers	Non-Voters	new	regular
NW	Alfred Oosenbrug	Nieuwe Wegen	New Ways	new	regular
OP	Hero Brinkman	OndernemersPartij	Entrepreneur Party	new	regular
PvdA	Lodewijk Asscher	Partij van de Arbeid	Labour Party	government	regular
PvdD	Marianne Thieme	Partij voor de Dieren	Party for the Animals	opposition	regular
PP	Ancilla van der Leest	Piratenpartij	Pirate Party	new	regular
PVV	Geert Wilders	Partij voor de Vrijheid	Party for Freedom	opposition	populist
SP	Emile Roemer	Socialistische Partij	Socialist Party	opposition	populist
SGP	Kees van der Staaij	Staatkundig Gereformeerde Partij	Reformed Political Party	opposition	regular
SNL	Mario van den Eijnde	StemNL	Vote Netherlands	new	regular
VNL	Jan Roos	Voor Nederland	For Netherlands	new	nativist/ populist
VDP	Burhan Gökalp	Vrije Democratische Partij	Free Democratic Party	new	regular
VP	Norbert Klein	Vrijzinnige Partij	Free-Minded Party	new	regular
VVD	Mark Rutte	Volkspartij voor Vrijheid en Democratie	People's Party for Freedom and Democracy	government	regular

Source: Table created by Author

References

Aaldering, L., van der Meer, T., & Van der Brug, W. (2018). Mediated leader effects: The impact of newspapers' portrayal of party leadership on electoral support. *The International Journal of Press/Politics, 23*(1), 70–94. https://doi.org/10.1177/1940161217740696

Andeweg, R. B., & Berg, S. B. V. D. (2003). Linking birth order to political leadership: The impact of parents or sibling interaction? *Political Psychology, 24*(3), 605–623. https://doi. org/10.1111/0162-895X.00343

Barisione, M. (2009). So, what difference do leaders make? Candidates' images and the "conditionality" of leader effects on voting. *Journal of Elections, Public Opinion and Parties, 19*(4), 473–500. https://doi.org/10.1080/17457280903074219

Bates, D. M. (2010). *lme4: Mixed-effects modeling with R*. New York: Springer.

Blumenthal, S. (1980). *The permanent campaign: Inside the world of elite political operatives*. Boston, MA: Beacon Press.

Bordewijk, J. L., & Van Kaam, B. (1986). Towards a new classification of tele-information services. *Intermedia, 14*, 16–21.

Bystrom, D. G., Robertson, T., Banwart, M. C., & Kaid, L. L. (Eds.). (2004). *Gender and candidate communication: VideoStyle, WebStyle, NewStyle* (1st edition). New York: Routledge.

Cambria, E. (2017). *A practical guide to sentiment analysis*. New York: Springer Berlin Heidelberg.

Carlson, T., Djupsund, G., & Strandberg, K. (2013). Taking risks in social media campaigning: The early adoption of blogging by candidates. *Scandinavian Political Studies, 37*(1), 21–40. https://doi.org/10.1111/1467-9477.12011

Emanuele, V. (2015). Dataset of electoral volatility and its internal components in Western Europe (1945–2015). GESIS Data Archive. Retrieved August 15, 2018, from http://dx.doi.org/10.7802/1112

Gattermann, K., & De Vreese, C. H. (2017). The role of candidate evaluations in the 2014 European Parliament elections: Towards the personalization of voting behaviour? *European Union Politics, 18*(3), 447–468. https://doi.org/10.1177/1465116517704519

Graham, T., Jackson, D., & Broersma, M. (2016). New platform, old habits? Candidates' use of Twitter during the 2010 British and Dutch general election campaigns. *New Media & Society, 18*(5), 765–783. https://doi.org/10/cv2q

Hale, S. A. (2017, October 1). Twitter trials 280 characters, but its success in Japan is more than a character difference – Oxford Internet Institute. Retrieved October 2, 2017, from www.oii.ox.ac.uk/blog/success-is-more-than-a-character-difference/

Haynes, J. (2014, March 6). Cameron's "on-the-phone-to-Obama" selfie tweet parodied by celebrities. *The Guardian*. Retrieved August 22, 2018, from www.theguardian.com/politics/2014/mar/06/celebrities-parody-camerons-on-the-phone-to-obama-selfie-tweet

Helms, L. (2012). Democratic political leadership in the new media age: A farewell to excellence? *The British Journal of Politics and International Relations, 14*(4), 651–670. https://doi.org/10.1111/j.1467-856X.2011.00495.x

Hermans, L., & Vergeer, M. (2013). Personalization in e-campaigning: A cross-national comparison of personalization strategies used on candidate websites of 17 countries in EP elections 2009. *New Media & Society, 15*(1), 72–92. https://doi.org/10.1177/1461444812457333

Jockers, M. (2017). syuzhet: Extracts sentiment and sentiment-derived plot arcs from text (Version 1.0.4). Retrieved January 21, 2018, from https://cran.r-project.org/web/packages/syuzhet/index.html

Kearney, M. W. (2016). rtweet: Collecting Twitter data (Version 0.3.6). Retrieved November 11, 2016, from https://CRAN.R-project.org/package=rtweet

Kiesraad (2017, April 18). Results general elections 2017 [Uitslag Tweede Kamerverkiezing 2017 in ODS-bestandl] [rapport]. Retrieved April 18, 2017, from www.kiesraad.nl/adviezen-en-publicaties/rapporten/2017/3/proces-verbaal-zitting-kiesraad-uitslag-tweede-kamerverkiezing-2017/uitslag-tweede-kamerverkiezing-2017-in-excel

Kriesi, H. (2012). Personalization of national election campaigns. *Party Politics*, *18*(6), 825–844. https://doi.org/10.1177/1354068810389643

Kriesi, H. (2014). The populist challenge. *West European Politics*, *37*(2), 361–378. https://doi.org/10.1080/01402382.2014.887879

Lang, C. (2017, March 16). This politician is being dubbed the "Dutch Justin Trudeau." Retrieved August 21, 2018, from http://time.com/4704610/jesse-klaver-dutch-justin-trudeau/

Lijphart, A. (1989). From the politics of accommodation to adversarial politics in the Netherlands: A reassessment. *West European Politics*, *12*(1), 139–153. https://doi.org/10.1080/01402388908424727

Meeks, L. (2016). Gendered styles, gendered differences: Candidates' use of personalization and interactivity on Twitter. *Journal of Information Technology & Politics*, *13*(4), 295–310. https://doi.org/10.1080/19331681.2016.1160268

Metag, J., & Marcinkowski, F. (2012). Strategic, structural, and individual determinants of online campaigning in German elections: Determinants of online campaigns in Germany. *Policy & Internet*, *4*(3–4), 136–158. https://doi.org/10.1002/poi3.14

Mirman, D. (2014). *Growth curve analysis and visualization using R* (1st edition). Boca Raton, FL: Chapman and Hall/CRC.

Mudde, C. (2004). The populist Zeitgeist. *Government and Opposition*, *39*(4), 541–563. https://doi.org/10.1111/j.1477-7053.2004.00135.x

Mudde, C. (2018, January 4). Six persistent misunderstandings about populism [Zes hardnekkige misverstanden over populisme]. Retrieved August 25, 2018, from https://decorrespondent.nl/7786/zes-hardnekkige-misverstanden-over-populisme/3122938789410-3988f8ec

O'Brien, D. Z. (2015). Rising to the top: Gender, political performance, and party leadership in parliamentary democracies. *American Journal of Political Science*, *59*(4), 1022–1039. https://doi.org/10.1111/ajps.12173

Poushter, J. (2017, April 20). Not everyone in advanced economies is using social media. Retrieved February 5, 2018, from www.pewresearch.org/fact-tank/2017/04/20/not-everyone-in-advanced-economies-is-using-social-media/

Rooduijn, M. (2016, December 6). Are VNL, FvD and GeenPeil populistic? [Zijn VNL, FvD en GeenPeil populistisch?]. Retrieved August 25, 2018, from http://stukroodvlees.nl/zijn-vnl-fvd-en-geenpeil-populistisch/

Rooduijn, M., Lange, S. L. de, & Brug, W. van der. (2014). A populist Zeitgeist? Programmatic contagion by populist parties in Western Europe. *Party Politics*, *20*(4), 563–575. https://doi.org/10.1177/1354068811436065

Strandberg, K. (2013). A social media revolution or just a case of history repeating itself? The use of social media in the 2011 Finnish parliamentary elections. *New Media & Society*, *15*(8), 1329–1347. https://doi.org/10.1177/1461444812470612

Thelwall, M., Wilkinson, D., & Uppal, S. (2010). Data mining emotion in social network communication: Gender differences in MySpace. *Journal of the American Society for Information Science and Technology*, *61*(1), 190–199. https://doi.org/10.1002/asi.21180

Van Dijk, J. A. G. M. (2012). *The network society* (3rd Revised edition). London: Sage.

Vergeer, M., & Hermans, L. (2008). Analysing online political discussions: Methodological considerations. *Javnost – The Public*, *15*(2), 37–56.

Vergeer, M., & Hermans, L. (2013). Campaigning on Twitter: Microblogging and online social networking as campaign tools in the 2010 General Elections in the Netherlands. *Journal of Computer-Mediated Communication*. https://doi.org/10.1111/jcc4.12023

Vergeer, M., Hermans, L., & Cunha, C. (2013). Web campaigning in the 2009 European Parliament elections: A cross-national comparative analysis. *New Media & Society, 15*(1), 128–148. https://doi.org/10.1177/1461444812457337

Vergeer, M., Hermans, L., & Sams, S. (2013). Online social networks and micro-blogging in political campaigning. The exploration of a new campaign tool and a new campaign style. *Party Politics, 19*(3), 477–501. https://doi.org/10.1177/1354068811407580

Walter, A. S. (2014). Negative campaigning in Western Europe: Similar or different? *Political Studies, 62*, 42–60. https://doi.org/10.1111/1467-9248.12084

PART 3

Social Media and Grassroots Politics

10

'TWITTER WAS LIKE MAGIC!'

Strategic Use of Social Media in Contemporary Feminist Activism

Kaitlynn Mendes

Introduction

On 8 March 2016, British feminist Carolyn Criado Perez was jogging through London when she noticed that among the 11 statues in Parliament Square, none were of women. This wasn't the first time Criado Perez had noticed and brought attention to the absence of women in the public sphere. In 2012, she rose to prominence after protesting that Elizabeth Fry, the only woman featured on a British banknote other than the Queen, would be replaced by Winston Churchill. Although the campaign was a success, with author Jane Austen appearing on £10 banknotes in 2017, it led to a mass trolling campaign against her (Criado Perez 2013). Traumatized by these events, her first reaction was to let this issue of the statues go. But after running back through Parliament Square on her route home, she reflected how deeply wrong it was, that in 2016, there were no female statues in this historic space:

> But as I carried on running through St. James's Park, I couldn't get those 11 statues of men out of my head. As I rounded Green Park, I realized I was composing the campaign text in my head. When I came back around to Buckingham Palace, I gave in to the inevitable: I sat on the ground, and set up a petition on my phone.
>
> *(Criado Perez 2018)*

Tweeting the campaign link, the petition garnered 85,000 signatures, and on 1 May 2018, the statue of suffragist Millicent Fawcett was unveiled. While not all feminist campaigns lead to such tangible or high-profile outcomes, Criado Perez' story is just one example of the ways contemporary feminists are harnessing

154 Kaitlynn Mendes

social media in their campaigns for gender equality. Since around 2011, with the rise in what is often known as the 'fourth' wave of feminism (see Baumgardner 2011; Rivers 2017), we have witnessed a rise in popular movements and initiatives from 'tech-savvy and gender-sophisticated' (Baumgardner 2011) feminists who challenge rape culture, sexism, harassment and misogyny in and through digital technologies.

While fourth-wave feminists make use of many digital technologies and platforms, this chapter explores the ways and experiences of feminist leaders who harness social media to organize, launch and communicate their feminist views to a range of stakeholders, participants and authority figures. Although the chapter provides new insights into *why* and *how* feminist leaders use social media in their activism, it raises broader questions about the use and effectiveness of social media to instigate social, cultural and ideological change.

Methodology

This chapter draws on evidence derived from over a decade studying high-profile feminist social movements or initiatives such as Hollaback!, Everyday Sexism, Who Needs Feminism?, *The Vagenda* and SlutWalks, all of which gained popularity after going 'viral' across 'legacy' mainstream or alternative feminist media. Drawing from an ethnographic approach which makes use of various methods (Reinharz 1992), I have conducted close observations of dozens of on and offline communities, semi-structured interviews with over fifty feminist leaders and textual analysis of nearly 2,000 pieces of digital data, including tweets, Facebook posts, blogs and memes. Although as scholars we of course have much to learn from studying social media texts, ethnographic approaches have long been favoured by feminist scholars for making the lives, voices and experiences of participants visible (Mitchell and Reid-Walsh 2008; Reinharz 1992). When applied in the context of digital practices, ethnographic approaches simultaneously offer the capacity to 'contextualise media engagements as part of a broader social terrain of experience' (Gray 2009, 14). An ethnographic approach therefore helps researchers make sense not only of feminist leaders' practices, but also of their experiences and motivations of using social media for activist purposes. As a highly rich and diverse dataset, methods such as qualitative content and thematic and critical discourse analysis were used to analyse various modes of communication within, between and across social media sites, campaigns and actors.

Why Social Media?

Like other contemporary grassroots activists, feminists are drawn to social media because they are already using these platforms and they are free, easy to use and have the potential to spread one's message to a large audience while maintaining control of their message. These themes were repeated time and again throughout

'Twitter was Like Magic!' **155**

my interviews with various feminist leaders. As Heather Jarvis, co-founder of the anti-victim-blaming movement SlutWalk, told me:

> We knew quickly that with an online world and social media there are distances you can cross that couldn't have been crossed 20 years ago. . . . We started a Facebook page, Twitter account and a website, and it says a lot about how we share our messages. People have communities and connections online so social media is important. We didn't have money or head offices, and we were not an official organisation and we didn't have status. So, the best way to function was online. When we are not doing events at a physical location with an attendance, our discussions take place online.

After the first SlutWalk took place in 2011 in response to a Toronto police constable advising that 'women should avoid dressing like sluts in order not to be victimized' (Kwan 2011), marches soon sprang up organically in over 200 cities around the world (Mendes 2015). David Wraith, an organizer for SlutWalk St. Louis, also confirmed the importance of social media: 'I don't know how we would have done it [organized the SlutWalk] without the internet, without Facebook and Twitter.' These comments are particularly significant given that all the initiatives under study here gained their popularity after going viral – often in response from one simple tweet or Facebook post which was picked up, shared and amplified through digital technologies.

While some of my interview participants stepped up as 'leaders' after an initiative became popular, many more could be considered 'founders' of their respective campaigns. Although founders such as Heather Jarvis (SlutWalk), Laura Bates (Everyday Sexism) and Emily May (Hollaback!) were aware of the *potential* of social media to spread their message, they were truly surprised at its power in spreading their message so quickly, to people all over the world. This rang true for Rhiannon Lucy Cosslett, co-founder of the satirical British feminist blog *The Vagenda*, which pokes fun at mainstream media's treatment of women. After launching the blog, went viral overnight, Cosslett reflected:

> It had 30,000 hits overnight on the first night we launched it. By the next day, I was looking at it and it kept going up and up and up and up and it was really crazy. We didn't really publicise it. We didn't even have a Twitter when it launched. . . . I think people saw something that they found really resonated with them, and they started sharing it on social media amongst themselves. And that's why more and more people started looking at it.

In recent years, there has been a growing body of scholarship exploring affect in media cultures. This scholarship has extended to the role of affect in social movements and the ways it travels and makes content salient in digital spaces (see Bore et al. 2018; Hillis et al. 2015; Kuntsman 2012; Mendes et al. in press;

156 Kaitlynn Mendes

Papacharissi 2015). Scholars such as Sara Ahmed (2004) have noted the way affective content, such as that discussed by Cosslett above, forge 'sticky' and emotional entanglements between contributors and readers who share, like and comment on these posts. From a practical perspective, many feminist leaders (current and aspiring) use social media not only because it is free at the point of access (there is more to be said about resources needed to buy technological infrastructure in the first place), but also potentially powerful, affective and capable of reaching a wide audience.

Where this section drew from interviews with feminist leaders to explain *why* feminist leaders use social media, the next section unpicks *how* feminist leaders use it, focusing on three key organizational purposes: 1) to launch feminist initiatives; 2) to recruit participants and fellow leaders; and 3) to communicate with a variety of stakeholders.

Launching Feminist Initiatives

As discussed in the previous section, social media has been a key space through which most fourth-wave feminist initiatives are launched. Closely tied in with why they are relying on these platforms, many leaders explained that they used social media because they lacked other resources (financial), knowledge (digital literacy) or skills (coding/web design/writing a press release) which previous feminist leaders may have used to launch or initiate action (see for example Barker-Plummer 2000). Significantly, most of the organizers interviewed were not already part of established feminist organizations or communities, and many did not even identify as feminists until several weeks or months into their campaign (see also Mendes et al. in press). Instead, many were simply 'moved' (Jasper 1997) by an event or experience such as blatant or ubiquitous sexism in their lives, irked by statements that feminism is irrelevant or angered by the ways victims are blamed for being sexually assaulted, and used social media to vent their frustration or issue a call to arms.[1]

As mentioned above, SlutWalk was founded when Heather Jarvis read a news article via Facebook about a police officer's advice that women could avoid being raped if they did not dress like 'sluts.' Angered by the ways such statements reinforced victim-blaming myths, Jarvis responded by posting a message on Facebook asking if anyone wanted to march to the Toronto police station to protest. A friend of a friend responded, and as Jarvis recounted, the first march was soon advertised via Facebook, Twitter and a website. Who Needs Feminism? experienced a similar genesis when it began at Duke University in 2012 as a class project. Here, students hung posters around campus featuring photographs of students holding hand-crafted signs explaining why feminism was relevant. After some posters were defaced, the class decided to publish these photos online via Facebook and Tumblr, accepting submissions from the public (see Mendes et al. in press; Seidman 2013). Their project soon went viral and to date, the official

'Twitter was Like Magic!' **157**

Who Needs Feminism? Tumblr blog has received over 5,000 submissions, with over sixty other universities worldwide starting their own Who Needs Feminism? campaigns and separate websites (Seidman 2013).

Because social media plays such a key role in spaces where many people socialize, connect and, increasingly, find information about the world, it therefore makes sense that contemporary activists are harnessing its power, relative affordability and ease of use to launch and publicize various initiatives. Social media are also key tools used to recruit fellow leaders, participants and allies.

Recruiting Leaders and Participants

Throughout semi-structured interviews, surveys and informal conversations with around 300 participants at feminist events, social media emerged as key spaces to recruit leaders, participants and other allies. As discussed above, SlutWalk co-founder Heather Jarvis was only one of many organizers who connected with her co-founder via social media. The two key organizers of SlutWalk Bangalore, Asqeer Sodhi and Dhillan Chandramowli, met when a mutual friend shared Dhillan's Facebook message 'asking if anyone wanted to get involved' with the SlutWalk. Recounting how their local march started, Dhillan jokingly remarked: 'It pretty much started over a [Facebook] status update.'

While dispersed yet pre-existing social networks played a key role in connecting organizers such as Asqeer and Dhillan, in this age of 'communicative capitalism' (Dean 2009), it is important to recognize the role algorithms play in what users are exposed to. SlutWalk Seattle organizer Laura Delgado first became aware of the local march when it appeared on her Facebook feed as something she might be interested in, prompting her to do further research and eventually get involved:

> I first heard about it [SlutWalk] on social media, on Facebook. It popped up as a page that I might like, and that's how I first found out about it. I then found the website and . . . decided to volunteer.

Although there has recently been much criticism of the ways social media algorithms shape the content (and advertising) on our news feeds (see Beer 2009; van Dijck and Poell 2013), one may optimistically interpret Delgado's experience as a positive effect of communicative capitalism for providing an opportunity to learn more about feminist initiatives and become involved. In the words of SlutWalk Newcastle organizer Lizi Gray, social media has made feminism 'more accessible for those who wouldn't consider themselves feminists or perhaps the "femi-curious."'

For those organizers who, rather than founding their respective campaign, became involved after it was up and running, it is significant that only a few first heard about it via legacy media. Significantly, even when hearing about it from

158 Kaitlynn Mendes

friends, it was rarely through literal 'word of mouth,' but through information shared via social media. Such findings indicate the importance of online communities and 'digital socialities' (Postill and Pink 2012) in spreading news of feminist activism, information and mobilization. Both surveys and informal conversations with hundreds of participants at various SlutWalk events in the UK and USA further highlighted the role social media played, not only for recruiting (potential) leaders, but participants as well. Many participants I spoke with discussed the way they not only learnt about feminist events via social media but also used it to coordinate their attendance and travel plans to various events.

Taking a phenomenological approach, I was particularly interested in the ways participants used social media, and how they made use of opportunities and features enabled by its technological affordances and architecture. Facebook is of significance here because in addition to one's own individual page which hosts a timeline, 'about' section, list of friends and photos, it also allows the creation of 'events' to which individuals are invited and asked to indicate if they are 'interested,' attending or not (they can also select 'maybe'). As many participants told me, being able to quickly identify which if any friends were 'interested' or 'attending' an event was a significant deciding factor on their participation. This unique affordance of Facebook was not only important for raising the profile and coordination of people to offline events, but also played a significant role in mainstream coverage of the movement, where the press frequently commented on how many people indicated via Facebook that they planned to attend, as a means of adding credibility to the movement (see Mendes 2015).

While the previous sections have discussed how feminist leaders make use of social media to organize events or initiatives, recruit leaders and participants, we of course cannot overlook the ways these platforms are used to communicate with a range of stakeholders. Conceptually, we may think of their communication as speaking 'out' to the public, 'across' to stakeholders and 'up' to power.

Speaking 'Out' to the Public

A basic scan across the social media accounts of various high-profile feminist initiatives demonstrates the highly active nature of these 'fourth-wave' feminists. Although feminist leaders often engage in composing original tweets or messages, a key activity is to share mainstream media content which they believe will be of interest to (potential) supporters or participants. When speaking about the sharing of various news articles, features or think pieces, David Wraith of SlutWalk St. Louis stated that sharing content on their Facebook page was as important way of engaging public interest and support to issues around rape culture and victim-blaming year-round, rather than the few times per year when a march or event takes place. This sort of engagement is important for community building – and for creating affective ties and what Dean (2009) calls 'feelings' of community. Although scholars (Dean 2009; Fuchs 2014) have argued that these

'Twitter was Like Magic!' **159**

affective feelings are coupled with mere *fantasies* of participation through feeling political, other research challenges such assertions, arguing that affective connections, even if they may result in no tangible changes to policy or law, nevertheless directly change and shape participant's experiences, interactions, expectations and everyday lives in profound ways (Mendes et al. in press).

Many feminist leaders I spoke with were cognisant and aware of the highly affective nature of content they share on social media, and often posted or shared links to pieces to deliberately cause outrage and indignation. As SlutWalk St. Louis organizer David Wraith explained:

> Whenever I see an article or news article which I think is relevant and I post it on the Facebook page and we get a lot of feedback and views. . . . For better or worse the SlutWalk page gives us an outlet for less cheery news.

Wraith's comments here support scholars who note how anger and outrage are useful emotions to foster when trying to instigate social change because most people will only become 'open to the possibility of protest' in response to a 'moral shock' or something truly upsetting or disturbing (Jasper 1997). As one SlutWalk St. Louis tweet with an accompanying hyperlink read: 'CNN Reports on The "Promising Future" of Rapists, Who Are "Very Good Students" fb.me/2fDogiNqn.' Such tweets are not only meant to highlight the existence of a rape culture and prevalence of victim-blaming attitudes, but to mobilize the public and 'curate' (Fileborn 2018) feelings of anger which can be harnessed to demand cultural change. In curating these highly charged emotions, feminist leaders are furthermore facilitating the emergence of *affective publics* (Papacharissi 2015). As Papacharissi explains:

> Social media facilitate engagement in ways that are meaningful. Most notably they help activate latent ties that may be crucial to the mobilization of networked publics. . . . On a secondary level, networked publics are formed as crowds coalesce around both actual and imagined communities. The connective affordances of social media then not only activate the in-between bond of publics but enable expression and information sharing that liberates the individual and the collective imaginations.
>
> *(Papacharissi 2015, 20–23)*

Digital networks, then, are useful for solidifying experiences and connecting otherwise disparate social media users through highly affective ties which scholars are wise to not simply dismiss because they may not lead to immediate policy change.

For example, in my recent interviews with those who have used the #MeToo hashtag to share personal experiences of violence and harassment, participants are

160 Kaitlynn Mendes

adamant that sharing their stories have led to small but noticeable changes in their lives, including making men in their lives more aware of what constitutes violence or harassment, and feeling more confident to call it out. As one 30-something participant based in the Netherlands told me after sharing her #MeToo story via Facebook:

> I am probably even more vocal about it [sexual harassment] now. I was probably a feminist my entire life and fighting this battle against sexism my entire life, and since #MeToo I have been even more aware of it, and I am also more willing to share my story. Just three weeks ago we were on a trip and a friend of ours was there and we were talking about #MeToo, and he was saying that he didn't understand it, all these stories coming out, and it's getting way out of hand. I just went to Facebook and I grabbed my phone and I said read this [my story] . . . and that sort of immediately shut him up and made him realise he was talking shit. So once your story is out there it is easier to talk about it.

Although movements such as #MeToo may not lead to tangible policy changes, there is no doubt amongst my participants that it has led to small but meaningful changes in their everyday lives.

Speaking 'Across' to Stakeholders

In addition to communicating to the public, feminist leaders make use of platform affordances to connect with one another – both publicly and privately. Regarding the former, an examination of many feminist social media pages provides evidence of the ways these groups regularly comment, share items, posts or news stories from relevant stakeholders and 'speak across' to one another through their social media accounts (see also Mendes 2015). This speaking across to one another is done through different tactics depending on the platform. On Twitter, for example, it is common to see @replies. According to Honeycutt and Herring (2009), the use of @users is a form of 'addressivity' used to gain specific people's attention to facilitate conversation or activism (cited in boyd et al. 2010, 2). In other cases, feminist leaders share or re-tweet content, including news of upcoming events, fundraising initiatives or comments which 'talk back' to a larger rape culture, as a means of making such content (and communities) visible (boyd et al. 2010; hooks 1989; Mendes 2015). According to scholars, such 'copying and rebroadcasting' is in fact part of a 'conversational ecology in which conversations are composed of a public interplay of voices that give rise to an emotional sense of shared conversational context' (boyd et al. 2010, 1).

Social media was used not only to speak with fellow organizers, but also to make connections with other stakeholders and feminist allies. For example, in May 2012, the Who Needs Feminism? Facebook page shared a link to Hollaback!, enticing readers to click through to the site by asking 'Did you know that "62% of women are harassed on college campuses? . . . Take a look." ' My analysis of nearly 2,000 tweets, Facebook posts and memes shows how feminist initiatives or campaigns regularly speak out to feminist organizations, charities or other feminist initiatives. Clearly, then, feminist groups are forming communities not only amongst themselves, but also with a range of other feminist organizations, individuals and communities who are committed to challenging patriarchy and other forms of oppression. As SlutWalk Newcastle organizer Lizi Gray argued, one of the most important aspects of social media was the way it allowed them to 'get in touch with other existing feminist groups that we didn't know were out there.'

What is not visible through textual analysis, but was regularly discussed throughout interviews with feminist leaders, is their reliance on social media to communicate privately with one another and other relevant stakeholders. For example, many SlutWalk organizers made use of Facebook's closed and secret groups to form organizer communities. The architecture of Facebook allows for the creation of group pages where users can post updates, poll the group and start group chats. Group pages offer three security levels: secret groups (only members can see that the group exists, who is in it and what is posted); closed groups (anyone can see that the group exists and who is in it, but not what members post); open groups (anyone can see that the group exists, who is in it and what is posted) (Facebook 2014). As Heather Jarvis explained on the use of secret groups:

> It's wonderful we can connect and share resources. If we are having problems with permits, others within these groups can help. Or people use these groups to answer things like 'How do people deal with the challenge with the media?' or 'What are great slogans for signs?'

Indeed, although difficult to access, sometimes let alone know they exist, scholars have recently highlighted the growing importance of these closed and 'safe spaces' to organize, congregate and support one another as they do feminism 'in the network' (Clark-Parsons 2017; Mendes et al. in press; Rentschler and Thrift 2015).

Speaking 'Up' to Power

Although the previous sections have challenged assertions that social media engagement leads to mere fantasies of participation or *feelings* of community rather than tangible social change (see Dean 2009; Fuchs 2014), it is worthwhile pointing out that many feminist initiatives and communities *do* regularly use social media to speak 'up' to power in the hope of achieving tangible changes in policies, laws and practices. Indeed, in my interviews, several feminist leaders discussed how they successfully used social media to communicate with key stakeholders when traditional tactics such as email and letters didn't work. Melanie Keller from Hollaback! Baltimore explained how she had been emailing local businesses to

162 Kaitlynn Mendes

take part in a safety programme for LGBT communities but had no response – but when they used Twitter, they got an immediate response. As Melanie reflected: 'I was, like, are you effing kidding me, I literally e-mailed you four times and got no response. But Twitter was like magic.' In this example, Twitter was instrumental in connecting Hollaback! Baltimore with key stakeholders whom they had previously been unable to reach and recruiting them to take part in their community programme.

While working with local businesses may help create tangible changes for those within discreet geographical locations, there is ample evidence of how feminist initiatives and movements regularly (attempt to) speak with powerful figures such as politicians, policy makers or the police. In April 2018, the main Hollaback! chapter tweeted an advert for a forthcoming National March Against Rape Culture, including an @reply to US Republican and Secretary of Education Betsy Devos, who attracted feminist critiques for dismantling protection for campus sexual assault survivors. The tweet read: 'All survivors deserve protection and support from their institutions. By marching we are demanding that @Betsydevos and the Trump administration uphold Title IX for survivors. buff.ly/2HzrJoW#NMARC.'

Similarly, it's quite common to see feminist campaigns 'talk back' (hooks 1989) to mainstream media through tagging or @ing them in their social media posts. On 19 April 2018, Everyday Sexism wrote an @reply to *The Sun* newspaper for its sexist coverage of New Zealand Prime Minister Jacinda Ardern. Responding to the article titled: 'Sadiq Khan poses for selfie with right-on Canadian leader Justin Trudeau and New Zealand's pregnant leftie PM,' the tweet read: 'Hey guess what? @sunpolitics? Jacinda Ardern has a name too! #everydaysexism.' This tweet is an example of the ways feminist leaders regularly use social media to highlight sexist or inaccurate coverage, presumably to raise consciousness, hold others to account and transform existing practices and ideologies.

What is less known, however, is how effective these tactics are. Although scholars have documented instances where mainstream media responded to feminist critiques (see Durham 2013; Shaw 2012) in general, it is not clear how much attention they pay to feminist critiques or their social media interactions. In this case, I found no evidence that *The Sun* either responded to Everyday Sexism's tweet or altered this headline, but this does not mean that such critiques are ignored or don't result in long-term change. In recent years, scholars have shown the way vocal feminists have become increasingly 'visible, forceful, and . . . effective' at using digital technologies to secure alternative forms of justice and ideological change (see Jane 2017b, 2; Durham 2013; Fileborn 2017; Salter 2013; Shaw 2012). Indeed, many activists have indicated that rather than targeting specific policy or legal changes, 'changing people's hearts and minds' is a key goal (see Keller 2013, 6). Such change is achieved through 'discursive activism' – or 'political speech . . . that intervenes in hegemonic discourses, and that works at the level of language to change political cultures' (Shaw 2011; see also Mendes 2015; Mendes et al. in

'Twitter was Like Magic!' **163**

press; Shaw 2012; Young 1997). Taking a Foucauldian approach, discursive activism understands that 'power is everywhere' (Foucault 1991, 63), and that hegemonic ideologies are not only reinforced by those in official positions of power but are instead dispersed and pervasive. If discourses are powerful, then, ideologies can only be challenged through discursive interventions, which require talking, listening and debate. Ideological change takes time, may not be immediately evident and can be hard to trace. This, however, does not mean that change is not happening, only that we as scholars must broaden our tools to detect it, such as through longitudinal analysis of content, and ethnographic approaches which allow us to interrogate the values, ideologies and practices of those in power.

Conclusion

Through semi-structured interviews with over fifty feminist leaders of high-profile campaigns; close observations of dozens of on and offline communities; and textual analysis of nearly 2,000 digital feminist texts, this chapter provided insights into how and why feminists are turning to social media as part of their activist campaigns. Although much can be learnt about social media practices through textual analysis, ethnographic approaches provide significant 'behind the scenes' understanding of some very practical ways and reasons why social media platforms have been enthusiastically adopted by contemporary feminists as they seek to disrupt patriarchal ideologies and practices. The chapter revealed the importance of social media as a key space to launch feminist initiatives, recruit fellow leaders and participants, communicate with a range of stakeholders and, ultimately, (attempt to) shift fundamentals of power in important ways. Indeed, this chapter demonstrates how social media has given a voice to those with few resources and little money, who would otherwise have little-to-no means of talking back to a sexist society or inserting feminist views and counter-discourses. In this sense, social media has had a profound impact on the terrain of modern feminist activism.

While it is of course important and interesting to explore how and why contemporary activists use social media, a more fundamental issue at stake is how effective these tools and modes of communication are at disrupting oppressive structures and practices – in a sense, how they speak to power to achieve social change. When answering this question, it is important to take a Foucauldian approach which recognizes the diffuse nature of power. Therefore, in addition to examining the ways feminist leaders speak 'up' to politicians and media organizations, we must not forget the ways that speaking out to the public and across to stakeholders are necessary steps in transforming powerful ideologies which, for example, maintain rape culture, rape myths and patriarchal power structures. It is through looking at these communicative practices, and through speaking with leaders and participants, that we may better understand what contemporary feminist initiatives can achieve beyond broad headlines, or victories won by those such as Criado Perez which opened the chapter.

164 Kaitlynn Mendes

Finally, while initiatives such as #MeToo, Hollaback! and Everyday Sexism are regularly celebrated in mainstream media, particularly for their creative use of digital technologies, interviews with leaders demonstrate the unglamorous and often painful work of activism. This includes the ways they are regularly subjected to highly sexualized trolling, harassment and abuse (see Mendes 2015; Mendes et al. in press). As highly affective work, many leaders suffer from burn-out and fatigue, which has left some with mental health issues and has caused others to withdraw from activism all together (Mendes et al. in press). As a result, work is needed on the short, medium and long-term impact of activism, and their range of both self-care and 'digital defence' strategies (Mendes and Ringrose 2018) used to cope with arising challenges. Moving forward, while it is of course important to ask questions about what digital feminist activism *does*, it is increasingly important to ask questions about how it's felt and experienced, going beyond big data trends or mass media analysis to explore the *lived experiences* of participants as they engage in activism.

Note

1 Beyond the scope of this study, Alyssa Milano's 2017 tweet that those who have experienced sexual harassment or assault should reply to her message with the words 'me too' demonstrates the often unexpected and powerful ways the public become mobilized in and through social media.

References

Ahmed, Sara. 2004. *The Cultural Politics of Emotion*. Edinburgh: Edinburgh University Press.

Barker-Plummer, Bernadette. 2000. "News as a feminist resource? A case study of the media strategies and media representation of the National Organization for Women, 1966–1980." In *Gender, Politics and Communication*, edited by Annabelle Sreberny and Liesbet van Zoonen, pp. 121–59. New York: Hampton Press Inc.

Baumgardner, Jennifer. 2011. *F'em, Goo, Gaga, and Some Thoughts on Balls*. Berkeley: Seal Press.

Beer, David. 2009. "Power through the algorithm? Participatory web cultures and the technological unconscious." *New Media & Society* 11(6): 985–1002.

Bore, Inger-Lise, Anne Graefer, and Allaina Kilby. 2018. "This pussy grabs back: Humour, digital affects and women's protest." *Open Cultural Studies* 1(1): 12–29. https://doi.org/10.1515/culture-2017-0050

boyd, danah, Golder, Scott, and Lotan, Gilad. 2010. "Tweet, tweet, retweet: Conversational aspects of retweeting on Twitter." *Proceedings of HICSS-42*, Persistent Conversation Track. Kauai, HI: IEEE Computer Society, January 5–8.

Clark-Parsons, Rosemary. 2017. "Building a digital Girl Army: The cultivation of feminist safe spaces online." *New Media & Society*: 1–20. /doi.org/10.1177/1461444817731919

Criado Perez, Carolyn. 2013. "After the Jane Austen announcement I suffered rape threats for 48 hours, but I'm still confident the trolls won't win." *New Statesmen*, 27 July. www.newstatesman.com/media/2013/07/after-jane-austen-announcement-i-suffered-rape-threats-48-hours-im-still-confident-tro.

Criado Perez, Carolyn. 2018. "Despite a barrage of hate, I put a statue of a woman where only men stand." *CNN*, 24 April. https://edition.cnn.com/2018/04/24/opinions/millicent-fawcett-statue-caroline-criado-perez-intl/index.html.

Dean, Jodi. 2009. *Democracy and Other Neoliberal Fantasies: Communicative Capitalism and Left Politics*. Durham, NC: Duke University Press.

Durham, Meenakshi Gigi. 2013. "Vicious assault shakes Texas town." *Journalism Studies* 14(1): 1–12.

Facebook. 2014. "Groups." *Facebook*, www.facebook.com/about/groups.

Fileborn, Bianca. 2017. "Justice 2.0: Street harassment victims' use of social media and online activism as sites of informal justice." *British Journal of Criminology* 57: 1482–501.

Fileborn, Bianca. 2018. "Naming the unspeakable harm of street harassment: A survey-based examination of disclosure practices." *Violence Against Women*. doi.org/10.11 77/1077801218768709

Foucault, Michel. 1991. *Discipline and Punish: The Birth of a Prison*. London: Penguin.

Fuchs, Christian. 2014. *Digital Labour and Karl Marx*. New York and Oxford: Routledge.

Gray, Mary. 2009. *Out in the Country: Youth, Media, and Queer Visibility in Rural America*. New York: NYU Press.

Hillis, Ken, Susannna Paasonen, and Michael Petit. 2015. *Networked Affect*. Cambridge, MA: MIT Press.

Honeycutt, C. and Herring, S. (2009). 'Beyond microblogging: Conversation and collaboration via Twitter', *Proceedings of the Forty-Second Hawai'I International Conference on System Sciences* (HICSS-42), pp. 1–10.

hooks, bell. 1989. *Talking Back: Thinking Feminist, Thinking Black*. Boston, MA: South End Press.

Jane, Emma A. 2017a. *Misogyny Online: A Short (and Brutish) History*. London: Thousand Oaks and New Delhi: Sage.

Jane. Emma A. 2017b. "Feminist digilante responses to a slut-shaming on Facebook." *Social Media + Society:* 1–10. doi.org/10.1177/2056305117705996.

Jasper, James M. 1997. *The Art of Moral Protest: Culture, Biography, and Creativity in Social Movements*. Chicago, IL: University of Chicago Press.

Keller, Jessalynn M. 2013. ""Still alive and kicking": Girl bloggers and feminist politics in a "postfeminist" age." PhD Dissertation. Austin: University of Texas at Austin.

Kuntsman, Adi. 2012. "Introduction: Affective fabrics of digital cultures." In *Digital Cultures and the Politics of Emotion*, edited by Athina Karatzogianni and Adi Kuntsman, 1–17. New York: Palgrave.

Kwan, Raymond. 2011. "Don't dress like a slut: Toronto cop." *Excalibur*, 8 February, www.excal.on.ca/dont-dress-like-a-slut-toronto-cop/.

Mendes, Kaitlynn. 2015. *SlutWalk: Feminism, Activism & Media*. Basingstoke: Palgrave Macmillan.

Mendes, Kaitlynn, and Jessica Ringrose. 2018. "Mediated misogyny, trolling and digital defense strategies." *Public Feelings, Dissent Acts*. Goldsmiths University, 18 June.

Mendes, K., J. Ringrose, and J. Keller. In press. *Digital Feminist Activism: Girls and Women Fight Back Against Rape Culture*. Oxford: Oxford University Press.

Mitchell, Claudia and Jacqueline Reid-Walsh, Eds. 2008. *Girl Culture: An Encyclopedia*. Westport, CT: Greenwood Press.

Papacharissi, Zizi. 2015. *Affective Politics: Sentiment, Technology, and Politics*. Oxford: Oxford University Press.

Postill, John and Sarah Pink. 2012. "Social media ethnography: The digital researcher in a messy web." *Media International Australia* 145(November): 123–34.

Reinharz, Shulamit. 1992. *Feminist Methods in Social Research*. Oxford: Oxford University Press.

Rentschler, Carrie and Samantha Thrift. 2015. "Doing feminism in the network: Networked laughter and the 'Binders Full of Women' meme." *Feminist Theory* 16(3): 329–59. https://doi.org/10.1177/1464700115604136

Rivers, Nicola. 2017. *Postfeminism(s) and the Arrival of the Fourth Wave: Turning Tides*. Basingstoke: Palgrave Macmillan.

Salter, Michael. 2013. "Justice and revenge in online counter-publics: Emerging responses to sexual violence in the age of social media." *Crime Media Culture* 9(3): 225–42.

Seidman, Rachel. 2013. "Who needs feminism? Lessons from a digital world." *Feminist Theory* 39(2): 549–62.

Shaw, Frances. 2011. "(Dis)locating feminisms: Blog activism as crisis response." *Outskirts*, 24(May), www.outskirts.arts.uwa.edu.au/volumes/volume-24/shaw.

Shaw, Frances. 2012. "'Hottest 100 women': Cross-platform discursive activism in feminist blogging networks." *Australia Feminist Studies* 27(74): 373–87.

van Dijck, José, and Thomas Poell. 2013. "Understanding social media logic." *Media and Communication* 1(1): 2–14. https://ssrn.com/abstract=2309065

Young, Stacey. 1997. *Discourse, Politics and the Feminist Movement*. London and New York: Routledge.

11

#UNSETTLING CANADA 150, ONE TWEET AT A TIME

How Indigenous Leaders Use Twitter to Resist and Reframe Mainstream News in Canada

Brad Clark

When Canada Day arrived in 2017, marking the 150th anniversary of Confederation, the contrast to the nation's centennial 50 years earlier could hardly have been starker. Back in 1967, Canadians were streaming through the exhibits at Expo '67 in Montreal, waving flags and humming along to Bobby Gimby's upbeat ode to the nation: "CA-NA-DA, one-little-two-little-three Canadians, we love thee . . ." For a young, sparsely populated country of just 20 million people, it was just as much a source of pride as the bicentennial in the United States nine years later. In 2017, Canada's sesquicentennial was similarly marked with songs, block parties, barbecues and fireworks, but this time there were thousands of people on the sidelines of the celebrations. On Parliament Hill in Ottawa, traditional First Nations dancers performed near a big "Canada 150" banner, not far from a teepee erected as part of a larger "reoccupation" protest to the festivities. Later that day Prime Minister Justin Trudeau conceded to reporters that "everyone needs to understand that even as we celebrate, people have different perspectives and that there are a large number of Indigenous people who don't feel like celebrating" (Coyle, 2017). For many First Nations, Métis and Inuit people, marking 150 years of Confederation, a period of coerced relocation and reserves, prohibition of cultural practices, residential schools and forced assimilation seemed profoundly inappropriate and insulting and failed to take into account their own histories dating back thousands of years. In the months leading up to Canada Day, Indigenous peoples, led by a group of loosely affiliated activists, worked to recast the 150th narrative and "succeeded in defining the sesquicentennial as an occasion to consider past harms, unmet promises and unfinished business" (Coyle, 2017).

This chapter examines the grassroots campaign to shift the narrative of nationhood and bring Indigenous perspectives to the social media sphere and beyond in the months leading up to the 150th anniversary. Hashtags of Indigenous resistance

168 Brad Clark

are traced through the Twitter accounts of nine Indigenous leaders and activists and two group accounts, with significant social media followings. That activity is then compared with coverage of Canada 150 in the digital editions of the *National Post*, the *Toronto Star* and the *Globe and Mail*. An analysis of the two datasets shows frames that appeared in the tweets of the Indigenous account holders show up in the mainstream news discourse, and with much greater frequency than has historically been afforded Indigenous points of view. Similar to the findings by the authors in other sections of this book, this study shows that social media tools in the hands of an informal but active network of "soft leaders" have the power to shape perceptions of issues in society, or at least in this case, in the way they are represented in mainstream news media. In a theoretical sense, the analysis points to an emerging model of transmedia agenda-setting and gatekeeping in which Indigenous leaders have disrupted and decolonized news production norms, at least to some degree, making space for Indigenous perspectives so often under-represented or missing in news content. Practically, however, the study suggests that in the digital age Indigenous leaders are recontextualizing the narrative of European colonization, forcing the nation to debate the morality of long cherished icons and images.

Mainstream News, Indigenous Peoples and Social Media

Studies have shown that mainstream news coverage of First Peoples in Canada has long been characterized by stereotypes, sensationalism and racist preconceptions (see Harding, 2010; Anderson & Robertson, 2011; Fleras, 2011; Pierro et al., 2013; Clark, 2014). CBC journalist Duncan McCue, a member of the Chippewas of Georgina Island First Nation in southern Ontario, captures this on the website he developed for reporting on Indigenous communities with the "WD4 Rule on How Indians Make The News": as Warriors, Drunk, Drumming, Dancing or Dead (McCue, 2015). On a theoretical level, scholars have identified an "us-versus-them" binary, a "colonial dichotomy," settler versus Indian in the 19th century, law-abiding citizen versus protester in the context of blockades and demonstrations in the present (Lambertus, 2004; Wilkes, Corrigall-Brown, & Ricard, 2010, cited in Clark, 2014). At the same time, mainstream media are also prone to under-representing Indigenous peoples (Clark, 2013). An analysis of news coverage in 171 print and online news organizations in the province of Ontario over three years found "Aboriginal-related stories are barely on the radar of most media outlets" (Pierro et al., 2013, p. 17). The analysis shows just .28 per cent of all the news stories produced were about Indigenous issues.

For First Nations, Métis and Inuit in Canada, Indigenous media have offered content that better represents their perspectives, cultural practices and issues. News organizations – such as the Aboriginal Peoples Television Network (APTN), *Windspeaker* and *Wawatay News*, to name a few – challenge the tropes of First Peoples through self-representation, revealing their own culture and "historical

#Unsettling Canada 150 **169**

realities to themselves and the broader societies that have stereotyped or denied them" (Ginsburg, 1994, p. 378). For Alia (2003), self-representation is necessitated by the "poverty and distorting of mainstream coverage," making it "imperative for indigenous people to develop their own news outlets" (p. 37). When "the means of production" are controlled by Indigenous storytellers, power binaries and long-held stereotypes are replaced by authentic Indigenous voices and perspectives. Social media functions much the same way. Indigenous users have total control over the content they share. There is no mainstream gatekeeper in place determining whether any given post meets a broad test of newsworthiness; friends and/or followers receive the message unfiltered. McMahon (2013) describes this as "digital self-determination" where Indigenous peoples challenge "oppressive structures" through the use of "networked digital infrastructures" – including social media – to "shape their own community-based media organizations". Others have noted that Indigenous peoples often lack the political resources or power to influence governments but can use social media as "mobilising grounds for Indigenous connective activism" (Duarte, 2017, p. 2). Burrows (2016) explains how the "Indigenous mediasphere" now includes traditional forms (print and broadcast) as well as "user-generated" content, allowing leaders and activists – as well as their followers – to "debate, challenge and provide counter-discourses to government policy and practice and mass media representations of their communities" while countering "the mass media's exclusion of Indigenous voices" (p. 13). In other words, unfiltered messages in social media can influence and potentially foster awareness, activism and political change. The most often cited example of this is the Idle No More movement, launched primarily by three Indigenous women in 2012 (John, 2015, p. 41). It started in an internet chat room over concerns about an omnibus bill, C-45, and its impact on treaty rights, resource development and the environment. To raise the alarm, the hashtag #IdleNoMore was used to spread the word about a series of teach-ins and demonstrations: "Digital tactics included flash mob prayer rallies at locations defining neoliberal reach, including highways, busy city intersections in financial districts, shopping malls, and border crossings" (Duarte, 2017, p. 5). The movement gained momentum and spread through Canada and the United States as the hashtag was shared over and over again.

Notably, Idle No More organizers and participants have been wary of official Indigenous leadership such as the Assembly of First Nations (AFN), a national body in Canada modeled after the United Nations, criticizing "the representation of the chiefs and advocat[ing] for a more basic democratic organization of First Nations" (John, 2015, p. 43). Idle No More remains a "grassroots movement" operating outside official First Nations leadership over concerns of co-option by Indigenous and non-Indigenous governments, politicians and corporate interests (Duarte, 2017, p. 5). This grassroots model of leadership has served as a template for other activist campaigns, such as the #Sealfie promotion of the Inuit seal hunt, calls for a national inquiry into Missing and Murdered Indigenous Women

(MMIW) across Canada or the Dakota Access Pipeline encampment in Standing Rock in 2016 (see Rodgers & Scobie, 2015; Felt, 2016; Martini, 2018).

Scholars – including some of the authors in this volume – have described this form of direction from behind the scenes in social media movements as "soft leadership." The term is not pejorative of the commitment to a given cause, but rather a feature common to egalitarian, collective action. A study examining the campaign for an MMIW inquiry conceptualizes soft leadership broadly as the "users who generate viral tweets, especially those retweeted daily by countless other users in an otherwise leaderless network" (Felt, 2016, p. 4). Gerbaudo (2012) suggests that soft leadership takes advantage of "the interactive and participatory character of the new communication technologies" in order to bring "a degree of coherence to people's spontaneous and creative participation in the protest movements". Castells (2015) has considered social movements in the digital age and links a non-hierarchical network of activists to the "digital mediation" of collective action. He looks at the Occupy movement and the Arab Spring, but his findings also apply to the leadership behind many Indigenous campaigns, in which "the careful and strategic uses of digital media to network regional publics, along with international support networks, have empowered activists in new ways". Indigenous social actors have successfully utilized this approach.

"Settler–Indian" Binary Extended: Canada 150–#Resistance150

Commemoration of Canada's sesquicentennial was steeped in politics right from the start. The Conservative government of Stephen Harper initiated plans for a celebration on the theme "strong, proud and free," but when the Liberals under Justin Trudeau took office, "they redrew public servants' marching orders to focus on diversity, reconciliation with Indigenous peoples, the environment and youth" (Hannay, 2017, p. A1). The additional focus on Indigenous peoples was undoubtedly motivated by the release – just as the Liberals took office – of the final report of the Truth and Reconciliation Commission, established as part of the Indian Residential School Settlement Agreement between school survivors and the federal government "to learn the truth about what happened in the residential schools and to inform all Canadians" (Truth and Reconciliation Commission of Canada, 2015a). The commission spent six years traveling the country and heard from over 6,000 witnesses who described being forced to leave their families, often for years, and to abandon their cultural practices, religion and languages, and who suffered all manner of abuse. The report concludes the system was intended "to indoctrinate children into a new culture – the culture of the legally dominant Euro-Christian Canadian society, led by Canada's first prime minister [John A. MacDonald]" (Truth and Reconciliation Commission of Canada, 2015b).

The commission's findings, which labeled government policy towards Indigenous peoples as "cultural genocide," undoubtedly forced the new Liberal government to broaden the mandate – at least officially – to recognize the role of Indigenous peoples in nationhood. The more inclusive remit came with a budget of a half-billion dollars to cover infrastructure programs and websites promoting events, but also projects deemed frivolous, such as a "red couch tour" in which two artists toured the country with a sofa to gather testimonials from Canadians (Hannay, 2017). The federal government urged Canadians to celebrate "what it means to be Canadian" and communities from coast to coast to coast organized hundreds of events.

Many Indigenous people across Canada strongly objected to the notion that the anniversary was something to celebrate. In their experience, European settlers took over their lands and traditional territories, while Ottawa imposed the reserve system of segregation, outlawed cultural practices and separated families, brutally enforcing assimilation through residential schools. The lives of First Nations, Métis and Inuit in Canada are often much different than those of non-Indigenous Canadians: many communities are without potable water; Indigenous people are murdered at seven times the national rate and incarcerated at disproportionately high levels; they experience "jaw-dropping" rates of suicide; and their life expectancy is 10 to 15 years shorter than in the wider population (Selley, 2017). Moreover, the nation's nominal age of 150 years excludes the long history of First Peoples in Canada, which obviously predates Confederation. As one writer notes, the "birth" of Canada also marks the "end of a way of life and the beginning of a new reality that was grim, painful and murderous" (Renzetti, 2017).

Towards the end of 2016, as the federal government and many Canadians began to gear up for 150th festivities, a group of Indigenous activists was laying the groundwork for a campaign to counter the dominant narrative implicit in Canada 150. As in the case of Idle No More, these leaders did not represent specific nations, band councils or national bodies. Tanya Kappo, a Cree activist; Anishinaabe artist and storyteller Isaac Murdoch; Michif visual artist Christi Belcourt; and well-known Métis author Maria Campbell decided they could not commemorate a "a history that ignores the tumultuous relationship between indigenous peoples and the rest of Canada" (Dunham, 2017). They came up with the hashtag #Resistance150 "as a way to inspire other indigenous people to reclaim what they lost during colonization" and to draw attention to issues of climate change and resource extraction. Around the same time, another group of Indigenous leaders was discussing a similar campaign. An initiative called "Unsettling Canada 150," with ties to the Idle No More movement and the Defenders of the Land Network, established a comprehensive website with videos, news releases, readings, a "call to action" form and links to Facebook events (Unsettling Canada 150, 2017). See Figure 11.1.

The digital activism associated with #Resistance150 and Unsettling Canada 150 included a consistent presence on Twitter. An account dedicated to the anti-colonial message, @Resistance150, included hashtags underscoring Indigenous perspectives on Canada 150, including #Unsettle150, #Colonialism150,

172 Brad Clark

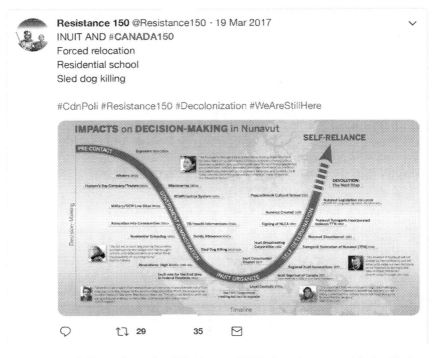

FIGURE 11.1   A Tweet from the @Resistance150 Twitter Account with the Hashtag #Canada150

Source: https://twitter.com/search?l=&q=%23Canada150%20from%3AResistance150&src=typd&lang=en

#Genocide150, #Racism150 and #Reoccupation. The account has put out over 3,300 tweets since it was established in January 2017 (twitter.com, 2017a). These tweets often contain memes, graphics or statements detailing inequalities between non-Indigenous people and Inuit or First Nations citizens related to drinking water, suicide rates, income and employment and education. They explicitly reject the assumption that Canada has existed for only 150 years, as captured in this tweet: "Get over #Canada150, it's #Canada15000 mofos" (@Resistance 150, 2017b). Particularly in the seven months leading up to Canada Day 2017, Twitter became the site of digital resistance to Canada 150, an expression of social media activism led by grassroots organizers that would be shared by Indigenous peoples from nations, settlements and communities in all parts of Canada.

Canada 150 and Indigenous Activism on Twitter

The Twitter activity around themes of Indigenous activism, resistance and resilience and Canada 150 was extensive. For purposes of this analysis, data from 11 Twitter accounts are considered. Nine users were selected based on connections as organizers of the Unsettle/Resistance movements, their prominence as Indigenous leaders or artists or their recognition as prolific social media activists in Canada. Almost all of them tally followers in the tens of thousands. The other two accounts are associated with activist groups, Idle No More and Unsettling Canada 150, referenced earlier. The individual accounts belong to: Tanya Tagaq, the well-known musician, artist and author from Iqaluktuutiaq, Nunavut; Pam Palmater, a Mi'kma lawyer from the Eel River Bar First Nation in New Brunswick, a prominent social justice advocate and associate professor at Ryerson University in Toronto; Cindy Blackstock, a member of the Gitksan First Nation, an academic, and the Executive Director of the First Nations Child and Family Caring Society of Canada; Chelsea Vowel, who uses the name @âpihtawikosisân on Twitter, a Métis writer and educator from manitow-sâkahikan (Lac Ste. Anne), Alberta; Terrill Tailfeathers, a Blackfoot activist from Treaty 7 territory in southern Alberta; and Christi Belcourt, Isaac Murdoch, Tanya Kappo and Russ Diabo, all discussed above as people behind the initial #Unsettle social media campaigns.

Tweets from those accounts were collected on the basis of hashtags that would emerge in the social media campaign. These included: #Colonialism150, #Resistance150, #Genocide150, #Unsettling150 and of course #Canada150. Versions of these, such as #UNsettlingcanada150 or #fuck150, were also included in the data if the other hashtags had not been included in the tweet. A content analysis of the tweets was conducted to identify frames using an inductive, constant comparative approach (Straus & Corbin, 1998), and a frames matrix was developed (Van Gorp, 2010). The tweets in the sample were coded for the specific frames that emerged. The most common frame, labeled the "not a celebration" frame, casts the sesquicentennial as a symbol of cultural genocide and historic and ongoing oppression against Indigenous peoples. Associated frames identified include: the timeless (more than 150 years) history of Indigenous cultures, settler racism, acts of resistance, longstanding inequality, the residential school legacy and cultural celebration/resilience. These frames were identified in the Twitter data with a view to compare them to frames in the news coverage from the same time period.

In the last five months of 2016, after the July 1 celebration of the 149th anniversary of Confederation, Canada 150 shows up in an Indigenous context in only 15 tweets among the accounts analyzed here, 12 tweets from Russ Diabo. That changes dramatically early in the new year. Between January 1 and July 2, 2017, those 11 accounts would generate 553 tweets using one of the identified hashtags, with retweets and likes totaling 13,480 and 18,100 respectively (see Table 11.1). On January 5, 2017, Pam Palmater sent her first tweet on the issue: "#Canada150 is perverse celebration of many 1000s FNs raped scalped murdered tortured oppressed abused & neglected for wealth #genocide500" (Palmater, 2017).

The @Resistance150 account debuted in late January (see Figure 11.2). A series of tweets featured memes of old black and white images of First Nations people with text promoting the group's core messages, for example: "JOIN IN. NO ACT IS TOO BIG OR TOO SMALL. 150 ACTS OF RESISTANCE. Celebrating

174 Brad Clark

TABLE 11.1 Tweets Using Hashtags Associated with Canada 150 between January 1 and July 2, 2017

Twitter account	Tweets	Retweets	Likes
Tanya Tagaq	7	1041	1567
Russ Diabo	108	1880	1863
Pam Palmater	44	443	614
Cindy Blackstock	5	539	608
âpihtawikosisân	25	560	1123
Christi Belcourt	78	2651	3476
@IdleNoMore4	42	681	706
Tanya Kappo	27	336	733
Isaac Murdoch	26	771	1043
@Resistance150	138	3223	5118
Terrill Tailfeathers	53	1355	1249
TOTALS	**553**	**13480**	**18100**

Source: Table created by Author

Indigenous resistance, resilience, resurgence, rebellion, and restoration. Starting February 1, 2017" (@Resistance150, 2017a). Such memes were common in many of the tweets about Canada 150, a way of challenging the mainstream narrative through Indigenous remediation. Scholars describe this as a media tactic whereby Indigenous artists re-appropriate existing images or texts associated with colonial "reductive constructions of Indigenous identities" and assert their own messages. Christi Belcourt takes remediation beyond tweets – though her work was shared through Twitter – in a poem/film using the Canada 150 theme. Her two-minute video features black and white photos of Indigenous children at residential schools and First Nations people from the last century in traditional dress, as well as early paintings of Indigenous people with their faces painted. There are also many images of contemporary First Peoples celebrating their lives and cultures, despite the historical record. Belcourt's narration begins "Canada, I can cite for you 150 lists of the dead, 150 languages no longer spoken, 150 rivers poisoned . . ." (Belcourt, 2017). The poem moves on to highlight resistance and Indigenous commitment to a brighter future: "Canada, I can cite for you 150 summers coming of resurgence, 150,000 babies' birthing ceremonies . . . 150,000 children with braids and feathers in their hair . . ." (Belcourt, 2017).

Throughout the sample period, the social media discourse followed a familiar pattern of contextualizing Canadian history, and even government policy, through an Indigenous lens. Cindy Blackstock was the least prolific tweeter in the sample group, but used #Canada150 to contrast spending on celebrations on the lack of

#Unsettling Canada 150 **175**

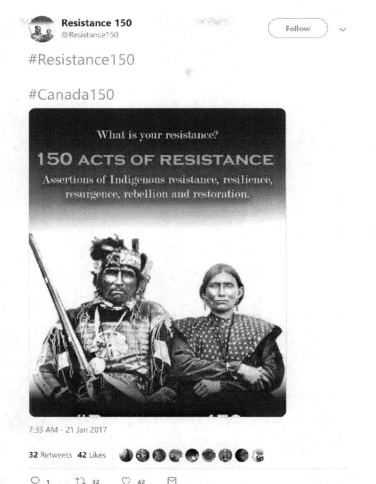

FIGURE 11.2 A Tweet from @Apihtawikosisan with the Hashtag #Canada150

Source: https://twitter.com/search?l=&q=%23Canada150%20from%3Aapihtawikosisan&src=typd&lang=en

drinkable water on First Nations across Canada. Blackstock comments on a tweet by a Cree woman from an Ontario First Nation describing how her family pays $10 for a jug of water to make formula for her niece: "This is where #Canada150 money should have gone. Clean water for babies". That one tweet was retweeted 399 times and drew 478 likes. A government report on housing in the north was given additional context in this tweet from @Resistance150: "Why is this normal, #Canada150? 15+ people, including young children, live in small & crumbling 3 bdrm units" (@Resistance150, 2017b).

Tweets featured in the data from the 11 accounts discussed here represented not just Indigenous points of views but also a range of media content from First Nations, Métis and Inuit sources, another expression of digital self-determination. Speeches and interviews featured on YouTube from First Nations leaders – Art Manuel, Romeo Saganash, Pam Palmater, Derek Nepinak – were frequently linked to tweets. Documents and newsletters put out by band councils or Indigenous agencies were often disseminated, as were infographics that help support the Canada 150 counter-narrative (see Figure 11.3). Indigenous media are frequently referenced, too, whether in the form of news stories from APTN or podcasts from Indigena Media, Resistance 150 or blog posts from Indigenous writers. In that sense, the tweets are decolonizing not just as textualized discourse, but also in spreading Indigenous content in the digital media sphere.

The most common theme running through these tweets is a demand to see the sesquicentennial as something other than a Canada Day party, to consider Canadian Confederation's impact on Indigenous peoples, and (based on that) to address

FIGURE 11.3 A Tweet from the @Resistance150 Account

Source: https://twitter.com/resistance150?lang=en

#Unsettling Canada 150   177

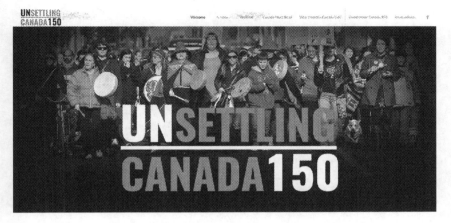

FIGURE 11.4   A Screen Shot of the Unsettling Canada 150 Home Page
Source: http://unsettling150.ca/

the longstanding and ongoing inequities in a meaningful way. A tweet from @Resistance150 captures this most succinctly: "To celebrate #canada150 would be to celebrate our own genocide" (@Resistance 150, 2017a). Âpihtawikosisân tweeted the screen shot of a list of criteria for Canada 150 grants from the City of Edmonton, noting "Lots of money out there for folks to celebrate #Canada150 #colonialism. Not critique. Only celebrate".

The 11 Twitter accounts under analysis undoubtedly played a substantive role in disseminating the counter-narrative, with additional Twitter users in the Indigenous networked-public extending that reach with prolific retweeting (see Figure 11.4). The next section explores whether the creation and amplification of these Indigenous voices were such that mainstream media heard their stories and started to share them with the broader public.

National News Media and Canada 150

For the purposes of this analysis, news content was considered from three of Canada's biggest English-language newspapers by digital reach: the *Toronto Star*, the *Globe and Mail* and the *National Post*. Despite the technological disruption associated with legacy media and especially the impact on print revenues, these organizations have significant digital audiences and are routinely listed among the top news websites in Canada based on social media, search and internet metrics. While these news operations have moved well into multimedia production, the content they produce is largely text-based, affording research efficiencies in finding and analyzing stories.

News content from the three newspapers is broken into two samples – the last five months of 2016 and seven months leading into the sesquicentennial – allowing for comparisons with the Twitter data collected over the same periods. In the months leading into 2017, the three newspapers produced 34 stories related to Canada 150, excluding the coverage related to Canada Day 2016. In that same time frame, the 11 accounts included in the Twitter analysis put out 15 tweets on the issue. Seven of the 34 news items included mentions of First Nations and/or Métis or Inuit peoples. However, none of those articles framed the coming anniversary in Indigenous terms, specifically two key frames from the Twitter data: the "not a celebration" frame nor the "timeless Indigenous history" frame. The news discourse in the first sample period, when only 15 tweets were disseminated from the 11 Indigenous Twitter accounts, reveals very little awareness of the Indigenous perspectives on Canada 150, prior to the new year.

In the next seven months, as the sesquicentennial approaches, the newspapers coverage of Canada 150 ramps up considerably. There is reporting on issues related to the politics, spending and government initiatives, but also considerable space devoted to Canadian history, culture and events. Advanced searches of the Canadian Newsstream data base show that between January 1 and July 2, 2017, the *Toronto Star* ran 99 stories containing the term "Canada 150," while the *Globe and Mail* and the *National Post* carried 88 and 39 items respectively. Those 226 stories were examined to see if they included the two most common Indigenous frames from the Twitter analysis, that Canada 150 was no cause for celebration and that First Peoples' history predates Confederation. The analysis found 69 of those 226 stories – about 30 per cent – contained one or both of those frames. Previous studies, as noted earlier, have documented severe under-representation in mainstream news regarding Indigenous issues and communities – as low as .28 per cent, according to Pierro et al. (2013). Given such low rates of Indigenous representation in the past, the high degree of inclusion of Indigenous perspectives in Canada 150 stories is striking.

A closer look at the coverage captured in this study shows that Indigenous frames identified in the Twitter data also appear in the news content. In an article defining Canada 150 as "the end of a way of life," Inuk filmmaker Alethea Arnaquq-Baril stated "every single time I see a Canada 150 logo, I want to take a Sharpie and add a couple zeros to the end of it" (Renzetti, 2017). That timeless Indigenous cultures frame is routinely featured in stories that appeared in news content from media outlets outside the sample as well, but a *Globe and Mail* article opens with the observation that "while the rest of Canada throws itself a half-billion dollar 150th birthday this weekend, Jess Housty could justifiably celebrate the 14,000th birthday of her nation – the Heiltsuk Nation in Bella Bella, B.C." (Bascaramurty, 2017). As in the Twitter data, there were multiple references in the news discourse to frame Canada 150 in terms of its federal price tag. When student groups announced they were pulling out of Canada 150 celebrations, this Ryerson University student argued that "to spend half a billion dollars on Canada 150, while, Indigenous communities are without basic necessities such as clean drinking water or safe adequate housing . . . where is the reconciliation?" (Kerr, 2017).

The three news publications generally dedicate quite a bit of space to the arts, and this is where frames of resistance and resilience often appear, whether in stories about publications by Indigenous artists and writers, live theatre productions, film or other forms of media. A venture involving the Toronto International Film Festival and the ImagineNATIVE Film and Media Arts Festival is featured in the *Globe and Mail* and was said to have been created in response to Canada 150. The project was called "2167" and is described as a virtual reality installation inviting "people to step inside the perspective of Indigenous artists to experience their visions of life in Canada 150 years in the future" (McGinn, 2017). Two of the three newspapers include lengthy features on Cree artist Kent Monkman, who created a project called "Shame and Prejudice: A Story of Resilience" that largely focused on residential schools, a deliberate response to the celebrations associated with Canada 150. Monkman explained to the reporter: "It's a turning point for the country . . . All of this was whitewashed and it left generations of Canadians in the dark. How do we move forward as a society when the whole founding mythology is false, exclusive, one-sided?" (Whyte, 2017).

From a research design perspective (discussed in the next section), it is impossible to determine the extent to which the Twitter campaign did or did not shape mainstream news content. However, it was the view of at least one writer in the newspaper sample that Indigenous peoples in Canada transformed Canada 150 from a "celebration without a theme" to something much deeper in meaning:

> First Nations succeeded in defining the sesquicentennial as an occasion to consider past harms, unmet promises and unfinished business. In the recurring message that the human experience on what is now Canada is a great deal more than 150 years, and that the century and a half of Confederation has inflicted cruelty, suffering and sorrow on First Nations, the sesquicentennial was by and large framed.
>
> *(Coyle, 2017)*

The analysis here points to a possible nexus – correlation, not causation – between the loose coalition of leaders and activists associated with the Indigenous social media campaign and the mainstream news. Indigenous voices have been chronically under-represented in the news discourse, yet the frames associated with the #Unsettle150, #Resistance150 and related hashtags frequently appear in the news sample.

Discussion

There is growing evidence that leaders from a variety of backgrounds can influence the news discourse through their use of social media, particularly Twitter. Maxwell McCombs, who pioneered agenda setting theory, describes how media define what is important in the public sphere "through their day-to-day selection and display of the news" (2014, p. 1). News organizations, in the course of dissemination, identify what is important to audiences through a host of "salience cues," everything from where stories are placed in a newspaper or newscast, to the length of the news item. Salience cues also work within journalistic practice to set the agenda for stories within news media. Stories by prominent organizations, such as the *New York Times* or the BBC, are signals to journalists in other newsrooms that these are issues that ought to be reported in their publications, too. This intermedia agenda setting is very much at play in a world where journalists are keen observers of social media in order to see what news is breaking and trending, and who might have initiated those trends.

In examining the connection between Twitter and mainstream news media, the research method of choice is usually a form of computer-assisted time series analysis, tracking mainstream news feeds temporally against Twitter data, and establishing correlations through content analysis (Conway, Kenski, & Wang, 2015). Some studies have concluded that mainstream news sets the agenda for digital media more often than the other way around (see Meraz, 2011; Conway, Kenski, & Wang, 2015; Rogstad, 2016; Harder et al., 2017). However, researchers note their findings are limited "based on the choice of issues studied" (Meraz, 2011, p. 188); most have focused exclusively on political events or election campaigns, or fail to take into account stories that fall outside the traditional news emphasis on "current affairs relating to crime and accidents, as well as international politics and foreign events" (Rogstad, 2016, p. 153). At the same time, most (if not all) intermedia agenda-setting analyses acknowledge an increasing influence by platforms such as Twitter on the news agenda: "It is clear that *all* media types set and follow each other, at least to some extent" (italics in the original, Harder, Sevenans, & Van Aelst, 2017, p. 287). More pointedly, as more people turn to digital sources for news, Conway et al. ask: "Have traditional media completely lost their agenda-setting power?" (2015, p. 275). Their answer is no, but the power of social media to influence news content in some capacity is evident in previous studies, as well as this one.

Intermedia agenda-setting scholarship clearly articulates the distinction between correlation and causation in considering the influence of one medium over another. While time series analyses connect specific Tweets to specific news stories and measure time lags, this study qualitatively traces the flow of specific frames disseminated from Indigenous leaders and activists and observes the appearance of those frames in the mainstream news discourse with considerable uptake. However, Harder et al. concisely capture the essential limitation of this type of work: "We can simply not be sure that one platform or medium 'caused' the other medium to cover a certain news fact" (2017, p. 290).

What previous research *has* clearly articulated is Twitter's fundamental utility in bypassing "the journalistic gatekeepers" and generating "social media 'buzz'" (Harder, Sevenans, & Van Aelst, 2017, p. 280). As a result, a number of scholars

#Unsettling Canada 150 **181**

assert that Twitter allows the leaders of social movements to place "neglected issues" in front of a broader audience, "thus potentially shaping the larger political discourse (Bogard & Sheinheit, 2013; Farrell & Drezner, 2008; Gunter et al., 2009; Wallsten, 2007, cited in Rogstad, 2016, p. 153). This is precisely the appeal of social media to the Indigenous leaders considered in this analysis. First Nations, Métis and Inuit Twitter users are free to share authentic, decolonized messages in the public sphere, free of some of the mainstream sourcing and news selection norms that privilege official sources at the expense of marginalized voices (Entman & Rojecki, 2001).

If bypassing the news gatekeepers can boost the salience of an issue on the public agenda, direct access to those same journalists through Twitter can also influence coverage. Studies have established the micro-blogging platform as the social medium most preferred by reporters (Parmelee, 2013). Tweets by political leaders or – in this case, Indigenous leaders and activists – can influence journalists in a process known as "agenda-building" (2013, p. 293). Status as a leader in the Twittersphere is influenced by readily available data, namely the number of tweets, followers and likes associated with the leader's account, another salience cue in the agenda-setting process. The leader's Twitter stream acts as a form of "information subsidy" to target reporters and "shape coverage." The research shows tweets "can influence which issues get covered by journalists and how those issues are presented" (p. 293). This appears to be true in this case study as well. Tweets from the accounts of prominent Indigenous leaders followed by journalists act as information subsidies, often drawing attention to a specific act of resistance, or Indigenous media production (blog, YouTube video, podcast), or text asserting Indigenous context against the historical record.

While legacy news media – such as the newspapers under analysis in this study – continue to work through the technological disruption that has obliterated their business models, newsrooms have contracted. Chaseten Remillard points out in another chapter in this volume that the diminished state of news organizations has allowed social media to fill the void as a "primary source" of information for the public. However, it is also true that Twitter and other platforms have become a primary source for journalists, an additional "information subsidy" in an era of limited resources for reporting. When a hashtag such as #Canada15000 or #Genocide150 starts to trend (a salience cue), the tweet takes on the role of a news release, providing background, links, video or photographs and easy access to the author by direct messaging. First Nations, Métis and Inuit leaders and activists rarely enjoyed that kind of access to journalists before social media's wide adoption.

Tanya Tagaq is perhaps the most famous of the people featured in this study's Twitter data. However, neither she, nor anyone else in the Twitter sample, could be described as the "face" of the movement to challenge Canada 150 colonialism. This would seem to have been the perception of the mainstream media as well. Out of the 226 stories in the three newspapers, only Diabo and Palmater are

182 Brad Clark

quoted in the context of Canada 150, and only on two occasions. The informal nature of the social media campaign reflects Castells' (2015) assertion that social media movements are often "leaderless." As with Idle No More, the activism in this study was grassroots in nature, guided by a soft leadership bridging languages and cultures associated with dozens of Indigenous communities across Canada. There was no involvement with the official leadership in the AFN; Grand Chief Perry Bellegarde had only one tweet in reference to Canada 150.

Features of the soft leadership and digital populism behind the Unsettle 150 campaign also emerge in a much different cause under analysis by Patrick McCurdy in his chapter. McCurdy examines a Canadian energy industry fight to ensure a monument in Ottawa, the Centennial Flame, continued to be fueled by natural gas, and not an LED light. Oil and gas industry groups sought to characterize any government move away from gas as "unCanadian" and engaged social media using the hashtag #KeepCanadasFlame. McCurdy references Ernesto Laclau's (2005) work on populism whereby a community unites against a "common enemy," specifically "unresponsive political elites" (Gerbaudo, 2018, p. 3), in this case, the Canadian federal government. Ottawa is similarly targeted in the Canada 150 campaign. There is no one pan-Indigenous viewpoint in Canada, but there is consensus through many Indigenous nations, communities and settlements that Canadian governments have failed to address ongoing inequities, or to listen to their views. McCurdy extends the battle analogy further, describing the social media mobilization and coordination of energy workers as a "ground campaign." Similar to the work of the Indigenous activists behind the Canada 150 movement, the energy industry's soft leadership in social media messaging creates an "emotional space" that motivates the rank and file, and at the same time provides the forum for reaction.

Social media have also emerged as an important tool in "transforming powerful ideologies," including historic iconography, according to Kaitlynn Mendes, in her chapter on feminist activism in Britain. Mendes cites the example of a campaign to add a woman to the 11 men featured as statues in London's Parliament Square, resulting in the unveiling of a monument of suffragist Millicent Fawcett two years later. While not every social media campaign, as Mendes notes, results in such clear outcomes, the ongoing challenges to ideology can also shift perspectives in society. The challenges to Canada 150 shared by Indigenous leaders influenced the media framing of the event, but the counter-narratives on Canadian history resonate beyond sesquicentennial. Against the backdrop of a movement to remove statues of Confederate leaders in the southern United States, icons of Canadian Confederation became the center of a similar debate. Bridges and buildings named after politicians associated with the residential school system have in many cases been changed, often in the wake of concerted social media campaigns. While it is difficult to measure the impact of these digital tactics, and to separate their influence from other factors, the traditional tale of Canada's origins has been profoundly disrupted. This is perhaps best reflected in the counter-narrative of Sir

John A. MacDonald, Canada's first prime minister. Often celebrated for "building a nation," MacDonald is also associated with policies that caused severe famine among First Nations, and he has been labeled by some historians as "the" architect of Indian residential schools (Carleton, 2017). This challenge to the founding father narrative has been controversial, but has also resulted in – for example – the removal of MacDonald's statue from city hall in Victoria, British Columbia (Brown, 2018). Such a move even ten years earlier might have been unthinkable.

Whether it is Confederation or treaty rights or celebrations of resiliency, the Indigenous social media leaders featured in this analysis, and their thousands of followers, have sought to bring an often overlooked message to social media, to other Indigenous peoples and to wider society. Based on this analysis, they seem to be enjoying some success in that mission.

Conclusion

This chapter illustrates the power of Indigenous leaders to deploy Twitter to circumvent traditional mainstream media gatekeeping, disrupt traditional models of intermedia agenda-setting and bring Indigenous perspectives to the media discourse. A pattern of tweets bearing Indigenous themes, shared by a like-minded group of "soft leaders" and redistributed through their extensive networks of followers, shifted the narrative on Canada 150 and shook the origin story of Canadian nationhood. This study establishes that social media can provide a direct conduit for the views and ideas of Indigenous leaders to journalists – and broader Canadian society – that was never in reach before.

References

@Resistance150. (2017a, March 19). #Canada150 from:@Resistance150. *Twitter*. Retrieved from https://twitter.com/search?l=&q=%23Canada150%20from%3AResistance150&src=typd&lang=en

@Resistance150. (2017b, January 20). #Resistance150 from:Resistance150. *Twitter*. Retrieved from https://twitter.com/search?l=&q=%23Resistance150%20from%3AResistance150&src=typd&lang=en

Alia,V. (2003). Scattered voices, global vision: Indigenous peoples and the new media nation. In K. H. Karim (Ed.), *The media of diaspora* (pp. 36–50). New York, NY: Routledge.

Bascaramurty, D. (2017, June 30). 'A horrible history': Four Indigenous views on Canada 150. *The Globe and Mail*. Retrieved from www.theglobeandmail.com/news/national/canada-150/canada-day-indigenous-perspectives-on-canada-150/article35498737/

Belcourt, C. (2017, February 4). CANADA, I can cite for you 150. *YouTube*. Retrieved from www.youtube.com/watch?v=Y6U9JV5-bA8

Blackstock, C. (2017, June 13). #Canada150 from:cblackst. *Twitter*. Retrieved from https://twitter.com/search?l=&q=%23Canada150%20from%3Acblackst&src=typd&lang=en

Bogard, C. J., & Sheinhet, I. (2013). Good ol' boy talk versus the blogosphere in the case of former Senator George Allen. *Mass Communication and Society, 16*, 347–368. doi:10.1080/15205436.2012.724141

Brady, M. J., & Kelly, J. M. (2017). *We interrupt this program: Indigenous media tactics in Canadian culture.* Vancouver: UBC Press.

Brown, S. (2018, August 9). Victoria to remove statue of Sir John A. Macdonald, a 'painful reminder of colonial violence', from city hall. *National Post.* Retrieved from https://nationalpost.com/news/local-news/victoria-removing-john-a-macdonald-statue-from-city-hall/wcm/66fe917b-347f-4333-a1c0-ee899a34f16d?utm_campaign=Echobox&utm_medium=Social&utm_source=Twitter#Echobox=1533755352

Burrows, E. (2016). Revitalising indigenous resistance and dissent through online media. *IAFOR Journal of Media Communication & Film*, 1–19. doi:10.22492/3.1.08

Carleton, S. (2017, July 9). John A. Macdonald was the real architect of residential schools. *The Toronto Star.* Retrieved from www.thestar.com/opinion/commentary/2017/07/09/john-a-macdonald-was-the-real-architect-of-residential-schools.html

Castells, M. (2015). *Networks of outrage and hope, social movements in the Internet age* (2nd ed.). Cambridge: Polity Press.

Clark, B. (2013). Reflecting which Canada? A source analysis of Canadian network television news. *International Journal of Diverse Identities, 12*(1), 33–45.

Clark, B. (2014). Framing Canada's Aboriginal peoples: A comparative analysis of indigenous and mainstream television news. *The Canadian Journal of Native Studies, XXXIV*(2), 41–64.

Conway, B. A., Kenski, K., & Wang, D. (2015). The rise of Twitter in the political campaign: Searching for intermedia agenda-setting effects in the presidential primaries. *Journal of Computer-Mediated Communication, 20*, 363–380. doi:10.1111/jcc4.12124

Coyle, J. (2017, July 1). Indigenous discontent gives 150th anniversary a defining theme. *The Toronto Star.* Retrieved from www.thestar.com/news/canada/2017/07/01/indigenous-discontent-gives-150th-anniversary-a-defining-theme.html

Duarte, M. (2017). Connected activism: Indigenous uses of social media for shaping political change. *Australasian Journal of Information Systems, 21*, 1–12.

Dunham, J. (2017, June 27). Resistance 150: Why Canada's birthday celebrations aren't for everyone. *CTV News.* Retrieved from www.ctvnews.ca/canada/resistance-150-why-canada-s-birthday-celebrations-aren-t-for-everyone-1.3478004

Entman, R., & Rojecki, A. (2001). *The black image in the white mind: Media and race in America.* Chicago, IL: The University of Chicago Press.

Farrell, H., & Drezner, D. W. (2008). The power and politics of blogs. *Public Choice, 134*(1–2), 15–30. doi:10.1007/s11127-007-9198-1

Feedspot. (2018, May 26). Top 60 Canadian News Websites. *Feedspot.* Retrieved from https://blog.feedspot.com/canadian_news_websites/

Felt, M. (2016). Mobilizing affective political networks: The role of affect in calls for a national inquiry into Murdered and Missing Indigenous Women during the 2015 Canadian federal election. *SM Society*, 1–8. doi:10.1145/2930971.2930978

Gerbaudo, P. (2012). *Tweets and the streets: Social media and contemporary activism.* London: Pluto Press.

Gerbaudo, P. (2018). Social media and populism: An elective affinity. *Media, Culture & Society*, 1–9. doi:10.1177/0163443718772192

Ginsburg, F. (1994). Embedded aesthetics: Creating a discursive space for Indigenous media. *Cultural Anthropology, 9*(3), 365–382.

Gunter, B., Campbell, V., Touri, M., & Gibson, R. (2009). Blogs, news and credibility. *New Information Perspectives, 61*(2), 185–204.

Hannay, C. (2017, January 5). Ottawa spending half a billion dollars for country's anniversary. *The Globe and Mail*, p. A1.

Harder, R. A., Sevenans, J., & Van Aelst, P. (2017). Intermedia agenda setting in the social media age: How traditional players dominate the news agenda in election times. *The International Journal of Press/Politics, 22*(3), 275–293. doi:10.1177/1940161217704969

John, S. (2015). Idle No More – Indigenous activism and feminism. *Theory in Action, 8*(4), 38–54. doi:10.3798/tia.1937–0237.15022

Kerr, J. (2017, June 30). Ryerson students' union chooses not to celebrate Canada 150. *The Toronto Star.* Retrieved from www.thestar.com/news/gta/2017/06/30/ryerson-students-union-opts-not-to-celebrate-canada-150.html

Laclau, E. (2005). *On Populist Reason.* London: Verso.

Lambertus, S. (2004). *Wartime images, peacetime wounds: The media and the Gustafsen Lake standoff.* Toronto, Canada: University of Toronto Press.

Martini, M. (2018). Online distant witnessing and live-streaming activism: Emerging differences in the activation of networked publics. *New Media & Society, 20*(11), pp. 4035–4055. doi:https://doi.org/10.1177/1461444818766703

McCombs, M. (2014). *Setting the agenda: Mass media and public opinion* (2nd ed.). Malden, MA: Polity Press.

McCue, D. (2015, December 21). News stereotypes of aboriginal peoples. *Reporting in Indigenous Communities.* Retrieved from http://riic.ca/the-guide/at-the-desk/news-stereotypes-of-aboriginal-peoples/

McGinn, D. (2017, June 22). Indigenous artists create virtual-reality vision of a future Canada. *The Globe and Mail.* Retrieved from www.theglobeandmail.com/arts/indigenous-artists-create-virtual-reality-vision-of-canada-in-the-future/article35436268/

McMahon, R. (2013, May 31). Digital Self-determination: Aboriginal Peoples and the Network Society in Canada. *Simon Fraser University Summit Institutional Repository.* Retrieved from http://summit.sfu.ca/item/13532

Meraz, S. (2011). Using time series analysis to measure agenda-setting influence in traditional media and political blog networks. *Journalism and Mass Communication Quarterly, 88*(1), 176–194.

Palmater, P. (2017, January 5). #Canada150 from:Pam_Palmater. *Twitter.* Retrieved from https://twitter.com/search?l=&q=%23Canada150%20from%3APam_Palmater&src=typd&lang=en

Parmelee, J. H. (2013). Political journalists and Twitter: Influences on norms and practices. *Journal of Media Practice, 14*(4), 291–305. doi:10.1386/jmpr.14.4.291_1

Pierro, R., Barrera, J., Blackstock, C., Harding, R., McCue, D., & Metatawabin, M. (2013). Buried voices: Media coverage of Aboriginal issues in Ontario. *Journalists for Human Rights.* Retrieved from www.jhr.ca/en/aboutjhr/downloads/publications/buried_voices.pdf

Renzetti, E. (2017, June 3). Look away from the giant duck and listen to real concerns over Canada 150. *The Globe and Mail.* Retrieved from www.theglobeandmail.com/opinion/look-away-from-the-giant-duck-and-listen-to-real-concerns-over-canada-150/article35189264/

Rogstad, I. (2016). Is Twitter just rehashing? Intermedia agenda setting between Twitter and mainstream media. *Journal of Information Technology and Politics, 13*(2), 142–158. doi: 10.1080/19331681.2016.1160263

Selley, C. (2017, June 30). Facile 150 bash begs for havoc; Teepee protest more coherent than Hill party. *Proquest.com.* Retrieved from http://libproxy.mtroyal.ca/login?url=https://search.proquest.com/docview/1914988859?accountid=1343

Straus, A., & Corbin, J. (1998). *Basics of qualitative research: Techniques and procedures for developing grounded theory* (2nd ed.). Thousand Oaks: Sage Publications.

Truth and Reconciliation Commission of Canada. (2015a). *About Us*. Retrieved from Truth and Reconciliation Commission of Canada: http://www.trc.ca/about-us.html

Truth and Reconciliation Commission of Canada. (2015b). Honouring the truth, reconciling for the future: Summary of the final report of the Truth and Reconciliation Commission of Canada. *NCTR.ca*. Retrieved from http://nctr.ca/assets/reports/Final%20Reports/Executive_Summary_English_Web.pdf

twitter.com. (2017a, January 11). Resistance 150. *Twitter*. Retrieved from https://twitter.com/resistance150?lang=en

twitter.com. (2017b, July 1). from:perrybellegarde since:2017–01–01 until:2017–07–02. *Twitter*. Retrieved from https://twitter.com/search?l=&q=from%3Aperrybellegarde%20since%3A2017-01-01%20until%3A2017-07-02&src=typd&lang=en

Unsettling Canada 150. (2017, January 31). Unsettling Canada 150. *Unsettling Canada 150*. Retrieved from http://unsettling150.ca/

Van Gorp, B. (2010). Strategies to take subjectivity out of framing analysis. In P. D'Angelo, & J. A. Kupers (Eds.), *Doing News Frames Analysis: Empirical and Theoretical Perspectives* (pp. 84–109). New York, NY: Routledge.

Vowel, C. (2017, February 22). #Canada150 from:apihtawikosian. *Twitter*. Retrieved from https://twitter.com/search?l=&q=%23Canada150%20from%3Aapihtawikosisan&src=typd&lang=en

Wallsten, K. (2007). Agenda setting and the blogosphere: An analysis of the relationship between mainstream media and political blogs. *Review of Policy Research, 24*(6), 567–587. doi:10.1111/j.1541-1338.2007.00300.x

Whyte, M. (2017, January 22). Kent Monkman fills in the blanks in Canadian history. *The Toronto Star*. Retrieved from www.thestar.com/entertainment/visualarts/2017/01/22/kent-monkman-fills-in-historys-blanks-with-humour-and-horror.html

12
FANNING FLAMES OF DISCONTENT

A Case Study of Social Media, Populism, and Campaigning

Patrick McCurdy

On May 3, 2018, Timothy Egan, the President and CEO of the Canadian Gas Association (CGA), penned an open letter to Prime Minister Justin Trudeau expressing concern over reports that the federal government was considering the conversion of the Canadian Centennial Flame from natural gas to LED lighting (Canadian Gas Association 2018). The letter, sent via email, was simultaneously shared as a paid press release via Canadian News Wire, and was promptly amplified by the Canadian Association of Petroleum Producers (CAPP) as part of their ongoing Canada's Energy Citizens (CEC) campaign. Egan's letter marked the start of the short-lived but successful #keepcanadasflame campaign, which resulted in the federal government backpedalling on plans to explore less carbon-intensive options for the Centennial Flame. This chapter uses #keepcanadasflame as a case study to examine the role and power of social media in the campaigning practices of Canada's fossil fuel lobby within the ongoing struggle over Canada's oil/tar sands development. Of particular interest is CAPP's turn to the use of "soft leadership" and its invocation of emotive, affect-laden and populist discourse as a means to mobilize specific, targeted publics via social media. However, before exploring details of this specific campaign, the broader contours of the media-saturated struggle over the oil/tar sands in Canada are first established along with the theoretical orientation towards these events.

(Social) Media as a Site of Struggle

The mediated representations of social and political issues are both sites *and* sources of political contention (Castells 2009; Couldry 2012; Silverstone 1999, 2007). Media create representational arenas where actors with competing ideas and resources actively engage in "symbolic contests" with parties deliberately

188 Patrick McCurdy

packaging and framing issues to best represent their stance and stake in the matter at hand (Gamson and Wolfsfeld 1993). While Gamson and Wolfsfeld envisioned political adversaries duking it out through traditional, often analogue, news media outlets such as newspapers, television, and radio, the turn to digitalization and ubiquity of social media platforms have created what Andrew Chadwick calls a "hybrid media system". For Chadwick, our contemporary media system consists of a confluence of traditional media (e.g. television, radio, newspaper) and social media (e.g. Facebook, YouTube, Twitter) platforms. This system is "built upon interactions among older and newer media logics – defined as technologies, genres, norms, behaviours and organisational forms – in the reflexively connected fields of media and politics" (2017, p. 4).

This chapter takes particular interest in the affordances of social media within the hybrid media system regarding their ability to segment, target, and provide space for fragmented publics, cultivate soft leadership amongst targeted publics, and, as a result, further divisiveness. Indeed, there is a burgeoning body of research on the use of social media by social movements as a tool for mobilization, message amplification as well as network building and maintenance (Cammaerts 2018; Gerbaudo 2018; Kavada 2018; Treré 2018). Social media, then, as both a *platform* embedded with specific logics, rhythms, and practices and a *resource* for stakeholders, movements, and their supporters and detractors, have altered the strategies and tactics of political campaigning at time of "deep mediatization".

Couldry and Hepp (2017) refer to deep mediatization to capture the multiple ways in which media has become embedded in cultural practice. From a mediatization perspective, media become arenas for social and political struggles which unfold in both mediated and material realms. Ultimately, as Castells (2007, p. 238) reminds us, "the fundamental battle being fought in society is the battle over the minds of the people". Castells' use of the word 'battle' is particularly apropos in the context of the ongoing struggle over the future of Canada's bitumen sands and that of the environment more broadly, where there is an established pattern of using war-fuelled language on all sides. For example, in June 2014 Richard Berman, a top US public-relations executive, was speaking at the Western Energy Alliance Annual meeting to a collection of big oil companies and described the struggle big oil has with environmentalists and climate change campaigns as an "endless war" (Lipton 2014). Later, in the same speech, which was leaked online, Berman also acknowledged "you have to play dirty to win" (ibid.).

While Berman's audience was principally fracking companies, war references have also been used to characterize the struggle over the oil/tar sands, such as journalist Chris Turner's (2012) feature article "The Oil Sands PR War" or Geo Takach's (2017) recent book *Tar Wars: Oil, Environment and Alberta's Image*. The Canadian Gas Association magazine *Energy* referred to the struggle over the controversial Kinder Morgan Trans Mountain pipeline as the "Trans Mountain Infinity War" or, in French, "La guerre sans fin de Trans Mountain", the 'war without end' (Sands 2018). Meanwhile, the April 2015 "Engagement" issue of CAPP's industry-focused Context Magazine also used war-like language. It referred to

Fanning Flames of Discontent **189**

CAPP campaigners as "road warriors" working on the "front lines" of oil issues and differentiated between its "air campaign", which concerns its TV and print advertising, and its "ground campaign", which refers to CAPP's in-person engagement, including the use of social media. Thus, there is both precedence and merit in framing the struggles over the oil/tar sands as a war. A war of position. A war of statistics. A war of images. A war over identity. A war over extraction. A war over the environment. A war which unfolds in the theatres of mainstream *and* social media. From a media communications perspective, it is a war which involves 'air campaigns', guerrilla tactics, and 'ground campaigns'. The next section provides an overview of these tactics and gives a brief history of the mediated war over Canada's oil sands of which #keepcanadasflame is a part.

A Selective History of the Oil/Tar Sands War

One of the first shots in the war over the tar/oil sands was fired on January 17, 2008 when a group of activists from Stop the Tar Sands (STS) erected a sculpture out in front of Calgary, Alberta's Telus Conference Centre, where the 5th annual Canadian Oil Sands Summit was being held (McCurdy 2017). The protest sought to raise environmental and climate concerns around bitumen production through a media-stunt style protest attuned to the visual logic and temporal rhythms of mainstream news media. STS's action marked the beginning of a barrage of "image events" (Deluca 1999) developed and deployed in the battle over bitumen.[1] Almost two years passed before oil industry lobby group CAPP launched *Oil Sands Today*, its communications response to mounting anti-oil sands activism. *Oil Sands Today* was a polished, multi-platform internet, print, television, and even outdoor advertising "air campaign" launched by CAPP in the spring of 2010 and ran until at least 2013. The campaign sought to combat negative public perceptions of the oil sands through a reasoned mass media campaign where "real, live oil patch workers [and executives] from a range of companies explain their jobs, most of which involve reducing the industry's environmental footprint or cleaning up the mess its extraction work leaves behind" (Turner 2012).[2]

Individual oil companies supplemented CAPP's *Oil Sands Today* with their own slick multi-platform advertising campaigns. The most notable of these was Suncor's 2013/14 "See What Yes Can Do" advertisement, which relays the challenges of meeting modern energy demands in ways which are efficient, collaborative, reflexive, and respectful of nature (Suncor 2013, 2014). The 30-second "TV Spot" version of "See What Yes Can Do", which also ran as YouTube "pre-roll" advertisement, has acquired over 1.4 million views (Suncor 2014).[3] In June 2014, Suncor's "air campaign" was met with a social media guerrilla campaign launched by Canadian environmental NGO Sum of Us. The eNGO recut and edited the two-minute version of Suncor's "See What Yes Can Do" (2013) to produce their own culture jammed version, aptly titled "See What Yes Is Doing" (Sum of Us 2014). The narrator in the Sum of Us' anti-oil sands subvertisement has a similar voice and delivery to that of Suncor's, while the script and visuals work together

190 Patrick McCurdy

to portray Suncor's original advertisement as corporate "greenwash": deceptive advertising meant to deflect from the company's real environmental impact (McCurdy and Thomlison 2019). CAPP and Alberta were caught in a war of position over the oil sands and they were losing. Their expensive, expansive yet dull campaigns were quickly subverted and exploited in the battle over bitumen.

Whereas well-funded lobby groups like CAPP and large oil and gas companies such as Suncor have the financial capital to create and disseminate slick corporate advertisements, eNGOs and activist groups are much leaner. As such, guerrilla media tactics such as the semiotic hijacking of mass media advertising campaigns are more appealing and achievable. Indeed, the uptake of the personal computer and the availability of cheap or free digital editing software together with the rise of networked communication – and the technological tools that came with it – have all reduced barriers to the practice of culture jamming.[4] Moreover, the rise and ubiquity of social media have increased the ability to create and disseminate culture jammed content, ultimately providing a low cost and powerful symbolic resource to combat the heavy assault of mass media "air campaigns" (Sandoval-Almazan and Gil-Garcia 2014;Van Laer and Van Aelst 2010).

Social media have become an essential component of "ground campaigns" in the war over the oil/tar sands. Traditionally, the concept of "ground campaigns" has referred to a literal 'boots on the ground' approach to mobilizing and coordinating supporters. However, more recently, scholars have recognized that "campaigning on the ground no longer depends solely on grassroots organising and coordination in physical settings, but also on the integration of online and offline tools and endeavours" (Vaccari and Valerian 2016, p. 20). Thus, physical ground campaigns have evolved in tandem with the affordances of digital and social media, which allow for increased segmentation, micro-targeting, and rapid and real-time responses (Nielsen 2012). They also offer political actors the ability to create or capitalize on digital spaces which bring likeminded people together to feed them targeted messaging, offer content which may be shared across their social networks, and provide an opportunity for targeted publics to converge and engage political actors and each other. This chapter is particularly interested in CAPP's "Canada's Energy Citizens" campaign, the "ground campaign" of which involved physical meetings such as a rallies and barbeques as well as online activities underwritten by social media. The uptake of CEC marked the moment when the Canadian oil and gas lobby embraced the social media shift from mass publics to targeted and winnable publics. I discuss the CEC campaign and its link to #KeepCanadasFlame in the next section.

The Centennial Flame, #KeepCanadasFlame, and Canada's Energy Citizens

The Centennial Flame sits out front of Parliament Hill in Ottawa, Ontario, and was first lit on January 1, 1967, to help mark the state of celebrations commemorating Canada's centennial. Conceived as a temporary installation, a public campaign in 1968 made the flame into a permanent fixture (Egan 2006). Working off the results of an Access to Information Request, veteran CBC journalist Dean Beeby (2018) broke the news on April 22, 2018, that Public Services and Procurement Canada was exploring options to convert the natural-gas-powered Centennial Flame into something more environmentally friendly. While a Canadian government spokesperson confirmed Beeby's story on the 'Greening of the Centennial Flame' project, he did not appear to raise any concerns that this 'green sky thinking' might become controversial.

Although powered by natural gas, the fact that the Centennial Flame uses *Canadian* gas was not part of its original intended symbolism. However, 11 days after CBC revealed the flame might be extinguished, the Canadian Gas Association (CGA), a gas distribution lobby group, launched its #KeepCanadasFlame. The campaign sought to associate the flame's status as a signifier of Canadian pride with pride in the country's fossil fuel industry. At its core, the campaign took the position that converting the Centennial Flame to a less carbon-intensive energy source was unCanadian in light of the country's vast natural resources, the global demand for these resources, and what they framed as the socially and environmentally responsible methods of resources extraction (Canadian Gas Association 2018; Fitzgerald, Myers, Ward and Skehar 2018).

The #KeepCanadasFlame campaign involved legacy media coverage via paid newswire posts and newspaper editorials but also included social media. When the campaign began on May 3, the CGA used its official Twitter account (@GoSmartEnergy) to share the CGA's open letter with Prime Minister Trudeau. The letter concluded by pointing to three bespoke social media campaign assets: a Twitter account (@Canadasflame), a Facebook account, and Instagram account (keepcanadasflame). However, these CGA accounts had limited content and nominal reach. The @Canadasflame Twitter account had a total of 51 tweets between May 3, 2018, and June 19, 2018, amassed 31 followers, and followed 80 accounts. The Facebook page had 12 posts and four followers and followed five accounts; meanwhile, the Instagram account had a total of three posts and eight followers and followed zero accounts. Whereas as the CGA was not successful in their efforts to gain traction for their bespoke social media accounts, they had a powerful political and social media ally in CAPP and its Canada's Energy Citizens campaign.

First launched in 2015, CAPP describes its CEC initiative as "[bringing] like-minded Canadians together by building an online community that supports Canada's energy. The Canada's Energy Citizens movement provides individuals with industry facts and information" (CAPP 2018). Wood (2018) describes Energy Citizens as an "amalgam of corporate public relations and citizen political participation" from sharing memes, to sharing thoughts, to sharing petitions on multiple platforms, including the campaign's Facebook page "Canada's Energy Citizens", which has over 228,000 likes. The campaign is what Edward Walker (2014), in his book *Grass Roots for Hire*, calls "grass roots from the top down" (p. 9). Energy Citizens involves a subsidized public whereby the professionally executed campaign "lower[s] the costs of participation for targeted activists groups" but unfolds in a similar fashion to progressive and environmental NGOs (p. 10). Moreover, CEC targets a heavily incentivized public: those who work in or have a connection to the oil and gas industry. Those whose livelihoods are at stake. Not only does the Canada's Energy Citizens campaign use public relations or propaganda – which is indeed part of CAPP's "air campaign" but they also seek to activate their target audience through a "ground campaign" which involves social media.

When CEC launched, CAPP framed it as "an important step towards building the kind of active engagement needed to balance public debate" (CAPP 2015). As much empirical research attests, social media campaigning does not often encourage rational debate. Instead, current social practices often seek to mobilize, activate, and communicate with publics using affect-heavy tactics designed to tap values. Moreover, since 2013 CAPP has taken a taken a communications approach with their communications involving "fact based & emotive messaging" that is "not apologetic or defensive" (CAPP 2013). Canada's Energy Citizens is an offensive campaign with national pride at its foundation.

CAPP's application of nationalism is barefaced. CEC uses both a maple leaf and the colours of the Canadian flag as a means to "transfer" (Lee 1945) the respect and pride many Canadians feel for Canada to a pride of working in energy and even our energy lifestyle. Indeed, CAPP is explicit in its desire to cultivate "pride" and forge a common identity amongst its members, together with a "desire to stand up and be heard" (CAPP 2015). If we accept Benedict Anderson's (1983) argument that the creation of nations is linked to historical forces which merge with political and ideological contestation, then we can see CAPP as tapping Canadian nationalism as a means to continue fossil fuel development in Canada. Rather ingeniously, the CEC campaign cast a purposefully wide net, encouraging anyone who works in the fossil fuel industry or uses fossil fuels in their lives. In the throes of an endless war over the oil/tar sands. Energy Citizens belong to the same nation. Energy Citizenship creates boundaries between insiders and outsiders. Through a repertoire of digital resources, the CEC campaign allows CAPP to share messages with supporters, publish calls to action, and engage its support base as well as enlist new supporters. As the next section details, #keepcanadasflame fit entirely within the scope, remit, and messaging of the CEC campaign.

The Centennial Flame, Energy Citizens, and Soft Leadership

Two days after the CGA launched #keepcanadasflame, CAPP sent a direct email to Canada's Energy Citizens subscribers with the evocative subject: "You won't believe this". The email disclosed the perceived threat to Centennial Flame, hyperlinked to a CBC news story (Beeby 2018a), and encouraged readers to "send a letter today to Prime Minister Trudeau asking him to Keep Canada's Flame alive".

The letter writing request hyperlinked to a webpage with a customizable form email which asked the Prime Minister to "keep Canada's Flame burning and to support our natural gas industry" (Canada's Energy Citizens 2018a)

CAPP's communications were sent via NationBuilder, a political engagement platform which McKelvey and Piebiak (2018) describe as an "all-in-one solution: one platform to manage the campaign's email, website, voter database, donations, volunteer coordination, and communications" (p. 902). NationBuilder also provides campaign owners with detailed information about user activities on their platform as well as on social media through, among other things, the platform's integration with Facebook (ibid., p. 910). This data-driven practice ultimately enables campaigners to construct detailed individual profiles which may be aggregated, segmented, and targeted as desired. CAPP's uptake of NationBuilder is evidence of how sophisticated, customizable, and targeted digital campaign tools continue to underwrite political campaigns. Moreover, it suggests that while in the past such tactics may have been the domain of progressive or upstart political campaigns (e.g. Bimber 2014; Kreiss 2012), their professionalization points to the further convergence of political engagement with consumer relations and, ultimately, the continued uptake of political marketing in Canada (see: Lees-Marshment and Marland 2012).

From the start of the #keepcanadasflame campaign on May 6, 2018, to the government's step back on May 15, 2018, CAPP only four of 54 CEC Facebook posts concerned the Centennial Flame campaign. While this number is quite small, CAPP also paid for #keepcanadasflame posts to appear as sponsored content on Twitter, Facebook, and Facebook Messenger. #keepcanadasflame launched against the backdrop of a much larger CAPP/CEC campaign in support of the Kinder Morgan Trans Mountain pipeline. In fact, all 50 of the remaining Facebook posts published during the period in question were in some way related to the CEC's Trans Mountain campaign, which used NationBuilder resources and involved a similar coordinated social media and lobbying effort.

While the #keepcanadasflame campaign was relatively small, it can be folded into the broader struggle over energy politics around Kinder Morgan and of the fossil fuel industry's future in Canada more generally. Moreover, its tone and use of nationalism is consistent with CAPP's CEC campaigning media strategy. Of particular interest is the political and symbolic manoeuvring which transformed the Centennial Flame from an empty signifier into a focal point, and rallying point, for the fossil fuel lobby and its supporters. Key to the campaign's success is CAPP's status and influence as a "soft leader" on the issue of Canadian energy politics via its Canada's Energy Citizens Facebook page.

Writing about the impact of social media on progressive "leaderless" social movements, Gerbaudo (2012) conceptualizes the role of what he calls "soft leaders", those who control/admin a movement's social media resources and thus become "involved in setting the scene, and constructing an emotional space within which collective action can unfold" (p. 5). Gerbaudo's point is that "leaderless movements" have leaders, and they exert "soft leadership". Gerbaudo's notion

194 Patrick McCurdy

of soft leadership is also relevant to formal groups or organizations that also seek to "exploit the interactive and participatory character of the new communication technology" (2012, p. 13). Thus, "soft leadership" is a social media practice whereby social media channels such as Twitter streams or Facebook pages are "not simply channels of information but also crucial emotional conduits through which organisers have condensed individual sentiments of indignation, anger, pride and a sense of shared victimhood and transformed them into political passions driving the process of mobilisation" (p. 14).

Gerbaudo's concept may be extended to CAPP's efforts to stir sentiment via its CEC page and the Centennial Flame campaign in particular. On May 8, CEC shared a post proclaiming: "The federal government is thinking about replacing Canada's Centennial flame with LED lights. Tell Ottawa that's a bad idea!" (Canada's Energy Citizens 2018b). Accompanying the post was a photo of the Centennial Flame, showing parliament in the background. Superimposed slightly above the brightly burning centennial flame was a red text box containing white text with the prompt "Tell Ottawa: Keep Canada's flame burning". On May 9, CEC shared the *Financial Post* editorial "Extinguishing the Centennial Flame – a Canadian icon – is no way to meet emissions targets", penned by three CAPP board members. The editorial was shared under the headline "Some common sense right here. SHARE to show your support! Send a letter to Ottawa telling them to Keep Canada's flame alive here: http://energycitz.in/keepcanadasflame" (Canada's Energy Citizens 2018c).

The tone of both posts and the inclusion of online petitions mimics the well-heeled strategies of progressive organizations (the type Gerbaudo was studying) but are instead employed by the well-funded fossil fuel lobby. Both posts are also consistent with CAPP's broader social media strategy of stoking a corporate petro-nationalist pride amongst its digital nation of Energy Citizens. Recognizing the symbolic work undertaken to twin Centennial Flame's iconic status of embodying Canadian values and pride with pride in Canada's fossil fuel energy sector, the threat of transitioning the Flame off of fossil fuels – in a similar way to the fact that Canada must transition off of fossil fuels – becomes a threat to the values and economic model of the Energy Citizens nation. The CEC Facebook posts demonstrate CAPP's practice of soft leadership by creating an "emotional space", emotively framing a threat to a self-selected community and then providing a space as well as encouraging reaction.

The Centennial Flame campaign is a populist one. Gerbaudo (2018, p. 3), paraphrasing Laclau (2005), sees populism as "a political logic that involves an appeal to the entirety of the political community against a common enemy, and in particular against unresponsive political elites". The elites in this case are the Liberal Trudeau government who, as conveyed in the *Financial Post* editorial, have targeted the Centennial Flame in a virtue signalling exercise: "Landmarks and symbols of Canadiana – such as the Centennial Flame – should not be compromised so the federal government can appear to be meeting its climate change agenda" (Fitzgerald et al. 2018). Of course, the fact that the editorial is penned by fossil fuel executives who are elites in and of themselves must not go unnoticed but may be masked in the creation of a shared antagonism via the Centennial Flame. Related, Gerbaudo (2018, p. 7) also summarizes Laclau's (2005) view on symbolism in populist politics, noting "movements often make use of an 'empty signifier', allowing to fuse together disparate demands in a single platform and campaign". Following Laclau, constructing the Centennial Flame as a symbol of enduring pride in Canada's oil and gas industry is barefaced populism. This calculated communicative practice seeks to construct the Trudeau Liberal government as a "common enemy" willing to sacrifice symbols of national pride for the sake of performative politics. Of course, these symbols, as argued above, have already been comprised to move forward the fossil fuel lobby's political agenda.

Waisbord (2018) has recently written about our "populist moment", noting that "current populist rhetoric resonates with anti-elite sentiments, frustration and disenchantment with the failings of democracy as well as anxieties and opposition to aspects of globalisation – major shifts in labour and employment, breakdown of social welfare policies, immigration, and multiculturalism" (p. 18). Waisbord sees a Weberian "'elective affinity" between populism and what he labels "post truth" politics. That is, a politics whereby "objective facts are less influential in shaping public opinion than appeals to emotion and personal belief" (Waisbord 2018, p. 19). Gerbaudo also explicitly identifies an "elective affinity" but sees it between social media and populism, arguing that "social media has favoured populist against establishment movements by providing the former a suitable channel to invoke the support of ordinary people against the latter" (2018, p. 2). Gerbaudo views social media as offering a "focal point around which the crowd can gather and millions of disaffected individuals, otherwise deprived of common organisational affiliation, can come together as an online crowd multiplying the power of each of its members" (ibid., p. 7). Although Gerbaudo and Waisboard do not cite each other's work, both scholars see an "elective affinity" or resonance between social media and contemporary – populist – political practice favouring emotion, emotional content, and emotional responses.

Gerbaudo suggests in his conclusion that "the underlying narrative and dominant value orientation of social media run counter to the key traits of establishment politics" (2018, p. 8). However, the Centennial Flame campaign, and the broader Canada's Energy Citizens campaign, is conducted by an establishment entity: CAPP, Canada's oil and gas lobby. As such, while the value orientation of social media may favour a logic and practice of emotive populism as a political strategy, *it is not* separate from establishment politics.[5] Instead, it is a practice adopted by establishment politics as captured by CAPP's social media campaigning. In the case at hand, CAPP has effectively used its CEC Facebook group to create a digital community of individuals affiliated with or with an affinity to Canada's oil and gas sector and are thereby mobilized to do industry bidding on and offline. Moreover, populism is not a "thin ideology" as Mudde & Kaltwasser (2017) insist but, instead, as Aslanidis (2016) notes, drawing from Laclau, a "discursive frame" deployed and drawn upon by political actors.

196 Patrick McCurdy

Repertories of contention evolve. Thus, it is not surprising that establishment entities adopt the discursive strategies of anti-establishment politics, especially if they have been proven effective. However, to further tease out the connection between Gerbaudo's and Waisboard's perspectives and link it to the case at hand, we must first acknowledge that social media is underwritten and filtered by platform-specific algorithms which automatically promote or bury content based on predetermined factors such as user engagement, reactions, and shares. Social media companies are for-profit corporations and thus keen to ensure users stay engaged with their platform and remain active, captive, harvestable, traceable, saleable audiences and commodities all in the name of profit. In our age of outrage, controversy has become a surefire topic to stimulate user engagement and has become hard codded into social media algorithms (Couldry and van Dijck 2015; Couldry and Mejias 2019; Fuchs 2017; Trottier 2016). Individuals, organizations, campaigners, and political parties who use social media platforms are equally keen to capture, maintain, and activate audiences. There are entire industries whose aim is to game social media to increase visibility, reach, and impact as part of the "like economy" (Gerlitz and Helmond 2013). Stakeholders can also, of course, pay social media companies directly for promoted or sponsored content.

Gerbaudo's view of the "value orientation" of social media and Waisboard's concept of "post truth" politics converge on the point of emotion. Social media are vital political platforms for emotion-fuelled post-truth politics, allowing political actors to bypass mainstream media and engage directly with their target audience. Moreover, emotion has proven to be a key means to connect with audiences with the rise of what Bennett (2012) terms the personalization of politics. Savvy political operatives craft social media content to game social media's algorithmic logic for maximum visibility and simultaneously elicit user reactions (views, shares, comments, likes) to foster virality and, ultimately, impact. Soft leadership involves crafting political messages to evoke emotional reactions such as anger via social media: a medium hard-coded to amplify and reward emotion.

While harnessing anger has been a key political strategy for mobilizing publics, cementing solidarity, and creating "others" for some time, anger has become a particularly potent political resource (Bennett 2012). Wahl-Jorgensen (2018) has recently written about the rise of "angry populism", which "seeks broad appeal through the deliberate expression of anger" (p. 1). The use or at least priming of strong emotions is well suited to the logics and audiences of social media. On May 8, CEC asked its community to "Tell Ottawa that is a bad idea!", referring to plans to green the flame (CEC 2018b). CEC's call to action is not excessive. Instead, it matches the tone of environmental movements which target the oil and gas industry. The post received 1,182 comments. The top replies to this Facebook post make clear that social media posts do not necessarily need to express unequivocal anger but, instead, create a space for emotion. The top-rated reply, with 522 reactions, read: "Let's replace the liberals with a candle it be a lot brighter"; a post with 183 reactions ends with "Worst government ever. Traitors".

Fanning Flames of Discontent **197**

Of interest is the fourth most reacted to reply, which said: "If the Liberals keep undermining our Canadian identity, they'll find themselves in a revolution". With 23 replies, this comment tied for the second most replied-to comment in the thread. Initial replies were affirmations such as "Amen brother" and "Yuppers". The most liked reply read: "Tooooo many imports in the government now! They have no concept of Canada but carry their countries, customs, etc. from their old lands and expect us to change every bloody thing!" (CEC 2018b). This comment is explicit in its "angry populism" and a xenophobic nationalism rooted in fears of immigration and multiculturalism. While less direct, the "revolution" comment which started the thread also exhibits these political tendencies. Comments such as expose the ugly underbelly of nationalist discourse.

This chapter is not suggesting that CEC or CAPP endorsed or espoused these views. However, their ongoing and permitted presence on CEC's Facebook page points to how soft leadership and specific discursive practices may harness 'angry populism' by creating, enabling, and promoting its expression for one's political end. Ugly comments still count as user interaction. They may also elicit activity amplifying content and campaign visibility. Just as with the adage "No news is bad news", in the like economy perhaps it could be said, "No posts are bad posts". Indeed, if in this process boundaries are overstepped, comments can be deleted, warnings issued, and even apologies made. To be sure, CEC has expressed outrage in the past, particularly against the University of Alberta's decision to award an honorary doctorate to environmental campaigner, scientist, television celebrity, and high-profile tar/oil sands critic Dr David Suzuki. However, soft leadership on social media encourages the building of a community – a fragmented, self-selected in-group – where soft leaders do not always need to express anger but, instead, create spaces for its expression.

Conclusion

On May 15, 2018, Canada's Energy Citizens sent out a NationBuilder email blast with the subject "You helped keep Canada's flame alive!" (CEC 2018d). The message thanked readers for their support, noting: "Because of you, they listened!" The political reality, however, was that it was easier for Trudeau's Liberal government to scrap the proposed Centennial Flame study to keep attention on the political war over Kinder Morgan's Trans Mountain pipeline, in which CAPP was also engaged.

Thus, CEC's victory was a symbolic one. Symbolic victories in battle can play important roles in validating a social movement's objectives and collective identity in the larger political wars. Social media have become key political weapons in the endless war over Canada's oil sands. This chapter explored a specific social media campaign – that of the Centennial Flame – which was part of a larger energy struggle in Canada. While the campaign was first initiated by the Canadian Gas Association (CGA), the CGA did not have an existing social media community

198 Patrick McCurdy

it could activate, and its bespoke social media accounts were ineffective. CAPP, on the other hand, had its large CEC Facebook community, who picked up and carried forward the campaign.

This chapter has argued that CAPP, via CEC, enacted a form of soft leadership in its social media posts. Thus, the political practice of soft leadership should not be seen as the sole domain of progressive movements but, instead, as a deliberate discursive practice which has become folded into the larger repertoire of political lobbying. Moreover, this practice is undertaken against the rise of populist political practices – of which the Centennial Flame's construction of a symbol of petro-nationalism is a part – whereby anger is a key resource to simultaneously satisfy social media logics and engage targeted users.

Having considered the presence and use of anger, this chapter agrees with Wahl-Jorgensen's (2018) call to take "seriously the role of emotion in mediated politics. This goes against the grain of much scholarship in political communication and media studies" (p. 2; also see Whal Jorgensen 2019). This chapter has focused on how Canada's oil lobby has, as part of its social media practice, retreated to a focus on partisan and winnable publics. Doing so has involved emotively fanning the flames of division as a strategy of engagement. As such, there is a troubling contradiction and indeed a wide gulf between our ideals of democratic political practice and the contemporary practice of politics. Indeed, a social media–infused politics has strayed far from the "good" or "ideal" citizen, who Wahl-Jorgensen (2013, 2018, 2019) reminds us is conceptualized as "rational, impartial and dispassionate" (ibid.), to that embodied by the Energy Citizen. A politics primed by affect, rooted in emotion, bifurcated, and inward looking. Social media politics is predicated on what Byung-Chul Han (2017) has polemically called a constant barrage of "shit storms": a relentless stream of outrage politics and manufactured crises designed to elicit outrage. Indeed, just as Mason (2018) has persuasively documented the "social" polarization of American politics into partisan, identity-driven camps, this chapter has presented a small Canadian case study which suggests similar practices are being used in Canada and driving polarization. – Thus while manufactured controversies such as that constructed around the Centennial Flame may mobilize public support in the short term as well as satisfy the algorithmic logic of social media, the practice of soft leadership twinned with a partisan populist approach does so at the peril of the rational, impartial, civic debate our democracy requires.

Notes

1 For a more detailed discussion of these events, see: McCurdy (2017).
2 For more on CAPP's advertising campaigns, see McCurdy (2018); McCurdy and Thomlison (2019).
3 The Suncor advertisement is now "unlisted" on YouTube, but, as of this writing, the URL is still active.
4 For more on culture jamming, see: Carducci (2006); Harold (2004).
5 Whereas Gerbaudo (2018) views left and right populism in tension with the establishment, Postill (2018) makes a convincing argument for "centrist populists" who challenge "the establishment and 'radical' populists" (p. 4). However, this chapter takes the

view that populism can also be viewed as a political discourse or political practice employed by establishment actors towards their own ends. Social media can play a particularly prescient role in this.

References

Anderson, B. (1983). *Imagined communities: Reflections on the origin and spread of nationalism.* London: Verso.

Aslanidis, P. (2016). Is populism an ideology? A refutation and a new perspective. *Political Studies, 64*(1_suppl), 88–104.

Beeby, D. (2018, April 22). 'Greening' project could end use of fossil fuel for Centennial Flame. CBC News. Retrieved from www.cbc.ca/news/politics/methane-natural-gas-centennial-monument-biogas-flame-bullfrog-enbridge-1.4626548

Bennett, W. L. (2012). The personalization of politics: Political identity, social media, and changing patterns of participation. *The Annals of the American Academy of Political and Social Science, 644*(1), 20–39.

Bimber, B. (2014). Digital media in the Obama campaigns of 2008 and 2012: Adaptation to the personalized political communication environment. *Journal of Information Technology & Politics, 11*(2), 130–150.

Carducci, V. (2006). Culture jamming: A sociological perspective. *Journal of Consumer Culture, 6*(1), 116–138.

Canadian Gas Association (2018, May 4). RE: Open Letter to the Prime Minister. News release. Retrieved from www.newswire.ca/news-releases/re-open-letter-to-the-prime-minister-681627871.html

CAPP (2013). CAPP Canadian upstream oil & natural gas industry overview. PowerPoint presentation. Retrieved from www.slideshare.net/InvestandRetire/capp-canadian-upstream-oil-natural-gas-industry-overview?qid=689a3d36-189c-4a87-a660-72525323d29a&v=&b=&from_search=5

CAPP (2015, April). The engagement issue. *Context Magazine, 3*(2). Retrieved from www.capp.ca/~/media/capp/customer-portal/publications/262007.pdf

CAPP (2018). Initiatives. Retrieved from www.capp.ca/initiatives

Cammaerts, B. (2018). *The circulation of anti-austerity protest.* Cham: Palgrave Macmillan.

Canada's Energy Citizens (2018a, May 5). "You won't believe this". Email.

Canada's Energy Citizens (2018b, May 8). The federal government is thinking about replacing Canada's Centennial Flame with LED lights. Tell Ottawa that's a bad idea!. Facebook post. Retrieved from www.facebook.com/story.php?story_fbid=1412280912251050&id=466158346863316

Canada's Energy Citizens (2018c, May 9). Some common sense right here SHARE to show your support! Send a letter to Ottawa telling them to Keep Canada's flame alive here: http://energycitz.in/keepcanadasflame. Facebook post.

Canada's Energy Citizens (2018d, May 15). You helped keep Canada's flame alive!. Email.

Castells, Manuel. (2009). *Communication power.* Oxford, UK: Oxford University Press.

Chadwick, A. (2017). *The hybrid media system: Politics and power.* Oxford: Oxford University Press.

Couldry, N. (2012). *Media, society, world: Social theory and digital media practice.* Cambridge: Polity.

Couldry, N., & Van Dijck, J. (2015). Researching social media as if the social mattered. *Social Media+ Society, 1*(2), 1–7.

Couldry, N., & Hepp, A. (2017). *The mediated construction of reality.* Cambridge: Polity.

Couldry, N., & Mejias, U. A. (2019). *The Costs of Connection: How Data is Colonizing Human Life and Appropriating it for Capitalism.* Stanford: Stanford University Press.

DeLuca, K. M. (1999). *Image politics: The new rhetoric of environmental activism*. New York: Routledge.

Egan, K. (2006, November 22). "Centennial Flame suffers burnout after 40 stressful years on the job." *Ottawa Citizen*. Retrieved from *Press Reader*. Retrieved from https://www-press reader-com.proxy.bib.uottawa.ca/canada/ottawa-citizen/20061122/282059092504416

Fuchs, C. (2017). *Social media: A critical introduction*. London: Sage.

Fitzgerald, M., Myers, P., Ward, P., & Skehar, J. (2018, May 3). "Extinguishing the centennial flame – a Canadian icon – is no way to meet emissions targets". *Financial Post*. http://business.financialpost.com/opinion/extinguishing-the-centennial-flame-a-canadian-icon-is-no-way-to-meet-emissions-targets

Gamson, W. A., & Wolfsfeld, G. (1993). Movements and media as interacting systems. *The Annals of the American Academy of Political and Social Science, 528*(1), 114–125.

Gerbaudo, P. (2012). *Tweets and the streets: Social media and contemporary activism*. London: Pluto Press.

Gerbaudo, P. (2018). "Social media and populism: An elective affinity?" *Media, Culture & Society*, 1–9. DOI: 10.1177/0163443718772192

Gerlitz, C., & Helmond, A. (2013). The like economy: Social buttons and the data-intensive web. *New Media & Society, 15*(8), 1348–1365.

Harold, C. (2004). Pranking rhetoric: "Culture jamming" as media activism. *Critical Studies in Media Communication, 21*(3), 189–211.

Han, B. C. (2017). *In the swarm: Digital prospects*. Cambridge: MIT Press.

Kavada, A. (2018). Connective or collective?: The intersection between online crowds and social movements in contemporary activism. In *The Routledge Companion to Media and Activism* (pp. 108–116). London: Routledge.

Kreiss, D. (2012). *Taking our country back: The crafting of networked politics from Howard Dean to Barack Obama*. Oxford: Oxford University Press.

Lees-Marshment, J., & Marland, A. (2012). Canadian political consultants' perspectives about political marketing. *Canadian Journal of Communication, 37*(2).

Lipton, Eric. (2014, October 30). Hard-nosed advice from veteran lobbyist: 'Win ugly or lose pretty'. *New York Times*, www.nytimes.com/2014/10/31/us/politics/pr-execu tives-western-energy-alliance-speech-taped.html

Lee, A. M. (1945). The analysis of propaganda: A clinical summary. *American Journal of Sociology, 51*(2), 126–135.

McCurdy, P. (2017). Bearing witness and the logic of celebrity in the struggle over Canada's oil/tar sands. In *Carbon Capitalism and Communication* (pp. 131–145). Cham: Palgrave Macmillan.

McCurdy, P. (2018). From the natural to the manmade environment: The shifting advertising practices of Canada's oil sands industry. *Canadian Journal of Communication, 43*(1), 33–52.

McCurdy, P. & Thomlison, A. (2019). Beyond Bitumen: How Advertising Sells the Myth of Canada's Oil/Tar Sands. In *Advertising, Consumer Culture and Canadian Society: A Reader*. Asquith, K. (ed). Toronto: Oxford University Press.

McKelvey, F., & Piebiak, J. (2018). Porting the political campaign: The NationBuilder platform and the global flows of political technology. *New Media & Society, 20*(3), 901–918.

Mason, L. (2018). *Uncivil agreement: How politics became our identity*. Chicago: University of Chicago Press.

Mudde, C., & Kaltwasser, C. R. (2017). *Populism: A very short introduction*. Oxford: Oxford University Press.

Nielsen, R. K. (2012). *Ground wars: Personalized communication in political campaigns*. Princeton, NJ: Princeton University Press.

Postill, J. (2018). Populism and social media: A global perspective. *Media, Culture & Society*, 1–12. http://journals.sagepub.com/doi/10.1177/0163443718772186

Sandoval-Almazan, R., & Gil-Garcia, J. R. (2014). Towards cyberactivism 2.0? Understanding the use of social media and other information technologies for political activism and social movements. *Government Information Quarterly, 31*(3), 365–378.

Sands, C. (2018). "The trans mountain infinity war | La guerre sans fin de Trans Mountain". Energy: Information, Insight, and Perspective on Energy. Published by the Canadian Gas Association. Retrieved from www.energymag.ca/wp-content/uploads/2018/06/energy_issue_2_2018.pdf

Silverstone, Roger. (2007). *Media and morality: On the rise of the mediapolis*. Cambridge, UK: Polity.

Silverstone, R. (1999). *Why study the media?* London: Sage.

Sum of Us (2014, June 24). See what yes is doing. [Video]. Retrieved from www.youtube.com/watch?v=kD-o365UbRA

Suncor (2013, October 27). Suncor – What yes can do [Video]. Retrieved from www.youtube.com/watch?v=JtYJDxy2-SI

Suncor (2014). Oil sands players no longer keeping it all bottled up [Photograph]. *Mediatoil*. Retrieved from http://mediatoil.ca/documents/details/843

Takach, G. (2017). *Tar wars: Oil, environment and Alberta's image*. Edmonton: University of Alberta.

Treré, E. (2018). *Hybrid media activism: Ecologies, imaginaries, algorithms*. London: Routledge.

Trottier, D. (2016). *Social media as surveillance: Rethinking visibility in a converging world*. Routledge: London.

Turner, Chris. (2012). The oil sands PR war. *Marketing Magazine*, Retrieved from http://marketingmag.ca/advertising/the-oil-sands-pr-war-58235/

Vaccari, C., & Valeriani, A. (2016). Party campaigners or citizen campaigners? How social media deepen and broaden party-related engagement. *The International Journal of Press/Politics, 21*(3), pp. 294–312.

Van Laer, J., & Van Aelst, P. (2010). Internet and social movement action repertoires: Opportunities and limitations. *Information, Communication & Society, 13*(8), 1146–1171.

Waisbord, S. (2018). The elective affinity between post-truth communication and populist politics, *Communication Research and Practice, 4*(1), 17–34. DOI: 10.1080/22041451.2018.1428928.

Wahl-Jorgensen, K. (2013). Future directions for political communication scholarship: Considering emotion in mediated public participation. In K.A. Gates (ed.), *Media Studies Futures* (pp. 455–478). New York: Blackwell.

Wahl-Jorgensen, K. (2018). Media coverage of shifting emotional regimes: Donald Trump's angry populism. *Media, Culture & Society*, 1–13. DOI: 10.1177/016344371877219.

Wahl-Jorgensen, K. (2019). *Emotions, Media and Politics*. Cambridge: Polity.

Walker, E. T. (2014). *Grassroots for hire: Public affairs consultants in American democracy*. Cambridge: Cambridge University Press.

Wood, T. (2018). Energy's citizens: The making of a Canadian petro-public. *Canadian Journal of Communication, 43*(1), 75–92.

13

NOT A LEADER!

Theresa May's Leadership Through the Lens of Internet Memes

Mireille Lalancette and Tamara A. Small

Introduction

On her 2018 African tour, British Prime Minister Theresa May was filmed 'awkwardly' dancing at two different events. While television news and the website of major British media featured the videos, memes of her dancing, where people added music or commentary, went viral on social media (entertainment.ie 2018). Memes are pieces of "digital content that spreads quickly around the web in various iterations and becomes a shared cultural experience" (Shifman 2013b, 18). Memes tend to be amusing and humorous while at this same time being sardonic (Shifman 2013a). While many memes focus on popular culture, politics is also an important topic. Research shows that political memes are new form of online activism, allowing groups and individuals to expand and complement their political action (Jenkins et al. 2009; Kligler-Vilenchik and Thorson 2015; Lievrouw 2011; Milner 2013; Penney 2017; Silvestri 2018). In this chapter, we explore a sub-section of political memes called 'leadership memes.' Leadership memes focus on personality or political action of a political leader, including heads of government or members of legislatures (Lalancette, Small, and Pronovost 2019, Lalancette and Small 2017). While considerable effort is spent by a leader and their team to cultivate and control the image presented to the public through photo-ops and social media (Marland 2016; Lalancette and Raynauld 2019), leaders cannot always control how they are presented. The media can provide one narrative of leadership that differs from the one presented by leaders (Trimble and Sampert 2004). Leadership memes are also uncontrolled; they are alternative and unconventional narratives about politicians and their leadership produced by citizens. In this sense, leadership memes are significant because they allow us to see how citizens feel about leadership – in a manner that did not exist pre-internet.

Focusing on the British Prime Minister, we ask: how is the leadership presented in the memetic form? Cloaked in the anonymity of the internet, meme creators can discuss and portray a leader in far different ways than the press or the leader themselves. Memes are therefore a useful way to assess citizens' expectations and opinions about leadership.

This analysis assesses to extent to which memes have altered the relationship between leaders and followers, by demonstrating a new method that the latter has in defining the former. In order reflect on the relationship, we conduct an analysis of memes featuring British Prime Minister Theresa May. May became Prime Minister in 2016 at one of the 'most turbulent times' in recent British political history – the Brexit referendum (Stamp 2016). David Cameron resigned as PM and party leader following the surprisingly narrow win for the 'leave side' in the referendum, which he had called for a campaign against. May was one of five candidates that ran for the leadership. She is an experienced parliamentarian – first elected in 1997, serving as Home Secretary since 2010, and the most senior woman in the Cameron cabinet. Consistent with the Westminster parliamentary system, May became Prime Minister after Andrea Leadsom dropped off the third and final ballot of the 2016 Conservative leadership race. Though not expected until 2020, May called a snap election in 2017. Selecting the date of an election is one of the prerogatives of the Westminster Prime Minister. The results of the 2017 election were disappointing for Conservatives, given that the polls showed that May's Conservatives had a significant lead over the Labour Party (Beauchamp 2017). While the Tories lost 12 seats and no longer held a majority in the House of Commons, they remained the governing party. May continued as PM in spite of what the *Economist* called a "big, disastrous gamble" (The Economist 2017).[1] May is Britain's second female prime minister, which allows us an opportunity to explore memes not only from a digital politics perspective but a gendered one as well. To be sure, there are issues of generalization because of the focus on a single case. However, we learned in our previous analyses that leadership memes tend to focus on the top of the leadership position, with memes of leaders of third or fourth parties existing in far fewer numbers.

In this chapter, we will first consider the ways in which political internet memes have altered the fundamentals of power. This will be accomplished through a discussion of the small body of research about political internet memes, including leadership memes. We will then move to explain our analytical process. At their core, political memes are about evaluation (Ross and Rivers 2017). In choosing to make a meme about a leader, a meme creator is making a statement about what is wrong with that leader and their leadership. In the case of Theresa May, memes were critical of her approach to governing. While the attacks were not overly personal or even gendered, they nevertheless used humour and sarcasm to express disapproval. While criticism and evaluation of leadership are not new, the format of political internet memes is. The virality of memes means that they can be shared and thus that citizens can be in contact with these critical assessments of leaders.

Memes and Politics

Given the theme of this book, it is important to recognize that memes are not social media per se. But their existence and popularity depend on it. Memes are shared on sites like Facebook, Twitter, Tumblr, YouTube, and Reddit. While some memes may only have been seen by a few people in a social network, others are rapidly shared and 'go viral.' When this happens, there is the potential that the legacy media picks up on the story and the memes get even more attention, as in the case of the dancing Theresa May meme (also see Bruner 2017; Ojogbede 2018). The creation of memes is facilitated by technology and digital tools, as well as websites dedicated to their construction (the most popular being memegenerator.net). From Grumpy Cat to the recent Tide Pod challenge, we can see that memes are focused on a variety of topics from the silly to the serious.[2] Animal, sports, fashion, popular culture, entertainment, and, as this chapter will discuss, politics are featured in memetic form.

A review of the literature shows memes have altered the fundamentals of power in a number of ways. First, meme making is part of the larger participatory culture where individuals take part in debates about socio-political questions in a personal way and with their own means (online and offline) (Jenkins, Ford, and Green 2013; Lievrouw 2011). Participatory culture can be defined as a culture "with relatively low barriers to artistic expression and civic engagement, strong support for creating and sharing one's creations, and some type of informal mentorship whereby what is known by the most experienced is passed along to novices" (Jenkins et al. 2009, 3). So, citizens can create memes; others can share them in order to express their views on a specific situation and/or political actor. In this sense, there is a political engagement component in both acts: the creation and the sharing of memes. Within electoral politics, meme making contributes to the promotional outreach of candidates (Penney 2017). While not a part of the official campaign organization, memes allow citizens to engage in promotion and persuasion about their preferred candidate. Overall, as Silvestri (2018, 2) notes, memes have the power to "promote civic awareness, and to connect individual creativity to collective expression."

Second, related to this notion of participatory culture, scholars suggest that memes open politics up to different types of participants. By making politics more "entertaining and accessible" (Penney 2017, 114), millennials, who have a unique relationship with social media and traditional politics, may get involved. Similarly, Heiskanen (2017) suggests that memes can allow ordinary people to get involved in politics and to participate. Denisova (2016) describes memes as a "fast-food media." Instead of reading a lengthy newspaper articles or blog post, meme messages can be digested within seconds and quickly liked or share. Memes make participation and consumption of politics easier.

Finally, and crucial to this argument of this chapter, memes have a argumentative significance (Sci and Dewberry 2015; Wiggins and Bowers 2015). By making memes, citizens provide support for and appraisal of political issues, events, and actions (Huntington 2015). Due to their humorous and sardonic nature, memes are seldom used in order to celebrate politics (Lalancette and Small 2017). Rather, they are more critical tools (Ross and Rivers 2017); memes provide citizens a venue by which they can negotiate society's norms (Gal, Shifman, and Kampf 2016), "challenge dominant narratives" (Silvestri 2018, 2), and discuss political issues like feminism and parity in politics (Rentschler and Thrift 2015) or, in our case, perceptions of political actors. Overall, political memes are a wonderful breeding ground for investigating discourses and expectations about politics and specifically about political actors. This vision is shared by Warnick and Heineman (2012, 72), who argue that political internet memes "can teach us more about the relationship between circulation of discourses and rhetoric in digital contexts."

There is a small but growing literature on political memes. One strand of research focuses on political protest. Scholars have explored political memes in the context of Occupy Wall Street (Milner 2012; Huntington 2015), #Black-LivesMatter (Clark 2016), and the Egyptian Arab Spring (Gerbaudo 2015). Other political issues examined include the memes created after the release of the Kony 2012 video (Kligler-Vilenchik and Thorson 2015), the 2014–15 outbreak of Ebola (Marcus and Singer 2017), or the Syrian refugee crisis (Olesen 2017). These studies show that the memes use humour and sarcasm to criticize politicians, police, and citizen behaviour in relation to the events discussed. Memes in political protest serve as powerful tools to raise consciousness and build communities around specific socio-political issues.

More specific to the topic of this edited volume, there are a few academic studies on the relationship between political leaders and memes. Sci and Dewberry (2015) examined Joe Biden memes created during and after a 2012 vice-presidential debate. This result suggests that memes provide a venue for citizen evaluation of Biden's performance and leadership skills. Another study showed how Donald Trump and Hillary Clinton memes produced during the 2016 United States presidential election served four delegitimizing purposes: authorization, moral evaluation, rationalization, and myth-making (Ross and Rivers 2017). Another 2016 election study explored how presidential candidates (Bernie Sanders, Hillary Clinton, Carly Fiorina, and Ted Cruz) were portrayed and framed in the memes. Both female and male politicians were portrayed negatively, though female politicians' policies, character, and skills were criticized. This research unravelled a gendered aspect to meme discourses more harshly. Also from that campaign, Penney (2017) argues that the memes such as #BabiesForBernie[3] created unofficial spaces of political marketing on behalf of one's preferred candidate. In this case, memes were created in support of a candidate rather than against. In two separate studies about leadership memes about Canadian Prime Ministers Stephen Harper and Justin Trudeau (Lalancette, Small, and Pronovost 2019; Lalancette and Small 2017), we found that memes were part of a normative debate about politics and political actions. Leadership memes were used to denunciate both the political

206 Mireille Lalancette and Tamara A. Small

actions and personalities of leaders. Though it is difficult to know for sure who the meme creators are, our research showed that they were certainly created by knowledgeable and highly politically engaged people/citizens. Memes were not created simply for laughing at the politician; they mostly refer to specific political decisions and were used to condemn some of the actions and decisions of both Harper and Trudeau. Our studies confirm "that meme creation is of larger grass-roots actions characterized by the possibility of spreading the message using various platforms. This enables citizens' appropriation and offers them the possibility to communicate in their own terms" (Bennett and Segerberg 2013, 37–38). In this chapter, we consider if our findings hold in leadership memes about Theresa May given the differences in political context.

Exploring Leadership Memes

While there are various types of memes, including hashtags, gifs, and video, the image macro meme is our focus (see Figure 13.1). Image macro memes usually have a phrase on the top of the image which sets up the context of the message and a bottom phrase with a witty message, a punchline, or a catchphrase. Image macro memes are extremely easy to make using a meme generator website such as memegenerator.net, knowyourmeme.com, or politicalmeme.com. These sites allow users to either select an image or upload their own and provide boxes to add text in the standard format of Impact font in capital letters, usually in black or white (Brideau and Berret 2014).

As an object of study, image macro memes present a number of methodological challenges. Image macros memes are unlike other digital artefacts such as tweets or online video. There is no single repository (e.g. Twitter or YouTube) where these memes, political or otherwise, are housed. Rather, memes are shared on various social media. Some memes may only be seen or shared with a handle of the meme creator's followers, while other go viral and are shared and shared. Not having a single home makes collecting political memes a challenge. Moreover, whereas a tweet or a YouTube video is associated with a particular user account, image macros memes may lose that information over time (if ever known). This means that data such as the original creator, date of creation, and number of views or shares does not readily exist.

Given these challenges, we used Google Images to locate memes using the search expression: "Theresa May political internet memes." A Theresa May meme is defined as one that directly or indirectly refers to the leader in the set-up, punchline, and/or image. This data collection method was selected because we wanted to mimic the strategy that a layperson would use to find memes of this type. Google Images, according to Google, is the most comprehensive image database in the world. Memes were collected in October 2017. Other scholars have used meme generator sites to select data. The discussion that follows is based on the assessment of 62 image macro memes collected in October 2017.[4] We do

FIGURE 13.1 Generic Image Macro Meme
Source: Lalancette, Small, and Pronovost (2019)

not claim that this is the entire universe of memes about May that exists on the internet. Other memes may exist using different search terms and/or using different meme sites. Nevertheless, as said earlier, our collection method allows us to analyse the memes most readily available to a layperson.

As a form of supply research (Norris 2003), we focus on the content produced by meme creators. A content analysis of the language and the visual component of the Theresa May memes was conducted. Content analysis is the

> measurement of dimensions of the content of a message or message in a context. Content analysis can be employed to describe a group of related messages, draw inferences about the sources who produced those messages, or draw inferences about the reception of those messages by their audience.
> *(Benoit 2011, 269)*

208 Mireille Lalancette and Tamara A. Small

By exploring Theresa May memes systematically, we can identify the trends and approaches taken by meme makers and learn how people view and assess her leadership. To be sure, this is a partial story. For the reasons above, we can only speculate some about meme creators and their process and objectives, because we know little about them. Moreover, without share statistics or view numbers, we speak little to the impact of a particular meme. That said, we believe that when a person chooses to make a meme about a leader, they are making a statement about what is right or wrong with that leader. Memes tells us about how some citizens are conceptualizing leaders, outside of polls and the media, and what aspects of leadership they are concerned with.

The coding scheme (Table 13.1) was based on our previous analyses, which explored leadership memes in two broad categories: political practices and personality. Political practice memes focused on political actions and policy decisions by a leader, while the personality-focused memes criticized more personal attributes, such as character, skill, or appearance (Lalancette, Small, and Pronovost 2019).[5] Like the chapter on Hillary Clinton in this volume, we situate this analysis in the gendered mediation literature. This literature suggests that "the mediated presentation of politics is gendered" (Sreberny-Mohammadi and Ross 1996, 103), that expectations are different for female and male politicians (for instance, Fox and Lawless 2011), and that gender stereotypes are often used when portraying women politicians (Kahn Fridkin 1996). This research shows that female and male politicians tend to be treated differently by the media, using masculine narrative as the norm.[6] Typical attributes of leadership like strength, intelligence, and toughness, which are often seen as masculine (Jamieson 1995), are assessed differently from their male counterparts (Gidengil and Everitt 2003; Drouin and Lalancette 2014) and framed as a novelty (Trimble 2018). There is evidence of gender mediation in the coverage of female candidates in British politics and elections (Ross 2002; Ross and Comrie 2012; Ross et al. 2013). Specific to this chapter, Garcia-Blanco and Wahl-Jorgensen (2012) found that the press focusses on Theresa May, then the Home Secretary's elegance – shoes and clothes.

We begin the analysis of each meme with assessing the main focus (Table 13.1). This allows us to get at what aspect of leadership, if any, is central in each meme. Both the image and the associated text are assessed. Is the meme focussed on May's skill or competence as a leader? Is the meme focussed on May's actions as Prime

TABLE 13.1 Meme Focus Coding Definitions

Skills or competences: discussion of the leader's aptness and political acumen
Character: discussion of the leader and their qualities as a person and for governing
Behaviour: discussion about the leader's actions
Gender: discussion about the leadership gender
Appearance: discussion of the leader's appearance

Source: Table created by Authors

Minister? Are May's qualities as either a person or a leader being questioned? We created different categories in order to assess the leadership of politicians. By dividing the assessment of leadership into questions of skills or competencies, character, behaviour, gender, appearance, and policy, we are able to identify the elements on which the evaluation of women's leadership were based.

We then consider the tone of the focus. Each meme was coded as to whether the focus positive, neutral, or negative. That is, a meme could comment positively on May's action or a policy issue or negatively on her inaction. As with our previous analyses, the meme needed to be very clearly positive or negative to be coded as such. Accordingly, some of the subtlest tone in the memes may have been missed. In addition, image type is analysed. As the name implies, altered images are those where something has been added or removed from the original image. Finally, a homemade meme image is one where two or more disparate images are put together to create a new image (Lalancette and Small 2017). Also, with regard gender, we consider the pictorial assessment representation of Theresa May, that is, if the image of May is positive, negative, or neutral.

Not a Leader: Theresa May in Memes

Research shows that citizens have very particular expectations of their leaders. As King (2002) points out, voters' perceptions of characteristics such as leadership abilities, honesty, intelligence, friendliness, sincerity, and trustworthiness play an important role when assessing politicians, especially during election time. Competence and responsiveness of a leader is also valued by citizens (Bittner 2011). The question of competence is key, as voters want political leaders to deliver tailored policies, understand the issues of the country, and be able to deal with unanticipated problems (Arbour 2014). Within the Conservatives, Theresa May's leadership has faced and continues face challenges from other politicians, including Boris Johnston, from pro- and anti-Brexit wings of the party (McTague 2018; Cooper and Dickson 2018). Calls for her resignation are frequent from within the party. In terms of leadership qualities, May was preferred candidate to Labour Party leader Jeremy Corbyn in the 2017 general election (Cowling 2017). Other polls show that while she was considered both competent and strong, she is not considered particularly likable or honest by voters (YouGov 2017). May remains more popular than Corbyn; however, satisfaction with her leadership among Conservative supporters has steadily declined since the 2017 election (Dixon 2018).

Given this, how do meme makers assess the British Prime Minister in memetic form? We begin our analysis by first exploring the rhetorical content of the memes, followed by an assessment of the images used. This is not because one is more important than the other. Indeed, image macro memes are a subtle synergy of image and text that work together to create the wit of the message. That said, for ease of analysis it is helpful to consider text and images independently. Overall, political internet memes provide a space for citizens to express disapproval of Theresa May's leadership. This disapproval is evidenced in both the purposely selected images and the crafted text. These memes provide a space for an alternative interpretation of leadership that differs from the self-presentation of politicians and by the traditional media.

The memes in our sample were overwhelming negative. Figure 13.2 presents examples of negative memes. Consistent with the genre of memes, May memes are not a tool for praise. When meme makers engage in this type of political activity, they use it as a forum to anonymously criticize May, from both personal and political standpoints. This is similar to the American research discussed earlier on leadership memes of Joe Biden, Hillary Clinton, and Donald Trump (Sci and Dewberry 2015; Ross and Rivers 2017).

Brexit, clearly one of the most important issue for May, was the main focus of two memes, though it was mentioned two other times in passing. Since May has been in power only for a short time, this could help explain the fact that policy issues were not the centre of attention of meme creators. Other policies featured in memes included internet regulation, austerity measures, and the scrapping of the Human Rights Act. The findings here differ somewhat from our previous analysis of Canadian Prime Ministers Stephen Harper and Justin Trudeau in Canada, where policy issues featured more prominently in memetic form. We find this less so with Theresa May. The consequence of this finding is that May memes are much more focussed on her leadership style, or lack thereof.

The most popular type of meme in the sample are those that make claims about May's behaviour. In general, May is portrayed as opportunistic, concerned with herself, uncaring of people, and mean-spirited. For instance, one meme featured May in the background saying: "I will starve your Granny/Then steal her house!" In this meme, May is framed as both mean-spirited and uncaring in her approach to governing. The memes that relate to austerity measures are similar to this. Figure 13.2 is shows May as being a hypocrite and also in another meme (not shown). In one, we can see a photoshopped image of May pictured with a cigarette in her mouth, beer and chips in her hands; she is presented as the champion of the working class. This photo of May was altered. In the original photo, May has a cone of French fries in one hand and a coffee in the other. The unflattering photo comes from a campaign stop during the 2017 election. The text reads: "Tabs. Beer. Chips. Theresa May: Champion of the Working Class" – suggesting that May is out of touch with the common people. Even without the alteration, May was criticized by the media for being "ill-at-ease" on the campaign trail (Belam 2017). This meme is clearly satirical and aimed at denouncing her behaviour and the fact that she is not as she presents herself. The image projected in the meme is clearly not of someone fit to be a leader.

In other behaviour memes, May is accused of political impropriety. For instance, one meme presents her along with her husband, and they are all smiles. The text reads: "Whilst her husband's £1.1 trillion investment company avoided U.K. tax/May got rid of 20,000 police, raised tax on the self employed & took away benefits for 160,000 disabled people." Her actions are not those of someone

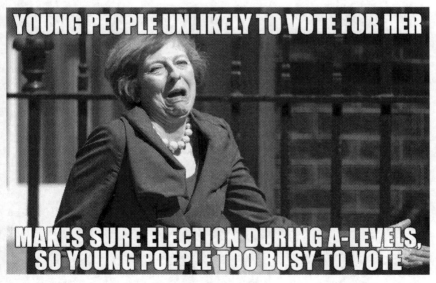

FIGURE 13.2 Examples of Theresa May Memes
Source: Memes created by Meme Generator

expected to lead with integrity and respect of the ethical rules. She is also accused of stealing the election in multiple memes. May is presented as unfit to lead the government. In other words, the memes discuss the fact that May's behaviour could be dangerous and detrimental for the country: behaviour that can be seen

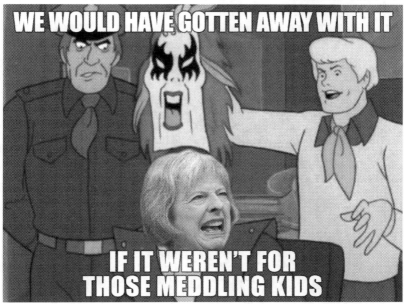

FIGURE 13.2 (Continued)

as opposite of the political attributes needed in a leader, such as honesty and trustworthiness.

This is important because, as a form of political communication, memes bring together both narrative and visual dimensions. Meme makers appear to carefully combine their image selection with political criticism of Theresa May. Our sample shows that they follow many conventions of the meme community while creating political memes (e.g. humour, stock photo uses, and popular culture references). A variety of images and image types were used in May memes. Despite the variety of images used, all seek to denigrate May's image as an effective leader. The most common type of image was a photo of Theresa May. While several different photos of May were used, the examples in Figure 13.2 are typical. They are typical in the sense that they are not the most flattering images of May. A lot of May photos were unflattering. Indeed, there are several different versions of 'mouth open' Theresa May. The purpose of such photos is to create a negative public perception. May comes off as arrogant, glib, and/or unfriendly. These depictions of May are contrary to what research suggests citizens value in a politician. This is consistent with the rhetorical messages discussed above. As Figure 13.2 shows, there is a purposeful synergy between May's open mouth and body language and the message of her not caring about young voters. We know that political leaders engage in significant image-making activities in order to generate favourable public perceptions (Lalancette and Raynauld 2019); leadership memes deviate from this considerably. It is worth pointing out that unflattering images did not feature our analysis of the two male Canadian Prime Ministers.[7]

And what about the assessment of leadership and gender? As noted, the gendered mediation literature shows that female and male leaders tend to be treated differently by the media, using masculine narrative as the norm. We wondered if meme makers would also engage in gendered mediation when creating their memes. Memes that were solely focused on gender were rare (only three of the 62 memes). These were quite misogynistic, including references to menstruation, that May was the man during sex with her husband, or that she was unattractive. Overall, there is little evidence to suggest that gender was at the forefront of criticism of Theresa May. One explanation for this is that leadership memes at their core are critiques of leadership. Politicians, regardless of gender, are seen as failing to live up to normative standards of good leadership. It is this belief that underscores the meme creator's desire to create the meme in the first instance. Bad leadership is bad leadership, whether the politician is male or female. Our results align with Spencer (2017), who found that memes did not support current stereotypes on gender in politics and that female politicians were not more negatively criticized than the men in her study. In the absence of possible comparison, it is difficult for us to say if she was more or less the object of scrutiny than her male counterparts. Nevertheless, memes and gender mediation could be the object of more systematic studies.

As with our earlier studies, broader meme conventions feature in May memes. Almost half of our sample featured a stock meme image. A stock image is one that comes from a popular (non-political) meme. The narrative structure of the meme is then applied to a new context, in this case political leadership. Stock image memes are easily created; these images are standard in meme generators. The meme creator selects the image and adds the text. Indeed, this is one appeal of memes; they "take images from dominant media structures, juxtaposing and remixing them to create new layers of meaning" (Huntington 2015, 78). These stock image memes seek to mock Theresa May within the context of popular culture. They use tropes and metaphor to again highlight what is wrong with May politically. Figure 13.2 provides two examples of stock image memes about Theresa May. The first is a variant of the 'Annoyed Picard'[8] meme, which is used to express exasperation and annoyance at someone's behaviour. This meme expresses disbelief of May's words, again suggesting an opportunism that is common in these memes. The second example in Figure 13.2 is an example of an altered stock image, where May is photoshopped into the meme. The 'Unmasking Villain' meme comes from the cartoon *Scooby Doo*. A common trope of the show is the unmasking of that show's monster to determine who the human villain is behind the monster's scam. In this case, the villain is Theresa May. Images from the *Matrix*, *South Park*, and *Pulp Fiction* are found in our sample. While meme generators do make the creation of memes quite simple, these altered memes take more effort and time, thus demonstrating a commitment on the part of the creator to this particular political message. The visuals are important in the creation of leadership memes. The images used convey significant amounts of information about Theresa May and are intimately tied to meaning making. May is presented in as evil, foolish, and uncaring of others. Moreover, the fact that meme creators are using popular culture references could help attract the attention of citizens all over the world, since these characters are renowned and have an attractive quality. Using them to condemn May's leadership could foster the propagation of the message and could also make the memes more viral and spreadable. Taken together, the different aspects of May leadership discussed in the memes offer a pretty hostile and antipathetic picture of her and how she might govern the country. This is interesting since we know that some citizens only get their information via social media platforms and thus are more likely to come across some of these memes. These memes would be shared by those they trust in their personal social networks, which gives them potentially greater weight. As noted in the introduction, memes are the enemy of image managers and political marketing experts who are trying to craft the perfect image of their leader.

Discussion and Conclusion

In this chapter, we explored the extent to which political internet memes, a part of the social media environment, have altered the relationship between leaders and followers. As discussed by other scholars, leadership memes are a communication tool and thus have a rhetorical power to challenge dominant narratives; they are also a great way to raise awareness about specific issues and build communities around specific political topics. Memes are also a bottom-up type of expression. They are easily created and shared. "Memes [. . .] [are] uniquely shape[d] and [able to] capture the mood of the moment" (Silvestri 2018, 15). Memes alter the relationship between leaders and citizens by giving them a public tool to express their evaluations of leadership. In this sense, they help citizens and political actors to get a sense of the spirit of the moment and what is grabbing the attention of the electorate at a specific time and place. Since they also have a short temporal life, they are tools to intervene into a current debate rapidly and with efficacy (Rentschler and Thrift 2015). Memes are thus "a way for people to communicate affiliation with less social risk" (Silvestri 2018, 2). The uses of popular culture references in the meme text and images make them accessible and easy to understand. Their humorous nature also adds to the pleasure of sharing them with friends and family.

Politicians should be aware of these new communication tools allowing citizens to express themselves and be active politically from the comfort of their homes with only a smartphone in their hands. A quick internet search brings up memes for Donald Trump, Justin Trudeau, Emmanuel Macron, and Angela Merkel. Memes do not just stay in social media. As mentioned, when memes go viral, they sometimes get picked up by legacy media, such as dancing Theresa May. The mainstream media has also written stories about memes created after Donald Trump's visits to the Vatican, such as "13 Hilarious Memes of Pope Francis Looking Miserable with Donald Trump" (Gonzales 2017). Political scientists and communication scholars must continue to problematize these new phenomena and develop analytical tools in order to grasp their significance in the political communication process and relationships with citizens.

As Theresa May stepped down during the final process of editing this chapter, it is worth asking how her leadership will be perceived over time. Did the memes capture the spirit of the moment? Could the analysis of memes help predict the future of some politicians? How can memes help us understand how politicians are perceived by the population? These questions are certainly worth asking and could be the object of future studies.

There is much work to be done on the area of leadership memes. Comparative analysis might provide a more fulsome understanding of memes and leadership and highlight any country-specific factors that may occur. Memes about politicians also appear in gif and video form. Indeed, there are several YouTube videos that have poked fun at Theresa May. For instance, the techno music video "Theresa May Remix Strong and Stable" by Eclectic Method has been viewed more than 87,931 times.[9] Leadership meme research could go beyond image macro memes. As such, some form of demand research of memes that explores both sharers of memes and audiences would be useful (though methodologically challenging). A quick Google Image search of a head of state will result in memes, so it appears that political leaders are being criticized by people all over the world. Yet, we know surprisingly little about this political practice.

Notes

1 On May 24, 2019 she announced that she would be stepping down as PM as off June 7, 2019 following the fact that she was not able to reach an agreement about the Brexit.

216 Mireille Lalancette and Tamara A. Small

2 Grumpy Cat is a meme featuring a cat with a grumpy or annoyed facial expression. As a meme, it is use to express annoyance or a lack of enjoyment (https://knowyourmeme.com/memes/grumpy-cat). The Tide Pod challenge is a video meme that features people, usually teenagers, eating the laundry detergent pod (https://knowyourmeme.com/memes/tide-pod-challenge).
3 #BabiesForBernie were photos of babies dressed by their parents in Bernie Sanders' signature white hair and glasses. See https://berniesanders.com/babies-for-bernie/ for examples.
4 We did a secondary search in October 2018 and concluded that we had generally reached research saturation with image macro memes using these search criteria.
5 Coding scheme is available from authors upon request.
6 Ross et al. (2013) argue that it is the case when media portrayal systematically presents women politician as such. By using the prefix "women", it codifies them as the "other" and reveals that they are not the typical male politician (p. 7). See also Van Zoonen (2006) on this subject.
7 However, an unsystematic review of Donald Trump and Boris Johnson memes in Google Images does show a significant number of unflattering images in memes of the two male politicians. Is the choice of an unflattering image of Theresa May related to the broader question of gender mediation? Or might other factors play a role in image selection, such as respect for politicians within a political system? Further research should consider these possibilities.
8 Captain Jean-Luc Picard is a character *on Star Trek: The Next Generation*. The original meme was created in January of 2012, with the text "Oh come on, you don't even know what a meme is!" (Lockhart 2013).
9 See this page: www.youtube.com/watch?v=H-EV9BKHRgA. The statistics were collected when writing this chapter. This number does not include other ways of sharing that video – Twitter, Facebook, and other YouTube accounts.

References

Beauchamp, Zack. 2017. 'The Shocking UK Election Results, Explained – Vox'. Vox. 9 June. www.vox.com/world/2017/6/9/15767522/uk-election-results-hung-parliament.
Belam, Martin. 2017. 'Theresa May Awkwardly Eating Chips Could Be 2017's "bacon Sandwich" | Politics | The Guardian'. 2 May. www.theguardian.com/politics/2017/may/02/theresa-may-awkwardly-eating-chips-could-be-2017s-bacon-sandwich.
Bennett, W. Lance, and Alexandra Segerberg. 2013. *The Logic of Connective Action*. Cambridge: Cambridge University Press.
Benoit, William L. 2011. 'Content Analysis in Political Communication'. In *Sourcebook for Political Communication Research: Methods, Measures, and Analytical Techniques*, edited by Erik P. Bucy and R. Lance Holbert, 268–79. New York: Taylor and Francis.
Bittner, Amanda. 2011. *Platform or Personality?: The Role of Party Leaders in Elections*. New York: Oxford University Press.
Brideau, Kate, and Charles Berret. 2014. 'A Brief Introduction to Impact: "The Meme Font"'. *Journal of Visual Culture* 13 (3): 307–13.
Bruner, Raisa. 2017. 'The Internet Has Jokes on Theresa May's Interrupted Speech'. *Time*. 4 October. http://time.com/4968737/theresa-may-memes/.
Clark, Lynn Schofield. 2016. 'Constructing Public Spaces Participants on the Margins: Examining the Role That Shared Artifacts of Engagement in the Ferguson Protests Played Among Minoritized Political Newcomers on Snapchat, Facebook, and Twitter'. *International Journal of Communication* 10: 235–53.

Cooper, Charlie, and Annabelle Dickson. 2018. 'Boris Johnson's Brother Resigns and Demands Second Brexit Vote'. Politico. 9 November. www.politico.eu/article/boris-johnson-brother-jo-johnson-resigns-and-demands-second-brexit-vote-referendum-theresa-may/.

Cowling, David. 2017. 'How Much Do Leaders' Images Matter in British Elections?' The Independent. 15 May. www.independent.co.uk/news/uk/politics/election-2017-guide-what-do-the-opinion-polls-say-about-the-importance-of-leadership-the resa-may-a7735831.html.

Denisova, Anastasia. 2016. 'Memes, Not Her Health, Could Cost Hillary Clinton the US Presidential Race | The Independent'. Independent. 2 September. www.independent.co.uk/voices/hillary-clinton-health-pneumonia-political-memes-a7238581.html.

Dixon, Ruth. 2018. 'Leader Approval Ratings Give Neither Main Party Cause for Optimism If an Election Was Held in 2018'. *British Politics and Policy at LSE* (blog). 2 October. http://blogs.lse.ac.uk/politicsandpolicy/party-leader-satisfaction-ratings-2018/.

Drouin, Alex, and Mireille Lalancette. 2014. 'Se Faire Tirer Le Portrait: Représentations Des Acteurs Politiques En Contexte de Campagne Électorale'. In *Médias et Société : La Perspective de La Communication Sociale*, edited by Dans J. Luckerhoff, 97–114. Quebec: Presses de l'Université du Québec.

The Economist. 2017. 'Theresa May's Failed Gamble – Britain's Election'. The Economist. 10 July. www.economist.com/news/leaders/21723191-conservatives-botched-cam paign-will-bring-chaosand-opportunities-theresa-mays-failed-gamble.

entertainment.ie. 2018. 'Theresa May's Awkward Mum-Dancing Has Spawned Some Hilarious Memes'. Entertainment.Ie. https://entertainment.ie/trending/theresa-mays-awkward-mum-dancing-has-spawned-some-hilarious-memes-327091.

Fox, Richard L., and Jennifer L. Lawless. 2011. 'Gendered Perceptions and Political Candidacies: A Central Barrier to Women's Equality in Electoral Politics'. *American Journal of Political Science* 55 (1): 59–73.

Gal, Noam, Limor Shifman, and Zohar Kampf. 2016. '"It Gets Better": Internet Memes and the Construction of Collective Identity'. *New Media & Society* 18 (8): 1698–714.

Garcia-Blanco, Iñaki, and Karin Wahl-Jorgensen. 2012. 'The Discursive Construction of Women Politicians in the European Press'. *Feminist Media Studies* 12 (3): 422–41.

Gerbaudo, Paolo. 2015. 'Protest Avatars as Memetic Signifiers: Political Profile Pictures and the Construction of Collective Identity on Social Media in the 2011 Protest Wave'. *Information, Communication & Society* 18 (8): 916–29.

Gidengil, Elisabeth, and Joanna Everitt. 2003. 'Tough Talk: How Television News Covers Male and Female Leaders of Canadian Political Parties'. In *Women and Electoral Politics in Canada*, edited by Manon Tremblay and Linda Trimble, 194–210. Toronto: Oxford University Press Canada.

Gonzales, Erica. 2017. '13 Hilarious Memes of Pope Francis Looking Miserable with Donald Trump'. Harper's BAZAAR. 24 May. www.harpersbazaar.com/culture/features/a9923075/trump-pope-francis-meme/.

Heiskanen, Benita. 2017. 'Meme-Ing Electoral Participation'. *European Journal of American Studies* 12 (12–2).

Huntington, Heidi E. 2015. 'Pepper Spray Cop and the American Dream: Using Synecdoche and Metaphor to Unlock Internet Memes' Visual Political Rhetoric'. *Communication Studies* 67 (1): 1–17.

Jamieson, Kathleen Hall. 1995. *Beyond the Double Bind: Women and Leadership*. New York: Oxford University Press.

Jenkins, Henry, Sam Ford, and Joshua Green. 2013. *Spreadable Media: Creating Value and Meaning in a Networked Culture*. New York: NYU Press.

Jenkins, Henry, Ravi Purushotma, Margaret Weigel, Katie Clinton, and Alice J. Robison. 2009. *Confronting the Challenges of Participatory Culture: Media Education for the 21st Century*. Cambridge, MA: MIT Press.

Kahn Fridkin, Kim. 1996. *The Political Consequences of Being a Woman: How Stereotypes Influence the Conduct and Consequences of Political Campaigns*. New York: Columbia University Press.

King, Anthony. 2002. Do Leaders' Personalities Really Matter? In Anthony King, ed., *Leaders' Personalities and the Outcomes of Democratic Elections*. Oxford: Oxford University Press, 1–43.

Kligler-Vilenchik, Neta, and Kjerstin Thorson. 2015. 'Good Citizenship as a Frame Contest: Kony 2012, Memes, and Critiques of the Networked Citizen'. *New Media & Society* 18 (9): 1–19.

Lalancette, Mireille, and Vincent Raynauld. 2019. 'The Power of Political Image: Justin Trudeau, Instagram, and Celebrity Politics'. *American Behavioral Scientist*, 63(7): 888–924.

Lalancette, Mireille, and Tamara A. Small. 2017. 'Justin Trudeau – Love Em or Hate Em: Political Memes in the Sunny Ways Era'. presented at the Canadian Political Science Association Annual Conference, Ryerson University, Toronto, June 30.

Lalancette, Mireille, Tamara A. Small, and Maxime Pronovost. 2019. 'Trolling Stephen Harper: Internet Memes as Online Activism'. In *What's Trending in Canadian Politics? Understanding Transformations in Power, Media, and the Public Sphere*, edited by Mireille Lalancette, Vincent Raynauld, and Erin Crandall. Vancouver: UBC Press, 106–126.

Lievrouw, Leah A. 2011. *Alternative and Activist New Media*. Malden, MA: Polity.

Lockhart, Sam. 2013. 'The 50 Funniest Annoyed Picard Memes'. Complex. 30 June 2013. www.complex.com/style/2013/06/annoyed-picard-memes/.

Marcus, Olivia Rose, and Merrill Singer. 2017. 'Loving Ebola-Chan: Internet Memes in an Epidemic'. *Media, Culture & Society* 39 (3): 341–56.

Marland, Alex. 2016. *Brand Command: Canadian Politics and Democracy in the Age of Message Control*. Vancouver: UBC Press.

McTague, Tom. 2018. 'Brexiteer Calls for Leadership Challenge to Topple Theresa May'. Politico. 15 November 2018. www.politico.eu/article/jacob-rees-mogg-calls-for-leadership-challenge-to-topple-theresa-may/.

Milner, Ryan M. 2012. 'The World Made Meme: Discourse and Identity in Participatory Media'. Lawrence: University of Kansas.

Milner, Ryan M. 2013. "Pop Polyvocality: Internet Memes, Public Participation, and the Occupy Wall Street Movement." *International Journal of Communication* 7: 2357–2390.

Norris, Pippa. 2003. 'Preaching to the Converted? Pluralism, Participation and Party Websites'. *Party Politics* 9 (1): 21–45.

Ojogbede, Kemi. 2018. '23 Hilarious Memes about Donald Trump and Emmanuel Macron's "Bromance"'. Mirror. 25 April 2018. www.mirror.co.uk/interactives/50-shades-orange-most-hilarious-12425068.

Olesen, Thomas. 2017. 'Memetic Protest and the Dramatic Diffusion of Alan Kurdi'. *Media, Culture & Society* 40 (5): 656–72.

Penney, Joel. 2017. *The Citizen Marketer: Promoting Political Opinion in the Social Media Age*. New York: Oxford University Press.

Rentschler, Carrie A., and Samantha C. Thrift. 2015. 'Doing Feminism in the Network: Networked Laughter and the "Binders Full of Women" Meme'. *Feminist Theory* 16 (3): 329–59.

Ross, Andrew S., and Damian J. Rivers. 2017. 'Digital Cultures of Political Participation: Internet Memes and the Discursive Delegitimization of the 2016 US Presidential Candidates'. *Discourse, Context & Media* 16: 1–11.

Ross, Karen. 2002. *Women, Politics, Media: Uneasy Relations in Comparative Perspective*. New York: Hampton Press.

Ross, Karen, and Margie Comrie. 2012. 'The Rules of the (Leadership) Game: Gender, Politics and News'. *Journalism* 13 (8): 969–84.

Ross, Karen, Elizabeth Evans, Lisa Harrison, Mary Shears, and Khursheed Wadia. 2013. 'The Gender of News and News of Gender: A Study of Sex, Politics, and Press Coverage of the 2010 British General Election'. *The International Journal of Press/Politics* 18 (1): 3–20.

Sci, Susan. A., and David R. Dewberry. 2015. 'The Laughing Joe Biden Meme as Digital Topoi within Political Argumentation'. In *Disturbing Argument: Selected Works from the 18th NCA/AFA Alta Conference on Argumentation*, edited by Catherine H. Palczewski, 232–37. London: Routledge.

Shifman, Limor. 2013a. 'Memes in a Digital World: Reconciling with a Conceptual Troublemaker'. *Journal of Computer-Mediated Communication* 18 (3): 362–77.

Shifman, Limor. 2013b. *Memes in Digital Culture*. Cambridge, MA: MIT Press.

Silvestri, Lisa Ellen. 2018. 'Memeingful Memories and the Art of Resistance'. *New Media & Society* Online First. https://doi.org/10.1177/1461444818766092.

Spencer, Elizabeth Ann. (2017). *What Does It All Meme?: A Look into Gender Stereotypes and Traits in the 2016 Presidential Primary Campaign*. (MA Thesis). Department of Journalism, Public Relations and New Media, Baylor University, Waco, Texas.

Sreberny-Mohammadi, Annabelle, and Karen Ross. 1996. 'Women MPs and the Media: Representing the Body Politic'. *Parliamentary Affairs* 49 (1): 103–16.

Stamp, Gavin. 2016. 'Who Is Theresa May: A Profile of UK's New Prime Minister'. BBC News. 25 July. www.bbc.com/news/uk-politics-36660372.

Trimble, Linda. 2018. *Ms. Prime Minister: Gender, Media, and Leadership*. University of Toronto Press.

Trimble, Linda, and Shannon Sampert. 2004. 'Who's in the Game? The Framing of Election 2000 by The Globe and Mail and The National Post'. *Canadian Journal of Political Science* 37 (01): 51–71.

Van Zoonen, Liesbet. 2006. The personal, the political and the popular. A women's guide to celebrity politics. *European Journal of Cultural Studies* 9(3): 287–301.

Warnick, Barbara, and David S Heineman. 2012. *Rhetoric Online: The Politics of New Media*. Bern, Switzerland: Peter Lang.

Wiggins, Bradley E., and G. Bret Bowers. 2015. 'Memes as Genre: A Structurational Analysis of the Memescape'. *New Media & Society* 17 (11): 1886–906.

YouGov. 2017. 'Corbyn vs May: How the Public Sees the Two Leaders'. 6 June. https://yougov.co.uk/topics/politics/articles-reports/2017/06/06/corbyn-vs-may-how-public-sees-two-leaders.

14

TWITTER AND STUDENT LEADERSHIP IN SOUTH AFRICA

The case of #FeesMustFall

Tanja Bosch, Thierry M. Luescher, and Nkululeko Makhubu

Introduction

With the rapid proliferation of social media around the world, social networking platforms such as Facebook and Twitter are increasingly becoming easily accessible vehicles for political expression and the formation of online networks by citizens. Social media holds the potential to play a key political function in the provision of new political information, but also creates spaces for new forms of political participation. Globally, social movement activists have increasingly begun to use these platforms as central communication tools, challenging traditional forms of political participation.

In this chapter we concentrate on the #FeesMustFall student protests at the University of Cape Town (UCT) in South Africa in 2015 and 2016, focusing on Twitter and the role it played with respect to student leadership. The national student protests against an increase in university tuition, commonly known as "Fees Must Fall" by the campaign slogan the movement adopted, began in October 2015 on various university campuses around the country. The protests adopted this name after the widely used hashtag #FeesMustFall on social media platforms, primarily Twitter. The protests took the form of marches, sit-ins, and occupation of buildings, public mass meetings, and incidents of civil disobedience (e.g. setting off fire alarms). The closing down of academic activities on most university campuses around the country was unprecedented in scale in post-apartheid South Africa.

What made the 2015/2016 protests unique in a broader context of previous student protests in the country was the use of social media by student activists, giving the protests the character of an "internet-age student movement" (Luescher & Klemenčič, 2017; Luescher, Loader, & Mugume, 2017). Moreover, the campaign led to wide-ranging policy changes, including the freezing of tuition fees in public universities nationwide for 2016 along with other wide-ranging national and institutional policy initiatives to respond to the students' demands. At the height of the protests, Twitter played a key role in the movement, serving as a space for discussion, debate, and information sharing (Bosch, 2016). The viral hashtag #FeesMustFall alongside #NationalShutdown and campus-specific hashtags such as #UCTShutdown or #WitsFeesMustFall created a space for online conversations between students themselves, within and across universities, and also between students and the wider public. The prevalent use of the hashtag resulted in the strengthening of public discourse on the issue, comprising a form of "hashtag politics" (Davis, 2013).

In this chapter, we explore how student leaders used Twitter to further their protest action. Social movement scholarship has increasingly focused on how digital media contributes to protest events, with various studies asserting that the internet helps activists diversify their engagement repertoires, move beyond previous spatial and temporal confines, and organize and coordinate participation in protest events more effectively. Twitter, particularly, has been singled out for its capacity to help activists to manage the complexities of mass protest organization and coordination more effectively (Theocharis, Lowe, van Deth, & García-Albacete, 2015).

Using the concept of connective action, i.e. the use of social media for the mobilization of loose social movements (Bennett & Segerberg, 2015), we explore the digital trace data of social media content. We draw on data from the open source platform Mecodify[1] (available on GitHub) to explore the hashtag #UCT-Shutdown, triangulated with qualitative interviews with student protesters. This particular hashtag reflects a call to action, asking protesters and other students to "shut down" the university, i.e. to keep it closed for business until protesters' demands were met. On the ground, action to facilitate such a shutdown included a disruption of the academic program by interrupting lectures and exams, and protests at campus libraries prompting their closure.

Background and Context

In accounts of Fees Must Fall, various scholars have identified social media as central to both the emergence and function of the movement (Bosch, 2016; Hodes, 2016; Nyamnjoh, 2016a, 2016b; Luescher et al., 2017). Historically, the 2015/2016 wave of student protests in South Africa is frequently divided into two main phases and traced back to the Rhodes Must Fall (RMF) campaign at UCT (Jansen, 2017), whereby the first phase of "Fallist" student protests started with RMF on 9 March 2015, when a student soiled the prominent statue of Cecil John Rhodes on campus with human waste as part of a well-staged protest performance. In Hodes' terms, this action can be understood as part of a broader pattern of civic action, described as "poo politics", designed "to confront and incite the

222 Tanja Bosch et al.

public through an assault on the senses" (Hodes, 2016, p. 143). This provided the impetus for the formation of the RMF movement at UCT, which in turn inspired and actively supported the formation of similar "decolonization" movements on historically white, English-tuition university campuses such as Rhodes University and the University of the Witwatersrand (Wits), as well as on historically white, Afrikaans-tuition campuses such as Stellenbosch University and the University of the Free State (Jansen, 2017). While originally the RMF-inspired protests were against the colonial character, educational content, and small number of black professors at the old established English universities, there was a difference at the historically Afrikaans universities. Student protesters at those institutions targeted Afrikaans as a language of instruction as well. Within a month after protests began at UCT, the statue of Rhodes was removed from the campus, on 9 April 2015, while similar initiatives took place on other campuses around the country with buildings being renamed and policies reviewed.

Meanwhile, prior to Rhodes Must Fall, students at historically black universities had been protesting for years about the high cost of higher education, financial exclusion, and the inadequacies of the National Student Financial Aid Scheme (NSFAS). However, student discontent on historically black campuses, many of which are in remote and rural locations around the country, failed to garner mainstream media attention. In the wake of a Wits University Council decision in September 2015 to raise tuition fees at that university by double digit figures, which was followed by similar announcements at the University of Pretoria and other institutions, #WitsFeesMustFall, #TuksFeesMustFall, and eventually the generic hashtag #FeesMustFall were coined, borrowing heavily from the successful "Must Fall"-label used by the initial RMF protesters. On 19 October 2015, the campaign to halt the rise of university fee increases, raise public awareness about the high costs of higher education, and eventually demand free education had gained traction, to the extent of starting a national shutdown of universities by student activists. Thus, by October 2015 the rallying point for student activism had shifted from "decolonization" to financial exclusion and fees. This second phase of protest "was promptly dubbed with the enduring hashtag #FeesMustFall" (Jansen, 2017, xi). Unprecedented numbers of students mobilized behind the Fees Must Fall demands. On 21 October, students marched to Parliament in Cape Town, on 22 October to the headquarters of the ruling African National Congress party in Johannesburg, and eventually, on 23 October, to the seat of government in Pretoria where the South African President announced a freeze of all tuition cost increases in public universities. Finally, in December 2017, outgoing President Jacob Zuma promised free higher education for poor and working–class students. The massive protests and forced closure of universities that swept South Africa in late 2015 (and again in 2016) thus resulted in a huge victory for students (Naicker, 2016).

While Fees Must Fall was a nationwide campaign, with the shutdown of university campuses a major aspect of the protest repertoire, every university experienced its own movement process and protest dynamic, and on every campus, activists developed their own respective hashtag campaigns. The University of Cape Town is particularly interesting in this respect insofar as on that campus, Rhodes Must Fall provided an existing network for participating in the online and offline campaign. At the level of social media, the most significant hashtag used in 2015/2016 for the UCT-specific Fees Must Fall campaign was #UCT-Shutdown (which was used alongside #RhodesMustFall and the nationwide #FeesMustFall, as well as less widely used UCT-specific hashtags such as #UCT-Fees and #UCTFeesMustFall). In this chapter, we attempt to further explore the use of the hashtag to facilitate the crowd enabled network (Bennett, Segerberg, & Walker, 2014).

Theoretical Framework

A conceptual starting point in this study is Bennett and Segerberg's (2013) concept of connective action, which they coin to explain how social protest movements use digital media to enable personalized public engagement. The idea of connective action is based on personalized content sharing across media networks, which shapes the core dynamics of the action. Bennett and Segerberg (2013) argue that in the context of a global decline in civic and political organization membership, people are more likely to share personalized content through social media. They term this connective action, which occurs in contrast to the more common collective action. The latter relies on the formation of collective identities. Connective action instead refers to the idea that people share personal frames on social media which results in crowd-enabled action, versus organization driven or collective action. They distinguish between crowd-embedded networks and organizationally enabled networks as two types of connective action, and organizationally brokered networks as a type of collective action (Bennett & Segerberg, 2013, 81).

Methodology

In order to further explore the manifestation of connective action within the leadership of the Fees Must Fall movement at UCT, we drew on a multi-method approach, integrating quantitative (Twitter analysis) and qualitative empirical work (interviews). Social media research remains an emergent field, with ethical issues at the forefront, particularly with respect to large datasets. In the case of the quantitative analysis, we only accessed data that was publicly available on Twitter, i.e. open discussions in which people broadcast their opinions using hashtags. With regard to the qualitative interviews, we built informed consent into the research design and gave participants anonymity, particularly since many had been involved in illegal protest activities on the university campus. This study received ethical clearance from the Human Sciences Research Council.

224 Tanja Bosch et al.

Social Media Data and Social Network Analysis

Using the open source tool Mecodify, we searched for all tweets containing the hashtag #FeesMustFall between 2015 and 2016. Mecodify uses a script to crawl web search results on Twitter.com, allowing users to search for tweets older than seven days. It uses the Twitter search API to return permanent links to the returned tweets (Al-Saqaf, 2016). The data is produced as raw comma separated value files (.csv). Searching in this way for all tweets between 1 October 2015 and 31 December 2016 yielded a dataset of 462,769 tweets (1.6 million with retweets). In order to focus specifically on UCT, we narrowed our search to look for tweets within this dataset containing UCT-related tweets, focused specifically on protest action on that campus. To this end, we identified the tweets with #UCTShutdown and #UCT-FeesMustFall as the most prominent campus-specific hashtags. We then selected #UCTShutdown as a proxy for the hashtag most representing Twitter-related protest action at UCT, as it was the most widely used. The analysis in this chapter is based on a dataset of 11,967 tweets containing the hashtag #UCTShutdown (98,085 with retweets). We then downloaded the tweets and tweeter data as. csv files and used the open source software Kumu to conduct a social network analysis. Classic social network analysis measures such as in- and out-degree centrality were used to define the position and influence of certain actors within the network.

Qualitative Interviews

The social network analysis was followed by interviews with UCT students to probe their perspectives on the protests and on leadership within the movement. In-depth qualitative interviews were conducted with eight current and former students who self-identified as student activists on the campus of the University of Cape Town during 2015/2016. The students were identified via a snowball sampling method. In three cases, these were self-identified (and well-known) leaders of the campus-based Rhodes Must Fall movement, while the other five had been closely involved in Fees Must Fall at UCT with different roles, e.g. as live-tweeters. Five of the eight interviewees gave explicit consent to be personally identified in the study and allowed us to connect their public social media profiles to their transcripts. However, we decided to keep all participants anonymous. The interviews ranged in duration from 45 minutes to 1.5 hours and were conducted in English, transcribed verbatim, and thematically coded in relation to the research question.

Findings and Discussion

#UCTShutdown – A Brief Summary

Using the open source tool Mecodify, we collected 11,967 tweets (98,085 with retweets) using the hashtag #UCTShutdown between October 2015 and

December 2016. The prevalence of the hashtag during October/November each year, which is when the student protests took place on the UCT campus.

A total of 3,410 Twitter users tweeted using the hashtag #UCTShutdown. The top user tweeting using the hashtag #UCTShutdown was varsitynews, which is the handle of the official student newspaper *Varsity* of UCT. This was followed by UCTLawStudents and UCTMSA, i.e. the official twitter account of the Muslim Students' Association.

We also considered those users who were most retweeted and found that, interestingly, there was not a strong connection between those who tweeted the most using the hashtag, and those who were most retweeted. Retweets are a powerful affordance of Twitter, which allow messages to spread quickly and go viral as they spread across the network; and retweeting could be considered as a measure of importance within a network, as users retweet the tweets of those they consider to be credible sources. Retweeting is a common Twitter convention. Thus, boyd, Golder and Lotan (2010) argue that

> the practice contributes to a conversational ecology in which conversations are composed of a public interplay of voices that give rise to an emotional sense of shared conversational context. [...] Retweeting can be understood both as a form of information diffusion and as a means of participating in a diffuse conversation. Spreading tweets is not simply to get messages out to new audiences, but also to validate and engage with others.
>
> *(boyd et al., 2010, 1)*

Moreover, "retweeting draws attention to a message (and its resource link), while suggesting possible endorsement, adding longevity, and circulating it beyond the original network for which it was posted" (Bennett et al., 2014, 245). Five of the top ten tweeters using the hashtag #UCTShutdown were also among the top ten retweeted tweeters.

The interviewees highlighted that Rhodes Must Fall was a central element of the network. This is also evidenced by the fact that the account was the second most retweeted; however interestingly, the most retweeted user was dounia, a US-based user. Here the retweets are based on one single tweet, a reference to the shield provided by white students to black student protesters in October 2015. Bosch and Mutsvairo (2017) argued that one of the simplest explanations as to why this particular image attracted attention is related to the argument that activists' actions are brought together by a common agenda rather than central leadership:

> That is, both black and white students felt they had one common enemy so they decided to join hands to confront their shared problem. This particular emotional image also highlights a continuing and perpetuating discourse

226 Tanja Bosch et al.

of black bodies marked as dangerous, and it has become synonymous with the event itself.

(Bosch & Mutsvairo, 2017, 80)

In addition to exploring those who were most retweeted, we also measured engagement by looking at the top tweeters with the highest number of mentions and the highest number of responses. The user that was mentioned most was eNCA, a commercial television news channel. This was followed by Rhodes Must Fall, who we have already established to be a key user in the network. Among the top ten tweeters with the most mentions are also Independent Online or IOL, which is the online news website of the largest publisher of print material in South Africa, and other media houses like GroundUp News and ANN7tv. This corroborated the interviewees' assertions that Twitter was used for PR and to alert mainstream news outlets to the protests:

> When something trends on Twitter, all media houses want to know what is happening and they want to get involved. When they get involved, the idea is successful because we wanted the attention, we wanted the world to know that there's this thing happening within.
>
> *(Interviewee 4)*

Conversely, when we look at the top tweeters with the highest number of responses, the picture shifts and the UCT student newspaper becomes the user most engaged with, followed by a student activist who mostly tweeted information about protest activities. Others in the top ten of tweeters with the highest number of responses include Rhodes Must Fall and most of the top tweeting tweeters, as well as eNCA.

Leadership Structure

UCT students' participation in the Fees Must Fall campaign represents a special case insofar as, unlike on most other university campuses in South Africa, Fees Must Fall represents an extension and continuation of a student movement that had started a half year earlier on that campus: Rhodes Must Fall. Thus, as noted by a UCT activist:

> Fees Must Fall would not have happened if Rhodes Must Fall didn't happen. It was like a derivative of the Rhodes Must Fall movement, but just like focusing on fees and the destitute [. . . rather than on decolonised education. . .]. They were very interlinked[. . . .] Fees Must Fall was like a child of Rhodes Must Fall.
>
> *(Interview 6)*

The Fees Must Fall campaign may also be described as a new period in the life of Rhodes Must Fall. The above also suggests that the Fees Must Fall campaign at UCT represents the point where the "decolonial moment" defined by the early Rhodes Must Fall extended to fully embrace an intersectional agenda, that more emphatically included class in the movement's analysis and advocacy alongside race, gender, and disability.

Classic social movement studies caution against the use of concepts derived from organizational theory in the analysis of social movement processes (Della Porta & Diani, 2006, 25). Yet, for the analysis of UCT students' Fees Must Fall campaign, it seems appropriate to at least partially and critically apply an organizational lens to the inner workings of the movement and particularly its leadership structure and the roles of movement participants as part of the analysis of the role of social media in protesting.

The Rhodes Must Fall movement is typically described as having been made up of a number of individuals and campus-based informal groups and formations. Special interest groups on campus included gender-based advocacy groups such as the TransCollective and the feminist formation Patriarchy Must Fall, and the most prominent formal organizations included the Students' Representative Council (SRC) of the university, as well as partisan, campus-based student political organizations such as the South African Students' Congress (SASCO) and the Pan Africanist Students Movement of Azania (PASMA) (Interview 1).

Overall, however, the leadership structure of the movement can be described as flat and fluid, which is typical in social movements, and which may be credited to the push-back against the patriarchal political culture. If the leadership structure were fixed, it was argued, "there is going to be these people who are speaking on behalf of the others". This was avoided by agreeing that "there mustn't be a special core" and "you mustn't say, I'm leadership". Rather, relatively open meetings were held to constitute task groups so that "if today we are electing a task team, if yesterday you were a leader, today you might not be a leader. So everyone has an opportunity to emerge and to be seen by the world, to contribute equally" (Interview 4).

The flat and fluid leadership structure is also described strategically as a means to create a sense of ownership among participants and ensure that Rhodes Must Fall was different from existing structures: "If people don't feel like they are owning this, then it won't be different from the other protests and everything" (Interviewee 4).

Looking more closely at the network structure on Twitter, one can see that this closely reflects this notion of a flat and fluid leadership structure, in which there were no clear individuals as "celebrity" leaders, at the centre of the network. Using the network visualization tool within Mecodify, we can clearly see the centrality of certain key actors. In this instance, these key actors are mainstream news organizations (e.g. eNCA, Netwerk24Berig, TheCapeArgus) and UCT

228 Tanja Bosch et al.

organizations (RhodesMustFall, ShackvilleTRC, UCT_SRC) that we can see to be most connected, and central to information diffusion, within the network. This network is based on connections, meaning that the most connected users are those who were most engaged with (in terms of replies and mentions).

Divisions in the Movement

A deep understanding of, and commitment to, feminism and intersectional theory and related groupings and individuals could not keep deeply ingrained patriarchal tendencies in South African politics at bay, so that even Rhodes Must Fall, with its deep commitment to the transformation of dominant culture and structures, found itself with the dilemma of reproducing the same, in parts articulated in terms of patriarchy, heteronormativity, and cissexism. As one interviewee stated: "There were so many women I was looking up to as leaders in the movement; there were so many queer people I was looking up", but eventually even in the Rhodes Must Fall movement, "patriarchy sort of like made a few men salient as leaders" (Interviewee 2). Indeed, several respondents highlighted the power dynamics related to gender, and the prevailing argument that some narratives were privileged over others during the Fees Must Fall protests. One key finding from the interviews is that the leadership of the movement was, on the outside, predominantly male in terms of visible leadership. Meanwhile, women played a key role on the inside of the movement, in terms of mobilization and support, but they received less public visibility. Similarly, Ndlovu (2017, 128) argues that gender remained a "silenced oppression" during the protests, which resulted in the creation of the parallel movement, Patriarchy Must Fall, which "attempted to illuminate perpetually silenced sexism and violent heteronormative patriarchy within the student movements and broader institutional culture of UCT".

Patriarchy Must Fall argued that

> the RMF movement perpetuated the same injustices and oppressions they claimed to have been fighting against: exclusion, marginalization and silencing of voices. In the process of fighting against oppression, some of the RMF members themselves symbolized the face of the oppressor.

Ndlovu and Vraagom (2016) point out that incidences of sexual violence across UCT campuses during the 2015/16 protest action led to a growth in women's resistance movements on campus, with some notable examples including the topless protest by members of the Patriarchy Must Fall (PMF) and the TransCollective, and eventually the disruption of the Rhodes Must Fall exhibition in March 2016. "Even before the birth of FMF, divisions within the RMF movement raised the alarm to heteronormative double standards within the movement. In response to this, PMF was organized as a structure of feminist resistance within the oppressive student movement" (Ndlovu, 2017, 132). It was argued that class, race, and gender became the main focus of the protests, neglecting other forms of oppression and creating divisions within the movement "as those individuals who identified as queer, transgender or gender non-conforming felt alienated and marginalized" (Ndlovu, 2017).

Social Network Analysis of #UCTShutdown

In our quest to better understand the student leadership structure of UCT FMF, we exported the user file (nodes) and the (edges) database on #UCTShutdown from Mecodify and imported it into a free online SNA tool called Kumu. Kumu is a powerful visualization platform which allows one to show network maps. What we see from the network map reinforces the interviewees' descriptions of the flat leadership structure within the student protest movement. The network does not reveal individuals to be at the centre of the #UCTShutdown hashtags and conversation.

We looked more closely at the network that emerged from Twitter, using Kumu's social network analysis metrics. With respect to "closeness centrality", we found that the campus newspaper, *Varsity*, was the user with the highest degree of closeness centrality. Closeness centrality is a measure of the distance each user is from other users. In general, elements with high closeness can spread information to the rest of the network most easily and usually have high visibility into what is happening across the network. With respect to "betweenness centrality", *Varsity* also featured as the most prominent user. Betweenness centrality measures how many times an element lies on the shortest path between two other elements. In general, elements with high betweenness have more control over the flow of information and act as key bridges within the network. While mainstream news organizations were most mentioned in order for students to place issues on the mainstream public agenda, the local campus newspaper played a key role as an information bridge within the network and emerges as one of the key communities in the network.

Communities are informal self-organizing groups of users sharing a particular practice or interest in a particular area and represent informal knowledge flows. The emergence of a community takes place when the nodes of the network can be easily grouped into (sometimes overlapping) sets of nodes, such that each set of nodes is densely connected internally. We found a very diffuse network of user communities tweeting with #UCTShutdown. The four largest communities in the network (i.e. most connected users) were centred around the following users: Decolonialqueer, RhodesMustFall, eNCA, and *Varsity* news. This highlights the emergence of and potential of higher-level organization in crowd-enabled networks (Bennett et al., 2014).

When considering the "in-degree" and "out-degree" of the users in the network, the same pattern emerged. In-degree measures the number of incoming connections for an element. In general, elements with high in-degree are the

230 Tanja Bosch et al.

leaders, looked to by others as a source of advice, expertise, or information. Out-degree measures the number of outgoing connections for an element. In general, elements with high out-degree can reach a high number of elements and spark the flow of information across a network (but may not be the most efficient at spreading the information). Most of the top ten users with the highest in-degree values were campus-based students and student organizations.

Twitter and Beyond: UCT Fees Must Fall, WhatsApp, and Facebook

Divisions in the movement as well as its leadership structure can also be observed in the analysis of social media use. Given the fluid and flat leadership structure and relatively open face-to-face gatherings, a mix of personal and social media provided the alternative way of organizing, in the sense of "communication as organization" (Bennett & Segerberg, 2013, 8). Crucially, despite the assertion that there was no "core group", the classic organizational structuring of the student movement into a core of militants, a wider circle of sympathizers, and a large group of non-participants (cf. Hamilton, 1968, in Badat, 1999, 23) is reflected in the use of different media platforms. WhatsApp groups in particular structured the movement into overlapping groups of core militants and extended activist task teams and also provided a means to communicate with Fees Must Fall leaders on the other campuses in closed groups. Sympathizers, in turn, as well as interested non-participants, would follow the movement and negotiate their participation online by means of Facebook groups and Twitter.

> The processes and results of such communication resemble the self-organization of open peer production and open collaboration. . . . This is to be expected, as the logic at the heart of connective action, self-motivated sharing, is also the logic at the heart of much peer production.
>
> *(Bennett et al., 2014, 235)*

Moreover, the gendered nature of engagement and leadership also expressed itself online: "You'd hear from Twitter that this man who is a leader is trending instead of this woman who is being victimized or whatever that is happening" (Interviewee 2).

A leader of Rhodes Must Fall that we interviewed thus stated:

> For me, the real important communication was WhatsApp. WhatsApp was integral connecting us with comrades across the country, and connecting us as a group of people who identify with whether it be Fees Must Fall, or Rhodes Must Fall, or whatever, so that we could communicate more effectively with one another.
>
> *(Interviewee 1)*

WhatsApp is a Mobile Instant Messaging application for smartphones which allows users to send and receive images, video, audio, and location-based messages to individuals or groups using Wi-Fi or a pre-existing data plan and at no cost. WhatsApp groups thus provided a means to coordinate internally within a private and closed group. At the height of protests, numerous WhatsApp groups proliferated to coordinate actions: "Then there was a group of Rhodes Must Fall, then there was a group of Fees Must Fall, within WhatsApp", and so forth (Interviewee 4). Apart from these, there were numerous other WhatsApp groups, including more peripheral groups of sympathizers and non-students, who would have specific tasks such as providing food at occupations and transport and water for demonstrations. During recent years, WhatsApp has become a powerful and influential tool for political campaigns in the global South, as a primary means of delivery for political messaging, to spread information, or to shape political dialogues.[2]

A wider group of activists and sympathizers was reached by means of other platforms. Given their different functionalities as well as different audiences, Facebook and Twitter were the preferred media for wider engagement as well as personalized politics. Facebook tended to be used by the movement leadership for creating awareness, conscientization, and debate. "Facebook was useful for long statements, most of the time". It also tended to have a wider reach within the UCT student body – "because most UCT students use Facebook" (Interview 4) – and beyond UCT including other campuses. Facebook created spaces for sharing personal experiences and views, "to sort of vent the things that were happening" and for "matching in ideology [and for] congregating". It was also a place to elaborate a counter-narrative when media coverage of the movement turned towards negative sentiments. This is well illustrated by the following interviewee comment:

> When free education came as a call . . . we don't want a fee increment – we don't want fees at all . . . there was a lot of ostracization by general media. People refer to students as hooligans: why were people protesting during a period when exams were coming up, and things like that. So there was a lot of ostracization by general media, and social media became a platform to which students or people could actually tell their stories and sort of depict the truth; what they would believe was the truth at the time.
>
> And there were people who found themselves matching in ideology, would land up congregating. So even if . . . I would be a comrade from Cape Town and there would be comrades from Joburg, and we had never met in our entire lives, but we shared a common goal, if that makes sense.
>
> *(Interviewee 5)*

In this respect, social media in general, but Facebook in particular, created the space for the emergence of common ties across time and space, or what social movement theory calls a "collective identity" that involves a sense of being

232 Tanja Bosch et al.

elements of larger and encompassing processes of change among actors (cf. Bennett & Segerberg, 2013; Della Porta & Diani, 2006).

Facebook would therefore play a different and complementary role to that of Twitter, which reached a different audience than Facebook and had a limited character count and different functionalities. Several interviewees argued that Twitter was a more "elitist" platform than Facebook: "Most of the students, I can say black students, don't use Twitter. It's only middle-class and few poor students" (Interviewee 4). Rather, as argued above, Twitter was being understood and used specifically as a public relations tool: to communicate with "the rest of the world" by feeding information to the broader public and particularly to media houses such as eNCA, IOL, SABC News, ANN7.

Furthermore, given the more elitist student audience, Twitter also served as a tool to reach out to and mobilize sympathizers that were seen as more peripheral to the movement – as "protest cows to come and herd and just be in the masses" (Interviewee 6). In this respect, "Twitter [. . .] played a huge role in mobilizing. It was the best mobilizing tool" (Interviewee 4). It facilitated a reaching out to more peripheral sympathizers, the majority of more "elitist" UCT students, to ensure that mass gatherings and demonstrations were packed with numbers – such as during the Fees Must Fall demonstration at Parliament in Cape Town on 21 October 2015, a case that is specifically referred to (Interviewee 6).

To play this public relations function, movement Twitter handles were used to tweet to specific audiences by means of mentions, whereby "live-tweeters" would ensure that the student perspective on protest events was disseminated widely. Interviewees thus acknowledged that different social media platforms served different purposes, and Twitter in particular was used instrumentally for public relations purposes: to quickly and at short notice inform other students as well as a wider public about where to physically present themselves for marches or occupations. Twitter was thus clearly a platform for quick collective mobilization and broader communication, with online content designed to build the discursive parameters of the protest.

Conclusion

Using a mixed-methods approach to the #UCTShutdown component of the Fees Must Fall national student protests in South Africa, we see the importance of Twitter in facilitating the protest action. The data from qualitative interviews with student activists indicated that the leadership approach to the student protests made a deliberate attempt at a flat leadership structure. This is corroborated by our social network analysis, which shows that Twitter played a similar role in terms of encouraging a more diverse leadership base. The Twitter data gives insights into parts of the protest, and also highlights its "importance for dynamically connecting or stitching the multiple sub-networks into a large-scale movement" (Bennett et al., 2014, 239).

Moreover, the use of social media changed the nature of the protests as Twitter was used not only to communicate, organize, and coordinate #UCTShutdown activities (alongside other platforms like Facebook and WhatsApp), but also and specifically as a PR tool to relay news into mainstream media. Overall, the social media activity around #UCTShutdown represents a crowd-enabled network, enabling a large-scale and unconnected crowd to achieve widespread organization across multiple communities. In the case of #UCTShutdown, the use of Twitter demonstrates how social media was used to build connective action, resulting in a new kind of fragmented networked repertoire, only loosely associated with formal institutional structures. These structures, student leaders, and formal political organizations remained in the background and generated action frames that were taken up by the student body, personalized, and diffused across different social media networks.

Notes

1 www.mecodem.eu/mecodify/
2 https://ourdataourselves.tacticaltech.org/posts/whatsapp/

References

Al-Saqaf, W. (2016). Mecodify: A tool for big data analysis and visualisation with Twitter as a case study. Available online at www.mecodem.eu/wp-content/uploads/2018/09/Al-Saqaf-2016_Mecodify_-A-tool-for-big-data-analysis-and-visualisation-with-Twitter-as-a-case-study.pdf. Retrieved 10 September 2018.

Badat, S. (1999). *Black Student Politics, Higher Education & Apartheid: From SASO to SANSCO, 1968–1990*. Pretoria: HSRC.

Bennett, W., & Segerberg, A. (2013). *The Logic of Connective Action: Digital Media and the Personalization of Contentious Politics*. New York: Cambridge University Press.

Bennett, W., Segerberg, A., & Walker, S. (2014). Organization in the crowd: Peer production in large-scale networked protests. *Information, Communication & Society*, 17(2), 232–260.

Booysen, S. (2016). Two weeks in October: Changing governance in South Africa. In *Fees Must Fall: Student Revolt, Decolonisation and Governance in South Africa*. Edited by Susan Booysen. Johannesburg: Wits University Press.

Bosch, T. (2016). Twitter and participatory citizenship: #FeesMustFall in South Africa. In *Digital Activism in the Social Media Era: Critical Reflections on Emerging Trends in sub-Saharan Africa*. Edited by Bruce Mutsvairo. London: Palgrave Macmillan.

Bosch, T., & Mutsvairo, B. (2017). Pictures, protests and politics: Mapping Twitter images during South Africa's fees must fall campaign. *African Journalism Studies*, 38(2), 71–89.

boyd, D., Golder, S., & Lotan, G. (2010). Tweet, tweet, retweet: Conversational aspects of retweeting on Twitter. In *System Sciences (hicss), 2010 43rd Hawaii International Conference* pp. 1–10. IEEE, 2010.

Davis, B. (2013). Hashtag politics: The polyphonic revolution of# Twitter. *Pepperdine Journal of Communication Research*, 1(1), 4.

Della Porta, D., & Diani, M. (2006). *Social Movements: An Introduction* (2nd edn). Oxford: Blackwell.

234 Tanja Bosch et al.

Hamilton, W. (1968). Venezuela. In E. Donald (Ed.), *Students and Politics in Developing Nations*. New York: Praeger.

Hodes, R. (2016). Questioning 'fees must fall'. *African Affairs*, 116(462), 140–150.

Jansen, J. (2017). *As by Fire: The End of the South African University*. Cape Town, South Africa: Tafelberg Press.

Luescher, T., & Klemenčič, M. (2017). Student power in twenty-first century Africa: The character and role of student organizing. In *Student Politics and Protests: International Perspectives*. Edited by Rachel Brooks. London: Routledge, 113–127.

Luescher, T., Loader, L., & Mugume, T. (2017). #FeesMustFall: An Internet-age student movement in South Africa and the case of the University of the Free State. *Politikon: South African Journal of Political Studies*, 44(2), 231–245. https://doi.org/10.1080/0258 9346.2016.1238644

Naicker, C. (2016). From Marikana to #feesmustfall: The praxis of popular politics in South Africa. *Urbanisation*, 1(1), 53–61.

Ndlovu, M. (2017). Fees Must Fall: A nuanced observation of the University of Cape Town, 2015–2016. *Agenda*, 31(3–4), 127–137.

Ndlovu, M., & Vraagom, F. (2016). Intersecting oppression: Locating gender within #Fees-MustFall. *The Daily Maverick*, 25 October. Available online at www.dailymaverick. co.za/article/2016-10-25-intersecting-oppression-locating-gender-within-feesmust fall/. Retrieved 10 September 2018.

Nyamnjoh, F. (2016a). *#RhodesMustFall: Nibbling at resilient colonialism in South Africa*. Cameroon: Langaa Research and Publishing Common Initiative Group.

Nyamnjoh, F. (2016b). Prologue: Sir Cecil John Rhodes, pp 1–62; Ian Glenn, Standing up for injustice? Nine notes on #Feesmustfall, *Litnet*, 28 September, Available online at www. litnet.co.za/standing-injustices-nine-notes-feesmustfall/. Retrieved 27 October 2016.

Pillay, S. (2016). Silence is violence: (Critical) psychology in an era of Rhodes Must Fall and Fees Must Fall. *South African Journal of Psychology*, 46(2), 155–159.

Theocharis, Y., Lowe, W., van Deth, J.W., & García-Albacete, G. (2015). Using Twitter to mobilize protest action: Online mobilization patterns and action repertoires in the Occupy Wall Street, Indignados, and Aganaktismenoi movements, *Information, Communication & Society*, 18(2), 202–220. https://doi.org/10.1080/1369118X.2014.948035

Tufekci, Z. (2017). *Twitter and Tear Gas: The Power and Fragility of Networked Protest*. New Haven, CT & London: Yale University Press.

CONCLUSION

Richard Davis

Following the announcement of his opinion in the U.S. Supreme Court case of *McCulloch v. Maryland*, which reinforced federal supremacy over the individual states, Chief Justice John Marshall was distressed by the barrage of attacks on the decision by states' rights advocates. Opponents wrote essays in local newspapers to urge nullification of the decision. In response, Marshall used the same technique. He wrote 11 pseudonymous newspaper essays over a three-month period defending his own opinion and repudiating the attacks of his opponents. Marshall attempted to gain public support for his opinion through his writings.[1]

During World War II, Winston Churchill spoke to the English people through radio broadcasts, beginning with his classic "blood, toil, tears, and sweat" speech as he took office as prime minister in May 1940. Churchill knew that Britons turned to radio for news, information, and entertainment. His usage of this medium was intended to inform, reassure, and bolster the citizenry in support of his war policies as they suffered privations through rationing, endured bombings, and lost love ones.[2]

In 1968, a phenomenon called Trudeaumania swept Canada. The new prime minister, Pierre Elliott Trudeau, was only in his 40s and exuded youthfulness and a new generation of leadership. Realizing that Trudeau was telegenic, Liberal Party leaders adopted an unconventional style of campaigning that catered to television news crews and even featured the first televised leaders' debate. They wanted to boost Trudeau's political capital as prime minister through new communication tools.[3]

Over the course of history, political leaders have sought to communicate with citizens utilizing media forms common to the time. Leadership, they knew, was impossible without communication. And communication required utilizing the available technological tools for shaping public opinion.

236 Richard Davis

The 21st century is proving to be no different, even though the tools at leaders' disposal are significantly different than the ones used by past leaders. Not only do political leaders today rely on print and broadcast news media, but they also are incorporating new forms of political communication available through social media. This book documents those efforts by an array of types of leaders – electoral and institutional, as well as non-governmental.

Social media has a short history as a medium (less than two decades old). Indeed, scholars are just beginning to understand how social media platforms are being merged into traditional media uses for campaigning, governing, constituent communication, and grassroots information and mobilization. This volume is intended to expand that understanding by focusing on one relationship – political leaders and social media forms and the shift in power that this usage may create.

We have offered a picture of social media use by a variety of leader types and settings. These include leaders in electoral as well as non-electoral settings, executives like Donald Trump and Justin Trudeau, movement leaders like the #FeesMustFall students and the SlutWalk organizers, electoral candidates such as Marine Le Pen and Emmanuel Macron, as well as legislative leaders in the U.S. and Europe. We discuss a Canadian prime minister who used photobombing to gain social media attention, as well as a U.S. presidential candidate who embraced Twitter in an unprecedented way to communicate with his voter base. We examine populist and even non-populist leaders in various nations employing social media to communicate populist messages. Through these chapters, we see that leaders are found far beyond the traditional halls of power – in feminist groups and indigenous and environmental movements, as well as youth interest groups. They, too, have been the subjects of our analysis on how leaders are utilizing social media to achieve individual, institutional, or group objectives.

Even though we study a variety of leaders and leader settings, we can see some similarities in leader utilization of social media. They include bypassing traditional media forms, seeking to control the message, agenda setting (both public and traditional media), framing, communicating with specialized audiences, and sending populist messages. Let's take each in turn.

Bypassing Traditional Media Forms

A common theme in these chapters is the usage of social media as an alternative to traditional news media venues for communication with specific audiences. One reason for this shift is the high bar for getting placed on traditional media's agenda, particularly with regard to elite media sources. The bar is highest for social movements, particularly new ones still establishing themselves in the public sphere. However, even legislative leaders, candidates, and established groups must compete (often unsuccessfully) for the attention of traditional news organizations. Social media entail less cost and a higher likelihood of success at reaching the desired audience.

Another factor is the dynamic target audience of communicators. While traditional media offer a broad-based audience that reflects the broadcasting nature of traditional news outlets, those seeking communication with particular audiences may find that traditional media audiences are too broad. Instead, their desired audiences are more specific in nature. For example, during his presidential campaign, Donald Trump spoke directly to his voter base through Twitter. The messages he sent to them were intended to reinforce their support. Indeed, the number of followers to Trump's Twitter feed far surpasses the reach of most national media outlets put together.

However, Donald Trump not only bypasses the traditional media but also seeks to disparage it and destroy its credibility. He utilizes social media to attack traditional media. By doing so, he reinforces the attitude shared by his supporters that traditional media are corrupt and unable to transmit the information they wish to receive. That message enhances the credibility of his own messages and impels his supporters to rely on his social media messages for "accurate" information they will not obtain from the "fake news" Trump claims the traditional media provide.

As we learn from the Joshua Scacco and Eric Wiemer chapter, President Trump seeks to undermine the credibility of the traditional news media through his continued rhetorical attacks on those media sources, such as the *New York Times*, the *Washington Post*, and CNN. All become "fake media" that cannot be trusted. Citizens must rely on him for information exclusively.

At the same time that leaders have sought other venues, so have their audiences. Social media outlets now compete with traditional media for information dissemination roles for ordinary citizens. And, among millennials, the competition is decidedly in the favor of social media. Leaders are seeking to move towards the audiences' preferred information sources, which now include Facebook, Instagram, Twitter, and other social media platforms.

Bypassing traditional media in favor of social media expends fewer resources for leaders. Public relations firms are more expensive than Facebook accounts. For example, as Kaitlynn Mendes found, feminist groups discovered that social media platforms are "free, easy to use, and have the potential to spread one's message to a large audience while maintaining control of their message."[4]

Controlling the Message

Control of the message, or at least an attempt to do so, is another similarity across these studies. This applies to both content and distribution. The contrast with traditional media is stark. Message control is difficult for leaders when utilizing traditional media, particularly since a journalistic filter limits whether and how the message is transmitted. Social media usage allows leaders to determine what content will reach users and even how it will do so.

For example, Donald Trump as a presidential candidate was adept at communicating with supporters through his Twitter feed. As Jennifer Stromer-Galley

238 Richard Davis

showed, his Twitter feed became Trump's vehicle for his brand of rhetoric featuring synecdochic arguments and utilizing enthymeme to dramatic effect. Distribution control through social media meant that Trump could be assured that his tweets would be seen, unedited, by his supporters.

Yet, attempts to control the message sent by governmental leaders can be undermined by non-governmental forces. Thus, the image of leaders competes with those messages distributed by non-leaders. The chapter by Tamara Small and Mireille Lalancette demonstrates the problem for leaders who seek to set a particular message. Theresa May's controlled image created by the Prime Minister's Office and the central office of the Conservative Party was challenged by anonymous individuals with no government position. In a sense, meme creators on social media play the same role editorial cartoonists did in an earlier era. The difference is the ease in creating and disseminating a meme, particularly by individuals with no traditional media connection. To what extent memes influence public attitudes about political leaders is unknown. However, their presence suggests that message control is a complicated task in the social media age.

Agenda Setting

The agenda setting role of social media has become of increasing interest to scholars and practitioners.[5] As Jacob Straus and Raymond Williams show, leaders also utilize social media to shape the public's agenda. Republican and Democratic leaders of Congress stressed differing issue agendas in the wake of the president's own attempt at agenda setting through the annual State of the Union speech. Not surprisingly, Democrats sought to shift the agenda away from the Republicans' preferred agenda of taxes and towards the Democrats' main issue of immigration reform, particularly DACA (Deferred Action for Childhood Arrivals).

However, there is a significant problem for institutional leaders seeking to shape agendas when they are in competition with other leaders in the same institution, as well as an executive who not only speaks with a single voice but, in the case of Donald Trump, is an adept tweeter. Presidential tweets are far more likely to receive press attention than tweets by any member of Congress, including Congressional leaders. Practically, this is no different than the president and Congressional leaders' historical relationship with traditional media and is not just a product of Trump's proclivity for tweeting.

As Scacco and Weimer disclose, Donald Trump sought to shape the public agenda by focusing attention on the shortcomings of the traditional media. His tweets were intended to make traditional media bias a priority agenda item for the public.

Intermedia Agenda Setting

Of particular interest to scholars is agenda setting between traditional and social media.[6] Leaders also may seek to use social media to influence traditional media

Conclusion **239**

agendas. Brad Clark also details the attempts by indigenous organizations in Canada to reframe Canada's 150th anniversary celebration with a counter-narrative disseminated via social media. These endeavors appeared to have been successful in shaping some of the traditional news media coverage of the anniversary, since he finds that nearly one-third of the Canada 150 story included references to the indigenous population. However, it is difficult to know for sure what impact their social media campaign actually had or whether such references would have existed anyway.

Mendes saw a similar attempt by SlutWalk to talk back to the traditional media in order to shape that media's approach to gender issues. She also concluded that influence is a slippery concept. For example, she found no evidence that the group's critique of *The Sun* newspaper had an impact on news coverage.

Framing

Media framing – providing contextual information that may alter its interpretation – has been well documented in traditional news media forms.[7] Since the construction of a media message can impact how events and issues are viewed by an audience, leaders have sought to shape the news media's frame to serve their own purposes. As these chapters demonstrate, media framing has been transferred to social media as well. Maurice Vergeer found that candidates are tweeting extensively around election events. They are seeking to frame an event in a certain way that favors their party and its messages.

However, as mentioned above, social media offer publishing opportunities to others to challenge the frames leaders seek to create. Again, Small and Lalancette's chapter on memes regarding Teresa May shows leader framing may be undermined by others. Media framing efforts by leaders exist within an environment of challenge that negatively affect the ability of the leader to frame messages.

Communicating With, Identifying, and Mobilizing Specialized Audiences

Traditional media sources – television and radio news, newspapers, newsmagazines, etc. – are broadcast media that reach wide audiences. Many in those audiences are uninterested in the variety of messages disseminated. Social media reach smaller audiences that would be considered "niche" by traditional media. However, leaders may seek to communicate specifically with that more specialized audience rather than with others who are disinterested, or perhaps may be reinforced or mobilized in opposition if animated by such information.

As Mendes documents, the SlutWalk organizers used social media to communicate with other feminist groups. Indeed, they formed closed and secret Facebook groups to carry on more private conversations with other feminists who were not involved in the organization. This allowed networking in a "safe space" for organizing and communicating.

240 Richard Davis

Non-governmental groups also find social media a useful tool for supporter identification, reinforcement, and stimulation. As described in Patrick McCurdy's chapter, the Energy Citizens movement in Canada used social media to create an online community of individuals who would support the goals of the energy industry. Similarly, the Clinton campaign viewed Twitter as a forum for reaching strong supporters and mobilizing them. Their tweets, according to Shannon McGregor and Regina Lawrence, featured mobilization rhetoric, while Instagram, for Clinton, was the means for reaching voters who might be less policy-focused and more interested in the "human" aspect of the candidate. The specialized audience on that medium was women, as indicated by the strongly gendered message of her Instagram campaign. Similarly, according to Chase Remillard and his co-authors, Justin Trudeau's team considered Instagram as a more personal medium where he could display images of Trudeau's family life and increase positive affective responses towards the prime minister.

One specialized audience is the journalistic community. Twitter, particularly, is a vehicle for speaking to the press since journalists have incorporated Twitter into newsgathering routines. As McGregor and Lawrence concluded, the Clinton campaign relied on Twitter for communicating with the Clinton campaign press corps and providing information journalists desired in quick and highly accessible form.

Supporters are a critical audience for leaders. The SlutWalk organizers Mendes studied and the student group leaders examined by Tanja Bosch and her co-authors considered social media an important tool for identifying their supporters. The goal was not simply to convey unidirectional information. Rather, it was also to facilitate recruitment of leaders and participants in the movement. Social media usage, then, also becomes critical for leaders to mobilize individuals to follow the leader's direction to become engaged and not simply informed.

Sending Populist Messages

Social media forums lend themselves to populist messages by political leaders, as Sina Blassnig and her co-authors so ably demonstrated. These range from populist political parties and candidates, including Donald Trump, to social movements such as feminist groups and youth organizations. As McCurdy noted, even an establishment organization such as the petroleum producers of Canada employed populist rhetoric on social media to reverse a government decision.

However, populism is much more credible as a message from a populist candidate. In Peter Maurer's chapter, we see the difference between a genuinely populist candidate, Marine Le Pen, and a candidate who uses populist language but lacks populist credentials – Emmanuel Macron. Macron seeks to straddle his need to utilize populist rhetoric to address general public frustration with his own elite credentials both in government and business.

Maurer shows that populism is closely connected with the medium of Twitter. Both Macron and Le Pen rely on populist messages. However, more establishment candidates can use Twitter for mild populism that targets certain groups without having to become radicalized.

Conclusion **241**

One of the best purveyors of populist rhetoric, particularly on Twitter, is Donald Trump. As Stromer-Galley discussed, the U.S. president has developed a vulgar eloquence – meaning he uses his rhetoric to relate to ordinary Americans rather than elites. His verbal attacks on the establishment, including the elites of his own political party, are legend on Twitter. Trump's Twitter feed portrayed the world in Manichean terms. His opponents were evil – Crooked Hillary, Lyin' Ted, Mr. Meltdown (Marco Rubio), and low energy Jeb Bush – while news media outlets were biased, or New York City has the worst mayor who causes the city's crime, dirty streets, and homelessness. Trump's Twitter feeds have been classic populism.

Throughout this book we have posed some intriguing questions: Why and how are political leaders using social media? How have social media platforms become tools to achieve the objectives of the political leader, such as re-election, policy change, social transformation, etc.? In turn, how effective is this tool in shaping public opinion or elite opinion or in affecting public policy? How do usage and effects vary across types of leaders – electoral, executive, or non-governmental – and political system contexts?

What have we learned? Communication is a recurring need for democratic political leaders. As Mendes demonstrated, feminist group leaders, for example, have found social media critical to their efforts to communicate with supporters and fulfill their purpose of speaking "up" to power.

Each new communication tool possesses its own distinctive traits and introduces new effects on the users and the communication system generally. The political system is affected when political leaders are drawn to the new communication medium as another mechanism for influencing public agendas, attitudes, and behavior. The nature of the medium becomes a factor in the conduct of public discourse, the audience, and the effectiveness of the leader's efforts to shape others' attitudes and behavior.

Leaders have not abandoned traditional media as a vehicle for communicating. But, as this volume has demonstrated, they have added a new technological tool – social media – to the quiver of available communication fora. In some ways, they use social media in the same way they have employed traditional media. Yet, distinctive elements of social media have forced them to adapt to a new communications environment. Clearly, leaders have learned that social media brings its own advantages and disadvantages. But, even with its challenges, the world we live in does not give leaders the choice to ignore social media.

Notes

1 Jean Edward Smith, *John Marshall: Definer of a Nation*, New York: Henry Holt, 1996, pp. 449–452.

2 See Richard Toye, *The Roar of the Lion: The Untold Story of Churchill's World War II Speeches*, Oxford, UK: Oxford University Press, 2013; and William Manchester and Paul Reid, *The Last Lion, Defender of the Realm: 1940–1965*, New York: Bantam Books, 2012, p. 608.

242 Richard Davis

3 Ian Ward, "Trudeaumania and It's Time: The Early Use of TV for Political Communication," *Australian-Canadian Studies*, 19 (2001): 1–21.

4 Kaitlyn Mendes, "'Twitter Was Like Magic!': Strategic Use of Social Media in Contemporary Feminist Activism," in David Taras and Richard Davis, eds., *Power Shift?: Political Leadership and Social Media*, New York: Routledge, 2019: 154.

5 See, for example, Jayeon Lee and Weiai Xu, "The More Attacks, the More Retweets: Trump's and Clinton's Agenda Setting on Twitter," *Public Relations Review*, 44 (June 2018): 201–213; G. R. Boynton and Glenn W. Richardson, Jr., "Agenda Setting in the Twenty-First Century," *New Media and Society*, 18 (October 2016): 1916–1934; and Evan L. Frederick, et al., "A Shift in Set: Examining the Presence of Agenda Setting on Twitter During the 2012 London Olympics," *Communication and Sport*, 3 (September 2015): 312–333.

6 See, for example, Raymond A. Harder, et al., "Intermedia Agenda Setting in the Social Media Age: How Traditional Players Dominate the News Agenda in Election Times," *The International Journal of Press/Politics,* 22 (July 2017): 275–293; Christina Holtz-Bacha and Reimar Zeh, "Tweeting to the Press? Political Twitter Activity on Offline Media in the 2013 German Election Campaign," in Richard Davis, Marion Just, and Christina Holtz-Bacha, *Twitter and Elections around the World: Campaigning in 140 Characters or Less*, New York: Routledge, 2016, pp. 27–42; and Bethany A. Conway, et al., "The Rise of Twitter in the Political Campaign: Searching for Intermedia Agenda-Setting Effects in the Presidential Primary," *Journal of Computer-Mediated Communication*, 20 (July 2015): 363–380.

7 Robert M. Entman, "Framing: Toward Clarification of a Fractured Paradigm," *Journal of Communication*, 43 (Autumn 1993): 51–58; Zhongdang Pan, "Framing Analysis: An Approach to News Discourse," *Political Communication*, 10 (January 1993): 55–75; and Robert M. Entman and Andrew Rojecki, "Freezing Out the Public: Elite and Media Framing of the U.S. Anti-Nuclear Movement," *Political Communication*, 10 (January 1993): 155–173.

ABOUT THE CONTRIBUTORS

Lindsey M. Bertrand is a communications professional specializing in public engagement in complex issues. She has also worked as a digital rights campaigner and as a critic of freedom of information and privacy policy and law in BC and Canada. Lindsey has written and spoken extensively about a number of issues relating to democratic communication, including media and platform ownership, diversity of voices, reputation management, and consultation and moderation models. Currently Lindsey is the digital engagement specialist at the Canadian Centre for Policy Alternatives (an independent progressive research institute) and sits on the board of the BC Civil Liberties Association.

Sina Blassnig is a research and teaching assistant at the Department of International and Comparative Media Research at the University of Zurich, Switzerland. She is currently pursuing her PhD, in which she investigates populist communication by politicians, journalists, and citizens in digital media from a comparative perspective. Her research interests include populism, political online communication, and its effects on audience reactions.

Tanja Bosch is Associate Professor in Media Studies and Production at the Centre for Film and Media Studies, University of Cape Town, South Africa. She teaches and conducts research in social media, democracy, and politics. Her book, *Broadcasting Democracy*, explores the role of local radio in identity production in South Africa. She is currently conducting research on social media and everyday life in South Africa.

Brad Clark is an associate professor and Chair of the Journalism and Broadcast Media Studies programs at Mount Royal University in Calgary, Alberta, Canada.

244 About the Contributors

Before entering the academy, he spent 20 years working as a journalist in print and broadcast. His 16 years at the Canadian Broadcasting Corporation included reporting for an award-winning investigative team and six years as a national radio reporter, filing stories from such diverse locales as Tuktoyuktuk in the Arctic, Ottawa, Toronto, Washington, D.C., Houston, Seattle, and Caracas.

Richard Davis is Professor of Political Science and Director of the Office of Civic Engagement Leadership at Brigham Young University, USA. He is the author or editor of several books, book chapters, and articles on the Internet and American politics, including *New Media and American Politics* (1999, with Diana Owen), *The Web of Politics* (1999), *Campaigning Online* (2003, with Bruce Bimber), *Typing Politics* (2009), *Making a Difference: A Comparative View of the Role of the Internet in Election Politics* (2008, with Stephen Ward, Diana Owen, and David Taras), and *Twitter and Elections Around the World* (2016, with Christina Holtz-Bacha and Marion Just).

Sven Engesser is Chair of Communication at Technische Universität Dresden, Germany. He received his PhD from LMU Munich. He was a member of the Swiss National Center of Competence in Research on "Challenges to Democracy in the 21st Century" and the European COST Action on "Populist Political Communication in Europe". His fields of interest include populism in the media, political polarization, and digital political communication.

Nicole Ernst is a doctoral student in the Department of International and Comparative Media Research at the University of Zurich, Switzerland. In research and teaching, she focuses on populism and political communication in social media.

Frank Esser is Professor of International and Comparative Media Research at the University of Zurich, Switzerland and holds an adjunct professorship at the University of Oslo, Norway. His research focuses on cross-national studies of news journalism and political communication. His books include *Handbook of Comparative Communication Research* (2012), *Mediatization of Politics* (2014), and *Populist Political Communication in Europe* (2017).

Alina Fisher is an ecologist and science communicator specializing in conservation and wildlife issues. Her communications research centers around the use of social media for science communication and barriers to uptake. Alina writes and speaks extensively on biology, ecology, science communications, and research methods for a variety of academic and public audiences, and across various media. Currently Alina is Research Manager at the School of Environmental Studies at the University of Victoria and Associate Faculty in the School of Environment and Sustainability at Royal Roads University, and Alina began her PhD at the University of Victoria in 2019 that combines her two research interests – wildlife management and science communication.

About the Contributors   245

Mireille Lalancette is Full Professor of Political Communication at the Université du Québec à Trois-Rivières, Canada. She has published about the construction of the mediatized image of politicians, gender, and representation, and about the use and impact of social media by citizens, grassroots organizations, and political actors in Canadian and international research publications in French and in English. She is the primary investigator on the SSHRC project called "Uses of Social Media During Contested Projects Raising Social Acceptability Issues". Researcher for the Research Group in Political Communication (Groupe de recherche en communication politique, GRCP), she is also the author of *ABC de l'argumentation pour les professionnels de la santé ou toute autre personne qui souhaite convaincre* (with Marie-Josée Drolet and Marie-Ève Caty) and the editor (with Pierre Leroux and François Hourmant) of *Selfies and Stars: Célébrité et politique en Amérique et en Europe*. She is also the editor of *What's Trending in Canadian Politics? Understanding Transformations in Power, Media, and the Public Sphere* (with Vincent Raynauld and Erin Crandall).

Regina G. Lawrence is Professor and Associate Dean of the School of Journalism and Communication Portland and Director of the Agora Journalism Center at the University of Oregon, USA. Her research focuses on journalistic norms and routines and the role of the media in public discourse. She has been Chair of the Political Communication section of the American Political Science Association, book review editor of the journal *Political Communication*, and a fellow at the Shorenstein Center on the Press, Politics, and Public Policy at Harvard. Dr. Lawrence's books include *When the Press Fails: Political Power and the News Media From Iraq to Katrina* (2007, with W. Lance Bennett and Steven Livingston), winner of the 2016 Doris A. Graber Best Book Award from the Political Communication section of the American Political Science Association; and *Hillary Clinton's Race for the White House: Gender Politics and the Media on the Campaign Trail* (2009, co-authored with Melody Rose).

Thierry M. Luescher is Research Director for Higher Education and Development in Africa in the education and skills development research program of the Human Sciences Research Council (HSRC) of South Africa. He has secondary academic affiliation with the University of the Free State as Associate Professor in Higher Education Studies, where he previously worked as Assistant Director for Institutional Research. Thierry was a student leader at the University of Cape Town, where he also completed his PhD. He has studied student politics and higher education in Africa as part of a number of research groups, including the Higher Education Research and Advocacy Network in Africa (HERANA), African Minds, and the Mellon Project "From #RMF to #FMF". Recent publications include the book *Student Politics in Africa: Representation and Activism* (2016), which he edited with Manja Klemenčič and James Otieno Jowi.

246 About the Contributors

Nkululeko Makhubu is a master's research intern at the Human Sciences Research Council, Education and Skills Development department. He is also an MCom Information Systems student at the University of Cape Town. His current research on Information and Communications Technology for Development (ICT4D) is a case study on the #FeesMustFall student movement to describe the "soft power" influence Twitter had on the movement online and offline in South Africa's higher education climate.

Peter Maurer is currently Postdoctoral Fellow in Political Communication at NTNU Trondheim, Norway, where he's part of the research group Elections, Values, and Political Communication. He is also affiliated with the COST Action Populist Political Communication in Europe. From 2011 to 2016, he was a postdoctoral researcher at the Department of Communication of the University of Vienna. He obtained a PhD in Communication Science from the Faculty of Social Science of the Freie Universität Berlin in 2011 with a thesis comparing perceptions of media influence between French and German politicians and journalists. His research focuses on the mediatization of politics, populist communication in different media, and the interaction of journalists and political elites, including hostile media perceptions.

Patrick McCurdy is an associate professor in the Department of Communication, University of Ottawa, Canada. His research draws from media and communication, journalism, social movement studies, and environmental communication to examine media as a site and source of social struggle and contestation. He has studied the mainstream and social media strategies of various social movements, including the global justice movement and the Occupy movement, among others. His published work has also examined the implications of living in a media-saturated society, covering topics ranging from WikiLeaks to the rise and consequences of celebrity activism. Currently he is under contract for a manuscript provisionally titled *A Tar Sands Tale: The Holding Power of Fossil Fuels Over the Social Imagination* and holds a SSHRC Insight Grant (2018–2021) of the same. The book and SSHRC IG carry forward his interest in the mediated debate over Canada's oil/tar sands. His SSHRC-funded project Mediatoil (2014–2017) focused on the evolution of advertising and campaigning around Alberta's oil/tar sands from 1970 to 2015. In 2016, Mediatoil won first prize in Compute Canada/SSHRC's national competition The Human Dimensions Open Data Challenge.

Shannon C. McGregor is an assistant professor in the Department of Communication at the University of Utah, USA. Her research interests center on political communication, social media, gender, and public opinion. Her work has been published in the *Journal of Communication*, *New Media & Society*, *Political Communication*, *Information, Communication & Society*, *International Journal of Communication*, *Journal of Broadcasting and Electronic Media*, *Social Media + Society*, and *Journal of Media Ethics*.

About the Contributors **247**

Kaitlynn Mendes is an associate professor at the University of Leicester, UK. She is an expert in feminist media studies and has written extensively on representations of feminism in the media and feminist uptake of digital technologies to challenge rape culture. She is author of five books, including *Feminism in the News* (2011), *SlutWalk: Feminism, Activism and Media* (2015), and *Digital Feminist Activism: Girls and Women Fight Back Against Rape Culture* (in press, with Jessica Ringrose and Jessalynn Keller).

Chaseten Remillard is an assistant professor at Royal Roads University, Canada. He is a communications scholar interested in questions of social and environmental justice. With expertise in visual and professional communications, Remillard's research includes topics as varied as homelessness, Canadian artist Bill Reid, hockey art, the Alberta Oil Sands, and shark films. Despite this eclecticism, he consistently interrogates how images gain and transmit meaning and how these meanings serve to reinforce particular "ways of seeing" ourselves and the world around us.

Joshua M. Scacco is Assistant Professor of Media Theory and Politics in the Brian Lamb School of Communication, Purdue University, and courtesy faculty in the Department of Political Science at the same institution. He also serves as Faculty Research Associate with the award-winning Center for Media Engagement. His research is focused on how emerging communication technologies influence established agents in American political life, including news organizations and the presidency.

Tamara A. Small is an associate professor in the Department of Political Science at the University of Guelph, Canada. Her research focuses on digital politics: use and impact of the Internet by Canadian political actors. She is the co-author of *Fighting for Votes: Parties, the Media and Voters in an Ontario Election* (2015) and co-editor of *Political Communication in Canada: Meet the Press, Tweet the Rest* (2014) and *Mind the Gaps: Canadian Perspectives on Gender and Politics* (2013). Her work has been published in *Information Communication and Society*, *Party Politics*, and *Canadian Journal of Political Science*.

Jacob R. Straus is a specialist on Congress with the Congressional Research Service (CRS) at the Library of Congress. He works on lobbying, ethics, commemorations (including monuments and memorials), congressional advisory commissions, and congressional communications. Prior to joining CRS, he was Assistant Professor of Political Science at Frostburg State University (MD), USA. His work has been published in *Presidential Studies Quarterly*, *Journal of Legislative Studies*, *PS: Political Science & Politics*, and *Online Information Review*. He edited *Party and Procedure in the United States Congress* (2012 and 2016).

248 About the Contributors

Jennifer Stromer-Galley is Professor of Information Studies and Director for the Center for Computational and Data Science at Syracuse University, USA. She is an affiliated faculty member with the Department of Communication and Rhetorical Studies and with the Department of Political Science, and she is Past President of the Association of Internet Researchers. She was a fellow at the Tow Center for Digital Journalism at Columbia University. The fellowship supported a collaborative research project, Illuminating 2016, studying the 2016 presidential campaign by collecting and analyzing the candidates' and public's postings on social media. Stromer-Galley is Principal Investigator of an $5.2 million project called "Trackable Reasoning and Analysis for Collaboration and Evaluation" (TRACE) project. Funded by the Intelligence Advanced Research Program Activity (IARPA), the project aims to experiment with reporting and crowdsourcing techniques to improve reasoning and intelligence analysis.

David Taras holds the Ralph Klein Chair in Media Studies at Mount Royal University. He was formerly Ernest Manning Chair in Canadian Studies at the University of Calgary and has taught at the University of Toronto and the University of Amsterdam in the Netherlands. Taras served as a special advisor to the Government of Alberta on the constitution and was an expert advisor to the House of Commons Standing Committee on Canadian Heritage during its review of the Broadcasting Act. He is the author of, among other works, *Digital Mosaic: Media. Power and Identity on Canada* and *The Last Word: Media Coverage of the Supreme Court of Canada*. He was President of the Canadian Communication Association and served two terms on the Board of Governors of the University of Calgary. He is also a five-time winner of the University of Calgary Student Association Award for Teaching Excellence. His political commentaries can be seen and heard regularly on the Global Morning News in Calgary and on the Corus radio network.

Raymond T. Williams is currently a researcher with the Congressional Research Service at the Library of Congress. Previously, he worked at the University of Maryland's Department of Government and Politics, the David C. Driskell Center, and the Institute for Governmental Service and Research. He has been published in *Online Information Review* and has a forthcoming publication in *Presidential Studies Quarterly* (March 2020). He received his BS from East Carolina University and his MA and PhD in Political Science from the University of Maryland-College Park. His scholarship focuses on the unilateral presidency and U.S. political institutions.

Eric C. Wiemer is a doctoral student in the Brian Lamb School of Communication at Purdue University studying political communication. His research interests include the interrelationships between political entities, the news media, and the public in the current media landscape using both traditional and computational methods.

Maurice Vergeer is Media Researcher at the Department of Communication Science, Radboud University, the Netherlands. His research focuses on social media use by professionals in politics (politicians, candidates, and political parties) and news (journalists and news organizations) as well as audiences commenting on social (media) events. He developed an interest in methodologies involving social media data collection and analysis, particularly longitudinal analysis, network analysis, and text mining. He has a special interest in social media in East and Southeast Asia. His research has been published in journals such as *New Media & Society*, *Journal of Computer-Mediated Communication*, *Social Science Computer Review*, and *Information, Communication and Society*.

INDEX

activism 7–8, 11–12, 239–240; in Canada 167–183, 187–198; and criticism of leaders 203; feminist 153–164; and students 220–233; *see also* environmentalism; feminism; minorities; protests
advertisements 5–7, 26, 50, 65, 189–190
Africa 13, 220–233
agenda setting *see* congressional leaders; Twitter
algorithms *see under* social media platforms
Amazon 5, 42
anonymity 12, 203, 210, 238
anti-elitism *see* populism

Bezos, Jeff 42; *see also* Amazon
Britain *see* Great Britain
broadcasting *see* television

cable news networks 4
campaigns *see* activism; election campaigns
Canada 5, 235; activist movements 8, 12, 167–183, 187–198, 240; *see also* Trudeau, Justin
celebrity influence 53, 59, 127
censorship 18–19; *see also* media control
Centennial Flame *see* Keep Canada's Flame Alive movement
Churchill, Winston 7, 235
civic engagement: with activism 223; and campaigns 4, 64, 113–115, 133; and criticism of politicians 204–205,

214–215; with political leaders 2, 6–7, 20, 88, 98–99, 106, 128
Clinton, Hillary 7, 9, 20, 49–61, 205, 240
college tuition *see* tuition, college
congressional leaders 10, 20–21, 76–88, 238; *see also under* election campaigns
constitutive control 20, 21–22
control of media *see* media control

election campaigns: other 64–66, 79–80, 112–124, 126–127, 129–145, 209, 239; US presidential 7, 9–10, 34, 35, 38–47, 49–61, 239; *see also* fundraising
elites *see* populism
eloquence *see* vulgar eloquence
England *see* Great Britain
enthymeme 9, 40, 43, 44–45, 47, 238
environmentalism 8, 13–14, 83–84, 164, 188–192, 196–197; *see also* activism
equalization 65, 131
ethnography 154, 163
Europe 4, 5, 11, 130; *see also* France
Everyday Sexism movement 154, 155, 162, 164
extremists 8, 13, 31, 99

Facebook 5, 11, 59, 100, 158, 231; *see also* social media platforms
fake news 18, 22–30, 237
feminism 58, 60; activist movements 7–8, 11–12, 153–164, 228–229, 237; *see also* Everyday Sexism movement; gender

Index **251**

differences; Hollaback! movement; Me Too movement; SlutWalk movement; *Vagenda*; Who Needs Feminism? movement
filters *see under* Internet
fireside chats 2, 38
fossil fuels *see* oil industry
Fox News 4, 23, 28–29, 40, 45
France 2, 10–11, 112–124
fundraising 7, 53, 160; *see also* election campaigns

gas industry *see* oil industry
gatekeepers: journalists as 98, 113, 114, 169, 178, 182; leaders as 22, 29; social media as 5, 7
Gaulle, Charles de 2, 13
gay rights 229; *see also* activism; minorities
gender differences: and activism 228, 230; and politicians 129, 131, 145, 205, 208, 213; *see also* feminism
Germany 1, 5, 132
Google 5–6, 206; *see also* social media platforms, algorithms
grassroot politics *see* activism
Great Britain 12, 153; *see also* May, Theresa
gun control 85

harassment, online 12, 153, 164; *see also* journalism, attacks on
hashtags: activists' use of 159–160, 167–168, 169, 171–175, 191, 193, 220–221; politicians' use of 82–85, 86–87, 120–124; role of 114–115
healthcare 82–83
history of media 2, 38, 236
Hollaback! movement 154, 155, 161–162, 164
humanization 10, 50, 51, 56, 58, 59–60; *see also* Instagram
hyperbole 34, 40, 42

immigration 43, 84
incumbency 11, 131–134, 138, 140
Instagram 59–60, 60–61, 69–70; *see also* humanization; social media platforms
Internet: filters 6; permanence of 5–6; *see also* social media platforms
intersectionality *see* minorities

Jarvis, Heather 155, 156, 157, 161
journalism: attacks on 12, 17–18, 27, 34, 42, 45, 99, 237; attacks on leaders 3;

coverage of social media 86, 105–106, 121, 175–178, 238–239, 240; *see also under* control of media

Keep Canada's Flame Alive movement 187–198

leadership, definition of 2
legacy media *see* journalism
Le Pen, Marine 10–11, 101, 106, 112–113, 116–124, 240
LGBTQ rights *see* activism; minorities
Lincoln, Abraham 7, 18, 27

macro memes *see* memes
Macron, Emmanuel 10–11, 112–113, 116–124, 240
mainstream media *see* journalism
May, Theresa 12, 202–215
media control: consumer control 6, 19, 114–115, 238; journalist control 2–4, 19, 114–115, 229, 236, 237; leader control 2–3, 6–7, 9–11, 17–30, 112, 115, 129, 235–236, 237–238
memes 12, 113, 132, 173, 202–215, 238
Me Too movement 159–160, 164
minorities 56, 78, 101, 168–169, 222, 227–229; *see also* activism; feminism

nationalism 120–122, 192
Netherlands 1, 11, 99, 126–145
news cycle 4, 7
New York Times 17, 25, 27, 45, 177, 237
Nixon, Richard 17–18
normalization 11, 131

Obama, Barack 7, 17, 20–21, 38
oil industry 12, 179, 187–189

partisanship 4, 86–88, 99, 138, 139–140, 143
Perez, Carolyn Criado 6, 153, 163
platforms *see* social media platforms
poetic structure 9, 35, 40
political awareness *see* civic engagement
poo politics 221–222
popularity 11, 67–69, 100–101, 107, 210–213
populism 97–108, 240; and activist movements 194–198; in France 10–11, 113–124; in the Netherlands 130–131, 134, 138, 139–140, 143, 145
presidential accountability system 29–30

252 Index

President of the United States: and control of media 2–3, 7, 9, 17–19, 21–26, 28; and relationship with the press 3, 9, 17–18, 23–24, 27–30, 42, 45, 59
printing press 3
promotion of news sources 28–29
protests: in Canada 167–183, 187–198; feminist 154–164; and political leaders 46, 205; student 13, 220–233; *see also* activism
public record *see* Internet

question periods 3–4

radio 37, 235
Reagan, Ronald 37–38
Reddit 20, 24
rhetorical style 18, 34–36, 39–47, 237
Roosevelt, Franklin D. 2, 7, 38

search engines 5–6; *see also* Google
selfies 10, 64–66
showmanship 4, 5
SlutWalk movement 8, 11, 154–159
social media platforms: algorithms 5, 6, 7; comparison of 9–10, 50–61, 99, 104–105, 107, 113, 232; *see also* Facebook; Internet; Instagram; Reddit; Twitter; WhatsApp
soft leadership: in activist movements 179–180, 183, 187–188, 192–194, 196, 197–198; definition of 13, 168, 170
State of the Union address 10, 77, 80, 82, 84–85
student protests *see under* protests
stump speeches 37, 44, 53
synecdoche 35, 40, 44–45, 47, 238

taxes 84, 85
telegraph 2

television 3–5, 37–38, 127–128, 189–190, 235
trolling *see* harassment, online
Trudeau, Justin 10, 63–71, 235, 240
Trump, Donald: election campaign 3; message control 9, 17–30, 237–238; and populism 97; rhetorical style 33–35, 38–47, 241; State of the Union address 82–85
tuition, college 13, 220–233
Twitter: and activist movements 172–175, 221, 225–226, 232–233; and congress 10–11 (*see also* congressional leaders); and Donald Trump 38–39 (*see also* Trump, Donald); and election campaigns 129–130; influencing the news 59, 99, 177–178, 240; and populism 112–118, 122–124, 240–241; *see also* social media platforms

university tuition *see* tuition, college

Vagenda 154, 155
virality 6, 196; and activist movements 154–156; and leaders 10, 67–68, 70–71 (*see also* Trudeau, Justin); and memes 12, 202, 203–204, 206, 214–215; and Twitter 170, 221, 225
vulgar eloquence 9, 33–47

Washington Post 26, 27, 42, 45, 86, 237
Watergate 3, 17, 18, 87
WhatsApp 230, 231; *see also* social media platforms
Who Needs Feminism? movement 154, 156–157, 160
World War II 2, 235; *see also* Churchill, Winston

Printed in the United States
by Baker & Taylor Publisher Services